Living and Working in the
European Union

A Survival Handbook

by
Joanna Styles

SURVIVAL BOOKS • LONDON • ENGLAND

First published 2004

Survival Books Limited, 1st Floor,
60 St James's Street, London SW1A 1ZN, United Kingdom
☎ +44 (0)20-7493 4244, ▤ +44 (0)20-7491 0605
✉ info@survivalbooks.net
💻 www.survivalbooks.net
To order books, please refer to page 414.

British Library Cataloguing in Publication Data.
A CIP record for this book is available
from the British Library.
ISBN 1 901130 18 5

Printed and bound in Finland by WS Bookwell Ltd

ACKNOWLEDGEMENTS

M y sincere thanks to all those who contributed to the successful publication of this book, in particular numerous staff at the EU Direct website and government websites, Martin Hills (editing and proofreading), Kerry and Joe Laredo (desktop publishing), and everyone else who provided information or contributed in any way. Also a special thank-you to Jim Watson for the superb cover, illustrations and cartoons.

OTHER TITLES BY SURVIVAL BOOKS

Living And Working Series

Abroad; America; Australia; Britain; Canada; The Far East; France; Germany; The Gulf States & Saudi Arabia; Holland, Belgium & Luxembourg; Ireland; Italy; London; New Zealand; Spain; Switzerland

Buying A Home Series

Abroad; Britain; Florida; France; Greece & Cyprus; Ireland; Italy; Portugal; Spain

Other Titles

The Alien's Guide To Britain; The Alien's Guide To France; The Best Places To Live In France; The Best Places To Live In Spain; Buying, Selling & Letting Property; How To Avoid Holiday & Travel Disasters; Renovating & Maintaining Your French Home; Retiring Abroad; Rioja And Its Wines; The Wines Of Spain

Order forms are on page 414.

WHAT READERS & REVIEWERS

When you buy a model plane for your child, a video recorder, or some new computer gizmo, you get with it a leaflet or booklet pleading 'Read Me First', or bearing large friendly letters or bold type saying 'IMPORTANT – follow the instructions carefully'. This book should be similarly supplied to all those entering France with anything more durable than a 5-day return ticket. It is worth reading even if you are just visiting briefly, or if you have lived here for years and feel totally knowledgeable and secure. But if you need to find out how France works then it is indispensable. Native French people probably have a less thorough understanding of how their country functions. – Where it is most essential, the book is most up to the minute.

LIVING FRANCE

Rarely has a 'survival guide' contained such useful advice. This book dispels doubts for first-time travellers, yet is also useful for seasoned globetrotters – In a word, if you're planning to move to the USA or go there for a long-term stay, then buy this book both for general reading and as a ready-reference.

AMERICAN CITIZENS ABROAD

It is everything you always wanted to ask but didn't for fear of the contemptuous put down – The best English-language guide – Its pages are stuffed with practical information on everyday subjects and are designed to complement the traditional guidebook.

SWISS NEWS

A complete revelation to me – I found it both enlightening and interesting, not to mention amusing.

CAROLE CLARK

Let's say it at once. David Hampshire's *Living and Working in France* is the best handbook ever produced for visitors and foreign residents in this country; indeed, my discussion with locals showed that it has much to teach even those born and bred in l'Hexagone. – It is Hampshire's meticulous detail which lifts his work way beyond the range of other books with similar titles. Often you think of a supplementary question and search for the answer in vain. With Hampshire this is rarely the case. – He writes with great clarity (and gives French equivalents of all key terms), a touch of humour and a ready eye for the odd (and often illuminating) fact. – This book is absolutely indispensable.

THE RIVIERA REPORTER

A mine of information – I may have avoided some embarrassments and frights if I had read it prior to my first Swiss encounters – Deserves an honoured place on any newcomer's bookshelf.

ENGLISH TEACHERS ASSOCIATION, SWITZERLAND

Have Said About Survival Books

What a great work, wealth of useful information, well-balanced wording and accuracy in details. My compliments!

THOMAS MÜLLER

This handbook has all the practical information one needs to set up home in the UK – The sheer volume of information is almost daunting – Highly recommended for anyone moving to the UK.

AMERICAN CITIZENS ABROAD

A very good book which has answered so many questions and even some I hadn't thought of – I would certainly recommend it.

BRIAN FAIRMAN

We would like to congratulate you on this work: it is really super! We hand it out to our expatriates and they read it with great interest and pleasure.

ICI (SWITZERLAND) AG

Covers just about all the things you want to know on the subject – In answer to the desert island question about the one how-to book on France, this book would be it – Almost 500 pages of solid accurate reading – This book is about enjoyment as much as survival.

THE RECORDER

It's so funny – I love it and definitely need a copy of my own – Thanks very much for having written such a humorous and helpful book.

HEIDI GUILIANI

A must for all foreigners coming to Switzerland.

ANTOINETTE O'DONOGHUE

A comprehensive guide to all things French, written in a highly readable and amusing style, for anyone planning to live, work or retire in France.

THE TIMES

A concise, thorough account of the DOs and DON'Ts for a foreigner in Switzerland – Crammed with useful information and lightened with humorous quips which make the facts more readable.

AMERICAN CITIZENS ABROAD

Covers every conceivable question that may be asked concerning everyday life – I know of no other book that could take the place of this one.

FRANCE IN PRINT

Hats off to *Living and Working in Switzerland*!

RONNIE ALMEIDA

THE AUTHOR

Joanna Styles was born in London but has lived and worked for many years on the Costa del Sol, Spain. She is a freelance writer and the author of several books, including **The Best Places to Buy a Home in Spain, Buying a Home in Greece and Cyprus** and **Costa del Sol Lifeline,** all published by Survival Books. She also regularly contributes to and updates many other Survival Books publications. Joanna is married with two daughters.

CONTENTS

1. CHOOSING THE COUNTRY

2. FINDING A JOB & WORKING

3. ACCOMMODATION

4. HEALTH & SOCIAL SECURITY 109

5. FINANCE & INSURANCE 127

6. EDUCATION 153

APPENDICES   383

INDEX   405

ORDER FORMS   414

NOTES   419

IMPORTANT NOTE

All EU countries have their idiosyncrasies and most encompass a variety of ethnic groups, languages, religions and customs, not to mention continuously changing rules, regulations (particularly regarding visas, work and residence permits, and business), laws and costs. This is particularly true of the ten new EU states, which from May 2004 enter a period of change and adaptation to EU rules and regulations. **I cannot recommend too strongly that you check with an official and reliable source before making any major decisions or taking an irreversible course of action.** Don't, however, believe everything you're told or read – even, dare I say it, herein!

Useful addresses, publications and websites have been included in all chapters and in **Appendices A**, **B** and **C** to help you obtain further information and verify details with official sources. Country-specific sources of information are included in **Chapter 8**. Important points have been emphasised throughout the book in **bold** print, some of which it would be expensive or foolish to disregard. Unless specifically stated, the reference to any company, organisation or product in this book doesn't constitute an endorsement or recommendation.

AUTHOR'S NOTES

- Times are shown using am (Latin: *ante meridiem*) for before noon and pm (*post meridiem*) for after noon (see also **Time Difference** on page 213).

- His/he/him also means her/she/her (please forgive me ladies). This is done to make life easier for both the reader and (in particular) the author, and isn't intended to be sexist.

- All spelling is (or should be) British English and not American English.

- Warnings and important points are shown in bold type.

- The following symbols are used in this book: ☎ (telephone), 🖷 (fax), 🖳 (internet) and ✉ (email).

- Lists of **Useful Addresses, Further Reading** and **Useful Websites** are contained in **Appendices A, B** and **C** respectively.

- For those unfamiliar with the metric system of weights and measures, imperial conversion tables are included in **Appendix D**.

- A map of Europe showing the European Union members is in **Appendix E**.

INTRODUCTION

This book has been published to coincide with the expansion of the European Union (EU) on 1st May 2004 from 15 to 25 countries, encompassing most of the European continent. The concept of the EU is unique in the world: it provides a wealth of prospects for employment, trade and commerce, not to mention numerous benefits for EU nationals including the right to live and work in any of the 25 member countries. It's with these opportunities in mind that this book has been written to provide the essential information necessary for anyone considering living or working in an EU country.

General information isn't very difficult to find in most EU countries, provided, of course, that you're fluent in the local language. However, reliable and up-to-date information specifically intended for foreigners planning to live or work in the EU isn't so easy to find, least of all **in English and in one volume**. My aim in writing this book was to help fill this void and provide the comprehensive **practical** information necessary for a relatively trouble-free life. Adjusting to a different environment and culture, and making a home in any foreign country can be a traumatic and stressful experience. You need to adapt to new customs and traditions and discover the local way of doing things, for example, finding a home, paying bills and obtaining insurance. For most people finding out how to overcome the everyday obstacles of life in the EU has previously been a case of pot luck. **But no more!** With a copy of *Living and Working in the European Union* to hand, you'll have a wealth of information at your fingertips.

Adapting to life in a new country is a continuous process and although this book will help reduce your 'beginner's' phase and minimise the frustrations, it doesn't contain all the answers (most of us don't even know the right questions to ask). What it **will** do is help you make informed decisions and calculated judgements, instead of uneducated guesses and costly mistakes. **Most importantly, it will help you save time, trouble and money, and repay your investment many times over!**

Although you may find some of the information a bit daunting, don't be discouraged. Most problems only occur once and fade into insignificance after a short time (as you face the next half a dozen!). Most people who relocate to the EU (or to another country within the EU) would agree that the experience enriches your life and broadens your horizons – and may even please your bank manager! Hund reds of thousands of foreigners already live and work in the EU, many of whom are permanent residents, and most would agree that, all things considered, they relish life in their adopted country. I trust this book will help you avoid the pitfalls of life and smooth your way to a happy and rewarding future in your new home.

Good Luck!

Joanna Styles
April 2004

1.

CHOOSING THE COUNTRY

Before deciding where, when, or indeed, whether to live or work in the EU, it's important to do your homework thoroughly and investigate all the possibilities. It may be that you already know the country where you wish to live or work, but have you thought about the alternatives? Of course, if you're being posted abroad by your employer, you may have little or no choice about where you're going – and may not even be in a position to refuse! However, for anyone planning to retire in the EU or who has a choice of countries where they can work, it's important to do exhaustive research and (try to) make the right decision. It isn't uncommon for people to regret their decision after some time and wish they had chosen a different country. Unless you know exactly where you want to live or work abroad, it's advisable to spend some time getting to know a country or region. This is particularly important if you're planning to retire or start a business abroad.

As when making all major life decisions, it's never advisable to be in too much of a hurry. Many people make expensive (even catastrophic) errors when moving abroad, often because they don't do sufficient research, taking into consideration all the possibilities and the circumstances of each family member. It isn't unusual for people to uproot themselves and, after a few years, wish they had chosen a different country or even that they had stayed at home (many people who emigrate return home within a relatively short period).

This chapter will help you decide on a country and includes important considerations such as permits, retirement, working, starting a business, communications, getting there and getting around (particularly motoring).

The first question to ask yourself is exactly why you want to live or work abroad. If you've been offered a transfer abroad by your present employer, then the decision may be relatively straightforward – although you will still need to take into account the wishes and considerations of your family. On the other hand, if you're seeking a new life or career (or career development); starting a business; want to retire to a warmer climate; or simply wish to make more money (who doesn't!), then you can usually choose from a number of countries – and the decision will be much more difficult. If you're a young single person, the decision is usually easier than for families. Families need to take into account such considerations as job opportunities for spouses and children, the availability of suitable accommodation (at an affordable price), security, education, family health, leisure and sports opportunities, culture shock, the cost of living and many other matters.

Having decided exactly why you want to live or work abroad, the next thing you need to do is choose the country. Unless you're being transferred abroad by your employer, you could be faced with a wealth of choices. There is, of course, no perfect country for everybody, although most people manage to find their particular ideal country, possibly after a few false starts.

When choosing a country there are numerous considerations to take into account. For example, if you're planning to work abroad, what are the prospects in your profession or trade? Can you change jobs freely if the one you've been offered doesn't work out? If you're planning to start a business, what opportunities are available and can you realistically expect to make a good living? Would you have to leave the country if the business folded? Can you speak the language or are you willing to learn? What is the cost of living? Do you wish to buy a home (which may not be permitted for foreigners or is prohibitively expensive in some EU countries) and could you sell at a realistic price should the need arise? Do you need or wish to be 'close' (measured in driving or flying time) to your home country or another country? How important is the climate?

You may already have some preferences, possibly influenced by where you've spent a number of enjoyable holidays or countries where you have family and friends. If you're planning to start a new life, you should choose a country that suits your family's personalities and tastes, as this will be a key factor in your future enjoyment. Before deciding on a country, it's advisable to do as much research as possible and to read books written expressly for those planning to live or work in particular countries and buy a home abroad (particularly those published by Survival Books – see page 414). It will also help to read magazines and visit expatriate websites such as 🖳 www.escape artist.com and 🖳 www.internationalliving.com (see **Appendix C** for a list). **Bear in mind that the cost of investing in a few books or magazines (and other research) is tiny compared to the expense of making a big mistake!**

PERMITS & VISAS

Before making any plans to live or work abroad, you must ensure that you will be permitted to enter and leave a country freely; live there as long as you wish; become a resident; and do anything else you have in mind, such as work as self-employed, start a business or buy a home. In the EU, a national of one EU country (including all the new member states) can live in any other EU country, provided they have sufficient funds and health insurance or qualify for health insurance under a public scheme (i.e. they have made enough social security contributions in their home country). However, nationals from non-EU countries don't have an automatic right to live there. Generally they aren't permitted to live in the EU for longer than three months per year without an appropriate permit or visa.

If there's a possibility that you or any family member may wish to live or work in the EU permanently, you should enquire whether that would be possible before making any plans. In some EU countries, the rules and regulations governing permits and visas change occasionally (although these changes usually only affect non-EU nationals), therefore it's important to obtain up-to-date information from an embassy or consulate in your home country. **Permit infringements are taken seriously by the authorities in all countries. There are penalties for breaches of regulations, including fines and even deportation for flagrant abuses.**

For further information on visas and permits for individual EU countries see **Chapter 9 – Country Profiles.**

Visas

EU Nationals don't require a visa to visit any of the EU countries and the following information applies only to **non-EU nationals**.

Visits Under 90 Days

Citizens from the following countries don't require a visa to enter the EU for visits under 90 days: Andorra, Argentina, Australia, Bermuda, Bolivia, Brazil, Brunei, Bulgaria, Canada, Chile, Costa Rica, Croatia, El Salvador, Guatemala, Honduras, Israel, Japan, South Korea, Macao, Malaysia, Mexico, Monaco, New Zealand, Nicaragua, Panama, Paraguay, Romania, Singapore, the US, Uruguay and Venezuela. This information was correct in January 2004. Check with an EU member state's consulate or embassy in your home country for up-to-date information. Citizens from countries not named above require a visa to enter the EU. If you're planning to visit Austria, Belgium, Denmark, France, Finland, Germany, Greece, Iceland, Italy, Luxembourg, the Netherlands, Norway, Portugal, Spain or Sweden you should acquire a Schengen visa.

Schengen Visas

A total of fifteen countries in Western Europe are signatories to the Schengen agreement (named after a Luxembourg village on the Moselle River), which came into effect in 1994 and was intended to introduce an open-border policy between member countries. Schengen members include Austria, Belgium, Denmark, France, Finland, Germany, Greece, Iceland, Italy, Luxembourg, the Netherlands, Norway, Portugal, Spain and Sweden. Under the agreement, immigration checks and passport controls take place when you first arrive in a member country, after which you can travel freely between member countries without further checks. Schengen visa holders are entitled to stay in the above-mentioned 15 countries for a maximum of 90 days per six-month period during the visa's period of validity, although the holder may not undertake any gainful employment and the Schengen visa does not constitute a work or residence permit.

If you intend to visit one Schengen country only, you should apply to that country's embassy or consulate in your home country. If you intend to visit several Schengen countries, you should apply to the embassy or consulate of your main destination in your home country. If you plan to visit several Schengen countries but don't have a main destination, you should apply to the embassy or consulate of your first destination in your home country.

You will need to provide a valid passport (valid for up to three months after your trip); a completed visa form plus one passport photo; proof of the purpose of your trip (e.g. a letter of invitation or business references, if the purpose of your trip is business); proof of sufficient funds and accommodation; and a return or onward travel ticket.

Further information about Schengen visas is available from embassies and consulates of participating countries or from the Schengen website (💻 www. eurovisa.com). Schengen visas aren't valid for the Czech Republic, Cyprus, Estonia, Hungary, Ireland, Latvia, Lithuania, Malta, Poland, Slovakia, Slovenia or the UK.

Visits Over 90 Days

All non-EU nationals require a visa for visits over 90 days or for visits for employment purposes. The visa should be applied for well in advance of arrival. Most consulates take at least one month to process visa applications and some take considerably longer.

Residence Permits

EU Nationals

In most EU states, EU nationals require a residence permit if they plan to stay in the country for more than 90 days. At present Spain and the UK are the only countries that don't issue residence permits for salaried or self-employed EU residents. However, the residence permit is usually a mere formality, since all EU nationals have the right to reside in another EU country as long as they can provide proof of sufficient funds and health insurance.

Non-EU Nationals

All non-EU nationals require a residence permit in order to live in any EU country and this often forms part of a work permit (see below) and must be applied for before arrival in the country. If you don't plan to work, then you should apply for a residence permit as part of a retirement or non-working visa. Spouses and dependants usually require residence permits as well, which must also be applied for before arrival in the country where you plan to live. See **Residence Permits** under individual **Country Profiles** in **Chapter 9** for further information.

Work Permits

Whether you need a work permit to work in an EU country depends on your nationality.

EU Nationals

Under EU laws, any citizen from an EU country has the right to work in another EU country without restrictions and without the necessity of a work permit. This right is applied in principle to the new member states, but with restrictions during a transitional period of at least two years and a maximum of seven. During the first two years of membership, from May 2004 to May 2006, the original EU member states plus Cyprus and Malta will admit new EU nationals for employment under their current national regulations. So, in practice, new EU nationals will still require a work permit in order to work in any of the original member states plus Cyprus and Malta. The same practice will also apply to EU nationals wishing to work in the new member states. During the two-year period, however, nationals from new EU states will be given priority for employment over non-EU nationals and have access to help in finding a job and securing unemployment benefit (if they qualify).

After the two-year transitional period, member states will review the employment situation in their own countries and decide whether to remove work permit regulations for other EU nationals. It's expected that many countries will abolish the regulations in 2006, although much depends on the economy and labour market within the EU. Regulations regarding work permits for EU nationals are therefore as one of the following:

- **Nationals from original EU states plus Cyprus and Malta wishing to work in an original EU state plus Cyprus and Malta** – No restrictions and no work permit required. However, Malta has the right to restrict employment for EU nationals if the labour market in the country becomes saturated.

- **Nationals from original EU states plus Cyprus and Malta wishing to work in a new member state** – Restrictions apply and work permit required until at least May 2006.

- **Nationals from new member states wishing to work in an original EU state plus Cyprus and Malta** – Restrictions apply and work permit required until at least May 2006.

- **Nationals from new member states wishing to work in another new member state** – Restrictions apply and work permit required until at least May 2006.

Regulations may change and you should obtain up-to-date information from the authorities in the country in question.

Non-EU Nationals

All non-EU nationals require a work permit to work in the EU and in many cases the permit must be applied for **before** arrival in the country where you plan to work. It's generally quite difficult for non-EU nationals to obtain a work permit in any EU country, although in some countries certain nationalities may have fewer restrictions than others, e.g. citizens from Commonwealth countries in the UK; citizens from former French colonies in France; and many Latin Americans in Spain.

HOLIDAY HOMES & RETIREMENT

If you wish to retire or spend long periods each year abroad (e.g. in a holiday home), you must check whether this will be possible before making any plans and ensure that you will be able to afford to live abroad. If you don't qualify to live in a country by birthright, it may be impossible to obtain a residence permit.

EU Nationals

Retirees from any country in the EU (including the new member states) have the right to retire to any EU country as long as they have sufficient funds and health insurance. The amount that qualifies as 'sufficient funds' is vague in most countries, but must usually be equivalent to the country's minimum wage. Health insurance must be in the form either of private insurance (the insurance company must have an office in the country you're retiring to) or proof that you qualify for medical attention under the country's public health scheme (form E121).

Non-EU Nationals

Non-EU retirees must obtain a residence visa (often referred to as a 'retirement visa' or 'non-working visa') before arrival in the EU country where they wish to retire. Documentary requirements for obtaining the visa usually include: proof of private health insurance; proof of financial resources (usually at least €1,000 a month plus proof of property ownership or possibly long-term rental lease); certificate of good conduct; and a health certificate. Retirement visas aren't automatically granted (many are actually refused), although the wealthier you are and the larger your assets in the country, the greater your chances are of being accepted.

Advantages & Disadvantages

Despite the bureaucracy and red tape encountered in EU countries, increasing numbers of people are retiring abroad and the volume is expected to rise sharply in the future as more people choose early retirement. Many retirees seeking a home in an EU country are North Americans or northern Europeans who can often buy a retirement home abroad for much less than the value of their family home. This is particularly true of resort areas in southern EU countries such as France, Italy, Portugal and Spain. The difference between the money raised on the sale of your family home and the cost of a home abroad can be invested to supplement your pension, allowing you to live comfortably in retirement, particularly when a lower cost of living is taken into account.

However, before planning to live abroad permanently, you must take into consideration many factors including:

- The cost of living.

- Pension payments (pensions may be frozen in some cases if there's not a reciprocal social security agreement between your home country and the country to which you retire; further information is available from ⌨ www. pensionservice.gov.uk).

- Investment income.

- Local taxes.

Can you really afford to retire abroad? What of the future? Is your income secure and protected against inflation? There are both advantages and disadvantages to retiring abroad, although for most people the benefits far outweigh the drawbacks.

Advantages

The advantages of retiring abroad may include a more favourable climate; lower taxation; a lower cost of living; a higher standard of living; and the availability of a wide range of leisure and sports activities at an affordable cost. For most people, one of the principal benefits is the improved health that results from living in a warmer climate and a more relaxing environment (provided you don't expect things to be done the same way as 'at home'). Those who suffer from arthritis, colds, influenza and other illnesses exacerbated by cold and damp may live longer and enjoy a better quality of life in a warm climate, while those who suffer from stress are often advised to live in a country with a more relaxing way of life. However, if you're planning to retire abroad for health reasons, you should ask your doctor for his advice regarding suitable countries and locations (see also **Chapter 4**). For retirees (and many others) the advantages of living abroad usually add up to an improved quality of life and an increased life expectancy.

Disadvantages

The main disadvantages of retiring abroad may include separation from family and loved ones; language problems; boredom (what are you going to do all day?); the health dangers imposed by too much sun and alcohol, overeating and too little exercise; poor social services (e.g. little or no state support for the elderly and infirm); poor medical facilities in some of the new member countries; financial problems (e.g. high cost of living, high taxation, exchange rate fluctuations and poor investments); possible loss of pension indexation; homesickness (e.g. sadness or depression from missing friends and family); and culture shock. Before planning to live abroad you should also consider how you'd cope if your mobility was restricted and once you reach old age (some EU countries provide inadequate facilities and support for the aged and those with disabilities).

FAMILIES

Although many expatriates are single, experiencing life abroad before they settle down permanently in their home countries, they also include many families, who, usually because of the husband or wife's profession or career, find themselves relocating abroad (for an average of around four years), possibly several times in their lives. The implications are far-reaching, particularly for family members who are being uprooted for reasons alien to them and who may not want to leave what they regard as home.

The expatriate spouse is generally referred to here as the wife, simply because it's a woman who follows her husband abroad in most cases, although the points raised apply equally to expatriate husbands. This information includes specific considerations for women contemplating a move abroad, including how to find employment, using your time constructively, and (not least) making a period spent abroad a rewarding and enriching experience. There is also advice on how to make the move abroad as smooth and trouble-free as possible for children.

Family life may be completely different abroad and relationships can become strained under the stress of adapting and culture shock (see page 179). You shouldn't underestimate the consequences of culture shock, the effects of which can be lessened if you accept the condition rather than deny it – a popular tactic that's often used to save face in front of others. Your family may find itself in a completely new and possibly alien environment, your new home may scarcely resemble your previous one (it may be much more luxurious or significantly smaller) and the climate may be dramatically different from that of your home country.

Your new country may be much richer or poorer than your home country and you will need to adapt to this. This will be much more difficult if the country is significantly poorer, when the images and experiences confronting you may initially be distressing. If possible, you should prepare yourself for as many aspects of the new situation as you can and explain to your children the differences they're likely to encounter, while at the same time dispelling their fears.

Family members, particularly parents, often find that they assume a new role during a posting abroad. The father, who was more than likely the instigator of the relocation, becomes the most important member of the family. Decision-making may be almost entirely in his hands and he'll probably manage all financial matters, particularly if the wife doesn't work and banking transactions are performed through his company. The father will probably also be working longer hours, as his overseas posting may be a promotion involving increased responsibility and demanding more time and dedication to his job. As a consequence, he'll be spending less time with his family than previously.

The mother, particularly if she worked before moving abroad, will therefore find herself in a new situation where she's financially dependent on her partner, and where her children (through lack of time with their father) become much more dependent on her than previously. The mother may find herself alone, with solitude intensified by the fact that there are no close relations or friends on hand. The resulting situation can put tremendous strain on a family. However, if you're aware that this may arise beforehand, you can act on it and lessen its effects. Good communication between family members is vital and you should make time to talk about your experiences and feelings, both as a couple and a family. Questions should always be raised and, if possible, answered, particularly when asked by children.

However difficult the situation may appear at the beginning, it will help to bear in mind that it's by no means unique and that most expatriate families have experienced exactly the same problems and have managed to triumph over them and thoroughly enjoy their stay abroad.

There are numerous resources for families planning a move abroad, including *Living & Working Abroad: A Wife's Guide* (Kuperard), *Living & Working Abroad: A Parent's Guide* (Kuperard) and *Homeward Bound* (Expatriate Press), all written by Robin Pascoe; *Third Culture Kids* by David C. Pollock & Ruth E. Van Reken (Intercultural Press), plus many websites, including 🖳 www.out postexpat.nl, 🖳 www.expatexchange.com and 🖳 www.brookes.ac.uk/world wise. See also **Appendices A, B** and **C** at the end of this book.

Children

Expatriate children (known by sociologists as 'Third Culture Kids') run into hundreds of thousands around the world – an estimated 400,000 from the US alone! In general, children under 12 adapt much faster to new surroundings and tend to accept new realities and situations with far fewer difficulties than adults. However, this doesn't mean that children will take to living in a new country immediately, nor that they won't suffer similar culture shock and feelings of displacement to those of their parents.

A parent should never underestimate the effects a move abroad will have on children, particularly adolescents, and if you feel that relocation is likely to affect a child negatively (in the long term) rather than positively, then it's probably advisable not to make the move. Children rarely have a choice about a move abroad, yet their needs must be considered as one of your priorities when making the decision. If a child has learning difficulties or disabilities, relocation shouldn't usually be considered unless you're certain that you will find experts abroad to help you cope with the situation. A possible alternative for teenagers may be for them to attend a boarding school in your home country or to stay with their grandparents and attend a local school while you're abroad.

In order to make your children's move to another country as problem-free as possible, you should consider the following before leaving home:

● Provide your children with as much information as possible about the country you're going to. Look at maps, books, videos and websites together, and talk about what you're going to discover. It will help to investigate the possibility of finding your children pen pals in the new country a few months before you go.

- If the move involves learning a new language, it will help enormously if your children have language lessons beforehand and even, if time permits, arrange a cultural exchange (where your child exchanges his home for a period with a child in the country that you're moving to). This is particularly important for teenage children.

- Talk to your children and try to discover their expectations and fears (children's imaginations are vivid, particularly about the unknown). Answer all the questions that you can and try to correct any misconceptions they have.

- Try to find out about possible new schools and share the information with your children. If possible, contact other expatriate parents with children at the same school and ask their advice. It's worth noting that most international schools have a higher academic level and a greater sense of competitiveness than their equivalents at home. You may need to prepare your children for this. If possible, try to find a family locally who have been to the country you're moving to and arrange a meeting with them and encourage your children to ask as many questions as possible.

- If they're old enough, allow your children to organise their own farewell party for friends and make sure that they say goodbye to everyone (and everything) before you leave. Bear in mind that it may be impossible to take pets with you and you may need to leave them with friends or relatives or have them 'adopted'.

- Above all, you should try to be positive about the move – even if you aren't! Children are quick to pick up on any negative undercurrents or tensions within their parents and if you're openly nervous and apprehensive about a move, they will be too.

Teenagers will probably react negatively at first to the idea of relocation and certainly very differently from their younger siblings. Teenagers are at the stage when they feel they've got their lives sorted out and into a routine, where friends are of major importance and where they enjoy a certain independence from their parents. The thought of leaving their friends and their familiar references will probably be more overwhelming the older a child is. Teenagers will also have a much better idea of the world as it really is than younger children, whose experience is limited by age and knowledge. A teenager will probably already know something about the country and may have preconceived ideas or even prejudices. You will need to provide exact information for teenagers, as well as give them precise assurances to dispel their fears and apprehensions.

For example, you will need to know in advance what sort of independence you will be able to offer a teenager once you're settled in the new country. You will also need ready-prepared answers to questions such as: Will I be able to go shopping on my own or with my friends? Will I be able to get the bus on my own (or drive a car)? What sort of things will I be able to do with my friends?

An excellent book about moving abroad and adjusting, written expressly for expatriate children, is *Let's Make a Move* published by BR Anchor Publishing (🖳 www.branchor.com). For parents, *Living & Working Abroad, A Parent's Guide* by Robin Pascoe (Kuperard) provides practical advice regarding all aspects of your stay.

KEEPING IN TOUCH

The availability, quality and cost of local services such as post, telephone (including mobile phones and the internet/email) and fax may be an important consideration when living and working abroad, particularly if you wish to keep in close touch with family and friends, or need to work closely with business colleagues in other countries. The range of services and the reliability and speed of postal deliveries vary considerably according to the country. In some countries airmail letters can take weeks to be delivered, even to neighbouring countries, and thousands of items of post go astray each year.

Telephone

Most EU countries provide an excellent telephone service and a phone can be installed in days; while in a few others there may be a long wait to have a telephone line installed and the service may be antiquated and prone to breakdowns. The cost of international telephone calls varies considerably according to the country and can be very expensive, although the introduction of competition in the domestic telephone market in many EU countries has led to a marked reduction in prices. However, there are a number of ways to reduce the cost, including obtaining an international calling card, e.g. from a US telephone company, or using a callback or resale company (see below). If you will be absent from a home abroad for long periods, you should pay your telephone bill (and all other regular bills) by direct debit from a local bank or post office account. If you fail to pay a bill on time your service could be cut off and it can take weeks to have it reconnected.

Home Country Direct

You can obtain an international calling credit card from telephone companies in most countries. This allows you to make calls (at local rates) from as many as 120 countries and charge them to your telephone bill in your home country. All EU countries except Estonia, Latvia and Slovenia subscribe to a Home Country Direct service that allows you to call a special number giving you direct and free access to an operator in the country you're calling. The operator will connect you to the number required and will also accept credit card and reverse charge calls. However, you should be wary of making international reverse charge calls to some countries using this scheme, as you will pay at least double the cost of using a local payphone. For a list of countries served by the Home Direct service, consult your telephone directory or call the local operator.

International Calling Cards

You can obtain an international telephone calling card from telephone companies in many countries that allows you to make calls from abroad and charge them to your telephone bill in your home country. US long-distance telephone companies (e.g. AT&T, MCI and Sprint) compete vigorously for overseas customers and offer calling cards allowing customers to bill international calls to a credit card. The benefits of international calling cards are that they're fee-free; calls can be made to or from most countries; calls can usually be made from any telephone (including hotel telephones); and calls can be made via an English-speaking operator in the US (foreign-language operators are also available). Some companies offer conference call facilities that allow you to talk to a number of people in different countries simultaneously. Other features may include a 'world office' facility, allowing you to retrieve voice and fax messages at any time from anywhere in the world. If you do a lot of travelling, it's advisable to carry a number of calling cards, as the cheapest card often depends on the countries you're calling from and to.

Callback Or Resale Companies

Callback and resale telephone companies buy international line time at a cheap rate from major telephone companies, thus enabling them to offer inexpensive international calls. Callback works by a system whereby you simply dial a code before making a call, which connects you to the resale company's services. Using these companies may entail dialling a lot of numbers, although it can be reduced if you've a phone with a memory facility (highly recommended). Calls must usually be paid for with a credit card, possibly in advance, or by direct debit each month from a bank account or credit card.

Mobile Phones

Most EU countries provide a mobile phone service countrywide except for remote areas. A mobile phone is particularly useful in countries where there's a long wait for the installation of a fixed phone line. However, in many countries mobile phones are expensive to buy and operate, and have high connection fees, standing charges and call rates. **International tariffs can vary by hundreds of per cent according to your network provider and your contract.** In some countries, e.g. Denmark, you must have an address in the country in order to buy and operate a mobile phone. Digital mobile phones that subscribe to the Global System for Mobile (GSM) communications system can be used to make and receive calls in all EU countries (called 'international roaming'). For information about individual countries, see the internet (🖥 www.gsm world.com) or contact the GSM Association, 6-8 Old Bond Street, London, UK (☎ 020-7518 0530, 🖥 www.gsmworld.com).

Before using a GSM phone abroad, you must contact your service provider to make sure that your tariff allows this facility. You must also ensure that your phone will operate in the country you're planning to visit. When you take a GSM phone abroad, all calls made to your phone will go via the country where the phone is registered and you must pay for the call from that country to the country where you're located. For example, if your GSM phone is registered in the UK, a caller in the UK pays the standard call charge for calls to mobile phones and you pay for the call from the UK to where you are abroad. This is because callers have no way of knowing that you've taken your phone abroad (unless you tell them!). You can, however, divert all incoming calls to voicemail when abroad. Calls made from abroad are routed automatically via a local GSM service provider.

Internet 'Telephone' Services

The success of the internet is built on the ability to gather information from computers around the world by connecting to a nearby service provider for the cost of a local telephone call. If you've correspondents or friends who are connected to the internet, you can make international 'calls' for the price of a local telephone call to an internet provider. Once on the internet, there are no other charges, no matter how much distance is covered or time is spent on-line. Internet users can buy inexpensive software that effectively turns their personal computer into a voice-based telephone (both parties must have compatible computer software). You also need a sound card, speakers, a microphone and a modem, and access to a local internet provider. While the quality of communication isn't as good as using a telephone (it's similar to a CB radio) and you need to arrange call times in advance, making international 'calls' costs virtually nothing.

Fax Services

Fax machines are available in all countries, although the cost varies considerably. It may be possible to take a fax machine abroad, but you must check that it's compatible or that it can be modified at a reasonable cost. Most fax machines made for use in a European country will operate in most other European countries, although getting a fax machine repaired abroad may be difficult unless the same model is sold locally. Public fax services are provided by main post offices in many EU countries, although they may only send faxes, not receive them. Telexes can also be sent via post offices, and telexes and faxes can be sent and received via major hotels, business offices (providing business services) and newsagents in many countries.

Business Services

In major towns and tourist areas in most EU countries, there are offices (such as Mail Boxes etc.) offering a range of communications services, which may include telephone, fax (transmission and receipt), mailbox service, *poste restante*, post forwarding, call-in service and 24-hour access, stamps, envelopes, postcards, packing supplies, air shipping/receiving, postal metering, money orders and transfers, telegrams, voicemail, email, internet, telex, copy service, telephone message service and various other business services.

The Internet

The internet has seen a spectacular increase in its usage in the EU. This is due mainly to lower prices for both calls and computers, and EU nationals increasingly now use the internet daily at work and/or at home. Ratings vary enormously from country to country, however, and the amount invested by individual countries in the internet, particularly in broad band technology, differs greatly. In some countries, such as Finland and Ireland, investment is high and all primary schools are online. In others, particularly many of the new member states, the internet is still very much in its infancy.

Connecting to the internet in the EU generally costs the same as local calls, although many telephone companies offer package deals, which usually allow you to buy a fixed number of access hours per month at a discount. Broad band internet is available in most member states, although in some of the new member states there's little access and many rural areas throughout the EU don't have broad band facilities at all.

All EU countries have numerous internet servers – shop around for the best deals – and most towns and cities have internet café facilities. In many major cities, internet access is also available in public libraries.

GETTING THERE

Although it isn't so important if you're moving to a neighbouring country within a reasonable driving or flying distance of your family and friends, one of the major considerations when living in the EU is communications (road, rail, air and sea links) with your home country. How long will it take to get there, e.g. by air, taking into account journeys to and from airports? Is it possible to drive? One of the main advantages of being able to drive is that you can take much more luggage with you and the cost for a family may be significantly lower than flying. Could you travel by bus, train or ferry? What does it cost? How frequent are buses, flights, trains or ferries at the time(s) of year when you plan to travel? Is it feasible to travel home for a long weekend, given the cost and travelling time involved?

Scheduled airline fares are prohibitively expensive to some countries, while in others, charter flight companies can be unreliable and over-booking is often a problem in the high season. The advent of so-called budget or 'no-frills' airlines offering services to and from some countries in the EU, e.g. the UK, Germany, Italy and Spain, has revolutionised the flight market and you can now buy a relatively cheap flight at short notice to many destinations in those countries. If you intend to make frequent trips back home, it obviously makes sense to choose a country that involves a relatively short journey and isn't too expensive. It may be worth choosing a destination served by a budget airline, although the very nature of the budget airline market means that companies can (and do) discontinue services at very short notice. If a long journey is involved, you should remember that it takes most people a day or two to recover fully, particularly when a long flight (and possibly jet-lag) is involved.

Regular travellers, e.g. with ferry companies and airlines, can take advantage of travel clubs, season tickets, discount schemes for shareholders and special deals for frequent fliers. For example, those travelling between the UK and the continent by ferry can make savings by joining a 'Property Owners Club', such as those operated by Brittany Ferries for homeowners in France and Spain; and P&O shareholders receive discounts on most routes. There are, however, strict qualifying conditions for both schemes. If flying is your only alternative, remember that if you need to take a flight at short notice it can be expensive, as you may be unable to get a inexpensive charter or APEX flight. Also bear in mind that, in some countries, ferry services are severely curtailed outside the main holiday season and services are often cancelled altogether owing to bad weather.

Shop around for the lowest fares available, but don't forget that an advertised fare rarely includes airport taxes and credit card charges, which, when added to the flight price, can cost more than the ticket! For some destinations it may be cheaper to fly via another country, rather than take a direct scheduled flight, assuming that this is possible. This is a possibility worth investigating for travellers to Central and Eastern EU countries who may find it's cheaper to fly with a budget airline to southern Germany or Italy and then travel overland to Austria, the Czech Republic, Hungary, Slovakia or Slovenia. Bargain fares are often advertised in national newspapers such as *The Sunday Times*, *Observer* and London's *Time Out* entertainment magazine in the UK or the Sunday editions of the *New York Times*, the *Los Angeles Times* and the *Chicago Tribune* in the US.

Useful publications for frequent fliers include the Official Airline Guides (OAG) *Worldwide Pocket Flight Guide*, *The Complete Skytraveller* by David Beaty (Methuen), and *Fly Europe: The Complete Guide to Budget Airline Destinations* by Katie Wood (Aurum Press). Regular air travellers may be interested in subscribing to *Inside Flyer* magazine (☎ 1-800-767-8896 within the US or ☎ 719-597 8889 from outside the US; 🖳 www.insideflyer.com).

Allow plenty of time to get to and from airports, ports and railway stations, particularly when travelling during peak hours, when traffic congestion can be horrendous.

Passenger Rights

In October 2003 innovative legislation was passed by the EU regarding rights for air passengers, particularly those suffering over-booking, flight cancellations or long delays. The legislation covers both scheduled and non-scheduled flights, and will be applied to all airlines operating at EU airports as from 2004. The new regulations are as follows:

- **Overbooking** – Some 1 million passengers a year at EU airports are affected every year by overbooking. Under the new legislation, when there are more passengers than seats available, the airline must appeal for volunteers to surrender their seats in return for advantages and, if there are no volunteers, must compensate the passengers who cannot get on the flight with: €250 for flights under 1,500km; €400 for inter-EU flights of more than 1,500km and for other flights between 1,500km and 3,500km; or €600 for other flights. In addition, these passengers can also choose between reimbursement of their ticket and an alternative flight, and receive meals and hotel accommodation.

- **Cancellations** – When flights are cancelled by airlines or tour operators for causes attributable to them, compensation must be paid at the same rates as for overbooking (see above) and passengers must receive meals and hotel accommodation when a cancellation means an overnight stay, and reimbursement when a cancellation delays the passenger for at least five hours.

- **Long Delays** – When a flight suffers a long delay, the airline is obliged to give passengers meals and refreshments, hotel accommodation if the delay means an overnight stay and reimbursement when a flight is delayed for at least five hours.

PUBLIC TRANSPORT

For many people an important aspect of living abroad is being able to get around easily, relatively cheaply and safely. Public transport services in EU countries vary considerably from excellent to terrible or even non-existent, depending on where you live. In some countries, public transport is poor and there's no rail service and only an infrequent and unreliable local bus service. Public transport tends to be excellent to adequate in major cities, where there may be an integrated system encompassing buses, trains, trams and possibly a metro or ferry system. However, outside the main towns and cities, public transport can be sparse and most people who live in rural areas find it necessary to have their own car. Taxis are common and plentiful in most countries, although they can be prohibitively expensive. In some countries, e.g. Cyprus, there are inexpensive shared taxis or mini-buses, which pick up and drop off passengers at any point along their route.

If you don't drive or aren't planning to own a car abroad, you will usually need to live in a city or large town where there's adequate public transport. If you don't plan to drive abroad, you should investigate the frequency and cost of local public transport, such as buses, trains, ferries and taxis. If you don't have a car, you may need to use taxis to carry your shopping home or have it delivered.

Further information about public transport in individual countries can be found in the **Country Profiles** in **Chapter 9** and is also obtainable from tourist offices and any good guide book.

MOTORING

If you're wedded to your car (or at least to having your own transport), you probably wouldn't consider living anywhere you cannot get around independently. Having your own transport will also allow you a much wider choice of where you can live. However, it isn't always necessary to own a car and many people use taxis for local trips and hire a car for longer journeys.

Driving can be a nerve-wracking and even dangerous experience in some EU countries, and most people are more accident-prone when driving abroad. Driving in cities is often totally chaotic at the best of times, particularly when traffic drives on a different side of the road from that in your home country. A car can be a liability in towns if you don't have private parking and you will save a lot of money if you can manage without one (which is why many people on a limited budget live in towns).

If you're an EU national planning to become a resident, you may be able to import a new or second-hand car from another EU country, duty and tax-free, although the paperwork involved is time-consuming. Check the regulations in any country you must pass through to reach your destination. When buying a car for use abroad, you will often find that in most EU countries it pays to buy a diesel-engined car (diesel is cheaper than petrol in EU countries except Slovenia and the UK) and one with air-conditioning, which is a 'must-have' in southern EU countries in the summer. If you're planning to import a car (new or second-hand) into EU countries, it must be have local type approval and meet certain technical standards. You usually also need to have owned and operated a vehicle abroad for six months to qualify for tax-free importation. This isn't a problem when taking a car from one EU country to another, but can be when exporting a vehicle from the US or Japan to the EU, when it may need expensive modifications.

EU nationals moving to another EU country can use a vehicle registered in their home country abroad without time limits or paying local taxes. However, the period of use is determined by the time that a non-resident is permitted to remain in another EU country without becoming a resident, which is a maximum of six months (182 days) in a calendar year. You must be resident in some EU countries in order to own and operate a car on local registration plates.

For further information on importing a car in the EU see **Car Importation** on page 175.

Car Hire

The major multinational hire companies such as Alamo, Avis, Budget, Hertz and Thrifty have offices in EU countries, particularly at major airports and in large cities. There are also cheaper local hire companies. Car hire companies are listed in yellow pages and local companies are listed by town. You may be approached at airports by representatives of local hire companies, who may not be reputable (check their credentials). It's advisable to reserve a hire car before arriving abroad, particularly during peak periods. When booking, remember to specify an automatic model if you aren't used to a manual (stick-shift) gearbox, as many hire cars in EU countries are manual.

Car hire rates vary considerably and are generally higher in the EU than North America, although they vary according to the location and season, e.g. Spain and Portugal offer relatively cheap car hire, while it's expensive in Ireland. Many companies have lower rates for weekend hire, e.g. from 4pm on Fridays to noon on Mondays and for periods of 14 days or longer. The rates charged by major international companies vary little, although you may get a better deal by booking in advance. One of the advantages of using a national company is that you can hire a car in one town and drop it off in another, although you should check the cost of this service. Although cheaper, small local companies require you to return a car to the office you got it from or to the local airport. **Some of the cheaper hire companies cut corners on maintenance and repairs, and cars can sometimes be unsafe to drive.**

When comparing rates, check that prices are fully inclusive of insurance and taxes, that insurance cover (including personal accident) is adequate, and that there are no hidden costs. Also check whether any 'extras' are included in the basic price, such as collision damage waiver (CDW), theft cover, personal accident insurance (PAI), airport tax, roof rack, baby seat, air-conditioning, additional drivers and local taxes as well as value added tax. Some companies don't offer unlimited kilometres/miles, which usually works out to be more expensive unless you plan to cover relatively little distance. If required, check that you're permitted to take a car out of the country where you rent it, as you may need extra insurance.

When choosing a hire car, bear in mind that, where applicable, you should ensure that you've sufficient power for mountain driving, e.g. at least a 1.6 litre engine for two people and their luggage. If you're going to be doing a lot of driving in summer, air-conditioning is a must (which again requires a larger engine). Always check the contract and car (e.g. for body damage and to ensure that everything works) carefully before setting out.

To hire a car in the EU, you must be aged at least 20, although it's 21 in most EU countries and can be 25 for certain categories of cars. Some companies also have an upper age limit, e.g. 70. Drivers must produce a valid licence (a copy isn't acceptable) with a photo ID, and some drivers (e.g. non-EU nationals) may require an international driving permit. If more than one person will be driving a vehicle, all the drivers' names must be entered on the rental agreement. If a credit card isn't used, there's usually a high cash deposit and possibly the whole hire period must be paid for in advance. **When paying by credit card, carefully check your bill and statement, as unauthorised charges aren't unknown.** It may be possible to sign a credit card authorisation slip and then pay by cash when you return a car. However, if you do this, you must make sure that you obtain (and destroy) the credit card payment slip.

Hiring a car is expensive in some countries, particularly during the high season or for long periods. One way to reduce the cost is to rent a car through the US office of an international car hire company such as Alamo (☎ 1-800 462 5266, 🖥 www.alamo.com), Avis (☎ 1-800 230 4898, 🖥 www.avis.com), Budget (☎ 1-800 472 3325, 🖥 www.budget.com) or Hertz (☎ 1-800 654 3001, 🖥 www. hertz.com) and pay by credit card. This is a legitimate practice and can save considerably on local rates. The US freephone (800) numbers of other international rental companies can be obtained from international directory enquiries or the company's website. When dialling freephone numbers from abroad, you're charged at international rates.

Driving Licence

Ensuring that you're licensed to drive in some countries can be simple or infuriatingly complicated. This depends, not on your nationality, but on the country that issued your licence. All licences issued by EU member states are recognised in all other EU and most other European countries. However, if you're a non-EU citizen planning to live in an EU country, obtaining a local driving licence can be a frustrating experience (this applies to many Americans). In some EU countries you can drive with a foreign licence (possibly with a translation) for a limited period, although some EU countries require foreigners to have an international driving permit (IDP). EU nationals who become resident in another EU country often don't need to change their original licence for a new one, although this depends on the country in question. If the licence has to be changed, it's usually just a case of going to the local traffic authorities and doing a direct swap. You don't have to take a driving test. Non-EU nationals who become residents usually have a limited period (e.g. six months or a year) in which to exchange a foreign licence for a local one, after which it becomes invalid and you may have to take a theoretical and/or driving test.

If your current licence isn't recognised in the country where you're planning to live, it may be possible to obtain a licence from a country whose licences are recognised, although you must do this before taking up residence abroad. Recognition of your licence will depend on whether your home country (or the country or state that issued your licence) has a reciprocity agreement with the EU country where you're planning to live. If it doesn't, you may need to do any or all of the following: undertake a first-aid course; take a number of lessons with a local driving school; pass written and practical driving tests; undergo a medical and eye examination; provide a copy and official translation of your driving licence; supply a number of photographs; obtain a residence permit;

complete various forms; produce your passport; and pay a hefty fee. If you wish to drive a car with a manual (stick) shift and passed your test in a car with an automatic gearbox, you will need to take a driving test. Your existing licence may be stamped and returned to you, retained until you leave the country, or returned to the country of issue. If you will need it to drive in your home or another country, be sure to obtain a copy before going abroad.

If your driving licence isn't recognised in a country where you're planning to live, make sure that you start the process for obtaining a local licence as soon as possible after your arrival, as it can take some months to achieve. If you don't obtain a local licence by the deadline, you may be prohibited from driving or may need to take a driving test, even if one wasn't originally required.

Further information on driving licences in individual EU countries can be found under **Driving** in **Chapter 8 – Miscellaneous Matters** and in **Chapter 9 – Country Profiles**.

Buying A Car

If you're planning to be resident long-term in an EU country, it may be worth buying a car, which may be no more expensive and considerably less time-consuming than importing one. An EU national or EU resident has the right to buy a car anywhere within the EU and then use it in his country of residence. The servicing and warranty conditions given when you bought the car are applicable in your home country. So, if the car is faulty or you're entitled to a free service, you can have this done in your home country (provided the car manufacturer is represented there) without having to return the car to the country where you bought it.

If you're buying anything more than a small cheap car, it may be worth buying a car in another EU country since car prices vary greatly from country to country. Don't forget, however, to include in your price calculations the cost of travel to collect the car **and** the drive back to your home country. Obviously it's cheaper if you buy the car from a neighbouring EU country rather than one that's a huge distance away.

An EU survey in 2003 found huge differences in price in different countries for the same car model. Price differences ranged from 15 to 36 per cent for many car models. For example, the difference between the cheapest and most expensive country for a small car such as a Peugeot 106 was 30 per cent and nearly 23 per cent for a larger model such as a Ford Mondeo. In 2003, the cheapest cars in the EU were on sale in Finland, Greece and Denmark (the cheapest, with cars on average 7 per cent cheaper than those in Greece). The most expensive countries were Austria and Germany, where some 35 models had the highest prices in the EU. Prices in Ireland and the UK are no longer high compared to those in the rest of the EU but, if you buy a car in Ireland or the UK to drive in the rest of the EU, there's an additional cost of converting the car to left-hand drive. Irish or British residents buying a car in continental EU countries have to pay extra for the conversion to right-hand drive. Further information on car prices in the EU is available from ⌨ http://europa.eu.int/comm/competition/ car_sector/price_diffs/2003_05.pdf. This survey is updated annually. You need Adobe (Acrobat Reader) to read this file.

Car Insurance

When driving in the EU you must have valid car insurance. This is a complicated subject and the types of insurance, what is included and the costs vary considerably from country to country. **Never take it for granted that your motor insurance is sufficient for you and your passengers**, but check in advance and obtain it in writing – this is particularly important when hiring a car. When driving abroad, you should also consider motor breakdown insurance.

Motorists insured in one of the fifteen original EU countries, the Czech Republic, Hungary, Iceland, Liechtenstein, Norway, Slovakia and Switzerland, are automatically covered for basic third party liability in all the above countries. However, at the time of writing (early 2004), Cyprus, Estonia, Latvia, Lithuania, Malta, Poland and Slovenia weren't covered, although this is expected to change in the near future. Check with your insurance company for the latest information. **In any case, you should always check for any EU country, as some insurance companies may restrict the countries where you're covered.** In the EU, an international insurance certificate (green card) isn't compulsory, but is useful since a green card serves as internationally recognised proof that you've at least the minimum compulsory third party insurance cover and it makes it easier to claim compensation if you have an accident. A green card is available at no extra cost when you're insured in most western European countries and extends your normal insurance (e.g. fully comprehensive) to other countries (currently 43) covered by the green card agreement. Further information on the green card system is available from the website ⌨ www.cobx.org.

Breakdown Insurance

When driving in the EU it's important to have motor breakdown insurance (which may include holiday and travel insurance), including repatriation for your family and your car in the event of an accident or breakdown. If you're a member of a motoring organisation, you may be covered when travelling abroad by a reciprocal agreement with national breakdown services, although cover is usually fairly basic. In some EU countries, motor breakdown insurance is provided by car insurance companies. More comprehensive policies are available from motoring organisations in many countries. Many companies providing European breakdown insurance operate multilingual, 24-hour, emergency centres where assistance is available for motoring, medical, legal and travel problems.

Car Security

Most EU countries have a problem with car theft and thefts from cars, particularly in major cities and resort areas. In many countries, foreign-registered vehicles – especially camper vans and mobile homes – are targeted by thieves. If you drive anything other than a worthless wreck you should have theft insurance that includes your car stereo and personal belongings (although this may be prohibitively expensive). If you drive a new or valuable car it's wise to have it fitted with an alarm, an engine immobiliser (the best system) or other anti-theft device, and also to use a visible deterrent such as a steering or gear stick lock. It's particularly important to protect your car if you own a model that's desirable to professional car thieves, e.g. most new sports and executive models, which are often stolen by crooks to order.

The best security system (available in many EU countries) for a valuable car is a tracking device that's triggered by concealed motion detectors. The vehicle's movements are tracked by radio or satellite and the police are automatically notified and recover over 90 per cent of vehicles. Some systems can immobilise a vehicle while it's on the move (which may not be such a good idea!). The main drawback is that tracking systems are expensive, although many insurance companies offer a discount on comprehensive insurance when you have a tracking system fitted.

Few cars are fitted with deadlocks and most can be broken into in seconds by a competent thief. A good security system won't usually prevent someone from breaking into your car or even stop it from being stolen, but it will make it more difficult and may persuade a thief to look for an easier target. Radios, cassette and CD players attract thieves like bees to a honey pot everywhere. If you buy an expensive stereo system, buy one with a removable unit or with a removable control panel that you can pop into a bag or pocket. Never forget to remove it (and your mobile phone), even when parking for a few minutes. In some EU countries you will notice that cars in cities rarely contain stereo systems, as most drivers remove them when parking.

Thieves often smash windows (in some countries BMW stands for 'break my window') to steal stereo systems and other articles from cars, even articles of little value such as sunglasses or cigarettes. When leaving your car unattended, store any valuables, including clothes, in the glove box or boot (trunk). However, storing valuables in the boot isn't foolproof, particularly if the boot can be opened from inside the car. If a car is empty a thief may be tempted to force open the boot with a crowbar. Some people leave their car doors and boot unlocked (and empty!) to avoid having their windows smashed or the boot broken open. It's never advisable to leave your original car papers in your car (which may help a thief dispose of it). When parking overnight or when it's dark, it's advisable to park in a secure overnight car park or garage, or at least in a well-lit area.

If your car is stolen or anything is stolen from it, report it to the police in the area where it was stolen. You can usually report it by telephone, but must go to the station to complete a report. Don't, however, expect the police to find it or even take any interest in your loss. Report a theft to your insurance company as soon as possible.

Rules Of The Road

You may be unfamiliar with the road rules and regulations in the EU country where you're planning to live, which may differ considerably from those in your home country. The following tips are designed to help you survive driving in the EU:

- If you're taking a car with you, don't forget your car registration and insurance papers, test and tax certificates (if applicable). If you intend to drive to the country where you're planning to take up residence, ensure that you've sufficient local currency (for petrol, road tolls, food, traffic fines, etc.) for all the countries you will pass through.

- In many EU countries it's compulsory to carry your driving licence and/or vehicle registration documents with you when driving. Failure to do so can result in a fine.

- You're probably aware that not all EU countries drive on the same side of the road – in some countries drivers use both sides (when not driving in the middle!). It saves confusion if you drive on the same side as the majority. All EU countries except Ireland and the UK drive on the right. If you aren't used to driving on the left or right, take it easy until you're accustomed to it. Be particularly alert when leaving lay-bys, T-junctions, one-way streets, petrol stations and car parks, as it's easy to lapse into driving on the wrong side. It's helpful to display a reminder (e.g. 'Think Left!' or 'Think Right!') on your car's dashboard.

- Procedures following an accident aren't the same in all countries, although most EU countries use a standard accident report form provided by insurance companies. As a general rule, it's advisable to call the police to the scene for anything other than a minor accident.

- Drivers of foreign-registered cars must have the appropriate nationality plate (sticker) affixed to the rear of their car when motoring abroad, unless the nationality is already displayed on the number-plate (as it is on all new cars in the EU). In some countries you can be fined on the spot for not displaying it, although it isn't often enforced judging by the number of cars without them. Cars must show the correct nationality plate only and not an assortment.

- Ensure that your car complies with local laws and that you've the necessary equipment. For example, spare tyre, bulbs and fuses, warning triangle (in some countries, such as Spain, you need two), first-aid kit, fire extinguisher, reflective jacket (to be worn if you have to get out of your car on the road at night), petrol can (carrying a can of petrol, or petrol in plastic cans, is forbidden in some countries) and headlight beam deflectors. Check the latest regulations with a motoring organisation in your home country.

- Make sure that you've sufficient spares, particularly if you're driving a rare or exotic car (i.e. any car that isn't sold locally). A good map will come in handy, particularly when you're lost. Michelin produces comprehensive maps for all EU countries and you can also consult routes online (🖥 www. viamichelin.com). If your car runs on unleaded petrol, make sure that it's freely available locally and in all the countries you intend to visit or pass through – it is in most EU countries. If you need leaded or lead replacement petrol (LRP) and it isn't available locally, you may need to have your car's engine modified. Leaded petrol is available only in Lithuania and Malta, and will be phased out by the end of 2005. Make sure that you know the local name for the type of fuel you require, which can be confusing, e.g. *gasolio* in Italy is diesel (and not gasoline), while *gasolina* in Spain is petrol (gasoline)!

- Seat belts (front and back) must be worn at all times in EU countries. In some EU countries (e.g. Finland, Hungary and Sweden) dipped headlights (low beam) must be used at all times.

- If you're planning a long journey, a mechanical check-up for your car is advisable, particularly if it's a while since its last service.

- The legal blood alcohol level when driving varies according to the country and is 0.5g per 100ml of blood in most EU countries, although it's zero in some of the new member states. Alcohol is estimated to be a major factor in at least a third of all road accidents and in countries with a 'drink-drive culture' it's much higher. The strength of alcoholic beverages (and the size of drinks) varies considerably from country to country. The best policy is not to drink alcohol at all when you're driving. The **Driving** section in the **Country Profiles** provides the legal alcohol limit for each EU country (see **Chapter 9**).

- In continental Europe, where all traffic drives on the right, most main roads are designated priority roads, indicated by a sign. The most common type is a yellow diamond on a white background (the end of priority is shown by the same sign with a black diagonal line through it). On secondary roads without priority signs and in built-up areas, you must give way to all vehicles coming from your RIGHT. **Failure to observe this rule is the cause of many accidents.** If you're ever in doubt about who has priority, give way to trams, buses and all traffic coming from your RIGHT (particularly large trucks!). Emergency (ambulance, fire, police) and public utility (electricity, gas, telephone, water) vehicles attending an emergency have priority on all roads in most countries. In most EU countries at roundabouts (traffic circles) vehicles on the roundabout have priority and not those entering it. Usually this is indicated by a 'give way' sign.

- Never carry anything across an international border unless you're absolutely sure what it is, as it could contain drugs or other illegal substances. The same applies to any passengers (and their baggage) that you pick up on your journey. It's illegal in some countries to transport produce, plants, alcohol and under-age children (apart from your own) across international borders.

- There are toll motorways in Austria, Cyprus, France, Greece, Hungary, Italy, Portugal and Spain. Drivers using toll motorways in some EU countries (e.g. Austria and Hungary) must display a toll label or *vignette* on their vehicle. The label can usually be bought at major border crossings into the country and at large petrol stations.

- The use of a mobile phone while driving increases the risk of a fatal accident by five times. All EU countries either explicitly or implicitly prohibit the use of mobile phones while driving (although you wouldn't think so, judging by the number of drivers one sees chatting on them!). Some EU countries allow the use of hands-free devices.

- Speed limits vary throughout the EU, but all countries impose fines for exceeding them and many also impose penalty points on your licence. Make sure you know what the speed limit is for the road you're driving along. Speed limits for individual EU countries are included in the **Driving** section of **Country Profiles** in **Chapter 9**.

Information on driving regulations, compulsory equipment, tolls and general tips throughout Europe are available from the AA UK website and in the *European Motoring Advice* leaflet (💻 www.theaa.com/allaboutcars/overseas/europe_advice).

When driving anywhere, **never** assume that you know what another motorist is going to do next. Just because a motorist is indicating left doesn't mean he's actually going to turn left – in some countries he's just as likely to be turning right, stopping or about to reverse – and in many countries motorists make turns without any indication at all! Don't be misled by any semblance of road discipline and clearly marked lanes. Try to be courteous, if only in self-defence, but don't expect others to reciprocate.

The most dangerous countries in which to drive vary according to the newspapers and magazines you read and whose statistics they use, but according to official EU statistics, some 45,000 people are killed on EU roads a year and more than 1.5 million injured. What is indisputable is that the likelihood of having an accident is much higher in some EU countries, particularly the Czech Republic, Greece, Poland, Portugal and Spain (check the road accident statistics – which don't lie!). The Netherlands, Sweden and the UK have the best road safety records. Take extra care in winter, when ice and snow can make driving particularly hazardous. Driving in some EU countries is totally chaotic, a bit like a funfair dodgem car track without the fun, and nerve-racking at the best of times. If you're in doubt about your ability to cope with the stress or the risks involved, you'd be wiser to use public transport.

2.

FINDING A JOB
& WORKING

Before making any plans to work in the European Union (EU), you must ensure that it will be possible and under what conditions. If you don't qualify to live and work in a country by birthright or as a national of one of the countries that are members of the EU, obtaining a work permit may be impossible. Americans and others without the automatic right to work in the EU must have their employment approved by a country's Ministry of Labour and obtain an employment visa **before** arriving in an EU country.

Even when you don't require a permit, you shouldn't plan on obtaining employment in a particular country unless you've a firm job offer, special qualifications or experience for which there's a strong local demand. If you want a good job, you must usually be well qualified and speak the local language fluently. If you plan to arrive without a job (assuming it's permitted), you should have a detailed plan for finding employment and try to make some contacts before you arrive. Being attracted to a country by its weather, cuisine and lifestyle (etc.) is understandable, but doesn't rate highly as an employment qualification! It's extremely difficult to find work in many countries, particularly in rural and resort areas, and can even be difficult in cities and large towns.

Before planning to work in the EU, you should dispassionately examine your motives and credentials. What kind of work can you realistically expect to do? What are your qualifications and experience? Are they recognised in the EU? How good is your local language ability? Unless you're fluent, you won't be competing on equal terms with the locals (you won't anyway, but that's a different matter!). Most employers aren't interested in hiring anyone without, at the very least, an adequate working knowledge of the local language. Are there any jobs in your profession or trade in the country and region where you plan to live? Could you work in a self-employed capacity or start your own business? How will you survive while looking for work? The answers to these and many other questions can be quite disheartening, but it's better to ask them before moving to or within the EU rather than afterwards.

There are numerous books for those seeking a job abroad, including the *Directory of Jobs and Careers Abroad* (Vacation Work), *Getting a Job in Europe* by Mark Hempshell (How To Books), *International Jobs: Where they are and how to get them* by Eric Kocher and Nina Segal (Perseus) and *What Color is Your Parachute?* by Richard Nelson Bolles (Ten Speed Press). There are also many magazines and newspapers dedicated to particular professions, industries or trades (see **Appendix B**).

UNEMPLOYMENT

The local unemployment rate is generally an excellent guide to employment prospects, although a low rate is no guarantee that you will be able to find work with a reasonable salary, particularly if you've few qualifications and little experience. Unemployment fell considerably in most European countries in the mid to late '90s, and in 2001 stood at its lowest level for decades in many countries, although general recession in 2003 pushed figures higher, particularly in Germany. The average unemployment rate in the EU in 2003 was 8.8 per cent, ranging from 3.9 per cent in Luxembourg to 11.3 per cent in Spain. Figures vary according to age group: for example, the unemployment rate for under-25s in 2003 was considerably higher at nearly 16 per cent in the EU as a whole. It's worth bearing in mind that a low average unemployment rate may mask particularly high rates in some regions of a country, e.g. the average rate in Italy in 2003 was around 8 per cent, although it varied from a low of under 4 per cent in the north of the country to over 25 per cent in some parts of the south. When deciding where to live, you should check the economic forecasts for the region and whether unemployment is rising or falling. As a general guide, unemployment figures tend to be lower in areas around the capital and large cities. Areas that depend on one or two industries only, such as motor manufacturing, armaments and textiles, may not be the best choice from a long-term point of view. In today's ever-changing world, nobody is immune from unemployment and it's important for workers to have skills that are in demand and which are constantly updated with further education and training.

EU CITIZENS

Nationals of the original fifteen European Union countries (Austria, Belgium, Denmark, Finland, France, Germany, Greece, Ireland, Italy, Luxembourg, the Netherlands, Portugal, Spain, Sweden and the UK) plus Cyprus and Malta have the right to enter, live and work in any of the above member states without a work permit, provided they have a valid passport or national identity card and comply with the member state's laws and regulations on employment. Malta has agreed not to impose restrictions, but has the right to impose a safeguard on employment of EU nationals if there's a threat to its employment market.

Nationals from the other new member states (the Czech Republic, Estonia, Hungary, Latvia, Lithuania, Poland, Slovakia and Slovenia) will eventually have the same right to enter, live and work in any other member state without a work permit, as will other EU nationals in the new member states. However, the EU has imposed a transitional period of a minimum of two years and a maximum of seven to avoid massive or disruptive migration. Until May 2006 at least, EU nationals from new member states (except Cyprus and Malta) will require a work permit to work in the original EU states, as will EU nationals from the original states to work in the new member states.

EU nationals are entitled to the same treatment as local citizens in matters of pay, working conditions, access to housing, vocational training, social security and trade union rights, and immediate dependants are entitled to join them and enjoy the same rights. EU legislation is designed to make it easier for people to meet vocational training requirements in other member states. There are, however, still practical barriers to full freedom of movement and the right to work within the EU. For example, some jobs in various member countries require job applicants to have specific skills or vocational qualifications, and qualifications obtained in some member states aren't always recognised in others. Other more practical barriers include housing availability and cost, and the transfer of pension rights. There are also restrictions on employment in the civil service, when the right to work may be limited in individual cases on grounds of public policy, security or health. Employment in the civil service is usually restricted to nationals of the country in question. There may also be restrictions in the security services and armed forces.

Job Seeker's Allowance For EU Nationals

If you're an EU National and eligible for a job seeker's allowance in your home country, you may also be eligible for the equivalent allowance if you're looking for work in another EU country. Eligibility is based on the number of social security contributions you've made during your working life. If you've made enough, the social security authorities in your home country will provide you with form E303. When you register as unemployed and looking for work in another EU country, you should show this form to the authorities. Allowances in some countries may take some time to be paid, so it's advisable to have sufficient funds to live on until you receive the allowance. Countries participating in this scheme are Austria, Belgium, Finland, France, Germany, Greece, Italy, Portugal, Spain, Sweden and the UK. Some of the new member states are expected to join in the near future.

QUALIFICATIONS

The most important qualification for working in the EU is often the ability to speak the local language. Once you've overcome this hurdle, you should establish whether your trade or professional qualifications and experience are recognised in a particular country. If you aren't experienced, employers usually expect studies to be in a relevant discipline and to have included work experience (i.e. on-the-job training). Professional or trade qualifications are required to work in many fields, although requirements are much more stringent in some countries than in others.

Most qualifications recognised by professional and trade bodies in North America are accepted throughout the EU. However, recognition varies from country to country, and in some cases foreign qualifications aren't recognised by local employers or professional and trade associations. All academic qualifications should also be recognised, although they may be given less prominence than equivalent local qualifications, according to the country and the educational establishment where they were gained. In general, qualifications earned in developing countries aren't as acceptable abroad as those from western institutions. Some professionals and tradesmen are required to undergo special training or work under supervision for a period (possibly a number of years) before they're permitted to work unsupervised or as self-employed.

University qualifications obtained in one EU country may not be considered as the equivalent qualification in another. This is particularly true of British university degrees whose courses are often shorter than those in many other EU countries. For example, an engineering degree takes three years in the UK but five years in France and Spain. Consequently, British degree holders may find their degree isn't recognised as a full degree and they may need either to undertake further study or to accept lower pay.

All EU member states issue occupation information sheets, containing a common job description with a table of qualifications, which are published in the various languages of the member states. These cover a large number of trades and professions and are intended to help someone with the relevant qualifications look for a job in another EU country. In the UK, information about academic qualifications can be obtained from NARIC, ECTIS 2000 Ltd. (Oriel House, Oriel Road, Cheltenham, Glos. GL50 1XP, ☎ 01242-260010, 💻 www. naric.co.uk) and information about the recognition of professional qualifications is available from the Department of Trade and Industry (☎ 020-7215 5000, 💻 www.dti.gov.uk). You can also check whether trades and professions are officially recognised on the European Union website (💻 http://citizens.eu.int), where a series of fact sheets is available, called *Dialogue with Citizens & Business*, providing detailed information on European and individual country procedures for the recognition of experience and qualifications.

EMPLOYMENT AGENCIES

European Employment Service

The European Union (EU) runs a job mobility portal, known as EURES, a network designed to bring together the European Commission, public employment services and other bodies such as trade unions, employer organisations and local and regional authorities throughout the EU member states. The member states (plus Iceland and Norway) exchange information regularly on vacancies. Local EURES offices have access to comprehensive information on how to apply for a job and living and working conditions in each country – over the last two years some one million EU citizens have found employment via the service. The international department of your home country's employment service can put you in touch with a Euroadviser who can provide advice. Euroadvisers can also arrange to have your personal details forwarded to the government employment service in selected countries. Further information is available from ☎ 00-800 4080 4080 (freephone throughout the EU) or ☎ 0800-917155 in the UK and the EURES website 💻 http://europa.eu.int/eures.

National Employment Agencies

Most governments operate an official employment agency whose job is to provide assistance for the unemployed to find work, particularly long-term unemployed people, the disabled and the disadvantaged. It may also be responsible for paying unemployment benefit. Government employment services may place people directly in jobs and offer guidance and counselling so that you can find the best way to return to employment, e.g. through education or training. Most employment services have websites. Some countries, e.g. the UK, provide job centres where local companies advertise for employees (🖥 www.jobcentreplus.gov.uk).

Private Employment Agencies

In addition to government employment services, many countries also have private employment agencies, which generally fall into two main categories: recruitment consultants (or head-hunters) for executives and senior personnel, and staff employment agencies that may recruit full-time, part-time and temporary staff. These agencies usually abound in all major cities and towns in Europe and are big business. Most large companies are happy to engage consultants to recruit staff, particularly executives (head-hunters account for around two-thirds of all top level executive appointments in some countries), managers, professional employees and temporary office staff (temps).

Most agencies specialise in particular fields or positions (e.g. computer personnel, accounting, etc.), while others deal with a range of industries and professions. Some agencies deal exclusively with temporary jobs in fields such as office staff, baby-sitting, home care, nannies and mothers' helps, housekeeping, cooks, gardeners, chauffeurs, hairdressing, security, cleaners, labourers and industrial workers. Nursing agencies are also fairly common (covering the whole range of nursing services, including physiotherapy, occupational and speech therapy, and dentistry), as are nanny and care agencies. Many employment agencies, both government and private, have websites (see page 64) where vacancies are advertised.

SEASONAL JOBS

Seasonal jobs are available throughout the year in most EU countries, the vast majority in the tourist industry. Many jobs last for the duration of the summer or winter tourist seasons, May to September and December to April respectively in the EU, although some are simply casual or temporary jobs for a number of weeks. Local language fluency is required for all but the most menial and worst paid jobs, and is equally or more important than experience and qualifications (although local language fluency alone won't guarantee you a well paid job). Seasonal jobs include most trades in hotels and restaurants; couriers and travel company representatives; a variety of jobs in ski resorts; sports instructors; jobs in bars and clubs; fruit and grape picking and other agricultural jobs; and various jobs in the construction industry. A useful publication is *Working in Tourism - The UK, Europe & Beyond* by Verite Reily Collins (Vacation Work).

It's essential to check whether you will be eligible to work in your chosen country before making plans, and you may also need to obtain a visa. Check with a local embassy or consulate in your home country well in advance of your visit. Students studying abroad can usually obtain a temporary work permit for part-time work during the summer holiday period and between school terms. The main seasonal jobs available abroad include those described below.

There are many books for those seeking holiday jobs, including *Summer Jobs Abroad 2004* and *Summer Jobs in Britain 2004* (both published by Vacation Work).

If you're a sports or ski instructor, tour guide, holiday representative or are involved in any job that gives you responsibility for groups of people or children, you should be extremely wary of accepting an illegal job without a contract, as you won't be insured for injuries to yourself, the public or accidents while travelling. Seasonal workers have few rights and little legal job protection, and can generally be fired without compensation at any time.

See also **Temporary & Casual Jobs** below and **Holiday & Short-Term Jobs** on page 54.

Couriers & Resort Representatives

Resort representatives' or couriers' duties include ferrying tourist groups back and forth from airports, organising excursions and social events, arranging ski passes and equipment hire, and generally playing the role of Jack or Jill of all trades. A job as a courier is tough and demanding, and requires resilience and resourcefulness to deal with the chaos associated with the package holiday business. The necessary requirements include the ability to answer many questions simultaneously (often in different languages), to remain calm and charming under extreme pressure, and above all, to maintain a keen sense of humour. Lost passengers, tickets, passports and tempers are everyday occurrences. It's an excellent training ground for managerial and leadership skills, pays well and often offers opportunities to supplement your earnings with tips.

Couriers are required by many local and foreign tour companies in both winter and summer resorts. Competition for jobs is fierce and local language ability is usually required, even for employment with British tour operators. Most companies have age requirements, the minimum usually being 21, although many companies prefer employees to be older. In countries with a thriving winter sports industry, the majority of courier jobs are available during the winter season with ski-tour companies and school ski-party organisers. A good source of information is ski magazines, which contain regular listings of tour companies showing who goes to which resorts. It's wise to find out the kind of clients you're likely to be dealing with, particularly if you're allergic to children or yuppies (young urban professionals – similar to children but more immature). To survive the winter in a ski resort, it helps to be a keen skier or a dedicated learner, otherwise you risk being bored to death by ski bums.

Holiday Camps & Theme Parks

For those who like working with children, holiday camps offer a number of summer job opportunities, ranging from camp counsellors and sports instructors to administrative and catering posts. Summer school holidays vary according to the country, although most schools in EU countries have summer holidays during July and August. Many countries have a number of theme parks that rely to a large extent on seasonal staff. The larger parks may also provide on-site accommodation for employees (the cost is deducted from your wages). Positions range from maintenance and catering to performing in the shows and pageants that form part of the entertainment. Check local newspapers starting in January or February for job postings for the coming summer season. April is a popular month for parks to hold auditions for performing roles. Most theme parks have websites containing employment information, e.g. Disneyland Paris (🖳 www.disneylandparis.com) and LegoLand in Jutland, Denmark and Windsor, UK (🖳 www.legoland.com).

Hotels & Catering

Hotels and restaurants are the largest employers of seasonal workers, from hotel managers to kitchen hands, which are required year round. Experience, qualifications and fluent local language ability are required for all the best and highest paid positions, although a variety of jobs is available for the untrained and inexperienced. If accommodation with cooking facilities or full board isn't provided with a job, it can be expensive and difficult to find. Ensure that your salary is sufficient to pay for accommodation, food and other living expenses, and hopefully save some money. The best way to find work is to contact hotel chains directly, preferably at least six months before you wish to start work.

Fruit & Vegetable Picking

Fruit or vegetable picking jobs are available in many countries, particularly in the south of Europe, where a veritable army of workers is needed to bring in the harvest. Information can be obtained from local employment and information offices in wine regions and farming areas. One of the most popular jobs is grape picking, although it involves hard physical work and is poorly paid. Occupational hazards include mosquito and other insect bites, cuts from secateurs, rashes on your arms and legs from chemical sprays, and incessant back pain from bending all day long. Pay is usually on a piecework basis: the more you pick, the more you earn. Where provided, accommodation and cooking facilities may be extremely primitive, and the cost of food and accommodation is usually deducted from your pay. Many people provide their own transportation and camp while working.

Ski Resort Staff

A seasonal job in a ski resort can be a lot of fun and very satisfying. You will get fit, improve your foreign language ability, make some friends, and may even save some money. However, although a winter job may be a working holiday to you, to your employer it means exactly the opposite. Ski resorts require an army of temporary workers to cater for the annual invasion of winter sports enthusiasts. Besides jobs in the hotel and catering trades already mentioned above, many others are available, including couriers, resort representatives, chalet girls, ski technicians, ski instructors and guides. As a general rule, the better paid the job, the longer the working hours and the less time there is for skiing. Employment in a winter resort usually entitles employees to a discounted ski-pass. An invaluable book for anyone looking for a job in a ski resort is *Working in Ski Resorts – Europe and North America* by Victoria Pybus (Vacation Work).

Sports Instructors

Sports instructors are sought for a variety of sports, including bungee jumping, canoeing, diving, golf, hang-gliding, horse riding, mountaineering, parachuting, rock-climbing, sailing, scuba diving, swimming, tennis and windsurfing. Whatever the sport, it's invariably played and taught somewhere in most EU countries. Most jobs are available in the summer months. If you're a qualified winter sports instructor, you should contact winter resorts. Ski instructors and guides should also contact tour operators, large luxury hotels, and ski hire and service shops. Start applying from May onwards. Interviews usually take place from early September through to early November and successful candidates are on the job by mid-December. If you miss the May deadline, you could still apply, as many applicants who have been offered jobs drop out at the last minute.

TEMPORARY & CASUAL JOBS

Temporary and casual jobs are usually for a fixed period only, e.g. from a few hours to a few months, or work may be intermittent. In many EU countries, most companies use temporary staff at some time, mostly in summer when permanent staff are on holiday, and usually in clerical positions. Employers usually require your national insurance number and sometimes a tax code, therefore it isn't usually easy for non-residents to obtain legal employment. For information regarding your legal obligations, contact the local tax or social security office. Many employers illegally pay temporary staff in cash without making any deductions for tax or national insurance (see **Working Illegally** on page 73).

Casual workers are often employed on a daily, first come, first served basis. The work often entails heavy labouring and is therefore intended mostly for men, although if you're a female weightlifter there's no bar against the fairer sex. Pay for casual work is usually low and is almost always paid cash in hand. Those looking for casual, unskilled work in many EU countries must compete with locals and certain immigrant groups (possibly illegal), who are usually prepared to work for less money than anyone else, although nobody **should** be paid less than the minimum salary (if applicable). Temporary and casual work includes the following:

- Office work, which is usually well paid if you're qualified and the easiest work to find, owing to the large number of secretarial and office staff agencies in most countries.
- Work in the building trade, which can be found through industrial employment agencies and by applying directly to builders and building sites.
- Jobs at exhibitions and shows, including setting up stands, catering (waitresses and bar staff), and loading and unloading jobs.
- Jobs in bars, restaurants, clubs and discotheques at busy times of the year.
- Jobs in shops and stores over Christmas and during sales periods (usually during January, July and August).
- Christmas jobs for the post office.
- Gardening work, both in private gardens and in public parks for local councils. Jobs may be advertised in local newspapers, on bulletin boards and in magazines. Local landscape gardeners and garden centres are also often on the lookout for extra staff, particularly in spring and summer.
- Market research, which entails asking people personal questions, either in the street or house to house (ideal job for nosy parkers).
- Modelling at art colleges; both sexes are usually required and not **just** the body beautiful.
- Security work in offices, factories, warehouses and shopping centres, often demanding long hours for low pay.
- Nursing and auxiliary nursing staff in hospitals, clinics and nursing homes (often employed through agencies to replace permanent staff at short notice).
- Newspaper and magazine distribution.
- Courier work (own transport usually required, e.g. motorcycle, car or van).
- Labouring jobs in markets.
- Driving jobs, including coach and truck drivers, taxi drivers, and ferrying cars for manufacturers and car hire companies.
- Miscellaneous jobs as cleaners, baby-sitters and labourers are available from a number of agencies specialising in temporary work.

HOLIDAY & SHORT-TERM JOBS

Holiday and short-term jobs are provided by numerous organisations in many countries, ranging from a few weeks up to six months. Before planning to travel abroad for a working holiday or short-term job, it's essential that you check that you're eligible and will be permitted to enter the country under the immigration and employment regulations. You may be required to obtain a visa or work permit and should check the documentation required with a local embassy or consulate in your home country well in advance of your planned visit. If you plan to study full-time and to work during your holidays, you don't usually require a work permit, but you may need to obtain permission and evidence from your school or university that the employment won't interfere with your studies.

Some countries operate a working holidaymaker scheme for nationals of certain countries which, in the UK, include Commonwealth, British Dependent Territories and British Overseas citizens. It's primarily intended for single people aged from 17 to 30 who can come to the UK on an extended holiday for a maximum period of two years.

There are a number of websites that list holiday jobs in Europe, including the following:

- Pay Away (🖥 www.payaway.co.uk).
- Summer Jobs in Europe (🖥 www.jobs-in-europe.net/summer).
- Travel Job Search (🖥 www.traveljobsearch.com).

Students from North America wanting temporary jobs in France, Germany and Ireland should contact the Council of International Educational Exchange (CIEE), 7 Custom House Street, 3rd Floor, Portland, ME 04101, USA (☎ freephone 1-207 553 7600, 🖥 www.ciee.org).

Many other holiday jobs (as opposed to voluntary jobs) are available in a range of occupations, including couriers and representatives (e.g. in holiday camps), domestic staff in hotels, farmhands, supervisors and sports instructors, teachers, youth leaders, secretaries, nurses and shop assistants.

TRAINEES & WORK EXPERIENCE

EU Nationals

The EU runs several schemes for EU nationals to gain training and work experience in other EU countries, including the Leonardo da Vinci scheme under which EU nationals have the opportunity to complete their vocational training in another EU country for a period of between three weeks and a year. Details of the scheme are available from the EU website (🖥 http://europa.eu.int/comm/education/leonardo) or from the agencies run in each EU country (in the UK, Department of Education and Skills, EU Division, Level 5D, Caxton House, Tothill Street, London SW1H 9NA (☎ 020-7340 4488, ✉ phil.randall@dfee.gov.uk). General details about training and apprenticeship schemes in all EU countries are available from the EU Ploteus portal (🖥 www.ploteus.net).

Non-EU Nationals

Nationals of many non-EU countries, particularly developing countries, can work in the EU as trainees or gain practical work experience under training and work experience schemes. Schemes are intended to give greater flexibility to companies 'to assist their international business and trading links whilst maintaining adequate safeguards for local nationals'. Many are designed 'to assist the emerging democracies of Eastern and Central Europe by helping their citizens gain valuable training or work experience abroad'.

Applications for training are often considered even if the training is available in the applicant's home country. Training usually applies to professions or occupations in which the training leads to the acquisition of occupational skills or professional qualifications. Trainees must usually be aged between 18 and 54, and work experience applicants between 18 and 35 years (who must also be at the start of their careers). The training or work experience must be for a minimum of 30 hours a week and for a fixed length of time. Work experience is normally limited to a maximum of one year, although in exceptional circumstances it can be extended to two years. Trainees occupy full-time positions with a normal salary and conditions of employment for similar on-the-job training in the area.

Work experience differs from trainee positions in that it doesn't usually result in a formal qualification; the worker doesn't fill a full-time position; and wages are paid in the form of pocket money or a maintenance allowance, and are much less than would be paid to an ordinary employee (unless a statutory minimum wage is applicable). Applications are considered even when applicants have no previous employment related to the intended work experience, provided they have relevant qualifications and the work experience is closely related to their future career.

Although the training and work experience scheme is intended to develop the applicants' industrial and commercial experience, a secondary objective is to improve their knowledge of the local language, although applicants must have an 'adequate knowledge' before they're accepted. Applicants may not transfer from training or work experience to full employment and aren't usually permitted to take a regular job for at least two years after the completion of their training or work experience. Trainees must sign an undertaking to return to their home countries once they've completed their training or work experience.

For information about training and work experience schemes abroad, contact the government education or training authorities in your home country, or the local embassy of a country where you'd like to work.

AU PAIRS

Single people aged between 17 and 27, are eligible for a job as an au pair in most EU countries. For example, nationals of an EU country or Andorra, Bosnia-Herzegovina, Croatia, the Faroe Islands, Greenland, Iceland, Liechtenstein, Macedonia, Monaco, Norway, San Marino, Switzerland or Turkey, plus Canada and the US, can work as an au pair in the UK. Under-18s need their parents' written approval. Male au pairs are also accepted and many families prefer them (although some governments are reluctant to accept them). The au pair system provides you with an excellent opportunity to travel, improve your language ability, and generally broaden your education by living and working abroad.

Au pairs are usually contracted to work for a minimum of six months and a maximum of two years. You may work as an au pair on a number of separate occasions, provided the total period doesn't exceed two years. It's also possible to work for two or three months in the summer. Prospective au pairs that are nationals of EU countries can enter other EU countries with the minimum of formalities. Non-EU nationals must have a letter from an au pair agency or family confirming their invitation to work as an au pair, plus a letter confirming that they've had a recent medical examination. Au pairs from non-EU countries and those staying for longer than six months may need to register with the police.

As an au pair, you receive free meals and accommodation and have your own room. You're required to pay your own fare to and from the country where you will be working, although some families contribute towards the return fare for au pairs who stay six months or longer. You may also be entitled to a week's paid holiday for each six months of service. In some families, au pairs holiday with the family or are free to take Christmas or Easter holidays with their own families, but you must obtain permission before making arrangements to go home at these times. Most families prefer non-smokers (smokers aren't popular and aren't accepted by some families) and those with a driving licence.

Working hours are officially limited to five hours a day (morning or afternoon), six days a week (a total of 30 hours), plus a maximum of three evenings a week baby-sitting. You should have at least one full day and three evenings a week free of household responsibilities and should be free to attend religious services if you wish. Au pairs are paid the princely sum of around €60 or GB£40 pocket money a week (possibly more in major cities), which means you stand little chance of getting rich unless you marry a wealthy foreigner.

Au pair positions must usually be arranged privately, either directly with a family or through anagency – there are no official government agencies. There are dozens of agencies in many countries specialising in finding au pair positions (both locally and abroad) which are usually licensed and inspected. Some agencies offer a two-week trial period, during which either the au pair or the family can terminate the arrangement without notice. Write to a number of agencies and compare the conditions and pocket money offered. Agencies must provide a letter of invitation clearly stating your duties, hours, free time and pocket money (which must be shown to the immigration officer on arrival abroad). **Agencies aren't permitted to charge au pairs a fee, which is paid by the family.**

Unfortunately, abuses of the au pair system are widespread and you may be expected to work long hours and spend many evenings baby-sitting while the family is out having a good time. If you've any questions or complaints about your duties, you should refer them to the agency that found you your position (if applicable). You're usually required to give notice if you wish to go home before the end of your agreement, although this won't apply if the family has abused the arrangement.

It's possible for responsible English-speaking young women (even without experience or training) to obtain employment as a 'nanny' in many countries (many people don't know the difference between an au pair and a nanny). Duties are basically the same as an au pair, except that a position as a nanny is a real job with a real salary! A useful book for prospective au pairs is the *Au Pair and Nanny's Guide to Working Abroad* by Susan Griffith & Sharon Legg (Vacation Work). There are also numerous websites such as ⌨ www.aupairs.co.uk and ⌨ www.princeent. com/aupair (others can be found using a search engine).

VOLUNTARY WORK

The minimum age limit for voluntary work in most countries is between 16 and 18 (there's no upper age limit, provided you're physically fit) and disabled volunteers are also welcomed by many organisations. Many organisations require good or fluent spoken English and the minimum length of service varies from around one month to one year (there's often no maximum length of service). Special qualifications may be required, depending on the position – in recent years, countries have been increasingly seeking qualified professionals in fields such as engineering, health, social services and teaching. Voluntary work is unpaid, although meals and accommodation are usually provided, and some organisations also pay pocket money.

It's essential that, before planning a trip abroad to do any kind of voluntary work, you check whether you're eligible and whether you will be permitted to enter the country under the immigration and employment regulations. You may be required to obtain a visa or work permit, therefore check what documentation is required with a local embassy or consulate in your home country well in advance of your planned visit. The usual visa regulations apply to voluntary workers and your passport must normally be valid for at least one year. For temporary employment in international work camps, farm camps, other voluntary jobs and au pair positions (see **Au Pairs** on page 56), a work permit isn't usually necessary, but a letter of invitation from the voluntary organisation or your employer must be produced. This letter doesn't provide entitlement to any other kind of paid work abroad.

International work camps provide the opportunity for people from many countries to live and work together on a range of projects, including building, conservation, gardening and community projects. Camps are usually run for periods of two to four weeks between April and October. Normally, workers are required to work for six to seven hours a day, five or six days a week. The work is normally quite physically demanding and accommodation, which is shared with your fellow slaves, is usually fairly basic. Most work camps consist of 10 to 30 volunteers from several countries and English is generally the common language. Volunteers are usually required to pay a registration fee, pay for their own travel to and from the work camp, and may also be expected to contribute towards the cost of their board and lodging. An application to join a work camp should be made through the appropriate recruiting agency in your home country.

Information about volunteering in EU countries can be obtained from national associations and from a wealth of websites such as the EU Youth Portal (⌨ http://europa.eu.int/comm/youth), Voluntary Services Overseas (⌨ www.

vso.org.uk), the Peace Corps (🖳 www.peacecorps.com), the Relief Web (🖳 www.reliefweb.int) and World Service Enquiry (🖳 www.wse.org.uk/home.html). There are also plenty of books published for volunteers, including *Green Volunteers* and the *International Directory of Voluntary Work,* a guide to 400 agencies and sources of information on short to long-term voluntary work world-wide (both published by Vacation Work).

ENGLISH TEACHERS & TRANSLATORS

There's a high demand for English teachers, translators and interpreters throughout the EU, particularly in the new member states, where there's a high turnover of teachers in language schools and a constant demand for translators (and sometimes technical authors and copywriters) from local companies.

Language Schools

There are literally hundreds of English-language schools in the EU, many of which expect teachers to have a TEFL (Teacher of English as a Foreign Language) certificate or its equivalent, although this isn't always the case. Some schools will employ anyone whose mother tongue is English, provided they've had experience in teaching, while others have their own teaching methods and prefer to train their own teachers. Many of the best schools are members of a local Association of English Language Schools, a list of which is usually available from the British Council (🖳 www.britishcouncil.org) or local British or US embassies. Language schools generally pay less than you can earn giving private lessons, but they provide a contract and pay your taxes and social security. However, you may be able to obtain only a short-term contract or freelance work. You're usually paid by the hour and so should ensure that you've a guaranteed number of hours per week, but not usually more than 25.

Private Lessons

Many students tend to favour learning lots of grammar and you will also find that students know a lot about English literature, but cannot speak a word of it correctly! If you aren't up-to-date with grammar and you want to teach privately, you should stick to teaching conversation or children. Work is easy to find in some countries, particularly in university cities and towns, as students must usually study English as part of their course work. Many foreigners teach English privately and are paid cash in hand by students, much of which is never declared to the tax authorities. Most people find that, when they have a few students, they spread the word, and before you know it you have as much work as you can handle. You could also try placing an advertisement in local newspapers and magazines offering private English lessons, although you may receive some replies from men who think that 'English lessons' implies something other than language lessons! The going rate for private lessons varies and can be anywhere between €10/GB£7.50 and €30/GB£20 an hour.

Translators & Interpreters

These are other occupations that tend to come under the heading of English teaching, with many expatriates moving between the three professions quite easily. Professional translators and interpreters are in huge demand and are usually employed by agencies. Translators and interpreters are also in high demand at the EU institutions, particularly those that speak one or more languages of the new member states. For anyone speaking an EU language fluently and wanting to work in the country where it's the national language, it may be worthwhile training as a translator or interpreter. Professional translators are paid by the page (or line) and the average rate is around €20/GB£13 per page, although this varies considerably depending on the kind of translation. Translating is a long and tiresome business, you must usually work to stringent deadlines, the subject matter can be highly technical (requiring a special vocabulary) and translations must be precise. If you don't translate medical notes, legal papers or business documents accurately, any mistakes could have serious consequences! Interpreters are employed mainly for exhibitions, congresses and seminars, where you're paid either a daily flat rate or by the hour.

University Teaching

English is taught in most universities throughout the EU and positions for assistants in English language departments are usually open to foreigners with university degrees. Applications should be made directly to the Rector of the University, followed by the name of the town or city. There are also special institutes of modern languages, foreign universities and schools in many countries, which offer a range of job opportunities for qualified teachers.

A good book is *Teaching English Abroad* by Susan Griffith (Vacation Work). Useful websites include the Centre for British Teachers (🖥 www.cfbt.com), the British Council whose website provides a wealth of useful information about teaching English (🖥 www.britishcouncil.org) and 🖥 www.jobs.edufind.com.

JOB HUNTING

When looking for a job in the EU, it's best not to put all your eggs in one basket as the more job applications you make, the better your chances of finding the right job. Contact as many prospective employers as possible, either by writing, telephoning or calling on them in person, depending on the type of vacancy. Whatever job you're looking for, it's important to market yourself correctly and appropriately, which depends on the type of job you're after. For example, the recruitment of executives and senior managers is handled almost exclusively by consultants who advertise in local newspapers (and also abroad) and interview all applicants prior to presenting clients with a shortlist. At the other end of the scale, manual jobs requiring no previous experience may be advertised at government employment centres, in local newspapers and in shop windows, and the first suitable, able-bodied applicant may be offered the job on the spot.

When writing for a job, address your letter to the personnel director or manager and include your curriculum vitae (CV), and copies of all references and qualifications. However, writing for jobs from abroad is a hit-and-miss business and it's probably the least successful method of securing employment. If you're applying from abroad and can attend interviews abroad, inform prospective employers when you will be available for interview and arrange as many as you can fit into the allotted time. Your method of job hunting will depend on your particular circumstances, qualifications and experience, and the sort of job you're looking for, and may include the following:

- Visiting local government employment offices abroad (see page 49). This is mainly for non-professional skilled and unskilled jobs, particularly in industry, retailing and catering.

- Using the EU EURES network (see page 49).

- There are special information centres for job seekers in some countries, which provide useful information about jobs, job hunting, education and training. Main libraries also provide a range of resources for job seekers, although they may not specifically provide advice and assistance for the unemployed.

- Checking the internet (see page 63) and other bulletin boards, such as those provided by TV teletext services. The internet provides access to hundreds of sites for job seekers, including corporate websites, recruitment companies and newspaper job advertisements.

- Applying to international and national recruitment agencies (see page 49) and executive search consultants acting for companies in the country where you wish to work. These companies mainly recruit executives and key managerial and technical staff, and many have offices worldwide. Some agencies may find positions only for local nationals or foreigners with a residence permit (or the right to work in a country).

- Obtaining copies of daily newspapers, most of which have 'positions vacant' sections on certain days. The quality daily and Sunday newspapers all contain 'vacancies' sections for executive and professional employees, and also contain job advertisements dedicated to particular industries or professions, e.g. the computer industry, teaching and the media. Local and national newspapers may be available in the reading rooms of local libraries, therefore it isn't always necessary to buy them. Jobs are also advertised in industry and trade newspapers and magazines. Major foreign newspapers are also available abroad from international news agencies, trade and commercial centres, expatriate organisations and social clubs, although they don't always contain the 'appointments' or 'situations vacant' sections. Most major newspapers and magazines have websites where you can usually access 'situations vacant' sections free of charge.

- Most professions and trade associations publish journals containing job offers (see *Benn's Media Directory Europe*) and jobs are also advertised in various English language publications, including the *International Herald Tribune* and *Wall Street Journal Europe* and other local publications (see **Appendix B**). You can also place an advertisement in the 'situations wanted' section of a local newspaper in the area where you'd like to work.

- Local foreign Chambers of Commerce maintain lists of their member companies doing business (or with subsidiaries) in the EU and some allow you to file your CV with them (for a fee). An advertisement may also be posted on their website and included in their monthly newsletter.

- Most countries in the EU also maintain Chambers of Commerce, which are good sources of information, as are Euro Info Centres (EIC) found in the major cities of EU countries. A list of EICs is available from ▣ http://europa.eu.int/comm/enterprise/networks/eic/eic

- Applying directly to American, British and other multi-national companies with offices or subsidiaries in the EU and making written applications directly to companies. You can obtain a list of companies working in a particular field from trade directories, such as *Kelly's* (▣ www.kelly search.com) and *Kompass* (▣ www.kompass.com –annual directories are published for all countries in the EU except Cyprus and Malta), copies of which are available at main libraries and Chambers of Commerce abroad. The European Business Directory *Euro Pages* also provides a comprehensive listing of companies in many EU countries online (▣ www.europages.com). Making unsolicited job applications is naturally a hit-and-miss affair. It can, however, be more successful than responding to advertisements, as you aren't usually competing with other applicants. Some companies recruit a large percentage of employees through unsolicited résumés.

- Putting an advertisement in the 'Situations Wanted' section of a national newspaper or a local newspaper in an area where you'd like to work. If you're a member of a recognised profession or trade, you could place an advertisement in a newspaper or magazine dedicated to your profession or industry. It's best to place an advert in the middle of the week and avoid the summer and other holiday periods.

- Networking, which basically involves getting together with like-minded people to discuss business and make business and professional contacts. It can be particularly successful for executives, managers and professionals when job hunting, especially in countries where people use personal contacts for everything from looking for a job to finding accommodation. In fact, a personal recommendation is often the best way to find employment abroad (nepotism and favouritism are rife in some EU countries), where finding a job may depend more on **who** you know, rather than **what** you know. It's difficult for most newcomers to make contacts among the local community and many turn to the expatriate community, particularly in major cities. You can also contact or join local expatriate social clubs, churches, societies and professional organisations.

- Asking relatives, friends or acquaintances working abroad whether they know of an employer looking for someone with your experience and qualifications.

- Applying in person to employers (see below).

Personal Applications

Your best chance of obtaining certain jobs in the EU is to apply in person, when success is often simply a matter of being in the right place at the right time. Many companies don't advertise but rely on attracting workers by word of mouth and their own vacancy boards. Shops often put vacancy notices in their windows and newsagents may also display job advertisements from employers on a notice board, although these are generally only for temporary or part-time help. It's advisable to leave your name and address with a prospective employer and, if possible, a telephone number where you can be contacted, particularly if a job may become vacant at a moment's notice. Publicise the fact that you're looking for a job, not only with friends, relatives and acquaintances, but also with anyone you come into contact with who may be able to help. You can give lady luck a helping hand with your persistence and enterprise by:

- Cold calling on prospective employers.
- Checking 'wanted' boards.
- Looking in local newspapers.
- Checking notice and bulletin boards at large companies, shopping centres, embassies, clubs, sports centres and newsagents.
- Asking other foreign workers.

When leaving a job in the EU, it's advisable to ask for a written reference (which isn't usually provided automatically), particularly if you intend to look for further work locally or you think your work experience will help you obtain work in another country.

The Internet

The internet provides access to literally thousands of websites for job seekers, advertising millions of job vacancies, including recruitment companies, corporate websites, and newspaper and magazine job advertisements (you can use a search engine to find them). Millions of people use the internet to find a new job and many companies do the majority of their recruitment via their own websites. The rapid development of the internet has also led to a big increase in the number of online recruitment agencies and job search sites. Some sites charge a subscription fee to access their vacancy listings, but most permit job seekers to review and respond to listings free of charge.

It's also possible to post your CV online (again, usually free), but it's wise to consider the security implications of this move. By posting your home address or phone number in public view, you could be opening yourself up to nuisance phone calls or even worse. Some websites allow you to exclude certain categories in your CV, such as your present and previous employers. Some internet websites that list vacancies in EU countries are listed below:

- **Career Journal Europe** – 🖥 www.careerjournaleurope.com (vacancies in many EU countries plus useful job hunting advice).

- **Engineering Production Planning** – 🖥 www.epp.co.uk (vacancies in engineering).

- **Euro Jobs** – 🖥 www.eurojobs.com (all EU countries listed).

- **Jobsite** – 🖥 www.jobsite.co.uk (jobs in France, Germany, Ireland, Italy, Spain and the UK).

- **Manpower Abroad** – 🖥 www.manpowerabroad.com (most EU countries listed).

- **Michael Page International** – 🖥 www.michaelpage.com (most EU countries listed).

- **Monster Board** – 🖥 www.monster.com (links to sites for most EU countries).

- **Online Recruitment** – 🖥 www.onrec.com (recruitment sites for most EU countries).

- **Overseas Jobs** – 🖥 www.overseasjobs.com (all EU countries listed).

- **People Bank** – 🖥 www.peoplebank.com (vacancies in the UK only).

- **Planet Recruitment** – 🖥 www.planetrecruit.com (all EU countries listed).

- **Reed** – 🖥 www.reed.co.uk (vacancies in the UK only).

- **Riley Guide** – 🖥 www.rileyguide.com (comprehensive guide and links to finding a job on the internet).

- **Robert Walters** – 🖥 www.robertwalters.com (recruitment agency with offices in Belgium, France, Ireland, Luxembourg, the Netherlands and the UK).

- **Stepstone** – 🖥 www.stepstone.com (one of Europe's biggest online recruiters).

- **Top Jobs** – 🖥 www.topjobs.co.uk (vacancies in the UK only).

- **Total Jobs** – 🖳 www.totaljobs.com (mainly UK vacancies with some European).

- **University of London Careers Service** – 🖳 www.careers.lon.ac.uk/links (excellent links to many European and worldwide sites as well as EU country specific).

It's worth noting that foreign language sites may not include an English language version. However, if your foreign language skills are rudimentary, you can obtain a rough translation using the (free) Babel Fish translator provided by the search engine company Alta Vista. Enter 'http://babelfish.altavista.digital.com' in your browser, then enter the address of the website that you wish to visit in the Babel Fish dialogue box that appears. You will then be presented with an instant translation of the web page in question.

Curricula Vitae & Interviews

Résumés or curriculae vitae (CV) are of vital importance in many countries when looking for a job, particularly when jobs are thin on the ground and applicants are a dime a dozen. Never forget that the purpose of your résumé is to obtain an interview, not a job, and it must be written with that in mind. This means that it must be individually tailored to every job application, paying particular attention to any useful skills you may possess (adaptability, tolerance), language ability (spoken and/or written), international experience (work, travel), etc. If you aren't up to writing a good résumé, you can employ a professional résumé writer who will turn your boring working life into something that Indiana Jones would be proud of.

When writing for jobs, address your letter to the personnel director or manager and include your curriculum vitae (in the local language if you're applying to a foreign company), and copies of references and qualifications. If possible, offer to attend an interview and state when you will be available. Letters should be tailored to individual employers and professionally translated if your language ability isn't perfect. In some countries, companies request hand-written letters from job applicants and submit them to graphologists (employers may also use astrology, numerology and even wilder methods of selecting staff!). When writing from abroad, enclosing an international reply coupon may help elicit a response.

European Curriculum Vitae

The EU and EEA countries have produced a standard European CV, which aims to give an overview of educational attainments and work experience. The CV provides information about your language skills, work experience, education and training background, and additional skills. The CV is available in 13

European languages and can be downloaded from 💻 www.cedefop. eu.int/ transparency/cv.asp.

Job interviews shouldn't be taken lightly, as interviewing and being interviewed for a job is a science, and making a good impression can make the difference between being on the ladder of success or in the unemployment queue. Dress smartly, even if the interview is for a lowly position (if they like the look of you they may offer you a better job!). The secret is in preparation, so do your homework thoroughly on prospective employers and try to anticipate every conceivable question (and then some) you may be asked and rehearse your answers. Some employers require prospective employees to complete aptitude and other written tests. In addition to a good résumé, employers may require the names of a number of personal or professional referees (e.g. three), whom they will usually contact. It's also advisable to provide written references if you have any.

There is a wealth of books available detailing everything from writing a compelling résumé to how to answer (or field) questions during an interview, including *The Perfect Résumé: Today's Ultimate Job Search Tool* by Tom Jackson, *The Damn Good Résumé Guide* by Yana Parker, *Sweaty Palms: The Neglected Art of Being Interviewed* by H. Anthony Medley, and *Great Answers to Tough Interview Questions* by Martin Yate. You may also wish to peruse some of the websites listed in this chapter, many of which contain useful advice and information. One website of particular interest is Labour Mobility (💻 www.labourmobility.com), which contains useful tips for international job seekers.

SALARIES

It can be difficult to determine the salary you should command in the EU and getting the right salary for the job is something of a lottery. Salaries can also vary considerably for the same job in different parts of a country. Those working in major cities are usually the highest paid, mainly owing to the higher cost of living (particularly accommodation; although, if you're employed in a remote area, you may receive a 'hardship' allowance). Salaries are usually negotiable and it's up to you to ensure that you receive the level of salary and benefits commensurate with your qualifications and experience (or as much as you can get!). Minimum salaries exist in all EU countries except Austria, Denmark, Finland, Germany, Italy and Sweden, although these countries often have a statutory minimum wage for many trades and professions. Salaries in some companies, trades and professions (particularly for public sector government employees) are decided by national pay agreements between unions and the government. Getting a good salary is, however, generally a case of every man (or woman) for himself.

Your working hours abroad may be quite different from those in your home country and will vary according to your profession and employer. Most executive, professionals and 'white-collar' workers (those who don't get their hands dirty), usually officially work between 35 and 40 hours a week, while factory and other 'blue-collar' workers (those who find it difficult to keep their hands clean) may work much longer hours when overtime is included. However, there's a maximum 48-hour week in the EU, although this varies from country to country (e.g. France has introduced a 35-hour week).

There's usually a huge disparity between the salaries of the lowest and highest paid employees, which is much wider in some countries than in others, particularly those with a lower GDP. At the bottom end of the scale, employees may earn the minimum wage, which was just €116 a year in Latvia and GB£4.85 an hour in the UK in 2003. If you work illegally (see page 73), you're likely to receive even less. At the other extreme, executive and managerial salaries have been increasing in leaps and bounds in the EU in recent years. The average salary of the chief executive of a multinational company may be over €1 million a year, plus performance-related bonuses, share options and perks such as chauffeured company cars. Salaries for some professionals have also soared in recent years, e.g. top stockbrokers can earn millions of euros a year! Private sector salaries generally increase at a much faster pace than those in the public sector and there's a growing pay gap in many countries. This has made it difficult for local authorities to recruit and retain staff, with the result that there are thousands of public sector vacancies in some countries (e.g. the UK).

Many employees, particularly company directors and senior managers, enjoy a 'salary' that's much more than what they get in their monthly pay packet. Many companies offer a number of benefits for executives and managers that may even continue after retirement. These may include a free company car (possibly with a chauffeur); free health insurance and health screening; paid holidays; private school fees; cheap or free home loans; rent-free homes; free rail season tickets; free company restaurants; non-contributory company pensions; share options; interest-free loans; free tickets for sports events and shows; free subscriptions to clubs; and business conferences in exotic places (see also **Managerial & Executive Positions** on page 83). The benefits of board members in some companies may make up 50 per cent or more of their total remuneration (to keep it out of the hands of the taxman). In addition, executives often receive huge golden handshakes should they be sacked or resign, which can run into several million euros.

SELF-EMPLOYMENT

One of the easiest routes to working in the EU is to be self-employed, although you will still need a work permit and it can be difficult to become established and make a good living. If you're an EU national or a permanent resident with a residence permit, you can work as a self-employed person or as a sole trader in an EU country. If you want to be self-employed in a profession or trade in most EU countries, you must meet certain legal requirements and register with the appropriate organisation, e.g. a professional must become a member of the relevant professional association. In many countries, the self-employed must have an official status and it's illegal simply to hang out a sign and start business.

Members of some professions and trades must possess recognised professional qualifications and certificates, and may be required to take a written examination in the local language. You may also be required to attend a business administration course. You're subject to any professional codes and limitations in force, e.g. a medical practitioner must have his qualifications accepted by the medical association of the state or region where he intends to practise, and any controlling specialist bodies. You must also show that you're in good standing with the professional authorities in your home country. In certain professions, such as the law, it's unusual to be permitted to practise abroad without local qualifications.

As a self-employed person you don't have the protection of a limited company should your business fail, although there are certain tax benefits (e.g. lower tax rates in most countries). It may be advantageous to operate a limited company. Obtain professional advice before deciding whether to work as a sole trader or form a company, as it may have far-reaching social security, tax and other consequences. All self-employed people must register for income tax, social security and value added tax, and you may also need a fiscal or other identification number. Don't be in too much of a hurry to register, as from the date of registration you may be required to pay state social security, pension and health insurance payments, and are also liable for income and other taxes. **You should never be tempted to start work before you're registered as there are harsh penalties that may include a large fine, confiscation of machinery or tools, and even deportation and a ban from entering a country for a number of years.**

New businesses may enjoy a tax exemption for the first few years of trading, including sole traders. There are, however, drawbacks to being self-employed in many countries, which may outweigh any advantages. Social security contributions for the self-employed are usually much higher than for salaried employees and you receive fewer social security benefits. As a self-employed person you aren't entitled to unemployment benefits should your business fail and there may be no state benefits for accidents at work. It's advisable to join a local professional or trade association, which can provide valuable information and assistance and may also offer insurance discounts. In some countries it's possible to register a company abroad in order to reduce your taxes although, in most EU countries, businesses are liable for tax on their worldwide income.

Starting A Business

One of the easiest (and most expensive) ways to live and work in the EU is to start your own business. In some countries, this is virtually the only way that many non-EU foreigners can obtain a residence permit. The amount a business starter needs to invest varies considerably, e.g. from a few thousand euros to considerably more. Businesses that create jobs are welcomed with open arms, particularly in areas with high unemployment, and a business licence may be conditional on the employment of a number of local citizens.

Most people find doing business in a foreign country exceedingly frustrating and the bureaucracy associated with starting a business in many EU countries is often onerous. The red tape can be almost impenetrable, especially if you don't speak the local language, as you will be inundated with official documents and must be able to understand them. It's only when you come up against the full force of foreign bureaucracy that you understand what it really means to be a foreigner! It's difficult not to believe that the authorities' sole purpose in life is to obstruct business (in fact it's to protect their own jobs). Patience and tolerance are the watchwords when dealing with foreign bureaucrats and will also do wonders for your blood pressure!

Research

BEWARE! For many foreigners, starting a business in a foreign country is one of the fastest routes to bankruptcy known to mankind! In fact, many foreigners who start a business in the EU would be better off investing in lottery tickets – at least they would then have a chance of receiving a return on their investment. Many would-be entrepreneurs return home with only their shirts on their backs, having learnt the facts of life the hard way. If you aren't prepared to research the market thoroughly and obtain expert business and legal advice, then you shouldn't even think about starting a business in the EU.

Generally speaking, you shouldn't consider running a business in a field in which you don't have previous experience. It's often advisable to work for someone else in the same line of business to gain experience, rather than jump in at the deep end. Always thoroughly investigate an existing or proposed business before investing any money. **As any expert (and many failed entrepreneurs) will tell you, starting a business in the EU (or anywhere else for that matter) isn't for amateurs, particularly amateurs who don't speak the local language.**

Many small businesses exist on a shoestring, with owners living from hand to mouth, and they certainly aren't what could be considered thriving enterprises. Self-employed people usually work extremely long hours, particularly those running bars or restaurants (days off are almost impossible in the high season), often for little financial reward. In most countries many people choose to be self-employed for the lifestyle and freedom it affords (no clocks or bosses), rather than the money. It's important to keep your plans small and manageable, and work well within your budget, rather than undertake a grandiose scheme.

If you're planning to buy or start a seasonal business based on tourism, check whether the potential 'real' income will be sufficient to provide you with a living. This applies particularly to bars, restaurants and shops in holiday resorts, especially those run by foreigners relying on the tourist trade, hundreds of which open and close within a short space of time. Don't overestimate the length of the season or the potential income and, most importantly, don't believe everything a person selling a business tells you (although every word may be true). Nobody sells a good business for a bargain price, least of all one making huge profits. In most areas, trade falls off dramatically out of the main EU holiday season (e.g. June to September or December to February in ski resorts) and many businesses must survive for a whole year on the income earned in the summer months. The rest of the year you could be lucky to cover your costs.

Professional Help

Owing to the difficulties in complying with (or understanding) local laws and bureaucracy, there are agencies and professionals in many countries that specialise in obtaining documents and making applications for individuals and businesses. They act as a buffer between you and officialdom, and will register your business with the tax authorities, social security, companies register, Chamber of Commerce and other official bodies. A lawyer or notary can also do this, but will be much more expensive. If you're a professional, you may have to take a routine examination before you can be included on the professional register with the Chamber of Commerce. There are also business consultants and relocation agencies in many areas, which provide invaluable local assistance. International accountants such as Price Waterhouse (🖳 www. pwcglobal.com) and Ernst & Young (🖳 www.ey.com) have offices in most EU countries and are an invaluable source of information (in English) on subjects such as forming a company, company law, taxation and social security. Most EU countries maintain Chambers of Commerce, which are also a good source of information and assistance.

Legal Advice

Before establishing a business or undertaking any business transactions in a foreign country, it's important to obtain expert legal advice from an experienced lawyer and accountant (who speaks English or a language you speak fluently) to ensure that you will be operating within the law. There are severe penalties for anyone who ignores the regulations and legal requirements. Expert legal advice is also necessary to take advantage of any favourable tax breaks and to make sense of the myriad rules and regulations. It's imperative to ensure that contracts are clearly defined and watertight before making an investment because, if you become involved in a legal dispute, it can take years to resolve. Businesses must also register for value added tax (VAT). Most people require a special licence to start a business in the EU and no commitments should be made until permission has been granted. Among the best sources of local help and information are Chambers of Commerce and town halls.

Avoiding The Crooks

In addition to problems with the authorities, you may also come into contact with assorted crooks and swindlers who will try to relieve you of your money. You should have a healthy suspicion regarding the motives of anyone you do business with abroad (unless it's your mum or spouse), particularly your fellow countrymen. It's also generally best to avoid partnerships, as they rarely work and can be a disaster. In general, you should trust nobody and shouldn't sign anything or pay any money before having a contract checked by a lawyer. It's a sad fact of life, but foreigners who prey on their fellow countrymen are commonplace in some countries. In most cases you're better off dealing with a long-established local company with roots in the community (and therefore a good reputation to protect), rather than your compatriots. If things go wrong, you may be unprotected by the law, the wheels of which grind extremely slowly in some countries – when they haven't fallen off completely!

Buying An Existing Business

It's much easier to buy an existing business than to start a new one from scratch and it's also less of a risk. The paperwork for taking over an existing business is also simpler, although still complex. However, buying a business that's a going concern is difficult, as most people aren't in the habit of buying and selling businesses, which are usually passed down from generation to generation. If you plan to buy a business, obtain an independent valuation (or two) and employ an accountant to audit the books. **Never sign anything that you don't understand 110 per cent. Even if you think you understand it, you should still obtain unbiased professional advice, e.g. from local experts such as banks and accountants.** In fact, it's best not to start a business at all until you have the infrastructure in place, including an accountant, lawyer and banking facilities. There are various ways to set up a small business and it's essential to obtain professional advice regarding the best method of establishing and registering a business in the EU, which can dramatically affect your tax position. It's important to employ an accountant to do your books.

A New Business

Most people are far too optimistic about the prospects for a new business abroad and over-estimate income levels (it often takes years to make a profit) and under-estimate costs. Be realistic or even pessimistic when estimating your income and overestimate the costs and underestimate the revenue (then reduce it by 50 per cent!). While hoping for the best, you should plan for the worst and have sufficient funds to last until you're established (under-funding is the major cause of business failures). New projects are rarely, if ever, completed within budget and you need to ensure that you've sufficient working capital to survive until a business takes off. Banks are usually extremely wary of lending to new businesses, particularly businesses run by non-resident foreigners, and it's difficult for foreigners to obtain finance abroad without local assets. If you wish to borrow money to buy property or for a business venture abroad, you should carefully consider where and in what currency to raise finance.

Location

Choosing the location for a business is even more important than the location for a home. Depending on the type of business, you may need access to motorway (freeway) and rail links, or to be located in a popular tourist area or near local attractions. Local plans regarding communications, industry and major building developments, e.g. housing complexes and new shopping centres, may also be important. Plans regarding new motorways and rail links are usually available from local town halls.

Employees

Hiring employees shouldn't be taken lightly abroad and must be taken into account before starting a business. You must usually enter into a contract under local labour laws and employees often enjoy extensive rights. If you buy an existing business, you may be required to take on existing (possibly inefficient) staff who cannot be dismissed, or be faced with paying high redundancy compensation. It's very expensive to hire employees in many EU countries where, in addition to salaries, you may need to pay an additional 50 per cent or more in social security contributions, bonus months salary, four to six weeks paid annual holiday, plus pay for public holidays, sickness, maternity, etc.

Type Of Business

The most common businesses operated by foreigners in the EU include holiday accommodation, caravan and camping sites, building and allied trades (particularly restoring old houses), farming, catering, hotels, shops, franchises, estate agencies, translation and interpreting bureaux, language and foreign schools, landscape gardening, and holiday and sports centres. The majority of businesses established by foreigners are linked to the leisure and catering industries, followed by property investment and development. Many professionals, such as doctors and dentists, also set up practises abroad to serve the expatriate community. There are also opportunities in import and export in many countries, e.g. importing foreign products for the local and expatriate market, and exporting locally manufactured goods. You can also find niche markets in providing services for expatriates and others, which are unavailable locally.

Companies

Companies cannot be purchased 'off the shelf' in most countries and it usually takes a number of months to set one up. Incorporating a company in many EU countries takes longer and is more expensive and more complicated than, or different from, doing so in the UK or US. There are a wide range of 'limited companies' and business entities in many countries and choosing the right one is important. **Always obtain professional legal advice regarding the advantages and disadvantages of different types of limited companies.**

Grants & Incentives

A range of grants and incentives is available for new businesses in many EU countries, particularly in rural and deprived areas. Grants may include EU subsidies, central government grants, regional development grants, redeployment grants, and grants from provincial authorities and local communities. Grants may include assistance to buy buildings and equipment (or the provision of low-rent business premises), research and technological assistance, subsidies for job creation, low-interest loans and tax incentives. Contact Chambers of Commerce and embassies for information.

Wealth Warning

Whatever people may tell you, working for yourself isn't easy and requires a lot of hard work (self-employed people generally work much longer hours than employees); a sizeable investment and sufficient operating funds (most new businesses fail from lack of capital); good organisation (e.g. bookkeeping and planning); excellent customer relations; and a measure of luck – although generally the harder you work, the more 'luck' you will have. Don't be seduced by the apparent laid-back way of life in some countries – if you want to be a success in business you cannot play at it. Some two-thirds of all new businesses fail within three to five years and the self-employed enjoy far fewer social security benefits than employees.

WORKING ILLEGALLY

Illegal working thrives in many EU countries and is expected to increase when the new member countries join in May 2004. It's most common in industries that employ itinerant workers such as catering (bars and restaurants), construction, farming, tourism and textiles, and in jobs such as domestic work and language teaching. In some countries, officials turn a blind eye, as the black economy keeps many small businesses alive and the unemployed in 'pocket money', although this is increasingly rare as many EU countries are clamping down on illegal immigrants. In many countries, the long-term unemployed don't receive unemployment benefits and any other benefits paid are usually too low to live on. Moonlighting by employees with second or third jobs is also widespread in some EU countries, particularly among those employed in the public sector, who are generally low paid. However, unscrupulous employers also use illegal labour in order to pay low wages (below the minimum wage) for long hours and poor working conditions.

It's strictly illegal to work without a work permit or official permission in the EU. If you're tempted to work illegally, you should be very aware of the consequences, as the black economy is a risky business for both employers and employees. If you run a business and use illegal labour or avoid paying taxes, you will have no official redress if goods or services are substandard. Non-payment of income tax or social security is a criminal offence in the EU, and offenders are liable to large fines and imprisonment. Employees who work illegally have no entitlement to social security benefits such as insurance against work injuries, public health care, unemployment pay or a state pension. A foreigner who works illegally is liable to a heavy fine and deportation, while businesses can be fined, closed down and the owners imprisoned.

SPOUSES

When her husband announces that he has been offered a position abroad, perhaps the most difficult issue facing the expatriate wife is **her** job, something that can cause great resentment on the wife's part and put immense strain on a marriage. Many woman have their own career, profession or business in their home country, which has taken them many years and much effort to establish, and which provides them with status and recognition. They probably find their job enjoyable and fulfilling and may be financially independent. When faced with the prospect of relocation abroad because of her husband's job, a wife is often faced with a difficult dilemma: the most obvious option is to follow her husband abroad, thereby relinquishing her own career, although some take the rather drastic option of staying behind.

In the vast majority of cases, the former solution prevails, particularly if the relocation is long-term and/or long-distance. Thus the previous working wife, used to the stimulation and reward of her own career, often finds herself abroad with nothing to do, bored, with a lack of self-esteem and financially dependent on her husband. In addition to this negative situation, she's in a foreign country where she may not speak the language or have any friends.

As an expatriate, it may be difficult to find a full-time or even a part-time job, let alone one in your own field or profession. Local labour laws vary from country to country and may not even allow spouses to work, although this is the case only for non-EU nationals. Wages may be lower than you're used to and there will probably be intense competition among expatriates for any available positions.

If you're posted abroad, it isn't usually realistic to try to take your career with you, but is more practical to put it on hold and consider alternative employment. In any case, you should wait a few months after arriving in a country before accepting a job, as you will need time to organise your family, home and yourself, and to adapt to a new environment and situation. When you feel less alien in a country may be the time to look for some sort of employment.

However, before you go there's a lot you can do to prepare the ground for finding a job, particularly regarding maintaining your self-esteem and motivation after you've left your job or given up your business. There are numerous general books on careers that you can study before you go, which can help you dispassionately assess your achievements and examine your preferences. Many contain self-assessment exercises, which help you to identify your strong points, what you enjoy doing most and your long-term goals. Once you've a better idea of what you like doing and have an objective view of your skills, you will be in a better position to use this knowledge to find a job opportunity abroad.

Before you go, find out as much as possible about local etiquette, particularly regarding business protocol. Customs vary considerably from country to country, but if you're well versed in the local etiquette, particularly how to greet someone and introduce yourself, then the chances are that you will avoid unnecessary *faux pas* (a good website for business etiquette is 🖥 www. executiveplanet.com, which includes guides on business etiquette for 12 countries in the EU). The **Working** sections in the **Country Profiles** in **Chapter 9** contain brief notes on business etiquette in individual EU countries. If you have time, it's advisable to learn a few basic phrases of greeting and introduction in the language of the country you're moving to, or even take a course so that you can make simple conversation (easier with some EU languages than others!). Possible employers won't always expect you to be fluent in their language, but will certainly appreciate your attempts to speak it (however tortured).

Before you go, take time to study expatriate websites (see **Appendix C** and **Useful Websites** in **Chapter 9 – Country Profiles**), most of which provide useful contacts in the local expatriate network and allow you to post questions and queries that are answered by experienced expatriates. Take the opportunity to ask about job possibilities and the skills required, and to tap into other people's experiences so that you can use this knowledge later. There are also websites specifically for expatriate wives and some women's groups have their own websites where you can contact them abroad by email or normal post.

Above all, you should try to view your career being put on hold for a period as a positive move and an opportunity to explore new and exciting horizons, rather than a problem or an obstacle in your life. Although your career may not be moving along the same unerring upward path, you will undoubtedly learn new skills that may enhance your future job prospects.

Once you arrive in the country there are two main employment scenarios. You may be fortunate and be able to apply your skills to a ready-made local job, which is more likely if you speak the local language. Options such as health care, teaching (particularly English as a Foreign Language), office management, and the hotel and travel industries are a good place to start. One of your first priorities should be to find out as much as you can about employment opportunities beforehand. Have plenty of copies of your CV to hand (plus copies of educational qualifications and employment references) and be prepared to make numerous cold calls on schools, hotels, academies and offices. If they're interested in your application, they will contact you or put your CV on file for when a vacancy arises.

The second, possibly more likely scenario, particularly if you relocate to one of the countries in Eastern Europe, is that the ideal job for you simply doesn't exist. Under these circumstances you will need to rethink your position and how your skills can be applied to the local job market. You will have to be imaginative and resourceful, and may need to invent a job based on local demand. Go out and meet people by joining expatriate groups, of which there are usually many in the form of women's groups, sports and special interest clubs, or the parents association at your children's school. Have some business cards made and give them to anyone you think may be interested in your skills or know someone who could be. Listen to the expatriate grapevine and find out what they complain about or what they miss, which may provide an opportunity for you to fill.

Bear in mind that all societies have different needs and fulfilling one of these may provide you with a job. Try to stay motivated by setting yourself small, manageable tasks with achievable goals. Don't set yourself the goal of finding a job by the end of the first week, but instead give yourself the task of visiting say five different contacts in one week. Flexibility is paramount and you may need to compromise, but the chances are that you will find yourself with a rewarding job that you'd never have dreamed of doing in your home country. It's also possible that your new employment may be far more satisfying and enriching than your previous career!

There are many good career publications written with the expatriate in mind, including *A Career in Your Suitcase* by Joanna Parfitt (Summertime Publishing) and *What Color is Your Parachute?* (updated annually) by Richard Nelson Bolles (Ten Speed Press).

MANAGING WITHOUT A JOB

Depending on the country, you may find yourself unable to find a job or, if you're a non-EU national, not being allowed to work by the authorities, who may issue work permits to only one member of a family. You then face the question: What do I do now? You may well find yourself alone in a new home with your husband away all day in a fulfilling job, one that provides him with lots of human contact with colleagues who speak his language, and your children settled into school (possibly abroad). This is a difficult situation, particularly when you may be suffering from culture shock, including rejection of the new country and its people, and you find that your family members are experiencing an exciting new life while you sit at home wishing you had never come! You've two choices in your new country: you can either sit at home and sink into disillusionment, unhappiness and possibly depression, or you can motivate yourself to participate fully in your new country and lifestyle.

However, active participation may be easier said than done, particularly if you're naturally shy or unused to taking the initiative. Relationships abroad are different from those at home, where everyone is on common ground in a familiar environment, and where you've many people you can relate to. Abroad, foreigners are outside their usual environment ('like fish out of water') and usually need to make the first move in unfamiliar circumstances. There may also be a limited number of English-speaking expatriates in your local area and a relatively high turnover of foreigners. Relationships may be difficult to start, simply because everyone is experiencing the same adaptation difficulties and first impressions may be negative owing to the effects of culture shock and stress.

However, making friends is the first step to enjoying a new country and therefore it's necessary to go out of your way to be friendly to other expatriates you meet, whether at your children's school, your husband's business functions or even in local supermarkets or cafés. Bear in mind also that expatriate wives who have been in the country longer than you have will know just how you feel and will be able to offer advice on how they coped as newcomers. You will usually find that the expatriate community is close-knit, its members concerned about others and willing to go out of their way to help you.

The following list provides a number of ways to meet other expatriate wives and enjoy your time abroad:

- **Expatriate Clubs** – Most popular expatriate destinations have a network of clubs whose activities encompass a wide range of social, sporting and educational activities. These may include a number of women's clubs which organise specific activities for expatriates, such as the *Federation of American Women's Clubs Overseas* (⌨ www.fawco.org), an organisation with clubs in 14 EU countries (Austria, Belgium, Denmark, Finland, France, Germany, Greece, Ireland, Italy, Luxembourg, the Netherlands, Spain, Sweden and the UK). This was originally established by Americans, but welcomes all nationalities. Contact your local embassy or consulate for a list of clubs in your area.

- **School Or Childcare Facilities** – These provide a ready-made place for contact with other expatriate parents. If there's a parents association, it's well worthwhile becoming a member. There may also be a school café where you can drop in after ferrying your children to school and join other mothers for coffee. Look on the school notice board for news about forthcoming events and meetings (you could also offer to help).

- **Language Lessons** – Classes can offer a good place to meet expatriates, as well as offering the best way to integrate into the local community and culture.

- **Sports Clubs** – Even if you aren't particularly sporty, the local sports club or gymnasium will probably offer tuition in various sports and the opportunity to play at different levels. Many clubs also operate leagues where you can take part in regular activities.

- **Volunteer Work** – If you cannot find a paid job or obtain a work permit, you may wish to consider volunteer work (if you're a non-EU national, volunteer work also requires a work permit, although it's usually a formality). Volunteering includes everything from listening to younger children read at your children's school to teaching English to the locals; from working alongside local people in the establishment of a health clinic to helping co-ordinate aid work. Opportunities are usually plentiful and volunteers are welcomed with open arms. You will probably also gain huge satisfaction from your endeavours. Contact your local embassy or consulate or international voluntary organisations for information before you go to enquire about the possibilities. Publications providing useful contacts and information include *International Directory of Voluntary Work* (Vacation Work). For more information on volunteering see **Voluntary Work** on page 58.

EMPLOYMENT CONDITIONS

Working conditions in most EU countries are largely dependent on an employee's individual contract of employment and an employer's general employment conditions. Many aspects of working conditions are set by governments or by collective agreements reached by employers and unions. Although many employers' pay and conditions are more generous than the statutory minimum, employers may offer pay and conditions that are actually illegal. In some countries, there's a huge disparity between the conditions of hourly-paid workers and salaried employees (i.e. monthly-paid), even those employed by the same company. In most countries, managerial and executive staff generally enjoys a much higher level of benefits than lower paid employees. Employees hired to work abroad by a multinational company may receive a higher salary (including fringe benefits and allowances) than those offered by local employers.

EU nationals working in other EU countries have the same rights as local citizens, for example with regard to pay, conditions, vocational training and trade union membership. The employment conditions of non-EU nationals are generally the same as for EU nationals, although employment is usually subject to the granting of a work permit and its renewal.

Negotiating an appropriate salary is only one aspect of your remuneration which, for many employees, consists of much more than what they receive in their pay packet. When negotiating the terms of employment for a job abroad, the checklists on the following pages should prove useful. The points listed under **General Positions** below apply to most jobs, while those listed under **Managerial & Executive Positions** (on page 83) may apply only to executive and top managerial appointments.

The term 'employment conditions' (as used here) refers to an employer's general employment terms and conditions (including benefits, rules and regulations) which apply to all employees, unless otherwise stated in individual contracts of employment. General employment conditions are usually referred to in employment contracts and employees usually receive a copy on starting employment (or, in some cases, beforehand). Certain subjects, such as health insurance and company pension plans, may be detailed in separate documents.

Employment conditions may include the validity and applicability; place of work; salary and benefits; extra months salary and bonuses; working hours and flexi-time rules; overtime and compensation; travel and relocation expenses; social security; company pension plan; accident insurance; unemployment insurance; salary insurance; health insurance; miscellaneous insurance; use of company cars; notification of sickness or accident; sick pay and disability benefits; annual and public holidays; compassionate and special leave of absence; allowances and paid expenses; probationary and notice periods; education and training; health and safety; pregnancy and confinement; part-time job restrictions; changing jobs and confidentiality; acceptance of gifts; retirement; military service; discipline and dismissal; severance pay; and trade union membership.

General Positions

Salary

- Is the total salary adequate, taking into account the cost of living (see page 147)?
- Is it index-linked or protected against devaluation and cost of living increases? This is particularly important if you're paid in an EU currency that may fluctuate or could be devalued, although this is unlikely within the EU.
- Are you paid an overseas allowance for working abroad?
- Does it include an allowance for working (and living) in an expensive area or a 'hardship' allowance for working in a remote or inhospitable region?
- How often is the salary reviewed?
- Does the salary include commission and bonuses?
- Does the employer offer profit-sharing, share options or share-save schemes?
- Is overtime paid or time off given in lieu of extra hours worked?
- Is the total salary (including expenses) paid in local currency, or is it paid in another country (in a another currency) with expenses for living abroad? Many employers pay expatriate employees' salaries into an offshore account, possibly with living expenses paid locally, which can have tax advantages.

Relocation Expenses

- Are relocation expenses or a relocation allowance paid?

- Do the relocation expenses include travelling expenses for all family members?
- Is there a maximum limit, and if so, is it adequate?
- Are you required to repay your relocation expenses (or a percentage) if you resign before a certain period has elapsed?
- Are you required to pay for your relocation expenses in advance (which may run to thousands in euros or other currencies)?
- If employment is for a fixed period, will your relocation expenses be paid when you complete or leave the job?
- If you aren't shipping household goods and furniture abroad, is there an allowance for buying furniture locally?
- Do relocation expenses include the legal and real estate agent's fees incurred when moving home?
- Does the employer use the services of a relocation company (see page 88)?
- Does the employer provide free briefing services before you leave?

Accommodation

- Will the employer pay for a hotel (or pay a lodging allowance) until you find permanent accommodation?
- Is subsidised or free, temporary or permanent accommodation provided? If so, is it furnished or unfurnished?
- Must you pay for utilities such as electricity, gas and water?
- If accommodation isn't provided by the employer, is assistance in finding suitable accommodation given? What does it consist of? Does it include an advance visit to find accommodation?
- What will accommodation cost?
- While living in temporary accommodation, will the employer pay your travelling expenses to your workplace?
- Are your expenses paid while looking for accommodation?

Working Hours

- What are the weekly working hours?
- Does the employer operate a flexi-time system? If so, what are the fixed (core time) working hours? How early must you start? Can you carry forward extra hours worked and take time off at a later date, or carry forward a deficit and make it up later?
- Are you required to clock in and out of work?
- Can you choose to take time off in lieu of overtime worked or to be paid for it?

Part-time Or Periodic Working

- Is part-time or school term-time working permitted?
- Are working hours flexible or is part-time working from home permitted?
- Does the employer have a job-sharing scheme?
- Are extended career breaks permitted with no loss of seniority, grade or salary?

Leave Entitlement

- What is the annual leave entitlement? Does it increase with age or length of service?
- What are the paid public holidays?
- Is free air travel to your home country or elsewhere provided for you and your family, and if so, how often? Are other holiday travel discounts provided?
- Is paid maternity/paternity leave provided?
- Is compassionate and special leave of absence permitted?

Insurance

- Is health insurance or regular health screening provided for you **and** your family? What does it include (see page 119)?
- Is free life assurance provided?
- Is accident or any special insurance provided by your employer?
- For how long is your salary paid if you're ill or have an accident?

Company Pension

- Is there a company pension scheme and what is your contribution?
- Are you required or permitted to pay a lump sum into the pension fund in order to receive a full or higher pension?
- What are the rules regarding early retirement?
- Is the pension transferable (portable) and do you receive the company's contributions in addition to your own? If not, will the employer pay into a personal pension plan?
- Is the pension index-linked?
- Do the pension rules apply equally to full **and** part-time employees?

Employer

- Have you checked the prospective employer's status? Is it legal?

- What are the employer's future prospects?
- Is his profitability and growth rate favourable?
- Does he have a good reputation as an employer?
- Does he have a high staff turnover?

Women

- What is the employer's policy regarding equal opportunities for women?
- How many women hold positions in middle and senior management or at board level? If the percentage is low in relation to the number of women employees, perhaps you should be wary of the company.
- Does the employer have a policy of reinstatement after childbirth (a legal requirement in most EU countries)?

Family

- Will the employer employ your partner or help her/him find a job?
- Is private schooling for your children paid for or subsidised? Will the employer pay for a boarding school locally or in another country?
- Does the employer provide a free nursery or subsidised crèche for children who are below school age or a day care centre for the elderly (granny crèche)?

Training

- What initial or career training does the employer provide?
- Is training provided in-house or externally and will the employer pay for training or education abroad, if necessary?
- Does the employer have an ongoing training programme for employees in your profession (e.g. technical, management or language)? Is the employer's training recognised for its excellence (or otherwise)?
- Will the employer pay for the cost of non-essential education, e.g. a computer or language course?
- Will the employer allow paid day release for you to attend a degree course or other study?
- What are the promotion prospects?

Amenities

- Are free or subsidised language lessons provided for you and your spouse (if necessary)?

- Is a free or subsidised employee restaurant provided? If not, is a lunch allowance paid? Is any provision made for shift workers, i.e. breakfast or evening meals?
- Is a travel allowance paid from your home to your place of work?
- Is free or subsidised parking provided at work?
- Are free work clothes, overalls or uniforms provided? Does the employer pay for the cleaning of work clothes (both workshop and office)?
- Does the employer offer cheap home loans, interest-free loans or mortgage assistance? A cheap home loan can be worth many thousands of euros or a year.
- Is a company car provided? What sort of car is it? Can it be used privately, and if so, does the employer pay for petrol? Does this affect your income tax liability?
- Does the employer provide any fringe benefits such as subsidised in-house banking services, car discount scheme, cheap petrol, travel discounts, product discounts, in-house store, sports and social facilities, or subsidised tickets for social and sports events?

Conditions

- Do you have a written list of your job responsibilities?
- Have your employment conditions been confirmed in writing?
- If a dispute arises over your salary or working conditions, under the law of which country will your contract be interpreted?
- Will the employer guarantee to employ you at the end of your assignment, either in your home country or in another country? Will the employer pay your repatriation expenses?

Managerial & Executive Positions

- Is a 'golden hello (similar to a 'golden handshake' when made redundant) paid, i.e. a payment for signing a contract?
- Is there an executive (usually non-contributory) pension scheme?
- Is a housing allowance paid or a rent-free house or apartment provided?
- Are paid holidays provided (perhaps in a company-owned property) or business conferences in exotic places?
- Are the costs incurred by a move abroad reimbursed (e.g. the cost of selling your home, employing an agent to let it or for storing household effects)?
- Will the employer pay for domestic help or towards the cost of a servant/cook?
- Is a car provided with a chauffeur?

- Are you entitled to any miscellaneous benefits such as club membership, free credit cards, or tickets for sports events and shows?

- Is there an entertainment allowance?

- Is extra compensation paid if you're made redundant or fired? Redundancy or severance payments are compulsory for all employees in many countries, but executives often receive a **very** generous 'golden handshake' if they're made redundant, e.g. after a takeover.

EMPLOYMENT CONTRACTS

In many countries, a 'contract of employment' exists as soon as an employee proves his acceptance of an employer's terms and conditions of employment, e.g. by starting work, after which both employer and employee are bound by the terms offered and agreed. The contract isn't always in writing, although employers must usually provide employees with a written statement containing certain important terms of employment and additional notes, e.g. regarding discipline and grievance procedures. A written contract of employment should usually contain all the terms and conditions agreed between the employer and employee.

You usually receive two copies of your contract of employment (which may be called a 'statement of terms and conditions' or an 'offer letter'), both of which you should sign and date. One copy must be returned to your employer or prospective employer, assuming you agree with the terms and want the job, and the other (usually the original) is for your personal records. There are generally no hidden surprises or traps for the unwary in a contract of employment provided by a bona fide employer although, as with any contract, you should know exactly what it contains before signing it. If your knowledge of the local language is imperfect, you should ask someone to explain anything you don't understand in simple English (employers rarely provide foreigners with contracts in a language other than the local language). Your contract (or statement) of employment may contain the following details:

- Names of the employer and employee.

- The date employment begins and whether employment with a previous employer counts as part of the employee's continuous period of employment.

- Job title.

- Salary details, including overtime pay and piece-rates, commission, bonuses and agreed salary increases or review dates.

- When the salary is to be paid, e.g. weekly or monthly.

- Hours of work.

- Holiday and public holiday entitlements and pay.

- Sickness and accident benefits.

- Pension scheme details.

- Probationary and notice periods (or the expiry date, if employment is for a fixed period).

- Disciplinary and grievance procedures (which may be contained in a separate document).

If there are no agreed terms under one or more of the above headings, this may be stated in the contract. Any special arrangements or conditions you've agreed with an employer should also be contained in the contract. If all or any of the above particulars are contained in a collective agreement, an employer may refer employees to a copy of this, including other documents such as work rules or handbooks, wage regulation orders, sick pay and pension scheme conditions, and the rules relating to flexible working hours and company holidays. Before signing your contract of employment, you should obtain a copy of any general employment conditions or documents referred to in the contract and ensure that you understand them.

Employment is usually subject to satisfactory references being received from your previous employer(s) and/or character references. In the case of a school-leaver or student, a reference may be required from the principal of your last school, college or university. For certain jobs, a pre-employment medical examination is required and periodical examinations may be a condition of employment, e.g. where good health is vital to the safe performance of your duties. If you require a work permit, your contract may contain a clause stating that the contract is 'subject to a work permit being granted by the authorities'. Employees must usually be notified in writing of any changes in their terms and conditions of employment, within a limited period of their introduction.

3.

ACCOMMODATION

In most EU countries, finding accommodation to rent or buy isn't difficult, provided your requirements aren't too unusual. There are, however, a few exceptions. For example, rented accommodation in major cities is usually in high demand and short supply, and rents can be very high. Accommodation usually accounts for around 25 per cent of the average family's budget, but can be up to 50 per cent in major cities. Property prices and rents vary considerably according to the region and city, and have increased steadily in most major cities in recent years. In most European cities and large towns, apartments are much more common than detached houses, which are rare and prohibitively expensive.

People in most EU countries aren't very mobile and move house much less frequently than the Americans and British, which is reflected in the fairly stable property market. It generally isn't worth buying a home abroad unless you plan to stay in the country for the medium to long term, say a minimum of five years and preferably 10 to 15. People in most countries don't buy domestic property as an investment (an exception is property in resort areas), but as a home for life, and you shouldn't expect to make a quick profit when buying property abroad.

RELOCATION COMPANIES

If you're fortunate enough to have your move abroad paid for by your employers, it's likely that they will arrange for a relocation company to handle the details. There are relocation companies in most EU countries, particularly in major cities. In some countries, there are different types of relocation companies, including corporate relocation ones (whose clients are usually large companies), commercial property companies and home-search companies, who act for individuals. The larger relocation companies may provide all three levels of service, while smaller companies may have just a few staff and offer only a home-search service.

The fees charged (and services provided) by relocation companies vary enormously, although most levy a registration (or administration) fee payable in advance, plus a daily fee for accompanied viewing of properties and other amenities. If finding a home is part of the service, a fee of 1 to 2 per cent of the purchase price is normal, with a minimum charge, e.g. €1,000 to €2,000 (GB£700 to £1,400). An all-inclusive international relocation package which includes the rental or purchase of an employee's home and advice on mortgages (for house purchasers), schools, insurance and other matters, can easily run to between €15,000 and €30,000 (GB£10,500 to £21,000). Home-search companies are becoming increasingly common and will undertake to find the home of your dreams. This can save buyers considerable time, trouble and money, particularly if you have special or unusual requirements. Some specialise in finding exceptional residences only, costing upward of €750,000 (GB£500,000), and can save buyers money by negotiating the price on their behalf.

Finding accommodation for single people or couples without children can usually be accomplished in a week or two, depending on the country and region, while family homes usually take a bit longer. You should usually allow at least two months between your initial visit and moving into a purchased property. Rental properties (see page 90) can usually be found in two to four weeks, depending on the location and your requirements. Relocation companies may provide the following services:

- **House Hunting** – This is usually the main service provided by relocation companies and includes both rented and purchased properties. Services usually include locating a number of properties matching your requirements and specifications, and arranging a visit (or visits) to view them.

- **Negotiations** – Consultants will usually help and advise with all aspects of house rental or purchase and may conduct negotiations on your behalf, organise finance (including bridging loans), arrange surveys and insurance, organise your move and even arrange quarantine for your pets (see page 199).

- **Schools** – Consultants can usually provide a report on local schools (both state and private) for families with children. If required, the report can also include boarding schools.

- **Local Information** – Most companies will provide a comprehensive data package for a chosen area, including information about employment prospects, state and private health services, local schools (state and private), estate agents, shopping facilities, public transport, amenities and services, sports and social facilities, and communications.

- **Miscellaneous Services** – Most companies provide advice and support (particularly for non-working spouses) both before and after a move. Orientation visits for spouses, counselling services for domestic and personal problems, help in finding jobs and even marriage counselling services.

Although you may consider a relocation consultant's services expensive, particularly if you're footing the bill yourself, most companies and individuals consider it money well spent. You can find a relocation consultant in most countries through the yellow pages or via the internet (using a search engine). There's an Association of Relocation Agents in some EU countries, such as the ARA in the UK (⌨ www.relocationagents.com).

If you just wish to look at properties for rent or sale in a particular area, you can make appointments to view properties through estate agents in the area where you plan to live and arrange your own trip abroad. However, you must make absolutely certain that agents know exactly what you're looking for and obtain property lists in advance.

TEMPORARY ACCOMMODATION

On arrival abroad, it may be necessary to stay in temporary accommodation for a few weeks or months, e.g. before moving into permanent accommodation or while waiting for your furniture to arrive. Some employers provide rooms, self-contained apartments or hostels for employees and their families, although this is rare and is usually only for a limited period. Many hotels and bed and breakfast establishments cater for long-term guests and offer reduced weekly or monthly rates. In many areas, particularly in major cities, service and holiday apartments are available. These are fully self-contained furnished apartments with their own bathrooms and kitchens, which are cheaper and more convenient than a hotel. Service apartments are usually rented on a weekly basis. Self-catering holiday accommodation is available in resort areas in many EU countries, although it's prohibitively expensive during the main holiday season (e.g. June to August).

Hotels

Hotel rates vary according to the time of year, the exact location and the individual establishment, although you may be able to haggle over rates outside the high season and for long stays. A single room in most EU countries (excluding major cities) costs from around €50 (GB£35) and a double room from around €75 (GB£50) per night. You should expect to pay at least double these rates in a major city, where cheap hotels are often used as permanent accommodation. Hotels aren't usually a cost-effective solution for anyone planning to stay in a country long term, although in some EU countries (particularly the new member states) they may be the only alternative and may offer special low rates for long-term residents. Bed and breakfast accommodation is also available in many countries, although it isn't always budget accommodation, when you need to choose a hostel or pension, which may have self-catering apartments or studios.

RENTED ACCOMMODATION

If you're planning to spend only a few years abroad, then renting is usually the best decision. It's also the answer for those who don't want the trouble, expense and restrictions associated with buying a property. **In fact, it's prudent for anyone looking for a permanent home abroad to rent for a period until you know exactly what you want, how much you wish to pay and where you want to live.** This is particularly important for retirees who don't know a country well. Renting allows you to become familiar with an area, its weather, amenities and the local people; to meet other foreigners who have made their homes abroad and share their experiences; and, not least, to discover the cost of living at first hand.

Most EU countries have a strong rental market and it's possible to rent every kind of property, from a tiny studio apartment to a huge rambling castle. However, rental properties in most EU capitals are in short supply. Outside the capitals, the situation is generally better, it's easier to find a property and you will probably have a choice. Rental properties are mostly privately owned, but include investment properties owned by companies and public housing owned by local councils. If you're looking for a home for less than a year, you're better off looking for a furnished apartment or house. Rental properties in most countries are let unfurnished, particularly for lets longer than one year, and long-term furnished properties are difficult to find. In some countries (e.g. Italy), unfurnished means a property will be completely empty, except perhaps for the bathroom porcelain and possibly a kitchen sink. There will be no kitchen cupboards, appliances, light fittings, curtains or carpets, although you may be able to buy these from a departing tenant. Semi-furnished apartments usually have kitchen cupboards and bathroom fixtures, and possibly a few pieces of furniture, while furnished properties tend to be fully equipped, including crockery, bedding and possibly towels (similar to renting a self-catering apartment).

Many EU countries have an abundance of self-catering accommodation. You can choose from cottages, apartments, villas, bungalows, mobile homes, chalets, and even castles and palaces, if your budget runs to them. Most property is available for short holiday lets only, particularly during the peak summer season, and little furnished property is let long-term. However, some owners let their homes long-term, particularly outside the peak summer period. When the rental period includes the peak letting months of July and August, the rent may be prohibitive. If you rent for a short period from an agent, you should negotiate a lower commission than the usual one month's rent, e.g. 10 per cent of the total rent payable. You can make agreements by fax or email when renting from abroad.

Standards vary considerably, from dilapidated ill-equipped cottages to luxury villas with every modern convenience. A typical holiday rental is a small cottage or self-contained apartment with one or two bedrooms (sleeping two to four and usually, including a sofa bed in the living room), a large living-room/kitchen with an open fire or stove, and a toilet and bathroom. Always check whether a property is fully equipped (which should mean whatever you want it to mean!) and whether it has central heating if you're planning to rent in winter.

For short-term lets, the cost is calculated on a weekly basis (usually Saturday to Saturday) and depends on the standard, location, number of beds and the facilities provided. For holiday rentals, the year is generally split into three rental periods: low (October to April), mid (May, June and September) and peak (July and August). Rents vary considerably according to the country, the region, the time of year and, not least, the size and quality of the property. As a rough guide, a rural property in Europe sleeping two costs from around €300 (GB£210) per week in the low season to €600 (GB£450) per week in the peak season. An urban property sleeping four costs from €300 (GB£210) per a week in the low season to €1,000 (GB£700) in the high season. At the top end of the scale, you can easily pay €3,000 to €6,000 (GB£2,100 to £4,200) or more per week for a large farmhouse or villa with a swimming pool in summer.

If you're looking for a rental property for a few months, it's best not to rent unseen, but to rent a holiday apartment for a week or two to allow you time to look around. Properties for rent are advertised in local newspapers and magazines, including expatriate publications, and can also be found through property publications in many countries. Many estate agents offer short-term rentals and builders and developers may also rent properties to potential buyers. Short-term rentals can be found through local and state tourist offices abroad, travel agents, the internet and many overseas newspapers.

Rental laws and protection for tenants don't usually extend to holiday lettings, furnished lettings or sub-lettings. For holiday letting, parties are free to agree such terms as they see fit concerning the period, rent, deposit and the number of occupants, and there's no legal obligation for the landlord to provide a written agreement. However, you shouldn't rent a furnished property long-term without a written contract, which is important if you wish to have a deposit returned.

Finding A Rental Property

Your success in finding a suitable rental property depends on many factors, not least the kind of rental you're seeking (a one-bedroom apartment is easier to find than a four-bedroom detached house), how much you want to pay and the area where you wish to live. There are a number of ways of finding a property to rent, including the following:

- If you have friends, relatives or acquaintances in the area, ask them to help spread the word. In many countries, the best properties are often found by word of mouth, particularly in major cities, where it's almost impossible to find somewhere with a reasonable rent unless you have connections.
- Check the advertisements in local newspapers and magazines (see below).
- Look for properties with a 'to rent' sign in the window.
- Visit accommodation and letting agents (listed in the yellow pages). Most cities and large towns have estate agents that also act as letting agents for owners. It's often better to deal with an agent than directly with owners, particularly regarding contracts and legal matters.
- Look for advertisements in shop windows and on bulletin boards in shopping centres, supermarkets, universities and colleges, and company offices.
- Check newsletters published by companies, colleges, churches, clubs and expatriate organisations, and their notice boards.

You must usually be quick off the mark to find accommodation through classified advertisements in local newspapers. Buy newspapers as soon as they're published and start phoning straight away. You can also view rental advertisements on the internet, where all major newspapers have websites. Other sources include expatriate publications published in major cities and classified advertisement newspapers. Some estate agents also provide apartment listings in magazines. You must be available to inspect properties immediately or at any time. Even if you start phoning at the crack of dawn, you're likely to find a queue when you arrive to view a property in a major city.

The best days for advertisements are usually Fridays and Saturdays. Advertisers may be private owners, property managers or letting agencies (particularly in major cities). You can insert a 'rental wanted' advertisement in many newspapers and on notice boards, but don't count on success using this method. Finding a property to rent in major cities in many EU countries is similar to the situation in London and Paris, where the best properties are usually found through personal contacts. The worst time to look is during

September and October when people return from their summer holidays and students are looking for accommodation.

Rents

Rents are very high in some countries, particularly in major cities where rental property is in high demand and short supply. Rents may also be astronomical in relation to the local cost and standard of living and foreigners may need to pay a high premium over what the locals pay. This is particularly true in the Baltic States and Poland. In most countries you must pay at least one month's rent in advance and landlords may demand a non-returnable deposit (called 'key money'), usually equal to at least one month's rent, simply for the 'privilege' of being able to rent a property.

Inventory

One of the most important tasks to perform after moving into purchased or rental accommodation is to make an inventory of the fixtures and fittings and, if applicable, the furniture and furnishings. When you've purchased a property, you should check that the previous owner hasn't absconded with any fixtures and fittings that were included in the price or anything that you specifically paid for, e.g. carpets, light fittings, curtains, furniture, kitchen cupboards and appliances, garden ornaments, plants or doors. It's common to do a final check or inventory when buying a new property, usually a few weeks before completion.

When moving into a long-term rental property, it's necessary to complete an inventory of its contents and a report on its condition. This includes the condition of fixtures and fittings, the state of furniture and furnishings, the cleanliness and state of the decoration, and anything that's damaged, missing or in need of repair. An inventory should be provided by your landlord or agent and may include every single item in a furnished property, down to the number of teaspoons. The inventory check should be carried out in your presence. If an inventory isn't provided, you should insist on one being prepared and annexed to the lease. If you find a serious fault after signing the inventory, send a registered letter to your landlord and ask for it to be attached to the inventory.

An inventory should be drawn up both when moving into and when vacating a rented property. If the two don't correspond, you must make good any damages or deficiencies or the landlord can do so and deduct the cost from your deposit. Although most landlords are honest, some will do almost anything to avoid repaying a deposit. **Note the reading on your utility meters (e.g. electricity, gas and water) and check that you aren't overcharged on your first bill.** The meters should be read by utility companies before you move in, although you may need to organise it yourself.

It's advisable to obtain written instructions from the previous owner concerning the operation of appliances, heating and air-conditioning systems; maintenance of grounds, gardens and lawns; care of special surfaces such as wooden, marble or tiled floors; and the names of reliable local maintenance men. Check with your local town hall regarding regulations about such things as rubbish collection, recycling and on-road parking.

BUYING PROPERTY

Buying property in most countries is usually a good long-term investment and is preferable to renting. However, if you're staying for only a relatively short term, say less than five years, you may be better off renting. For those staying longer than this, buying is usually the better option, particularly as buying a house or apartment is generally no more expensive than renting in the long term and could yield a handsome profit. Provided you avoid the most expensive areas (i.e. major cities and resort areas), property can be relatively inexpensive in many countries compared with the UK or the US, although the fees associated with a purchase usually add between 5 and 15 per cent to the cost.

Property ownership is high in some countries, e.g. as high as 80 per cent, although people in most countries don't generally buy property as an investment and you shouldn't expect to make a quick profit when buying property abroad. In most countries, property values increase at an average of around 5 per cent a year or in line with inflation, meaning that you must own a house for a few years simply to recover the fees associated with buying. The prices generally rise faster than average in some fashionable areas. The stable property market in most countries acts as a discouragement to speculators wishing to make a quick profit, as does capital gains tax.

It isn't advisable to be in too much of a hurry when buying a home. Have a good look around in your preferred area(s) and make sure that you have a clear picture of the relative prices and the kinds of properties available. There's a huge variety of properties for sale in most countries, ranging from derelict farmhouses and village houses requiring complete restoration, to new luxury apartments and villas with all modern conveniences. Some people set themselves impossible deadlines in which to buy a property (e.g. a few days or a week) and often end up bitterly regretting their impulsive decision.

Some EU countries have strict regulations governing the purchase of property by foreigners. In some countries, foreigners have to fulfil residence conditions or there may be a limit to the number (and size) of properties you're allowed to buy. For information on restrictions in individual countries, see the **Accommodation** sections in **Chapter 9 – Country Profiles**.

It's a wise or lucky person who gets his choice absolutely right first time, which is why most experts recommend that you rent before buying unless you're absolutely certain what you want, how much you wish to pay and where you want to live. To reduce the chances of making an expensive error when buying in an unfamiliar country or region, it's often prudent to rent for 6 to 12 months. This allows you to become familiar with the region and the weather, and gives you plenty of time to look around for a permanent home at your leisure. There's no shortage of properties for sale in most countries and whatever kind of property you're looking for, you will have an abundance to choose from. Wait until you find your dream home and then think about it for another week or two before signing a contract.

To get an idea of property prices, check those of properties advertised in English language property magazines and local newspapers, magazines and property journals (see **Appendix B**). In some countries, property price indexes for various regions are published by local property magazines, although these should be taken only as a rough guide. Before deciding on the price, make sure you know exactly what's included, as it isn't unusual for people to strip a house or apartment bare when selling and remove the kitchen sink, toilets, light fittings and even the light switches! If applicable, have fixtures and fittings listed in the contract.

For anyone planning to buy a home abroad, our sister publication, *Buying a Home Abroad* by David Hampshire, is essential reading. Survival Books also publishes books on buying a home in several EU countries, including Cyprus, France, Greece, Ireland, Italy, Portugal, Spain and the UK. The Survival Books *Living & Working* series includes information and advice on buying a home in Belgium, France, Germany, Ireland, Italy, Luxembourg, the Netherlands, Spain and the UK. See page 414 to order copies or you can order online (🖳 www. survival books.net). A comprehensive list of other books can be found in **Appendix B**.

Avoiding Problems

The problems associated with buying property abroad have been highlighted in the last few decades or so, during which the property market in some countries has gone from boom to bust and back again. From a legal point of view, some countries are much safer than others, although buyers have a high degree of protection under the law in most EU countries. However, you should take the usual precautions regarding contracts, deposits and obtaining proper title. Many people have had their fingers burnt by rushing into property deals without proper care and consideration. It's all too easy to fall in love with the beauty and allure of a home and sign a contract without giving it sufficient thought. If you're uncertain, don't allow yourself to be rushed into making a hasty decision, e.g. through fears of an imminent price rise or because someone else is interested in a property. Although many people dream of buying a home abroad, it's vital to do your homework thoroughly and avoid the dream sellers (often fellow countrymen) who will happily prey on your ignorance and tell you anything in order to sell you a home.

The vast majority of people who buy homes abroad generally don't obtain independent legal advice and most of those who experience problems take no precautions whatsoever. Of those who do take legal advice, many do so only after having paid a deposit and signed a contract or, more commonly, after they've run into problems. The most important point to bear in mind when buying property abroad is to obtain expert legal advice from someone who's familiar with local law. When buying property in any country, you should never pay any money or sign anything without first taking legal advice. You will find the relatively small cost (in comparison with the cost of a home) of obtaining legal advice to be excellent value for money, if only for the peace of mind it affords. Trying to cut corners to save a few pennies on legal costs is foolhardy in the extreme when a large sum is at stake.

There are professionals speaking English and other languages in most EU countries, and many expatriate professionals (e.g. architects, builders and surveyors) also practise abroad. However, don't assume that because you're dealing with a fellow countryman that he'll offer you a better deal or do a better job than a local person (the contrary may be true). It's wise to check the credentials of professionals you employ, whatever their nationality. It's never advisable to rely solely on advice proffered by those with a financial interest in selling you a property, such as a builder or estate agent, although their advice may be excellent and totally unbiased.

Declared Value

Don't be tempted by the quaint custom of tax evasion, where the 'official' sale price declared to the authorities is reduced by an 'under the table' cash payment. In some EU countries (e.g. Italy, Portugal and Spain), it's possible when buying a property direct from the vendor that he may suggest this, particularly if he's selling a second home and must pay capital gains tax on the profit. Obviously if the vendor can show a smaller profit, he pays less tax. **You should steer well clear of this practice, which is strictly illegal (although widespread).** If you under-declare the price, the authorities can re-value the property and demand that you pay the shortfall in tax plus interest and fines. If you're selling a property, you should bear in mind that if the buyer refuses to make the illicit payment after the contract has been signed, there's nothing (legally) you can do about it!

Among the most common problems experienced by buyers abroad are buying in the wrong area (**rent first!**); buying a home that's unsaleable; buying too large a property and grossly underestimating restoration and modernisation costs; not having a survey done on an old property; not taking legal advice; not including the necessary conditional clauses in the contract; buying a property for business (e.g. to convert to self-catering accommodation) and being too optimistic about the income; overcharging by vendors and agents (a common practice when selling to foreigners); taking on too large a mortgage; and property management companies going bust or doing a moonlight flit with owners' rental receipts.

Other problems include buying a property without a legal title (a particular problem in Slovenia); properties built or extended illegally without planning permission; properties sold that are subject to embargoes; properties that are part of the assets of a company, sold illegally by a bankrupt builder or company; undischarged mortgages from the previous owner; builders absconding with the buyer's money before completing a property; claims by relatives after a property has been purchased; properties sold to more than one buyer; and people selling properties they don't own. **Always take care when a property is offered at a seemingly bargain price by a builder, developer or other businessman, and run a thorough credit check on the vendor and his business.** One law that property buyers should be aware of is the law of subrogation, whereby property debts, including mortgages, local taxes, utility bills and community charges, remain with a property and are inherited by the buyer in some EU countries. This is an open invitation to dishonest sellers to cut and run. Of course, it's possible to check whether there are any outstanding debts on a property and your legal advisor must do this after you sign a contract and again a few days before completion.

It's advisable to have your finance in place before you start looking for a property abroad and, if you need a mortgage, to obtain a mortgage guarantee certificate from a bank that guarantees you a mortgage at a certain rate, usually subject to a valuation. However, in many countries, a buyer can withdraw from a contract and have his deposit returned if he's unable to obtain a mortgage. You will need to pay a deposit when signing a contract and must pay all fees and taxes on completion.

Summary

It's important to deal only with qualified and licensed agents, and to engage a local lawyer before signing anything or paying a deposit. A surveyor may also be necessary, particularly if you're buying an old property or a property with a large plot of land. Your lawyer will carry out the necessary searches regarding such matters as ownership, debts and rights of way. Enquiries must be made to ensure that the vendor has a registered title and that there are no debts against a property. It's also important to check that a property has the relevant building licences, conforms to local planning laws and that any changes (alterations, additions or renovations) have been approved by the local town hall. If a property is owned by several members of a family – as is common in some EU countries, particularly in those with strict inheritance laws (e.g. France, Greece and Spain) – all owners must give their consent before it can be sold. It's also important to ensure that a rural property has a reliable water supply.

Finally, if there's any chance that you will need to sell (and recoup your investment) in the foreseeable future, it's wise to buy a home that will be saleable. A property with broad appeal in a popular area will usually fit the bill, although it will need to be very special to sell quickly in some areas. A modest, reasonably priced property is usually likely to be much more saleable than a large expensive home, particularly one requiring restoration or modernisation.

CHOOSING A LOCATION

The most important consideration when buying a home is usually its location – or, as the old adage goes, the **three** most important points are location, location and location! A property in a reasonable condition in a popular area is likely to be a better investment than an exceptional property in a less attractive location. There's no point in buying a dream property in a terrible location. The wrong decision regarding location is one of the main causes of disenchantment among foreigners who have bought homes abroad.

Where you buy a property will depend on a range of factors, including your personal preferences, your financial resources and, not least, whether you plan to work. If you already have a job, the location of a home will probably be determined by the proximity to your place of employment. However, if you intend to look for employment or start a business, you must live in an area that allows you the maximum scope. Unless you have reason to believe otherwise, it would be unwise to rely on finding employment in a particular area. If, on the other hand, you're looking for a holiday or retirement home, you can live virtually anywhere. When seeking a permanent home, don't be too influenced by where you've spent an enjoyable holiday or two. A town or area that was acceptable for a few weeks holiday may be far from suitable, for example, for a retirement home, particularly regarding the proximity to shops, medical facilities and other amenities.

If you have little idea about where you wish to buy, read as much as you can about the countries and regions on your shortlist and spend some time looking around your areas of interest. Climate, lifestyle and cost of living can vary considerably according to the country, region and even within a particular region. Before looking at properties, it's important to have a good idea of the type of property you're looking for and the price you want, and to draw up a shortlist of the areas or towns of interest. If you don't do this, you're likely to be overwhelmed by the number of properties to be viewed. Estate agents usually expect serious buyers to know where they want to buy within a 30 to 40km (20 to 25mi) radius and some even expect clients to narrow it down to specific towns and villages.

The 'best' area in which to live depends on a range of considerations, including the proximity to your place of work, schools, bar, country or town, shops, public transport, bar, sports facilities, beach, bar, etc. There are beautiful areas to choose from in most countries within easy travelling distance of a town or city (and a bar). Don't, however, believe the travelling times and distances stated in advertisements and estate agents' brochures. According to some agents' magical mystery maps, every home is close to a city or large town, public transport and other amenities. When looking for a home, bear in mind travelling times and costs to your place of work, shops and local amenities such as restaurants and bars. If you buy a remote country property, the distance to local amenities and services could become a problem, particularly if you plan to retire abroad. If you live in a remote rural area you will need to be much more self-sufficient than if you live in a town. You will need to use the car for everything, which will add significantly to the cost of living. **The cost of motoring is high in most EU countries and may be an important consideration when buying a home.**

If possible, you should visit an area a number of times over a period of a few weeks, both on weekdays and at weekends, in order to get a feel for the neighbourhood (walk, don't just drive around!). A property seen on a balmy summer's day after a delicious lunch and a few glasses of wine may not be nearly so attractive on a subsequent visit on a dull day without the warm inner glow. If possible, you should also visit an area at different times of the year, e.g. in both summer and winter, as somewhere that's wonderful in summer can be forbidding and inhospitable in winter. On the other hand, if you're planning to buy a winter holiday home, you should also view it in summer, as snow can hide a multitude of sins! In any case, you should view a property a number of times before making up your mind to buy it. If you're unfamiliar with a country or area, most experts recommend that you rent for a period before deciding to buy (see **Rented Accommodation** on page 90). This is particularly important if you're planning to buy a permanent or retirement home in an unfamiliar area. Many people change their minds after a period and it isn't unusual for families to move once or twice before settling down permanently.

If you will be working abroad, obtain a map of the area and decide the maximum distance you wish to travel to work, e.g. by drawing a circle with your workplace in the middle. Obtain large-scale maps of the area where you're looking, which may even show individual buildings, thereby allowing you to mark off the places that you've seen. You could do this using a grading system to denote your impressions. If you use an estate agent, he'll usually drive you around and you can then return later to those that you like most at your leisure – provided you've marked them on your map!

There are many points to consider regarding the location of a home, which can roughly be divided into the local vicinity, i.e. the immediate surroundings and neighbourhood, and the general area or region. Take into account the present and future needs of all members of your family, including the following:

- For most people the climate is one of the most important factors when buying a home abroad, particularly a holiday or retirement home. Bear in mind both the winter and summer climate, the position of the sun, the average daily sunshine, plus the rainfall and wind conditions. You may also wish to check whether the area is noted for fog, which can make for hazardous driving conditions. The orientation or aspect of a building is vital; if you want morning or afternoon sun (or both) you must ensure that balconies, terraces and gardens are facing south.

- Check whether an area is particularly prone to natural disasters such as floods (which are common in some countries), storms (hurricanes, tornadoes, etc.), forest fires, landslides or earthquakes. If a property is located near a coast or waterway, it may be expensive to insure against floods, which are a constant threat in some countries. In areas with little rainfall, there are often severe water restrictions and high water bills. See also **Climate** on pages 111 and 190.

- Noise can be a problem in many cities and resort areas. Although you cannot choose your neighbours, you can at least ensure that a property isn't located next to a busy road, railway line, airport, industrial plant, commercial area, discotheque, night club, bar or restaurant (where revelries may continue into the early hours). Look out for objectionable properties that may be too close to the one you're considering and check whether nearby vacant land has been 'zoned' for commercial activities or tower blocks. In community developments (e.g. apartment blocks), many properties are second homes and are let short term, which means you may have to tolerate boisterous holidaymakers as neighbours throughout the year (or at least during the summer months).

- You stand to be inundated with tourists in summer or possibly all year if you live in a popular tourist area or city (e.g. Florence, Paris or Prague). They won't only jam the roads and pack the public transport, but may also occupy your favourite table at your local café or restaurant (heaven forbid!). Although a 'front-line' property on a beach or in a marina development may sound attractive and be ideal for short holidays, it isn't always the best choice for permanent residents. Many beaches are hopelessly crowded in the high season, streets may be smelly from restaurants and fast food joints, parking impossible, services stretched to breaking point, and the incessant noise may drive you crazy. Some people prefer to move inland or to higher ground, where it's less humid, more peaceful and you can enjoy panoramic views. On the other hand, getting to and from hillside properties is often precarious and the often poorly maintained roads (usually narrow and unguarded) in many countries are for sober, confident drivers only. Many country roads are suitable only for four-wheel-drive vehicles.

- Do you wish to live in an area with many of your fellow countrymen and other expatriates or as far away from them as possible? If you wish to integrate with the local community, avoid foreign ghettos and choose an area or development with mainly local inhabitants. However, unless you speak the local language fluently or intend to learn, you should think twice before buying a property in a village. The locals in some villages resent 'outsiders' buying up prime properties, particularly holiday home owners, although those who take the time and trouble to integrate into the local community are usually warmly welcomed. If you're buying a permanent home, it's important to check your prospective neighbours, particularly when buying an apartment. For example, are they noisy, sociable or absent for long periods? Do you think you will get on with them? **Good neighbours are invaluable, particularly when buying a second home.**

- Do you wish to be in a town or do you prefer the country? Inland or on the coast? How about living on an island? If you buy a property in the country, you will probably have to tolerate poor public transport (or none at all), long travelling distances to a town of any size, solitude and remoteness. You won't be able to pop along to the local bakers, drop into the local bar for a glass of your favourite tipple with the locals or have a choice of restaurants on your doorstep. In a town or large village, the market will be just around the corner, the doctor and pharmacy close at hand and, if you need help or have any problems, your neighbours will be close by.

In the country you will be closer to nature, will have more freedom (e.g. to make as much noise as you wish) and possibly complete privacy, e.g. to sunbathe or swim *au naturel*. Living in a remote area in the country will suit nature lovers looking for solitude who don't want to involve themselves in the hustle and bustle of town life. If you're after peace and quiet, make sure that there isn't a busy road or railway line nearby or a local church within DONGING distance. However, many people who buy a remote country home find that the peace of the countryside palls after a time and they yearn for the more exciting city or coastal nightlife. If you've never lived in the country, it's advisable to rent first before buying. While it's cheaper to buy in a remote or unpopular location, it's often much more difficult to sell.

● If you're planning to buy a large country property with an extensive garden or plot of land, bear in mind the high cost and amount of work involved in its upkeep. If it's to be a second home, who will look after the house and garden when you're away? Do you want to spend your holidays mowing the lawn and cutting back the undergrowth? Do you want a home with a lot of outbuildings? What are you going to do with them? Can you afford to convert them into extra rooms or guest or self-catering accommodation?

● How secure is your job or business and are you likely to move to another country or area in the near future? Could you find other work in the same country or area, if necessary? If there's a possibility that you may need to move in a few years' time, you should rent or at least buy a property that will be relatively easy to sell and recoup the cost.

● What about your partner's and children's jobs or your children's present and future schooling? What is the quality of local schools? Even if your family has no need or plans to use local schools, the value of a home is often influenced by their quality and location.

● What local health and social services are provided? How far is the nearest hospital with an emergency department?

● What shopping facilities are provided in the local neighbourhood? How far is it to the nearest sizeable town with good shopping facilities, e.g. a supermarket? How would you get there if your car was out of action? Many rural villages are dying and have few shops or facilities, and so aren't necessarily a good choice for a retirement home.

● What is the range and quality of local leisure, sports, community and cultural facilities? What is the proximity to sports facilities such as a beach, golf course, ski resort or waterway? Properties in or close to ski and coastal resorts are usually considerably more expensive, although they also have the best letting potential. If you're interested in a winter holiday home, which area should you choose? While properties in ski resorts are relatively expensive, they tend to appreciate faster than properties in many other areas and generally maintain their value in bad times.

● Is the proximity to public transport, e.g. an international airport, port or railway station, or access to a motorway important? Don't, however, believe all you're told about the distance or travelling times to the nearest motorway, airport, railway station, port, beach or town, but check yourself. Being on a local bus route is also advantageous.

- If you're planning to buy in a town or city, is there adequate private or free on-street parking for your family and visitors? Is it safe to park in the street? In some areas, it's important to have secure off-street parking if you value your car. Parking is a problem in many towns and most cities, where private garages or parking spaces are rare and can be expensive (although you may be able to rent a garage). An apartment or house in a town or community development may be some distance from the nearest road or car park. How do you feel about carrying heavy shopping hundreds of metres to your home and possibly up several flights of stairs? Traffic congestion is also a problem in many towns and tourist resorts, particularly during the high season.

- What is the local crime rate? In some areas, the incidence of housebreaking and burglary is high. Owing to the higher than average crime rate (see page 191), home insurance is higher in major cities and some resort areas. Check the crime rate in the local area, e.g. burglaries, housebreaking, stolen cars and crimes of violence. Is crime increasing or decreasing? Professional crooks like isolated houses, particularly those full of expensive furniture and other belongings that they can strip bare at their leisure. You're much less likely to be a victim of theft if you live in a village, where crime is usually virtually unknown – strangers stand out like sore thumbs in villages, where their every move is monitored by the local populace.

- Do houses sell well in the area? Generally, you should avoid neighbourhoods where desirable properties routinely remain on the market for three months or longer (unless the property market is in a severe slump).

MOVING HOUSE

After finding a home, it can usually take just a few weeks to have your belongings shipped within the EU. From anywhere else it varies considerably, e.g. around four weeks between the east coast of the US and the EU, six weeks between the US west coast or the Far East and the EU, and around eight to ten weeks between Australasia and the EU. Customs clearance isn't necessary when shipping your household effects from one EU country to another. However, when shipping your effects from a non-EU country, you should enquire about customs formalities in advance. When moving to some countries you must present an inventory (usually in the local language) of the items that you're importing to your local consulate, which must be officially stamped. **In any case, it's advisable to have an inventory to hand and/or to give to your shipper.** If you fail to follow the correct procedure, you can encounter problems and delays, and may be charged duty or fined. The relevant forms to be completed may depend on whether your home abroad will be your principal residence or a second home. Removal companies usually take care of the paperwork and ensure that the correct documents are provided and properly completed (see **Customs** on page 173).

It's advisable to use a major shipping company which has a good reputation. For international moves it's certainly best to use a company that's a member of the International Federation of Furniture Removers (FIDI, 💻 www.fidi.com) or the Overseas Moving Network International (OMNI, 💻 www.omnimoving.com), with experience in the country you're moving to. Members of FIDI and OMNI usually subscribe to an advance payment scheme providing a guarantee: if a member company fails to fulfil its commitments to a client, the removal is completed at the agreed cost by another company or your money is refunded. Some removal companies have subsidiaries or affiliates abroad, which may be more convenient if you encounter problems or need to make a claim.

You should obtain at least three written quotations before choosing a company, as costs vary considerably. Companies should send a representative to provide a detailed quotation. Most companies will pack your belongings and provide packing cases and special containers, although this is naturally more expensive than packing them yourself. Ask a company how they pack fragile and valuable items, and whether the costs of packing cases, materials and insurance (see below) are included in a quotation. If you're doing your own packing, most shipping companies will provide packing crates and boxes. Shipments are charged by volume, e.g. the cubic metre in Europe and the cubic foot in North America. You should expect to pay from €3,000 to €6,000 (GB£2,100 to £4,200) to move the contents of a three to four-bedroom house within the EU, e.g. from London to southern Spain. If you're flexible about the delivery date, shipping companies will quote a lower fee based on a 'part load', where the cost is shared with other deliveries. This can result in savings of 50 per cent or more compared with an individual delivery. Whether you have an individual or shared delivery, obtain the maximum transit period in writing, otherwise you may have to wait months for delivery!

Be sure to insure your belongings fully during removal with a well-established insurance company. Don't insure with a shipping company that carries its own insurance, as they may fight every penny of a claim. Insurance premiums are usually 1 to 2 per cent of the declared value of your goods, depending on the type of cover. It's prudent to make a photographic or video record of valuables. Most insurance policies cover for 'all-risks' on a replacement value basis. China, glass and other breakables can usually be included in an 'all-risks' policy only when they've been packed by the shipping company. Insurance usually covers total loss or loss of a particular crate only, rather than individual items (unless they were packed by the shipping company). If there are any breakages or damaged items, they should be noted and listed before you sign the delivery bill (although it's obviously impractical to check everything on delivery). If you need to make a claim, be sure to read the small print, as some companies require clients to make a claim within a few days, although seven is usual. Send a claim by registered post. Some insurance companies apply an 'excess' of around 1 per cent of the total shipment value when assessing claims.

If you're unable to ship your belongings directly abroad, most shipping companies will put them into storage and some allow a limited free storage period prior to shipment, e.g. 14 days. **If you need to put your household effects into storage, it's imperative to have them fully insured, as warehouses have been known to burn down!** Make a complete list of everything to be moved and give a copy to the shipping company. Don't include anything illegal (e.g. guns, bombs, drugs or pornographic videos) with your belongings as customs checks can be rigorous and penalties severe. Provide the shipping company with detailed instructions as to how to find your home from the nearest motorway or main road and a telephone number where you can be contacted.

After considering the shipping costs, you may decide to ship only selected items of furniture and personal effects, and buy new furniture locally. If you're moving household goods yourself, you can rent a self-drive van or truck. However, you will usually need to return it to the country where it was hired. If you plan to transport your belongings personally, check the customs requirements in the countries you will pass through. Most people find it isn't worthwhile doing their own move unless it's a simple job, e.g. a few items of furniture and personal effects only. It's no fun heaving beds and wardrobes up stairs and squeezing them into impossible spaces. If you're taking pets (see page 199) with you, you may need to ask your vet to tranquillise them, as many pets are frightened (even more than people) by the chaos and stress of moving house.

Bear in mind when moving home that everything that can go wrong often does, therefore you should allow plenty of time and try not to arrange the move from your old home on the same day as the new owner is moving in. That's just asking for fate to intervene! **Last but not least, if your new home has poor or impossible access for a large truck you should inform the shipping company (the ground must also be firm enough to support a heavy vehicle).** If furniture needs to be taken in through an upstairs window, you may need to pay extra. See also **Customs** on page 173. and the **Checklists** on page 184.

HOME SECURITY

When moving into a new home it's often wise to replace the locks (or barrels) as soon as possible, as you have no idea how many keys are in circulation for the existing ones. This also applies to new homes, as keys are often given out. In any case, it's advisable to change external locks or barrels regularly, e.g. annually, particularly if you let a home. If not already fitted, it's best to fit high security (double cylinder or dead bolt) locks. Modern properties may be fitted with high security locks that are individually numbered. Extra keys for these cannot be cut at a local store and you will need to obtain details from the previous owner or your landlord. Many modern developments have security gates and caretakers.

In areas with a high risk of theft (e.g. most major cities and coastal resorts), your insurance company may insist on extra security measures such as two locks on external doors, internal locking shutters, security bars on windows below a certain height from the ground, and grilles on patio doors. External doors should be of the armoured variety with a steel rod locking mechanism. An insurance policy may specify that all forms of protection must be employed when a property is unoccupied and, if security precautions aren't adhered to, a claim may be reduced by half. It's usually necessary to have a safe for any insured valuables, which must be approved by your insurance company.

You may wish to have a security alarm fitted, which is usually the best way to deter thieves and may also reduce your household insurance. It should cover all external doors and windows and use internal infrared security beams. It may also include a coded entry keypad (which can be frequently changed and is useful for clients if you let a home); and 24-hour monitoring (with some systems it's possible to monitor properties remotely from another country via a computer). With a monitored system, when a sensor (e.g. smoke or forced entry) detects that an emergency or panic button has been pushed, a signal is sent automatically to a 24-hour monitoring station. The duty monitor will telephone to check whether it's a genuine alarm (a number or password must be given) and, if he cannot contact you, someone will be sent to investigate.

You can deter thieves by ensuring that your house is well lit and not conspicuously unoccupied. External security 'motion detector' lights (that switch on automatically when someone approaches), random timed switches for internal lights, radios and televisions, dummy security cameras, and tapes that play barking dogs (etc.) triggered by a light or heat detector may all help deter burglars. In remote areas, it's common for owners to fit two or three locks on external doors, alarm systems, grills on doors and windows, window locks, security shutters and a safe for valuables. The advantage of grills is that they allow you to leave windows open without inviting criminals in (unless they're very slim).

You can fit UPVC (toughened clear plastic) security windows and doors, which can survive an attack with a sledge hammer without damage, and external steel security blinds (which can be electrically operated), although these are expensive. A dog can be useful to deter intruders, although it should be kept inside where it cannot be given poisoned food. Irrespective of whether you actually have a dog, a warning sign with a picture of a fierce dog may act as a deterrent. You should have the front door of an apartment fitted with a spy-hole and chain so that you can check the identity of a visitor before opening the door. **Remember: prevention is better than cure, as stolen property is rarely recovered.**

Holiday homes are particularly vulnerable to thieves and in some areas they're regularly ransacked. No matter how secure your door and window locks, a thief can usually obtain entry if he's sufficiently determined, often by simply smashing a window, breaking in through the roof or even by knocking a hole in a wall! In isolated areas, thieves can strip a house bare at their leisure and an unmonitored alarm won't be a deterrent if there's no-one around to hear it. If you have a holiday home, it isn't wise to leave anything of real value (monetary or sentimental) there.

If you vacate your home for an extended period, it may be obligatory to notify your caretaker, landlord or insurance company, and to leave a key with someone in case of emergencies. If there's a robbery, you should report it immediately to the police and you must make a statement. You will receive a copy, which is required by your insurance company if you make a claim.

When closing up a property for an extended period, you should ensure that everything is switched off and that it's secure. Another important aspect of home security is ensuring that you have early warning of a fire, which is easily done by installing smoke detectors. Battery-operated smoke detectors can be purchased for around €10 (GB£7). They should be tested periodically to ensure that the batteries aren't exhausted. You can also fit an electric-powered gas detector that activates an alarm when a gas leak is detected.

LETTING YOUR PRINCIPAL HOME

Many people planning to live abroad let their family home while they're away, to help pay the mortgage and running costs. It also ensures that the home is more secure and isn't neglected. The costs incurred when letting a home are usually tax deductible and there may also be other tax advantages such as reduced capital gains tax and being able to offset mortgage interest against income tax. You can let your home short term and use it yourself for holidays, or do as most people do when going abroad for a number of years, and let it long term. However, you need to be careful with contracts, as in some countries it can be difficult to evict long-term tenants if they refuse to vacate your home, which is why some people prefer short-term lets. Short-term lets are more lucrative if your home is situated in a major city or resort, but it will need to stand up to a lot more wear and tear.

You will also need a property management company that specialises in short or long-term letting. Before letting an apartment you must check that letting is permitted. Short-term lets may be prohibited and you may also need to notify the building's administrator, your mortgage lender and your insurance company if a property is let. You can let a property yourself, although this is generally advisable only if you're letting it to a close friend or relative. The alternative is to get a reliable friend or relative to handle the letting or use a professional agent, which is usually the best solution. You (or your agent) should never finalise letting agreements via the internet and should always interview tenants face to face, and obtain personal, professional and financial references.

If you plan to engage a management company and wish to have a tenant in situ as soon as possible after your departure, you will need to make arrangements two or three months in advance. A management company will charge commission based on a percentage of the gross rental income. This is usually around 10 to 15 per cent for letting and rent collection, and a further 5 to 10 per cent for management services. Take care when selecting a company and ensure that your income is kept in a separate bonded (escrow) account and paid regularly. It's essential to employ an efficient, reliable and honest company, preferably long-established. Ask for the names of satisfied customers and check with them. The rent is usually set in consultation with the management company and based on existing rents in the area for similar properties. It's usually non-negotiable, although the terms of the lease are generally negotiable. **The contract should be checked by your lawyer or solicitor!**

A management company's services should include rent collection and payment; arranging routine maintenance and essential repairs to the building and garden; notifying insurance companies (where applicable) and obtaining approval for essential repairs; regular inspections; paying taxes (e.g. property tax) and insurance premiums (if not done by the owner); and forwarding post. Give the company a telephone or fax number, or an email address so you can be contacted abroad, so that you can approve major repairs or resolve other matters. If you have your own maintenance people or companies, you should give their names to the management company, plus details of anything that's under warranty and the manufacturer's name and model numbers of major systems and appliances (e.g. heating and cooling systems, cookers, fridge-freezers, etc.).

The landlord is usually responsible for maintaining the structure, major installations and appliances such as the heating and cooling system, cooker, washing machine, refrigerator and freezer. Tenants are usually responsible for any damage other than fair wear and tear to fixtures and fittings, furniture and decoration, and for maintaining the garden. The landlord or agent should check the condition and state of repair of a property at regular intervals, and also make periodic checks when a property is empty (e.g. between lets) to ensure that it's secure and that everything is in order.

If you let a property, it's advisable to replace expensive furniture and furnishings and remove valuable personal belongings. Leave them with friends or relatives or put them into storage, and ensure they're insured for their full value with a reputable company (preferably not the storage company). When furnishing a property that you plan to let, you should choose hard wearing, dark coloured carpets that won't show stains, and buy durable furniture and furnishings. Simple, inexpensive furniture is best, as it will need to stand up to hard wear. You will also need to decide whether you wish to let to families with young children (which may result in damage to expensive contents and decor) or pets, sharers or smokers. Many people who are letting a luxury home insist on professional tenants or let only to companies. Letting to someone with diplomatic immunity can be risky, as they would be outside the jurisdiction of the local courts.

Other points to bear in mind are deposits (how much and who will hold them – usually a management company if you have one), and insurance. You will need a special contents insurance policy if you're letting (or leaving a property empty) and may need to obtain a policy from an insurance company that specialises in letting. Tenants should have third party insurance for damage caused to the building and its contents, and contents insurance for their own belongings. Draw up an itemised inventory of all contents and fixtures and fittings, and append it to the lease (a management company will usually arrange this for you). This must be checked and agreed by the tenants on moving in and when vacating the property.

Landlords must adhere to strict regulations in many countries, particularly regarding fire and safety matters, e.g. fire-resistant furniture, approved gas installations, fire and gas alarms and fire-fighting apparatus (e.g. fire extinguishers). It may be necessary to have a home inspected by an official inspector and to display a certificate confirming this in a prominent position in.

4.

HEALTH &
SOCIAL SECURITY

This chapter contains information on many aspects of health in the EU, including public health services, emergencies, hospitals, registering for a doctor and dentist, health insurance and reciprocal health agreements. Information is also provided on social security contributions made by employees and the self-employed in the EU countries.

One of the most important aspects of living abroad (or anywhere) is maintaining good health. The quality of health care and health care facilities varies considerably within the EU, although most countries provide excellent health care for those who can afford to pay for private treatment. However, there's a stark contrast between public and private health facilities in some countries, which have severely over-stretched and under-funded public health services. The provision of fully-equipped hospitals is rare in some countries (there may be few major general hospitals even in cities), and nursing care and post-hospital assistance are below what many westerners take for granted. Health facilities in remote areas, even in some of the richest EU countries, are often inadequate, and if you have a serious accident or need emergency hospital treatment in some countries, you will need to be evacuated to the nearest major city or possibly to another country.

PUBLIC HEALTH SERVICES

All EU countries have a public health service providing free or low cost health care for those who contribute to social security, including their families. Retirees from EU countries enjoy free public health services in other EU countries. All EU nationals contributing to social security in their home country are entitled to free or subsidised public health services in other EU countries. If you don't qualify for health care under a public health service, it's essential to have private health insurance (see page 119) – in fact it's usually impossible to obtain a residence permit without it. Private health insurance is often advisable in any case, owing to the shortcomings of public health services and long waiting lists in many EU countries. Non-EU visitors should have travel insurance (see page 149) if they aren't covered by a reciprocal health care agreement (see page 124). The World Health Organisation (⌨ www.who.int) publishes regular surveys in which it rates countries according to their health care and, in the latest survey, the top ten included five EU countries (Austria, France, Italy, Malta and Spain).

COMMON HEALTH PROBLEMS

Common health problems experienced by foreigners abroad may include sunburn and sunstroke; stomach and bowel problems (due to the change of diet and, water, but they can also be caused by poor hygiene); and various problems related to excess alcohol (including a high incidence of alcoholism in some countries). The dangers of disease and infection are considerably greater in some countries and precautions should be taken. All food must be thoroughly washed and tap water avoided in some countries (e.g. Slovakia).

There are also risks of illness or death from diseases such as AIDS, hepatitis, tetanus and tuberculosis. Although these diseases aren't widespread in EU countries, outbreaks do occur and hepatitis and AIDS in particular are problems in all EU countries. Health problems are also caused or exacerbated by the high level of air pollution in some countries (particularly in major cities), which affects asthma sufferers and others with respiratory problems. Before travelling to the EU it's not necessary to have particular vaccinations, although travellers arriving in Malta, the Azores or Madeira (Portugal) from areas with yellow fever must present a yellow fever certificate. It's also a good idea to keep your tetanus vaccinations up to date. For a worldwide vaccination guide see 🖥 www.tmvc.com.au or 🖥 www.who.int.

The World Health Organisation (🖥 www.who.int) provides a wealth of information for travellers and those moving abroad, including health topics, communicable/infectious diseases, disease outbreak news, vaccines, environment and health statistics. Other useful websites include the Medical Advisory Service for Travellers Abroad (🖥 www.masta.org) and the UK Government's Health Advice for Travellers (🖥 www.doh.gov.uk/traveladvice), which also offers a free booklet with the same name. Where applicable, health warnings are included under **Medical Facilities** in the **Country Profiles** in **Chapter 9**.

CLIMATE

The best climate in which to live is generally considered to be one without extremes of cold and heat and where the average temperature over the year has the smallest swings between the coldest and hottest days. Examples are areas such as the Algarve in Portugal, Cyprus, southern France and the Canary Islands, Costa Blanca and Costa del Sol in Spain. You may also wish to avoid the coldest countries in the EU, such as the Baltic States, Poland and Scandinavia, where winters can be severe, lasting five months or longer and driving conditions can be extremely hazardous. On the other hand, you may also want to shun those parts of southern European countries that experience hot conditions in the summer. If you aren't used to the hot sun, you should limit your exposure and avoid it altogether during the hottest part of the day (from noon to 5pm), wear protective clothing (including a hat) and use a sun block. Too much sun and too little protection will dry your skin and cause premature ageing, to say nothing of the dangers of skin cancer. Care should also be taken to replace the natural oils lost from too many hours in the sun, and the elderly should take particular care not to exert themselves during hot weather.

However, a warm climate is therapeutic, particularly for sufferers from rheumatism and arthritis, and those prone to bronchitis, colds and pneumonia. The generally slower pace of life in many hot countries is also beneficial for those prone to stress (it's difficult to remain uptight while lying in the sun), although it takes some people a while to adjust. The climate and lifestyle in any country has a noticeable affect on your mental health, and those who live in southern Europe with warmer climates are generally happier and more relaxed than people living in cold, wet climates (such as those found in Northern European countries).

RETIREES

Health and health insurance are important issues for those retiring abroad, many of whom are ill-prepared for old age and the possibility of health problems. There's a dearth of welfare and home-nursing services for the elderly in many popular retirement countries, either state or private, and many foreigners who can no longer care for themselves are forced to return to their home countries. In some EU countries there are few state residential nursing homes and no hospices for the terminally ill, although many EU countries offer private sheltered homes and retirement developments for those who can afford them. Provision for disabled travellers and wheelchair access to buildings and public transport is also poor in many EU countries. This is gradually changing: 2003 was the European Year of the Disabled, during which the 15 original member states pledged to improve provisions for the disabled in their respective countries.

PRE-DEPARTURE CHECK

It's advisable to have a complete health check (medical screening, eyes, teeth, etc.) before going to live abroad, particularly if you have a record of poor health or are elderly. There are no mandatory immunisations for visiting countries in the EU, although it's advisable to make sure your tetanus inoculations are up to date and, in most EU countries, children need to be immunised against a range of diseases in order to attend school. If you're already taking regular medication, you should note that brand names for drugs and medicines vary from country to country, and you should ask your doctor for the generic name. If you wish to match medication prescribed abroad, you will need a current prescription with the medication's trade name, the manufacturer's name, the chemical name and the dosage. Most drugs have an equivalent in other countries, although particular brands may be difficult or impossible to obtain.

It's possible to have medication sent from abroad and no import duty or tax is usually payable. If you will be living abroad for a limited period, you should take sufficient drugs to cover your stay or until you can find a source locally, or have it sent from abroad. However, it's illegal to import certain drugs into some countries, e.g. you aren't allowed to take codeine into Greece! In an emergency, a local doctor will write a prescription that can be filled at a local chemist's or a hospital may refill a prescription from its own pharmacy. It's also advisable to take some of your favourite non-prescription drugs (e.g. aspirins, cold and flu remedies, lotions, creams, etc.) with you, as they may be difficult or impossible to obtain abroad or may be much more expensive. If applicable, take a spare pair of spectacles, contact lenses, dentures or a hearing aid, plus a comprehensive first-aid kit (many kits are available off the shelf). Finally, if you have any serious medical problems you should make a note of the relevant details, including the treatment you were given with dates, and any drugs or medicines you're taking. You should also note your blood group and any drugs or medicines to which you're allergic.

There are many internet sites where medical advice is available, such as the UK sites Healthworks (⌨ www.healthworks.co.uk), Net Doctor (⌨ www.net doctor.co.uk) and Patient (⌨ www.patient.co.uk) and the US Combined Health Information Database (⌨ http://chid.nih.gov), Healthfinder (⌨ www.health finder.gov) and Medline plus (⌨ www.medlineplus.gov). However, published information, although usually approved or written by medical experts, shouldn't be used as a substitute for consulting a doctor. Internet 'doctors' and medical advice must be used with extreme caution.

Among the many useful health guides are the British Medical Association's *Complete Family Health Guide* (Dorling Kindersley), the *Merck Manual of Medical Information: Home Edition* (Merck), *International Travel and Health 2003-4* (World Health Organisation), the *Rough Guide to Travel Health* by Dr. Nick Jones, *Travel with Children* by Maureen Wheeler (Lonely Planet), *The ABC of Healthy Travel* (British Medical Journal), *Travellers' Health* by Dr. R. Dawood (OUP) and the *First Aid Handbook* (National Safety Council).

EMERGENCIES

The EU emergency number 112 has been adopted by many original member states and is currently being adopted by some new member states. In the UK, the emergency number is 999.

The action to take in a medical emergency depends on the degree of urgency. Keep a record of the telephone numbers of your doctor, local hospital and clinic, ambulance service, dentist and other emergency services (fire, police) next to your telephone. In many countries, emergency numbers are displayed at the front of telephone directories. If you're unsure whom to call, dial the emergency number and you will be put in touch with the relevant service. The appropriate course of action to take may include one of the following:

● In a life-threatening emergency, such as a heart attack or serious accident, call the free emergency number and request an ambulance. State clearly where you're calling from and the nature of the emergency, and give your name and the telephone number from which you're calling. Don't hang up until the operator tells you to. In many EU countries, ambulances are equipped with cardiac equipment and special cardiomobiles may be provided for emergency heart cases. There's also an emergency helicopter ambulance service in many countries, which may be privately operated with membership by subscription.

● If you're physically able, you can go to a hospital emergency or casualty department. All EU nationals have the right to be treated free of charge in an emergency in an EU country, irrespective of whether they have insurance. However, in order to qualify for this, you require form E111 (see page 125).

- If you're unable to visit your doctor's surgery, your doctor may visit you at home provided you call him during surgery hours. If he's away, his office will usually give you the name and number of a substitute doctor on call. Local newspapers usually list duty chemists (pharmacies) – in major cities some may be open 24 hours a day.

- If you need urgent medical treatment outside surgery hours and cannot get to your nearest casualty department, there may be a local duty doctor service or emergency telephone helpline.

Provided you call in response to a real emergency, you won't usually be charged for the use of the emergency services. In some countries, it's an offence to offer medical assistance in an emergency if you aren't a doctor or qualified in first-aid, although it may also be an offence **not** to assist someone in an emergency, e.g. by calling the emergency services or offering first-aid when qualified to do so.

If you have an existing medical problem that cannot easily be seen or recognised, e.g. a heart condition, diabetes, a severe allergy (e.g. to penicillin) or epilepsy, or you have a rare blood group, you may wish to join Medic-Alert. Medic-Alert members wear an internationally recognised identification bracelet or necklace, on the back of which is engraved details of your medical condition, your membership number and a 24-hour emergency phone number. When you're unable to speak for yourself, doctors, police or paramedics can obtain immediate, vital medical information from anywhere in the world by telephoning this number. Medic-Alert is a non-profit registered charity and members pay for the cost of the bracelet or necklace (from around GB£30) plus an annual fee of GB£10. For more information contact the Medic-Alert Foundation, 1 Bridge Wharf, 156 Caledonian Road, London N1 9UU, UK (☎ 020-7833 3034, 💻 www.medicalert.co.uk or 💻 www.medicalert.org in the US, or 💻 www.medicalert.ca in Canada).

DOCTORS

The training, proficiency and availability of doctors varies considerably according to the country or region where you live. Those who live in a city in an EU country have a far wider choice of practitioners (many English-speaking) than those living in rural areas, where the nearest doctor may be some distance away. Even in EU countries, the quality and choice of doctors in remote areas is often poor, and you may be faced with a long journey to the nearest surgery or hospital. Even though English-speaking doctors practise in most EU countries, it's still essential to have a working knowledge of the local language. In an emergency this could save your life. Embassies and consulates may keep lists of doctors and specialists in their area who speak English and other languages, and your employer, colleagues or neighbours may also be able to recommend someone. General practitioners or family doctors are also listed in the yellow pages in most countries.

If you're entitled to take advantage of a free or subsidised public health service, one of the first things to do after arrival in a country is to register at the nearest office. When registering you're required to choose a family doctor with a social security agreement and, if you have young children, possibly also a paediatrician. Local health authorities can provide you with a list of doctors with whom you can register and you can choose anyone who's willing to accept you (although there may be a requirement to register with a doctor within a certain distance of your home). Each adult member of a family is usually issued with a membership number and card, which you must take with you when visiting a doctor or other health practitioner. School-age children are usually listed on their mother's card. If you want a doctor to visit you at home, you must telephone during surgery hours. House calls made by public health service doctors are usually free during normal working hours.

If you have private health insurance, you can usually see a private doctor, specialist or consultant at any time, although (depending on your level of insurance) you may need to pay for their services. In some countries you're expected to settle the bill (usually in cash, although some doctors accept credit cards) immediately after treatment, even if you have health insurance, and you may need to prove that you can pay before any treatment is given. It's important to keep all medical receipts in some countries, which can be offset against your income tax bill.

There are certain health requirements for employees and schoolchildren in some countries. Employees who work in the food industry (bars, restaurants, food shops, factories producing food products, etc.) may need to obtain a health record book from the local public hygiene office and undergo an annual medical examination. Schoolchildren may need a health book in which compulsory immunisations are recorded and secondary school students may need to provide a medical certificate or undergo a medical examination before being allowed to participate in certain sports activities.

HOSPITALS & CLINICS

All cities and large towns have at least one clinic or hospital, usually indicated by the international sign of a white 'H' on a blue background. Public (state) hospitals may include community hospitals, district hospitals, teaching hospitals and university hospitals (or a combination of these). Major hospitals or general hospitals may be designated teaching hospitals, which combine treatment with medical training and research work, and are staffed and equipped to the highest standards.

Some hospitals and most clinics specialise in particular fields of medicine, such as obstetrics and surgery, rather than being full service hospitals. In addition, there may be specialist hospitals for children, the mentally ill and disabled, the elderly and infirm, and for the treatment of specific complaints or illnesses. There are also dental hospitals in many countries. Public hospitals may have a 24-hour accident, casualty or emergency department that provides treatment for medical emergencies and minor accidents, although this may apply only to major hospitals. In some countries there are also walk-in clinics (possibly 24-hour) where you can be treated on the spot for minor emergencies. Except in emergencies, you're normally admitted or referred to a hospital or clinic for treatment only after consultation with a doctor.

In addition to public hospitals, there are usually private hospitals and clinics in major cities and resort areas in many EU countries, which may include US, UK and international hospitals. There's a wide discrepancy between public and private hospital facilities (e.g. medical equipment, private rooms, catering, etc.) in a few EU countries, although in most there's generally little difference between the quality of medical treatment (e.g. surgery). The best hospitals are invariably found in the wealthiest suburbs of major cities and large towns. Therefore, if you wish to have a first class hospital on your doorstep, you may need to live in an up-market (i.e. expensive) area. The best public hospitals often have long waiting lists.

Your choice of hospital and specialist usually depends on whether you choose a public or private hospital and the treatment required. If you're treated in a public hospital under a state's public health service, you must usually be treated or operated on by the medical specialist on duty. If you request the services of a particular specialist or wish to avoid a long waiting list for an operation, you must usually pay the full cost of treatment. If you aren't covered by the public health service, you may be required to pay before you receive treatment, regardless of whether you have private health insurance. However, international health insurance companies usually have arrangements with certain hospitals and pay bills directly. Costs for private operations vary enormously, depending on the reputation of the specialists involved and the fees they command. Sometimes it's cheaper to have an operation abroad, e.g. in a neighbouring country. You should check the local hospital facilities in advance and, if necessary, ensure that your health insurance covers you for medical evacuation.

Basic accommodation in public hospitals normally consists of shared rooms, although single rooms are usually available with an en suite bathroom for a supplement or for private patients. In some EU countries, patients in public hospitals must bring everything they need with them, including towels, toiletries, night wear and dressing gowns, although meals are provided free of charge. However, the food may be inedible and you may need some outside assistance (food parcels) if you're to survive a stay! You may also need to get your family or friends to attend to your needs, as nursing services are sparse or non-existent in public hospitals in some countries. In contrast, in private clinics and hospitals, accommodation is generally on a par with a luxury hotel, with air-conditioned single rooms, TV and telephone, gourmet food and an extra bed for a relative if required. Public hospitals usually have restricted visiting hours of around two or three hours a day, while private hospitals and clinics may have no restrictions.

DENTISTS

Both the quality of dental treatment and its costs vary considerably from country to country. Many people are sceptical about the quality of foreign dentists and prefer to have treatment in their home country when they're on leave. In some countries few dentists speak English, which can be an added problem. However, your country's local embassy or consulate may keep a list of English-speaking dentists in your area, or your employer, colleagues or neighbours may be able to recommend a local dentist. Dentists are also listed in local telephone directories and the yellow pages, although only names and addresses may be listed and information such as specialities and surgery hours may not be provided.

There are public health dental services in some EU countries, although the treatment provided is usually basic and may consist only of check-ups and emergency treatment. Private dentists in some countries have a better reputation than those working for a public health service, although many dentists treat both public and private patients. You need to be wary of unnecessary treatment, which is a common practice in some countries, where dentists deliberately 'drill for profit'! If you have regular check-ups and usually have little or no treatment, you should be suspicious if a new dentist suggests you need a lot of fillings or extractions. In this case, you should obtain a second opinion before going ahead (however, two dentists rarely agree on exactly the same treatment).

Always try to obtain an accurate (preferably written) quotation before beginning a course of treatment, although few dentists will quote an exact fee for work, and often a rough estimate will prove to be only a fraction of the final bill. For extensive work, such as root canal treatment or cosmetic work, bills can be astronomical. As with private doctors, it's usual to pay a dentist before a course of treatment begins in most countries. If your family requires expensive dental treatment, e.g. crowns, bridges, braces or false teeth, it's worthwhile checking whether treatment is cheaper abroad, e.g. in your home country.

OPTICIANS

As with other medical practitioners abroad, it isn't necessary to register with an optician or optometrist. You simply make an appointment with the practitioner of your choice, although it's advisable to ask your friends, colleagues or neighbours if they can recommend someone. Opticians are listed in the yellow pages. The eye care business is competitive in most countries and prices for spectacles and contact lenses aren't controlled, so it's wise to shop around and compare costs. There are large optical chains in some EU countries, where spectacles can be made on the spot or within 24 hours, although if you have your prescription you can sometimes buy ready-made reading spectacles from pharmacies. Always obtain an estimate for contact lenses and ask about extra charges for fittings, adjustments, lens-care kits and follow-up visits.

To be treated under a public health service, it may be necessary to have your eyes examined by an eye specialist or oculist, for which you generally need to obtain a referral from your family doctor. An oculist can make a more thorough test of your eyesight than an optician and is able to test for certain diseases that can be diagnosed from eye abnormalities, e.g. diabetes and some types of cancer. If glasses are necessary, he will write a prescription you can take to an optician or spectacle maker.

It's advisable to have your eyes tested before going abroad and to take a spare pair of spectacles and/or contact lenses with you. You should also bring a copy of your prescription in case you need to obtain replacement spectacles or contact lenses urgently.

SEXUALLY-TRANSMITTED DISEASES

The spread of sexually-transmitted diseases, particularly AIDS, has caused a lot of anxiety in EU countries, although it's nothing compared with the problems in many African countries, where half the population (or more) is infected in some countries. AIDS is transmitted by sexual contact, needle sharing among drug addicts and, less commonly, transfused or infected blood. Groups considered to be most at risk are prostitutes, drug addicts and homosexuals, although nobody who has unprotected sex with a number of partners is free from the risk of infection. The best protection against AIDS is for men to wear a condom, although they're not foolproof (either against AIDS or pregnancy) and the only real protection is abstinence or monogamy. Condoms can be purchased from pharmacies, family planning clinics and vending machines in most EU countries.

Free and anonymous testing for HIV, which is usually conducted at least one month after patients have been at risk, is available in most EU countries at special clinics or departments of infectious diseases in public hospitals and other public health centres. A doctor's referral isn't usually required. In most EU countries there are free telephone helplines where you can obtain confidential advice. For the testing and treatment of other contagious diseases (e.g. hepatitis B and C, syphilis and gonorrhoea), it may be necessary to be referred by your family doctor, although there are free and confidential clinics in many countries.

CHILDREN'S HEALTH

If you qualify for treatment under a public health service, your children may be treated by your family doctor or you may be assigned a paediatrician, who generally treats children up to the age of around 14. Of course, if you're a private patient you can generally see any doctor or specialist you wish. In many EU countries, children must have a health record card and are required to have inoculations against various diseases such as diphtheria and tetanus (DT), polio and hepatitis B. These are usually provided free of charge and may be compulsory. Although they may not be mandatory, inoculations against whooping cough, measles, mumps, German measles (rubella) and HIB (which can cause serious illnesses such as meningitis) are also recommended. A whooping cough vaccination may be administered in combination with the diphtheria and tetanus vaccinations (called DTP). Also recommended is a multiple vaccination (called MMR) against measles, mumps and German measles. **It's important to ensure that you keep all inoculations up-to-date!**

When going to live abroad, you should take proof of immunisations with you, with official translations if necessary.

BIRTHS & DEATHS

Births and deaths abroad must be registered within a certain time, e.g. seven days, at the local births and deaths registry office of the town where they take place. Registration applies to everyone irrespective of their nationality and whether they are residents or visitors. In the case of births, registration is usually carried out by the hospital or clinic where a child is born. However, if you give birth at home, you will need to complete the registration yourself. A local birth certificate is usually issued automatically.

In the event of a death, all interested parties must be notified. If a death takes place in a hospital, the attending doctor will complete a certificate stating the cause of death; you should make several copies of this, as they will be required by banks and other institutions. If death occurs at home, you should call your family doctor or the local police. If a death occurs in suspicious circumstances, a post mortem (autopsy) must usually be performed. As with births, deaths must be registered in the town where the death occurred, although the undertaker (see below) will usually do this for you.

Dying abroad can be very expensive. Burial grounds are extremely limited in some countries, where it may be necessary to be buried in a tomb in a wall or in a communal burial ground, which is recycled after five or ten years and used for new burials. Cremation is possible in many EU countries, although you may be unable to keep the ashes at home or dispose of them as you wish. The body of a deceased person can usually be shipped to another country for burial. You will need to provide the funeral agent with the documents relating to the death and the identity of the deceased, so that he can obtain the necessary permits. Your local embassy may be able to help arrange this. In some EU countries (e.g. Spain and Greece) burial or cremation takes place the day after a person has died and in others (e.g. the UK) it's usual to wait several days after a person dies.

HEALTH INSURANCE

One of the most important aspects of living abroad is having adequate health insurance for your family, as the cost of being uninsured or under-insured can be astronomical and could even prove fatal! However, the cost of private health insurance can be prohibitively expensive in some countries. If you have a poor health record you may be unable to obtain insurance for an affordable premium. Long-stay visitors (e.g. up to six months) should have travel or long-stay health insurance or an international health policy. If your stay abroad will be limited, you may be covered by a reciprocal agreement between your home country and the country where you will be living.

The majority of residents in EU countries are covered for health treatment under public health service or compulsory private health insurance schemes. In the EU countries this also includes foreign retirees over the age of 65 who are covered by the public health scheme in their home countries. Many EU countries provide emergency treatment for visitors under reciprocal agreements (see page 124), although these don't apply to citizens of some countries, e.g. the US. Visitors spending short periods abroad should have travel health insurance (see page 149) if they aren't covered by a reciprocal agreement or an international health policy.

If you will be living abroad permanently and don't qualify for medical treatment under a public health service, it's usually imperative that you have private health insurance (unless you have a very large bank balance), which is compulsory for non-EU nationals applying for some visa categories in the EU. Even in countries with a public health service, those who can afford it often take out complementary private health insurance, which provides a wider choice of medical practitioners and hospitals, and frees you from inadequate public health services, waiting lists and other restrictions. Private insurance may also allow you to choose an English-speaking doctor or a hospital where staff speak English or other languages.

A health insurance policy should, if possible, cover you for all essential health care whatever the reason, including accidents (e.g. sports accidents) and injuries, whether they occur at your home, place of work or while travelling. Policies offered in different countries vary considerably in the extent of cover, limitations and restrictions, premiums, and the free choice of doctors, specialists and hospitals. **Don't take anything for granted, but check in advance.** Insurance companies in some countries can (and will) cancel a policy at the end of the insurance period if you have a serious illness with constant high expenses, and some companies automatically cancel a policy when you reach a certain age, e.g. 65 or 70. You should avoid such a policy like the plague, as to take out a new policy at the age of 65 or older for a reasonable premium is difficult or impossible in some countries.

International Policies

If you do a lot of travelling, it's advisable to have an international health policy. These generally offer wider cover than local policies although, if local medical facilities are adequate and you rarely travel abroad, they can be a waste of money. Most international health policies include repatriation or evacuation (although it may be optional). This may be an important consideration if you need treatment that's unavailable locally, but is available in your home or another country. Repatriation may also include shipment (by air) of the body of someone who dies abroad to their home country for burial. Some companies offer policies for different areas, e.g. Europe; worldwide excluding North America; and worldwide including North America. A policy may offer full cover anywhere within Europe and limited cover in North America and certain other countries, e.g. Japan. An international policy also allows you to choose to have non-urgent medical treatment in another country. Most companies offer different levels of cover, for example basic, standard, comprehensive and prestige.

There's always a limit on the total annual medical costs, which should be at least €500,000 or around GB£350,000 (most go up to €1.5 million/GB£1.05 million or higher), and some companies limit costs for specific treatment or costs such as specialist's fees, surgery and hospital accommodation. Some policies also include permanent disability cover, e.g. €150,000 or GB£100,000, for those in full-time employment. A medical isn't usually required for health policies, although pre-existing health problems are excluded for a period, e.g. one or two years. Claims are usually settled in all major currencies and large claims are usually settled directly by insurance companies (although your choice of hospitals may be limited). Always check whether an insurance company will settle large medical bills directly. If you're required to pay bills and claim reimbursement from an insurance company, it may take you several months to receive your money (some companies are slow to pay). It isn't always necessary to have bills translated into English or another language, although you should check a company's policy. Most international health insurance companies provide 24-hour emergency telephone assistance.

The cost of international heath insurance varies considerably according to your age, the extent of cover, the insurer, and your home country or the where you're resident. With most policies, you must enrol before you reach a certain age, e.g. between 60 and 80, to be guaranteed continuous cover in your old age. Companies may also have restrictions on where you live permanently and your nationality. Premiums can sometimes be paid monthly or quarterly, although some companies insist on payment annually in advance. When comparing policies, carefully check the extent of cover and exactly what's included and excluded (which may be in very small print), in addition to premiums and excess charges.

In some countries, premium increases are limited by law, although this may apply only to residents in the country where a company is registered and not to overseas policyholders. Although there may be significant differences in premiums, generally you get what you pay for and can tailor your premiums to your requirements. The most important questions to ask are: Does the policy provide the cover you need? and Is it good value for money? If you're in good health and are able to pay for your own out-patient treatment, such as visits to your family doctor and prescriptions, then the best value for money policy is usually one covering only specialist visits and in-hospital treatment.

Among the many companies offering international private medical insurance are BUPA International (🖥 www.bupa-intl.com), Expacare (🖥 www.expa care.net), Goodhealth (🖥 www.goodhealth.co.uk), InterGlobal Insurance Services (🖥 www.medicus.co.uk), International Private Healthcare (🖥 www.iph.uk.net), Medicare International (🖥 www.medicare.co.uk), Morgan Price International Healthcare (🖥 www.morgan-price.com), AXA PPP Healthcare (🖥 www.ppp healthcare.co.uk) and William Russell (🖥 www.william-russell.co.uk).

Make sure you're fully covered abroad before you receive a large bill. It's foolhardy for anyone living abroad (or even visiting) not to have comprehensive health insurance. If you or your family is inadequately insured, you could be faced with some **very** high medical bills. When changing employers or moving, you should ensure that you have uninterrupted health insurance and, if you're planning to change company, ensure that important benefits aren't lost.

Checklist

When comparing the level of cover provided by different health insurance schemes, the following points should be considered:

- Does the scheme have a wide range of premium levels and are discounts or special premium rates available for families or children?
- Is private, half-private (e.g. a two-bed room) and general hospital cover available? What are the costs? Is there a limit on the time you can spend in hospital? Are private and half-private rooms available in local hospitals?
- Is optional dental cover provided? What exactly does it include? Can it be extended to include extra treatment? Dental insurance usually contains numerous limitations and doesn't cover cosmetic treatment.
- Are accidents covered (e.g. sports injuries) and dental treatment, wherever and however they occur? As a general rule, health insurance includes cover for accidents, but may exclude car accidents and accidents incurred when participating in certain 'dangerous' sports, such as skiing and hang-gliding.
- What are the restrictions regarding hospitalisation in a region or country other than the one where you have your permanent home?
- What emergency ambulance or other transportation fees are covered?
- Is there a qualification period for specific benefits or services?
- What level of cover is provided in other countries? What are the limitations?
- What is the cover regarding pregnancy, hospital births and associated costs? What is the position if conception occurred before joining an insurance scheme?
- Are all drugs and medicines covered or are there restrictions?
- Are convalescent homes or spa treatments covered when prescribed?
- What are the restrictions on complementary medicine, e.g. chiropractic, osteopathy, naturopathy, massage and acupuncture? Are they covered? Must a doctor make a referral?
- Are possible extra costs likely and, if so, what for?
- Are spectacles or contact lenses covered, and if so, how much can be claimed and how frequently? Some insurance policies allow you to claim for a new pair of spectacles every two or three years.
- Is the provision and repair of artificial limbs and other health aids covered?
- Are evacuation and the cost of medical treatment abroad covered in full?
- Will the insurer provide a cash deposit or guarantee payment in advance if a hospital requires it?

SOCIAL SECURITY

The information in this section applies to the EU generally. Specific information for each member state can be found under **Social Security** in the **Country Profiles** in **Chapter 9**.

Contributions

All EU countries require employees and the self-employed to make social security contributions and workers in most countries require a social security number. Under EU legislation, contributions to social security in one EU country are usually valid in another and may be used to count towards unemployment benefits and pensions. When applying for benefits bear in mind the following:

- An allowance you receive in your home country may not be available in other EU countries or may be discontinued if you move abroad.

- For some allowances (e.g. sick pay, unemployment benefit and maternity benefit), an EU country may consult your contributions record in your home country to see if you quality for the benefit.

- If you qualify for an allowance in the EU country you move to, your application will take time (possibly months) to be processed and you should make sure you have sufficient funds to live on while you're waiting.

The new member states (Cyprus, Czech Republic, Estonia, Hungary, Latvia, Lithuania, Malta, Poland, Slovakia and Slovenia) aren't included in this legislation, although this is expected to change soon, since most are well on the way to implementing reciprocal social security. Some new member states already have reciprocal agreements with EU countries, e.g. Cyprus and Malta with the UK. Further information about social security contributions and allowances is available from social security offices. A useful guide, *Your Social Security Rights when Moving Within the EU*, is available from the EU website (🖳 http://europa.eu.int) and from social security offices in member states.

Exemption From Contributions

Under certain circumstances EU nationals who move to another EU country to work aren't required to contribute to that country's social security scheme when they first start work and continue to be insured under their home country's scheme. This is the case if:

- You work for your usual employer in another EU country for less than a year.
- The EU country where you start work has a reciprocal social security agreement with your home country.
- You're self-employed and work in another EU country for less than a year before returning to your home country.

If you fulfil any of the above conditions you should apply for form E101 (available from the social security authorities in your home country), which certifies you're insured under your home country's scheme. In exceptional circumstances you may continue under your home country's scheme for a further year (to a maximum of two years), in which case you require form E102. There are different regulations for construction workers and international transport workers.

Voluntary Contributions

If you plan to work in another EU country for a period, but later return to your home country, you may wish to consider making voluntary social security contributions to the social security scheme in your home country. Most EU countries allow you to do this, although you must usually start making the contributions within a short period of leaving the country. Voluntary contributions aren't valid for all allowances and benefits including healthcare.

Reciprocal Health Agreements

Many people are covered by reciprocal health agreements when living in the EU, although this may apply in emergencies only. For example, anyone insured under a public health scheme in an EU country is covered for medical expenses in other EU countries, provided certain steps are taken in advance. You must usually obtain a form (see **Forms** below) from your social security office before leaving home and must be covered by your home country's public health scheme to qualify. Full payment (possibly in cash) may have to be made in advance for treatment received abroad, although you will be reimbursed on your return home. **However, you can still receive a large bill, as your local health authority usually assumes only a percentage of the cost.**

This applies to all EU countries except the UK, where everyone receives free health care, including visitors. Even if you're covered for health care under a reciprocal agreement, it's advisable to take out travel insurance wherever you're travelling in the EU, as insurance provides more comprehensive medical cover than reciprocal health care agreements (and usually includes other services, such as repatriation). If you do a lot of travelling abroad, it's usually worthwhile having an annual international health insurance policy.

Further information about reciprocal health agreements is available from the social security authorities in your home country. British nationals planning to travel, work or retire to the EU can obtain information from the Inland Revenue National Insurance Contributions Office, International Services, Newcastle-upon-Tyne, NE98 1ZZ, UK. Further information is also available on the Department for Work and Pensions website (🖳 www.dwp.gov.uk).

In order to qualify for health treatment in most EU countries you must provide proof that you've contributed to the state health insurance scheme in your home country. If you cannot, then you must usually take out private health insurance. The following forms certify that you qualify for medical treatment:

- **E104** – This form states how much you've contributed to the state health insurance scheme in your home country.

- **E111** – This form is for a short-term stay (e.g. a holiday) in another EU country and usually covers urgent medical treatment. You may still have to pay for part of the treatment and this form is only temporary.

- **E128** – This form entitles the holder to full medical treatment. However, you may still have to pay for part of the treatment.

- **E119** – If you're receiving an allowance (e.g. Job Seekers) this form certifies that you're entitled to healthcare for the period covered by the allowance.

- **E121** – This form is for pensioners who usually receive free healthcare and, in many EU countries, free prescriptions.

The EU has announced plans to introduce an electronic health card for all EU nationals and residents. The card will contain data such as the holder's social security number, health number (if different) and contributions record. The card, which is expected to be introduced gradually in EU countries as from June 2004, will replace many of the above forms including the E111 and E121.

Long-Term Incapacity Benefit

If you qualify for this benefit in your home country, you will probably continue to receive it if you move to another country in the EU. The conditions and amount received depend on the country. In Belgium, France, the Netherlands, Ireland and Spain you will receive long-term incapacity benefit from that country only under the same conditions as its own nationals. This could mean your benefit is significantly reduced. In Austria, Denmark, Finland, France, Greece, Italy, Luxembourg, Portugal, Sweden and the UK, however, you will receive long-term incapacity benefit from both the country you move to and your home country.

Pensions

Social security contributions made towards a state pension scheme in any EU country count towards a state pension in another EU country. If you qualify for a state pension, you can claim it from any EU country where you made contributions or from the EU country you're living in when you retire. All EU countries have different regulations on qualifying age, number of contributions and amount paid. The country in which you apply for a pension will consult your social security contributions record in other EU countries and you may possibly qualify for a higher pension than the one normally paid where you apply. This process takes considerable time and you're advised to start the application process at least six months before you retire.

5.

FINANCE & INSURANCE

Finance is obviously a very important aspect of living abroad and includes everything from transferring and changing money to banking, mortgages and local taxes. If you're planning to invest in a property or business in the EU, financed with funds imported from another country, it's important to consider both the present and possible future exchange rates (don't be too optimistic!). On the other hand, if you live and work abroad and earn your income in the local currency, this may affect your financial commitments abroad (particularly if the local currency is devalued). **Your income can be exposed to risks beyond your control when you live abroad, particularly regarding inflation and exchange rate fluctuations. It's important to obtain expert financial advice before going to live abroad from an independent and impartial source, i.e. NOT someone that is trying to sell you anything else!**

In several EU countries, residents and non-resident foreigners with financial dealings there must have a fiscal or tax number, which must be used in all dealings with the tax authorities and in various other financial transactions. Without a fiscal number, you may not be able to register the title deed of a property, open a bank account or take out an insurance policy.

If you're a non-resident and own a home in the EU, it's advisable to employ a local professional, e.g. an accountant or tax adviser, as your representative to look after your local financial affairs and declare and pay your taxes. You can also have your representative receive your bank statements, ensure that your bank is paying your standing orders (e.g. for electricity, gas, water and telephone bills), and that you have sufficient funds to pay them. If you let a home abroad through a local company, they may perform these tasks as part of their services. In some countries it's mandatory for foreign non-resident property owners to appoint a fiscal representative, who automatically receives all communications from the local tax authorities.

If you plan to live abroad, you must ensure that your income is (and will remain) sufficient to live on, bearing in mind currency devaluations and exchange rate fluctuations (if your income isn't paid in the local currency); rises in the cost of living (see page 147); unforeseen expenses such as medical bills; or anything else that may reduce your income, such as stock market crashes and recessions! Foreigners, particularly retirees, often underestimate the cost of living abroad and some are forced to return to their home countries after a few years.

Although many people prefer to pay cash (which cannot be traced by the tax man!) rather than use credit or charge cards (see page 134), it's wise to have at least one credit card when visiting or living abroad. However, not all businesses accept credit cards (businesses in rural areas in EU countries rarely accept them), therefore you should check in advance.

This chapter includes information about the euro currency; importing and exporting money; banking; credit, debit and charge cards; mortgages; pensions; taxes (income, property, capital gains, wealth, inheritance and gifts); wills; the cost of living; and insurance.

To convert foreign currencies into your local currency you can use the universal currency converter (🖳 www.xe.com).

CURRENCY

The euro (€) is the EU's single currency and has been adopted by 12 of the original 15 member states (all except Denmark, Sweden and the UK, none of whose populations show any real desire to join). It was introduced in January 1999 and completely replaced member states' currencies in January 2002. Member states with the euro currency are known collectively as the eurozone. Many of the new member states have expressed their desire to join the euro, although this will depend on their fulfilling strict economic criteria. Prices for property are already quoted in euros in many Eastern European countries.

Euros are issued by the European Central Bank. Banknotes are the same throughout the EU and are issued in denominations of €5, €10, €20, €50, €100, €200 and €500 (worth around US$500 or GB£350!). Coins have a standard design on one side and a national motif on the other and are issued as 1, 2, 5, 10, 20 and 50 cents (there are 100 cents in a euro) and €1 and €2.

After a somewhat faltering start, the euro is now a strong currency (too strong according to some experts) and in February 2004 exchange rates with other major currencies were:

Currency	€1 =
GB Pounds	£0.69
US Dollars	US$1.26
Danish Krona	DK7.45
Swedish Krona	SEK9.14
Canadian Dollars	C$1.67
Japanese Yen	133.34 yen
Australian Dollars	AUS$1.62
Swiss Francs	CHF1.57

European Central Bank (ECB): The ECB controls the EU's monetary powers and, as such, regulates the eurozone interest rate (known as the EURIBOR) and the issue of euro banknotes and coins. Fiscal power remains, however, in the hands of individual member states and there are no national branches of the ECB. In February 2004, the euro interest rate was 2 per cent.

IMPORTING & EXPORTING MONEY

Exchange controls have been abolished in the last few decades in most countries, particularly western countries. However, many countries require foreigners to declare imports or exports of funds above a certain amount and have restrictions on the amount that can be imported or exported in cash, notes and bearer cheques in any currency, plus gold coins and bars. Where necessary, it's particularly important to declare large sums, e.g. for the purchase of a business or home abroad, as it may be impossible legally to export funds from some countries if they weren't declared when imported. These regulations are usually designed to curb criminal activities (e.g. money laundering) and tax evasion, and may also apply to travellers simply passing through a country. In some countries (e.g. Greece, Portugal and Spain), foreigners must declare the origin of funds used for the purchase of a business or property – **if you don't declare the funds, they may be subject to confiscation.**

In most EU countries, there isn't a lot of difference in costs between buying foreign currency or travellers' cheques or using a credit card to obtain cash. However, many people simply take cash when travelling abroad. This is asking for trouble, particularly if you have no way of obtaining more cash, e.g. with a credit or debit card. **One thing to bear in mind when travelling anywhere is not to rely on only one source of funds!**

International Money Transfers

Making money transfers between different countries can be a nightmare and can take anything from a few minutes to many weeks (or months if the money gets 'lost'), depending on the banks and countries involved. A bank to bank transfer can usually be made by a 'normal' postal transfer or via an electronic transfer (such as SWIFT). A normal transfer within the EU is supposed to take three to seven days, but in reality it often takes much longer, whereas a SWIFT telex transfer should be completed in a few hours, with funds being available within 24 hours. The cost of transfers varies considerably, not only the commission and exchange rates, but also transfer charges (such as the telex charge for a SWIFT transfer).

Most international transfers are slow and costly, even between banks and countries with sophisticated, state-of-the-art banking systems. The average time taken for international transfers within Europe is around five days and some transfers take many weeks or even get lost completely. Banks in some countries are notoriously slow and have been accused of deliberately delaying transfers in order to earn interest on money 'stuck in the pipeline'. The cost of transfers also varies considerably. Except for the fastest (and most expensive) methods, transfers between international banks are a joke in the age of electronic banking, when powerful financiers can move funds anywhere in the world almost instantaneously.

Shop around banks and financial institutions for the best deal and don't be afraid to change your bank if the service provided doesn't meet your requirements. Many banks subscribe to an international electronic network to facilitate fast and inexpensive transfers between members. You can also make transfers in Europe via euro giro (sometimes known as postcheques) from post offices, which takes four days. This facility is available between Belgium, the Czech Republic, Denmark, Finland, France, Germany, Ireland, Italy,

Luxembourg, the Netherlands, Slovakia, Spain, Sweden and the UK in the EU plus Switzerland. Euro giros can be made for amounts up to €1,900 or €3,000 depending on the country, but payments over £250 to the UK can be made only through a bank account. Telegraphic transfers can be made via specialist companies such as Western Union (🖳 www.westernunion.com) between some 200 countries. This is the quickest (around ten minutes!) and safest method, but also one of the most expensive. American Express (AE) operates a similar service for cardholders, who can send money via the AE Moneygram service (🖳 www. moneygram.com) between offices in Europe and North America in as little as 15 minutes.

Yet another way to transfer money is via a bank draft, which should be sent by registered post. However, in the unlikely event that it's lost or stolen, it's impossible to stop payment and you must wait six months before a new draft can be issued. In some countries, bank drafts aren't treated as cash and must be cleared like personal cheques through a bank. It's also possible to send a cheque drawn on a personal account, although these take a long time to clear (usually a number of weeks) and fees are high. When transferring small amounts, it's better to use a cheque or money order. **If you intend sending a large amount of money abroad for a business transaction such as buying a business or property, you should ensure that you receive the commercial rate of exchange rather than the tourist rate (shop around for the best rate).**

Personal Cheques

It's often possible to pay a cheque drawn on a bank in your home country into a bank account in the EU, although it can take a long time to clear. A personal cheque drawn on a European or US bank can take three or four weeks to clear, as it must be cleared with the paying bank. However, some banks allow clients to draw on cheques issued on foreign banks from the day they're paid into a client's account. Many foreigners living abroad keep the bulk of their money in a foreign account (perhaps in an offshore bank) and draw on it using a cash or credit card when abroad, which is a convenient solution for short trips abroad. Most US banks don't accept cheques drawn on foreign bank accounts written in a foreign currency.

Travellers' Cheques

Travellers' cheques are widely accepted in most EU countries, but may be restricted only to major currencies (if in doubt, buy them in euros or US$) and may be cashed only by banks in major cities. The commission for cashing travellers' cheques is usually 1 per cent (you need your passport), depending on the issuer and where you cash them. Lost or stolen travellers' cheques can be replaced in most countries (the easiest to replace are American Express), but you must keep a separate record of the cheque numbers.

BANKS

Although it's possible to live abroad without having a local bank account, by using credit and debit cards and traveller's cheques, this isn't advisable and is an expensive option. In any case, residents and homeowners usually need a local bank account to pay their utility and tax bills, which are best paid by direct debit. If you have a holiday home abroad you can usually have all documentation (e.g. statements) sent to your permanent home address. Many foreign banks have branches in major cities abroad, although few have extensive networks. Foreign banks in EU countries usually operate in exactly the same way as domestic banks, so you shouldn't expect, for example, a branch of Barclays or Deutsche Bank in Spain to operate like a branch in the UK or Germany.

Non-residents can open a bank account in many EU countries by correspondence, although it's best done in person in the country concerned and some countries will allow accounts to be opened only in person. Ask your friends, neighbours or colleagues for their recommendations and just visit the bank of your choice and introduce yourself. You must provide proof of identity (e.g. a passport or identity card), your address abroad and, in some countries, a fiscal or tax number. If you open an account while in your home country, you must obtain an application form from an overseas branch of your chosen bank or from a bank abroad. If you open an account by correspondence, you will also need to provide a reference from your current bank.

Banks in most countries make few or no concessions for foreign customers, e.g. the provision of general information and documentation such as statements in foreign languages and staff who speak foreign languages. However, some banks offer a multilingual service and go out of their way to attract foreign customers. In some countries there are restrictions regarding the type of accounts a non-resident foreigner may open, although residents can usually open any type of account.

Overdrawing a bank account without prior agreement (bouncing cheques) in some EU countries (e.g. France) is a criminal offence, and offenders can be barred from maintaining a bank account for a period (it will also severely damage your credit rating).

Offshore Banking

If you have a sum of money to invest or wish to protect your inheritance from the tax man, it may be worthwhile investigating the accounts and services (such as pensions and trusts) provided by offshore banking centres in tax havens such as the Caribbean islands, Channel Islands (Guernsey and Jersey), Gibraltar and the Isle of Man. Some 50 locations worldwide are officially classified as tax havens. Offshore banking has had a good deal of media attention in recent years, during which it has also been under investigation by the EU and the OECD. The major attractions are that money can be deposited in a wide range of currencies; customers are usually guaranteed complete anonymity; there are no double-taxation agreements; no withholding tax is payable; and interest is paid tax-free. Many offshore banks also provide telephone (usually 24 hours a day, seven days a week) and internet banking.

A large number of US, UK and other European banks and financial institutions provide offshore banking facilities in one or more locations. Most institutions offer high-interest, instant access accounts, deposit accounts for long-term savings and investment portfolios, in which funds can be deposited in most major currencies. It's also possible to invest in a range of bonds, funds, trusts, pensions, equities and other investment vehicles, which are usually intended for long-term investments. Many people living abroad keep a local account for everyday business and maintain an offshore account for international transactions and investment purposes. However, most financial experts advise investors not to rush into the expatriate life and invest their life savings in an offshore financial centre until they know what their long-term plans are.

Most accounts have minimum deposits levels which usually range from the equivalent of around €750 to €15,000 or GB£500 to £10,000, with some as high as €150,000 or GB£100,000. In addition to large minimum balances, accounts may also have strict terms and conditions, such as restrictions on withdrawals or high early withdrawal penalties. You can deposit funds on call (instant access) or for a fixed period, e.g. from 90 days to one year (usually for larger sums). Interest is usually paid monthly or annually. Monthly interest payments are slightly lower than annual payments but have the advantage of providing a regular income. There are usually no charges, provided a specified minimum balance is maintained. Many accounts offer a cash or credit card (e.g. MasterCard or Visa) that can be used to obtain cash from cash machines (ATMs) throughout the world.

When selecting a financial institution and offshore banking centre, your first priority should be for the safety of your money. In many offshore banking centres, bank deposits are guaranteed under a deposit protection scheme, whereby a maximum sum is guaranteed should the financial institution go to the wall (the Isle of Man, Guernsey and Jersey all have such schemes). Unless you're planning to bank with a major international bank (which is only likely to fold the day after the end of the world!), you should check the credit rating of a financial institution before depositing any money, particularly if it doesn't provide deposit insurance. All banks have a credit rating (the highest is 'AAA') and a bank with a high rating will happily tell you what it is (but get it in writing). You can also check the rating of an international bank or financial organisation with Moodys Investors Service (🖳 www.moodys.com). You should be wary of institutions offering higher than average interest rates; if it looks too good to be true it probably will be – like the infamous Bank of International Commerce and Credit (BICC) that went bust in 1992!

When choosing an offshore bank, you may also wish to consider its communications network (24-hour telephone banking, fax, email, internet banking), your personal contact (will you have one?) and the geographical location. It's best to choose a bank within roughly the same time zone (if possible), otherwise you may be calling your advisor in the middle of the night! Useful websites include Investors Offshore (🖳 www.investorsoffshore.com) and Tax News (🖳 www.tax-news.com).

CREDIT, DEBIT & CHARGE CARDS

'Plastic money' in the form of cash, debit, credit and charge cards is widely used in most EU countries, where banks are busy trying to create a cashless society. Cash and debit cards are issued by most banks and many can be used EU-wide via the American Express, MasterCard and Visa networks. With a cash/debit card (they're usually the same card), cash withdrawals and purchases are automatically debited from a cheque or savings account. All withdrawals or purchases are shown on your monthly statement and you cannot usually run up an overdraft or obtain credit (unless arranged beforehand).

Cards allow holders to withdraw cash, e.g. €150 to €750 or GB£100 to £500 (or the foreign currency equivalent) per day from automated teller machines (ATMs) and obtain account balances and mini-statements. Cash can also be obtained from the ATMs of networks other than the one your card belongs to, although there's usually a fee. Most ATMs accept a bewildering number of cards, which may be illustrated on machines, including credit (Eurocard, Mastercard, Visa) and charge (Amex, Diners Club). Although debit cards such as those belonging to the Visa network can be used to obtain cash abroad, they may be treated as credit cards and a charge levied. However, debit cards issued in some countries don't work outside that country, as is the case with Spanish debit cards for example.

Credit and charge cards are usually referred to collectively as credit cards, although not all cards are real credit cards, where the balance can be repaid over a period. Visa and MasterCard are the most widely accepted credit cards in most EU countries and are issued by most banks. Charge cards such as American Express and Diners Club aren't widely accepted in some EU countries, particularly by small businesses (who wisely prefer cash). Debit cards may use the American Express, MasterCard or Visa networks, but allow withdrawals or purchases to be made from a personal bank account that's in credit (or has an overdraft facility).

When using a credit card in some countries (e.g. France), you usually need to enter a PIN number into a machine. You also need a PIN number to withdraw cash abroad from an ATM with a credit card (there's a limit to the amount that can be withdrawn). Using a foreign credit card to obtain cash abroad is expensive as there's a standard charge (e.g. 1.5 per cent), a high interest rate, which is usually charged from the day of the withdrawal, plus possibly a poor exchange rate. Never assume that a business (such as a restaurant) accepts a particular credit or charge card or you may discover to your embarrassment that 'that won't do nicely, sir'! Small businesses in some EU countries don't accept credit cards and most businesses in rural areas don't either.

Even if you don't like credit cards and shun any form of credit, they do have their uses – for example, no-deposit car rentals; no prepaying hotel bills (plus guaranteed bookings); obtaining cash 24 hours a day; simple telephone and mail order payments; greater safety and security than cash; and above all, convenience. They're particularly useful when travelling abroad and you also need some form of credit card if you wish to make purchases by phone or via the internet. However, in the wrong hands they're a disaster and should be shunned by spendthrifts and politicians (in fact, by anyone who's reckless with money).

MORTGAGES

Mortgages or home loans for those buying a home in the EU may be available in your home country, the country where the property is situated, and possibly also from financial institutions in offshore banking centres. The amount that can be borrowed varies according to the country where the property is situated, the country where the loan is to be raised, the lender and, not least, your financial standing. In the last decade, lenders have tightened their lending criteria in many countries owing to the repayment problems experienced by recession-hit borrowers in the early '90s. Some lenders apply strict rules regarding income, employment and the type of property on which they will lend. Foreign lenders, such as banks in offshore financial centres, also have strict rules regarding the nationality and domicile of borrowers, and the percentage they will lend. In theory, lenders based in EU countries are allowed to make loans anywhere within the EU, but in practice a single market doesn't exist. Foreigners and non-residents may have difficulty obtaining a mortgage in some EU countries: in Greece and Cyprus, it's virtually impossible for non-residents to obtain a mortgage.

In some countries the law does not permit banks to offer mortgages or other loans where repayments are more than one-third of net income (which includes existing mortgage or rental payments). Joint incomes and liabilities are included when assessing a couple's borrowing limit (usually a bank will lend to up to three joint borrowers). Most banks require proof of your monthly income and all outgoings, such as mortgage payments, rent and other loans and commitments. Proof of income includes three month's pay slips for employees, confirmation of income from your employer and tax returns. If you're self-employed, you usually require an audited copy of your balance sheets and trading accounts for the past three years, plus your last tax return. However, 'no-income qualifier' loans are available in many countries up to around 60 per cent of a property's value. If you want a mortgage to buy a property for commercial purposes you must usually provide a detailed business plan. In many countries it's customary for a property to be held as security for a loan, i.e. the lender takes a first charge on the property which is recorded at the property registry.

Mortgages are granted on a percentage of a property's valuation, which itself may be below the actual market value. The maximum mortgage granted in most countries is 70 to 80 per cent of the purchase price, although it can be as low as 50 to 60 per cent for non-residents and buyers of second homes. Loans may be repaid over 5 to 30 years, depending on the lender and country, although the usual term in most countries is 10 to 20 years for residents and possibly less for non-residents. Repayment mortgages are the most common type in most countries, although endowment and pension-linked mortgages may also be offered. Repayments are usually made monthly or quarterly, although fortnightly payments (which reduce the interest considerably) are also possible in some countries.

You must add expenses and fees totalling from around 5 to over 20 per cent of the purchase price (depending on the country) to the cost of a property. There are various fees associated with mortgages, e.g. all lenders charge an 'arrangement' fee and, although it's unusual to have a survey in most countries, lenders usually insist on a 'valuation survey' before they grant a loan. **Always shop around for the best interest rate and ask the effective rate, including all commissions and fees.**

Buying Through An Offshore Company

This is (not surprisingly) popular among non-resident property buyers in some EU countries, as they can legally avoid paying wealth tax and inheritance tax. It is also an option in some of the new member states, where foreign individuals cannot buy property, but foreign companies can. Buyers can also avoid transfer tax or stamp duty when buying a property owned by an offshore company, which can be a good selling point. However, it isn't possible in all EU countries and the owners of properties purchased through offshore companies in some countries (e.g. Spain) must register their ownership with the authorities or face punitive taxes. However, there are still legitimate advantages for buying property through an offshore company in some countries, although you should obtain expert advice from an experienced lawyer before doing so. One possible disadvantage is that, since a company does not have a 'principal residence', any appreciation in value may in some countries attract high rates of capital gains tax when the property is sold.

Mortgages For Second Homes

If you have equity in an existing home, it may be more cost-effective to re-mortgage (or take out a second mortgage) on that property, rather than take out a new mortgage for a home abroad. It entails less paperwork and therefore lower legal fees and a plan can be tailored to meet your individual requirements.

Depending on the equity in your existing property and the cost of a home abroad, this may also enable you to pay cash for the second home. The disadvantage of re-mortgaging or taking out a second mortgage is that you reduce the amount of equity available in a property, which is useful if you need to raise cash in an emergency. When a mortgage is taken out on a home in many countries in the EU, it's usually charged against the property and not the individual borrower, which can be important if you get into repayment difficulties.

Foreign Currency Loans

It's generally recognised that you should take out a mortgage in the currency in which your income is paid or in the currency of the country where a property is situated. However, it's also possible to obtain a foreign currency mortgage in major currencies such as GB£, US$, euros or Swiss francs. In the '80s and '90s, high interest rates in many countries meant that a foreign currency mortgage was a good deal for many people. **However, most borrowers should be extremely wary of taking out a foreign currency mortgage, as interest rate gains can be wiped out overnight by currency swings and devaluations.**

The advantage of having a mortgage in the currency in which your income is paid is that, if the currency is devalued against the currency of the country where you own a property, you will have the consolation that the value of your home abroad will (theoretically) have increased by the same percentage when converted back into your 'income' currency. When choosing between various currencies, you should take into account costs, fees, interest rates and possible currency fluctuations. Regardless of how you finance the purchase of a home abroad, you should always obtain professional advice. If you have a foreign currency mortgage, you must usually pay commission charges each time you transfer currency to pay your mortgage or remit money abroad. If you let a home abroad, you may be able to offset the interest on your mortgage against rental income, but pro rata only. If you raise a mortgage abroad or in a foreign currency, you should be aware of any impact this may have on your tax allowances or liabilities.

Payment Problems

If you're unable to meet your mortgage payments, some lenders will renegotiate mortgages so that payments are made over a longer period, thus allowing you to reduce the amounts. Although interest rates have fallen in recent years, many lenders are slow to reduce their interest rates for existing borrowers and some try to prevent existing mortgage holders transferring to another lender offering a lower rate by imposing prohibitive fees. However, many EU countries have introduced legislation to enable borrowers with fixed rate mortgages to change their mortgage lender or re-negotiate a mortgage with their existing lender at a greatly reduced cost. A mortgage can usually be taken over (assumed) by the new owner when a property is sold, which can be advantageous for a buyer. If you stop paying your mortgage, your lender can embargo your property and could eventually force its sale at auction to recover his loan.

PENSIONS

Before deciding where, or indeed whether, to work in the EU, it's important to consider how this will affect your state and/or private pensions. In many EU countries, you can continue to contribute to social security when working there in order to qualify for a full state pension although, if the pension is insignificant, you may be better off not doing so. Company pensions in many countries are transportable between employers in the same country, but rarely transportable to another country (unless you remain with the same employer). You may, however, be able to continue paying into a private pension when you work abroad, although you will lose any tax benefits in your home country (most pension contributions are tax-free up to certain limits). This also applies in reverse, i.e. if you contribute to a company pension abroad, you won't be able to transfer it back home unless you remain with the same employer (and penalties may apply).

It's compulsory to contribute to the local social security system in practically all EU countries, which usually includes a state pension, although it may take 10 or 15 years of contributions to qualify for a part pension and the amount may be insignificant. However, when you leave the country you may be able to reclaim your pension payments or claim a reduced pension when you reach the local retirement age, e.g. 65. Retirement ages vary within the EU: for example, in Lithuania the retirement age for women is 57.5 years and 61.5 years for men, but in Spain it's 65 for both women and men. When you have a company or private pension abroad (which may be mandatory) that isn't transportable to another country, you will be able to reclaim the sum accrued in your pension fund (possibly, including your employer's contributions) when you leave.

One option worth investigating if a job abroad doesn't come with a company pension or a mandatory state pension (particularly for anyone who does contract work in different countries), is to contribute to an offshore pension fund or other investment. You can then continue to contribute to it irrespective of the country where you work, although you may not receive any tax benefits on your contributions.

Before making any decisions about pensions, it's important to consult an independent pensions advisor.

EU Nationals

EU nationals who have worked in EU countries and paid social security contributions are entitled to claim a pension from any EU country where they've worked or from the EU country they live in when they retire. The system is somewhat complicated and the pension may take time to approve, since the country you claim from or where you're resident must examine contributions made in other countries in order to decide if you qualify for a pension and how much you qualify for. All social security contributions made in EU countries during your working life count towards a retirement pension, although all EU countries have different pension systems and qualifying conditions.

TAXES

Before planning to live or work abroad, it's advisable to investigate the taxes that will be payable, particularly income tax, social security and other taxes incurred by residents. If you plan to buy a home abroad, you may also need to take into account property taxes (rates), capital gains tax, wealth tax and inheritance tax. For many people, moving abroad is an opportunity to reduce their overall taxes, particularly when moving from a high to a low-tax country. The timing of a move can be decisive. Some countries, such as Cyprus and Malta, encourage foreigners (e.g. retirees) to take up residence by offering tax incentives. Some EU countries provide tax incentives for foreigners employed for a limited period by a foreign company, although there are usually restrictive conditions that must be fulfilled in order to qualify.

Income Tax

Income tax is of particular interest (or concern!) to those planning to become residents abroad, although some EU countries also levy income tax on income earned by non-residents, such as the income from letting a home. The highest income tax in the EU is paid in Finland, Sweden and Denmark (the highest) and the lowest in the new member countries plus Greece, Portugal and Spain. If you're planning to live or work abroad permanently you should also take into account social security contributions, which are high in some countries, particularly for the self-employed. Contributions are particularly high in Germany (18.7 per cent), but are low in Denmark. The EU average is 14.4 per cent.

If you're planning to work or start a business in the EU, you should seek expert tax advice, both in your present country of residence (regarding your tax liability there) and the country where you plan to work. The combined burden of income tax, social security and other taxes can make a considerable hole in your income in some countries.

Liability

Under the law of most EU countries, you become a fiscal resident (liable to income tax) if you spend 183 days there during a calendar year, or if your main centre of economic interest, e.g. investments or business, is there. Temporary absences are usually included in the calculation of the period spent abroad, unless residence is shown to have been in another country for 183 days in a calendar year. If your spouse (and dependent minor children) normally resides in a country where you have a home, has a residence permit, and isn't legally separated from you, you may also be considered to be a tax resident in that country (unless you can prove otherwise). Some countries restrict the visits of non-residents over a certain period, e.g. the UK limits visits by non-residents to 182 days in any tax year or an average of 91 days per year over four consecutive tax years.

Dual Residence

It's possible for some people to have 'dual residence' and be tax resident in two countries simultaneously, in which case your 'tax home' may be resolved under the rules of international treaties, although this is increasingly difficult between two EU countries. Under such treaties you're considered to be resident in the country where you have a permanent home. If you have a permanent home in both countries, you're deemed to be resident in the country where you have the closest personal and economic ties. If your residence cannot be determined under these rules, you're deemed to be resident in the country where you have an habitual abode. If you have an habitual abode in both or in neither country, you're deemed to be resident in the country of which you're a citizen. Finally, if you're a citizen of both or neither country, the authorities of the countries concerned will decide your tax residence between them by mutual agreement!

Double-Taxation Treaties

Residents in most EU countries are taxed on their worldwide income, subject to certain treaty exceptions. Non-residents are usually taxed only on income arising in a particular country, e.g. non-residents of France pay tax only on income arising in France. Citizens of most countries are exempt from paying taxes in their home country when they spend a minimum period abroad, e.g. one year, although this doesn't apply to US citizens. EU countries have double-taxation treaties with many other countries, designed to ensure that income that has been taxed in one treaty country isn't taxed again in another. The treaty establishes a tax credit or exemption on certain kinds of income, either in the country of residence or the country where the income is earned.

Double-taxation treaties vary according to the countries concerned and, where applicable, have priority over domestic law. In the absence of a double-taxation treaty between your home country and the country where you're planning to live or work, check how this will affect you. In many cases, even when there's no double-taxation agreement between two countries, you can still usually obtain relief from double taxation. In this case, tax relief is usually provided through direct deduction of any foreign tax paid or through a 'foreign compensation' formula. If your tax liability in one country is less than in another, you may be required to pay the tax authorities the difference in the country where you're resident. If you're in any doubt about your tax liability in your home country or a country where you're living abroad, contact your nearest embassy or consulate for information. The US is one of the few countries that taxes its non-resident citizens on income earned abroad – Americans can obtain a copy of a brochure, *Tax Guide for US Citizens and Resident Aliens Abroad*, from US consulates.

Tax Havens

If you're looking for a tax haven or a low-tax country within the EU, you should investigate Cyprus or Malta, although neither country is on a par with some of the islands in the Caribbean or Channel Islands. Some tax havens within Europe (e.g. Andorra, the Channel Islands, Gibraltar and the Isle of Man) aren't part of the EU. You should also be aware that owning a home in a particular country won't necessarily qualify you for a residence permit and that to qualify as a resident you must usually spend at least 183 days a year in a country.

Planning

Before leaving a country for good, you usually need to pay any tax due for the previous year and the year of departure, and you may also need to apply for a tax clearance. A tax return must usually be filed before departure and must include your income and deductions for the current tax year up to the date of departure. The local tax office will calculate the taxes due and provide a written statement. In some countries, a tax clearance certificate is necessary to obtain a 'sailing or departure permit' or an exit visa. A shipping or moving company may also need official authorisation from the tax authorities before they can ship your personal effects abroad.

If you're planning to move abroad permanently, you should plan well in advance, as the timing of a move can make a big difference to your tax liabilities, both in your present and your new country of residence. Find out what you must do to become an official non-resident in your current country of residence and how long you will need to be resident in your new home to qualify as a resident for tax purposes. In most countries you automatically become liable for income tax if you spend longer than six months (183 days) there during a calendar year.

If you intend to live abroad permanently, you should notify the tax and social security authorities in your previous country of residence well in advance. You may be entitled to a tax refund if you leave during the tax year. This usually requires the completion of a tax return. The tax year is the calendar year in all EU countries except the UK, where it runs from 6th April to 5th April. The authorities may require evidence that you're leaving the country, e.g. evidence of a job abroad or of having purchased or rented a property. If you move abroad to take up a job or start a business, you must register with the local tax authorities soon after your arrival.

Property Taxes

Property taxes (also called real estate taxes or rates) are levied by local authorities in all EU countries – except Ireland, Lithuania and Malta, where property taxes don't exist; and the UK, where council taxes are paid instead. Property taxes are payable by all property owners, whether they're residents or non-residents, and may also be paid by tenants. In some countries (e.g. France) an additional 'residential' or local income tax is also paid by residents. Property taxes pay for local services which may include rubbish collection, street lighting, sanitary services (e.g. street and beach cleaning), local schools and other community services, local council administration, social assistance, community substructure, cultural and sports amenities, and possibly water rates. In some countries (or parts of some countries) an additional charge is made for refuse collection. Before buying a property, check the tax rate with the local town hall, as rates usually vary from community to community.

Property tax is usually payable whether a property is inhabited or not, provided that it's furnished and habitable. It may be split into two separate amounts, one for the building and another for the land, with tax on land payable whether it's built on or not. Before buying a property, you should check that there are no outstanding property taxes for the current or previous years as, in some EU countries, the new owner assumes all unpaid property related taxes and debts. You can, however, reclaim the tax from the previous owner – if you can find him! When you buy a property in any country, ownership must be registered at the local land registry, which is usually done by the lawyer or public notary officiating at the completion of the sale.

Property taxes are normally based on the fiscal or notional letting value of a property, which is usually lower than the actual purchase price or a property's market value. If the fiscal value of your property increases greatly, check that it has been correctly calculated. You can appeal against the valuation of your property if you believe it's too high, particularly if it's higher than that of similar properties in the same area. However, an appeal must be lodged within a limited period (check with the local town hall). **It's important that the fiscal value of your property is correct, as in some countries (e.g. Spain) a number of taxes are linked to this value, such as property letting tax, wealth tax, transfer tax on property sales and inheritance tax.**

Wealth Tax

Only five EU countries levy a wealth tax, which is usually applicable only to residents, although it sometimes also applies to non-resident property owners (e.g. Spain). Your wealth is generally calculated by totalling your assets and deducting your liabilities. When calculating your wealth tax, you should include the value of all property, including real estate, vehicles, boats, aircraft, business ownership, cash (e.g. in bank accounts), life insurance, gold bars, jewellery, stocks, shares and bonds. If you fail to declare your total assets you can be fined.

Assets that are exempt from wealth tax usually include *objets d'art* and antiques (provided their value doesn't exceed certain limits); the vested rights of participants in pension plans and funds; copyrights (as long as they remain part of your net worth); assets forming part of a country's historical heritage; and 'professional assets' in a business. Deductions are usually made for mortgages, business and other debts, and wealth tax paid in another country.

The level at which wealth tax is applicable varies greatly according to the country and whether you're a resident or non-resident. For residents in Spain, it's payable on assets above €108,182 (although couples are each entitled to the €108,182 exemption, making a combined exemption of €216,364, and principal residences are exempt up to the value of €150,253). In Finland, no tax is payable on assets below €135,000. Wealth tax may depend on your domicile, e.g. if you're domiciled in France, the value of your estate is based on your worldwide assets. If you're resident in France but not domiciled there, the value of your estate is based only on your assets in France.

Capital Gains Tax

Capital gains tax (CGT) is payable on the profit from sales of certain assets in all EU countries except Belgium and Greece. Assets affected may include real estate and also antiques, art and jewellery; stocks, bonds and shares; household furnishings; vehicles; coin and stamp collections and other 'collectables'; gold, silver and gems; and the sale of a business. International tax treaties usually decree that capital gains on real estate are taxable in the country where it's situated.

If you move abroad permanently and retain a home in another country, this may affect your position regarding capital gains there. Had you sold your home before moving abroad, you'd usually have been exempt from CGT, as it would have been your principal residence. However, if you establish your principal residence abroad, your property in your home country becomes a second home and thus you may be liable to pay CGT when it's sold. Capital gains tax can be a complicated subject and you should always obtain legal advice before disposing of property or buying property abroad. **The tax authorities in many EU countries cooperate to track down those who attempt to avoid capital gains tax.**

Most countries provide an exemption if gains don't exceed a certain amount. Certain gains are also exempt and may include gains as a result of the death of a taxpayer; gifts to government entities; donations of certain assets in lieu of tax payments; and the contribution of assets in exchange for a life annuity for those aged over 65. Capital losses can usually be offset against capital gains, but not against ordinary income. It's usually possible to carry forward capital losses (or a percentage) in excess of gains and offset them against future gains for a limited period (this may also be possible with business losses). In most countries, capital gains are treated as ordinary income for residents.

A property capital gain is based on the difference between the purchase price and the sale price. However, in most countries there are exemptions, which may depend on the number of years a property has been owned. If an asset has been owned for less than a certain period, e.g. two years in France (second homes) and Spain, capital gains are taxed in full. Most countries allow a tax exemption (called indexation relief) on the sale of your principal residence (e.g. France and the UK). Some, such as Spain, allow an exemption only if you buy another home within a limited period, and levy tax on any profits that aren't reinvested. However, residents of France don't pay CGT on a profit made on the sale of their principal home, provided they've occupied it since its purchase or for a minimum of five years. In Spain, residents aged over 65 are exempt from paying CGT. In Cyprus, there's a once in a lifetime exemption of CY£50,000 per individual on CGT from property. In some EU countries you may be exempt from CGT on a second home if you don't own your main residence (i.e. if you're a tenant or leaseholder), although this may apply only to the first sale of a second home.

In some countries, capital gains made by non-residents are taxed at a flat rate (e.g. 35 per cent in Spain) and there may be no reduction for the length of time you've owned a property. However, in most countries, the amount of CGT payable is reduced the longer you've owned a property until it's no longer applicable, e.g. after 22 years in France. Where applicable, a sum may be withheld by the official handling the sale in lieu of capital gains tax or the buyer must retain a percentage when the seller is a non-resident, e.g. 5 per cent in Spain.

You should keep all bills for the fees associated with buying a property (e.g. lawyer, real estate agent and surveyor), plus any bills for renovation, restoration, modernisation and improvements of a second home, as these can usually be offset against CGT and may be index-linked. If you work on a house yourself, you should keep a copy of all bills for materials and tools, as these also can be offset against CGT. Losses on rentals may also be able to be carried forward and offset against a capital gain when a property is sold. Costs relating to a sale can also usually be offset against any gain, as can interest paid on a loan taken out to purchase or restore a property. In some EU countries you can protect yourself and your survivors from capital gains tax by bequeathing appreciated property, rather than giving it away while you're alive.

Inheritance & Gift Tax

Dying doesn't free you (or more correctly, your beneficiaries) entirely from the clutches of the tax man. Most EU countries impose an inheritance (also called estate tax or death duty) and gift tax on the estate of a deceased person, although several, namely Belgium, Cyprus, Estonia, Italy, Latvia, Luxembourg, Malta and Portugal, don't. Usually both residents and non-residents are subject to inheritance tax if they own property abroad. Your domicile usually determines the country where you pay inheritance and gift tax. If you're living permanently abroad at the time of your death, you will be deemed to be domiciled there by the local tax authorities. If you're domiciled abroad, then inheritance and gift tax payable there will apply to your worldwide estate (excluding property). Otherwise, it applies only to assets held abroad, such as a second home. It's important to make your domicile clear so that there's no misunderstanding on your death.

Inheritance Tax

In most EU countries, inheritance tax is paid by the beneficiaries and not by the deceased's estate. This may mean that if you inherit a home abroad, you may need to sell it to pay tax. The rate of inheritance tax payable usually depends upon the relationship between the donor and the recipient, the amount inherited, and (in some countries) the current wealth of the recipient. Direct descendants and close relatives of the deceased usually receive an allowance before they're liable for inheritance tax. Some countries have strict succession laws (although they usually apply to nationals only) regarding permitted beneficiaries of your assets. To take advantage of lower tax rates, it's advisable to leave property to your spouse, children or parents, rather than to someone who is unrelated.

There are a number of ways to avoid or reduce inheritance tax depending on the country, including buying property through an offshore company or trust. Some EU countries don't recognise the rights to inheritance of a non-married partner, although there are a number of solutions to this problem (e.g. a life insurance policy), and the rights of non-married couples are improving throughout the EU. Some bequests are exempt from inheritance tax, including certain types of properties and legacies to charities and government bodies.

Gift Tax

Gift tax is calculated in the same way as inheritance tax, according to the relationship between the donor and the recipient and the size of the gift. A reduction is usually granted depending on the age of the donor (generally, the younger the donor the larger the reduction).

It's important for both residents and non-residents owning a business or property in the EU to decide in advance how they wish to dispose of it. If possible, this should be done **before** buying a home or other property abroad, as it can be complicated and expensive to change later. There are many ways to limit or delay the impact of restrictive inheritance laws, including inserting a clause in a property purchase contract allowing a property to be left in its entirety to a surviving spouse without being shared among the children. A surviving spouse can also be given a life interest in an estate in preference to children or parents, through a 'gift between spouses'.

Inheritance law is a complicated subject and professional advice should be sought from an experienced lawyer who's familiar with the inheritance laws of the country where you plan to buy a business or home and any other countries involved. Your will (see below) is a vital component in keeping inheritance and gift tax to the minimum or delaying its payment.

WILLS

It's an unfortunate fact of life that you're unable to take your hard-earned assets with you when you take your final bow (or come back and reclaim them in a later life!). All adults should make a will, regardless of how large or small their assets. The disposal of your estate depends on your country of domicile (see **Income Tax** on page 139). Most EU countries permit foreigners who aren't domiciled abroad to make a will in any language and under the law of any country, provided it's valid under the law of that country. A will must usually be in writing (but not necessarily in the hand of the testator) and can be in any language. Under international rules regarding conflict of law, the law that generally applies is the law of the country where the testator was a citizen at the time of his death.

However, immovable property (or 'immovables'), i.e. land and buildings, must usually be disposed of (on death) in accordance with local law. All other property abroad or elsewhere (defined as 'movables') may be disposed of in accordance with the law of your home country or domicile. Therefore, it's important to establish where you're domiciled. One solution for a non-resident wishing to avoid foreign inheritance laws may be to buy a business or property through a company, in which case the shares of the company are movable assets and are therefore governed by the succession laws of the owner's country of domicile.

In some EU countries (e.g. France, Greece and Spain), the law gives the immediate family (i.e. spouse, children and parents) an absolute right to inherit a share of an estate, and therefore it isn't possible to disinherit them as can be done in some other countries (e.g. the UK). However, a foreigner who wishes to dispose of his estate according to the laws of his home country can usually state this in his will. In many EU countries, marriage doesn't automatically revoke a will, as it does, for example, in the UK.

If you have a large estate in the EU, it's advisable to consult a lawyer when drawing up a will. It's possible to make two wills, one relating to property in your home country and another for any foreign property. Experts differ on whether you should have separate wills for property in different countries, written under local law, or have one will in your home country with a codicil (appendix) dealing with any foreign property. However, most lawyers believe that it's better to have a local will in any country where you own immovable property, which will speed up and reduce the cost of probate. If you have more than one will, you must make sure that they don't contradict each other.

You will also need someone to act as the executor of your estate, which can be particularly costly for modest estates. In some countries, many people appoint their bank, lawyer or other professional to act as the executor, although this should be avoided if at all possible as the fees can be astronomical. It's advisable to make your beneficiaries the executors, who can in turn instruct a lawyer after your death if they require legal assistance. Probate (the proving of a will) can take a long time in some countries.

Keep a copy of your will(s) in a safe place and another copy with your lawyer or the executor of your estate. Don't leave them in a safe deposit box, which in the event of your death may be sealed for a period under local law. You should keep information regarding bank accounts and insurance policies with your will(s), but don't forget to tell someone where they are!

Inheritance law is a complicated subject and it's important to obtain professional legal advice when writing or altering your will(s).

COST OF LIVING

No doubt you'd like to estimate how far your money will stretch abroad and how much you will have left after paying your bills. The cost of living has risen considerably in many EU countries in the last decade or so, and some countries that previously enjoyed a relatively low cost of living are no longer quite so attractive, particularly for retirees. A survey carried out in 2003 found that Denmark was the most expensive country in the EU and, among the original 15 states, Portugal was the cheapest. Of the new members, Hungary is the cheapest, although the cost of living in all new EU member states is expected to rise considerably once they become members.

If you spend only a few weeks abroad each year, you won't be too concerned about the local cost of living. However, if you plan to live abroad permanently you should ensure that your income is, and will remain, sufficient to live on, bearing in mind currency devaluations (if your income isn't paid in local currency); inflation; extraordinary expenses such as medical bills; and anything else that may drastically reduce your income (such as stock market crashes and recessions). If your pension is paid in a currency that's devalued, this could have a catastrophic affect on your standard of living (as it did on UK residents abroad when sterling was effectively devalued by some 20 per cent in 1992, after the UK withdrew from the European Monetary System). Some countries (e.g. the UK) freeze state pensions at the current rate for those going to live permanently in certain countries.

It's difficult to calculate an average cost of living for any country, as it depends very much on an individual's particular circumstances and lifestyle, and where you live. The EU's most expensive cities in 2003 were Oslo, London, Copenhagen, Milan, Dublin, Paris and Frankfurt, and the cheapest was Lisbon. In all EU countries it's generally cheaper to live in a rural area than in a large city or a popular resort area (and homes are also much cheaper). London has the EU's most expensive accommodation. The actual difference in your food bill will depend on what you eat and where you lived before moving abroad. Food in most southern EU countries is cheaper than in most northern European countries, although North Americans will find it costs around the same or more. The equivalent of around €300 or GB£210 should feed two adults for a month in most EU countries, including inexpensive local wine (if available), but excluding fillet steak, caviar and expensive imported foods. The price of consumer goods varies widely throughout the EU with goods in countries like France, Germany and Ireland costing around the EU average, but those in Sweden and the UK costing considerably more (some 20 per cent more in the case of the UK). Portugal has the cheapest consumer goods among the original member states.

A couple owning their home (with no mortgage) in many popular EU retirement countries (e.g. Spain, Cyprus and Malta) can 'survive' on a net income of as little as €600 or around GB£420 a month (some pensioners live on less) and most can live quite comfortably on an income of €1,000 or GB£700 a month – this applies mainly to basic needs and doesn't include luxuries. In fact, many northern Europeans (particularly Scandinavians) and North Americans find that, if they live modestly without overdoing the luxuries, their cost of living in many EU countries, particularly those in the south, is cheaper than that in their home countries.

Comparing prices and where feasible shopping abroad (possibly by post or via the internet – see page 203) for expensive items can yield huge savings. It may also be possible to make savings by buying clothes, general household items, furniture and furnishings, and even your car abroad. Where possible, foreign newspapers and magazines should be purchased on subscription. If you have a tight budget, you should avoid shopping in fashionable towns or shopping centres and tourist shops, which abound in some countries and may include supermarkets in areas inhabited mainly by foreigners. Ask the locals where to shop for the lowest prices and best value for money.

There are many websites providing cost of living comparisons between countries and major cities, including the Economic Research Institute (🖳 www. salariesreview.com), Runzheimer International (🖳 www.runzheimer.com), Expat Forum (🖳 www.expatforum.com) and Career Perfect (🖳 www.career perfect.com/careerperfect/salaryinfo) which includes good links.

INSURANCE

An important aspect of living abroad is insurance, including health, travel, home contents and third party liability insurance. In all EU countries, the government and local law provide for various obligatory state and employer insurance schemes. These usually include sickness and maternity; accidents at work and occupational diseases; invalidity, old age and survivors pensions; unemployment insurance; and family allowances. However, benefits vary greatly and in most countries there are qualifying conditions, e.g. you must pay a minimum number of contributions before you can obtain some benefits. It's unnecessary to spend half your income insuring yourself against every eventuality from the common cold to being sued for your last euro, but it's important to insure against any event that could precipitate a major financial disaster, such as a serious accident or your house falling down. Social security benefits in some EU countries (particularly the new member states) may be less than you're used to, and in most countries you'd be unwise to rely solely on state benefits to meet your needs.

As with anything concerning finance, it's important to shop around when buying insurance. Just collecting a few brochures from insurance agents, or making a few phone calls, could save you a lot of money. However, not all insurance companies are equally reliable or have the same financial stability, and it may be better to insure with a large international insurance company with a good reputation than with a small local company, even if this means paying higher premiums. Major international insurance companies have offices and representatives in most EU countries.

Read all insurance contracts before signing them. If a policy is written in a language that you don't understand, get someone to check it and don't sign it unless you clearly understand the terms and the cover provided. Some insurance companies will do almost anything to avoid paying out in the event of a claim and will use any available legal loophole. Therefore it pays to deal only with reputable companies – not that this provides a foolproof guarantee! Policies often contain traps and legal loopholes in the small print, and it's therefore essential to obtain professional advice and have contracts checked before signing them.

In all matters regarding insurance, you're responsible for ensuring that you and your family are legally insured abroad. Regrettably, you cannot insure yourself against being uninsured or sue your insurance agent for giving you bad advice! If you wish to make a claim on an insurance policy, you may be required to report an incident to the police within 24 hours (this may also be a legal requirement). You should obtain legal advice for anything other than a minor claim, as the law abroad may differ considerably from that in your home country or your previous country of residence, so **never** assume that it's the same.

See also **Health Insurance** on page 119 and **Car Insurance** on page 38.

Travel Insurance

Travel Insurance is recommended for all those who don't wish to risk having their journey spoilt by financial problems or to arrive broke. As you probably know, anything can and often does go wrong when travelling, sometimes before you even reach the airport or port (particularly when you **don't** have insurance). Travel insurance is available from many sources, including travel and insurance agents, motoring organisations, transport companies and direct from insurance companies. When you pay for your travel costs with some credit cards, your family (including children under the age of 25) are provided with free travel accident insurance up to a specified amount. **However, you shouldn't rely on this insurance, as it usually covers death or serious injury only.**

Level Of Cover

Before taking out travel insurance, carefully consider the level of cover you require and compare policies. Most policies include cover for loss of deposit or travel cancellation; missed flights; departure delay at both the start and end of a journey (a common occurrence); delayed baggage; personal effects and lost baggage; medical expenses and accidents (including repatriation home if necessary); personal money; personal liability; legal expenses; and protection against a travel company or operator going bust. You should also insure against missing your flight because of an accident or transport breakdown, as some 50 per cent of travel insurance claims are for cancellation. Some policies limit the amount you can claim for personal belongings to around €300 (GB£210) per item, which may be insufficient to cover your Rolex watch or digital camera.

Medical Expenses

Medical expenses are an important aspect of travel insurance and it isn't advisable to rely on reciprocal health arrangements (such as provided by form E111 in EU countries). You also shouldn't rely on travel insurance provided by charge and credit card companies, house contents policies or private medical insurance, none of which usually provide the necessary cover (although you should take advantage of what they offer). The minimum medical insurance recommended by most experts is around €400,000 (GB£280,000) in the EU. If applicable, check whether pregnancy-related claims are covered and whether there are any restrictions for those over a certain age, e.g. 65 or 70. Third-party liability cover should be €750,000 to €1.5 million (GB£525,000 to £1.05 million) in the EU. **Most travel and holiday insurance policies don't provide the minimum level of cover that most people need.** Always check any exclusion clauses in contracts by obtaining a copy of the full policy document, as not all relevant information is included in insurance leaflets.

Annual Policies

For people who travel abroad frequently or spend long periods abroad, an annual travel policy usually provides the best value, but always carefully check exactly what it includes. Many insurance companies offer annual travel policies for a premium of around €150 to €300 (GB£100 to £210) for an individual (the equivalent of around three month's insurance with a standard travel insurance policy), which is excellent value for frequent travellers. The cost of an annual policy may depend on the area covered (e.g. Europe; worldwide excluding North America; or worldwide including North America), although it doesn't usually cover travel within your country of residence. There's also a limit on the number of trips a year and the duration of each trip, e.g. 90 or 120 days. An annual policy is usually a good choice for owners of a home abroad who travel there frequently for relatively short periods. **However, carefully check exactly what's covered or omitted, as an annual policy may not provide adequate cover.**

Claims

Although travel insurance companies will gladly take your money, they aren't so keen to pay claims and you may have to persevere before they pay up. Fraudulent claims against travel insurance are common; therefore, unless you can produce evidence to support your claim, the insurers may think you're trying to cheat them. Always be persistent and make a claim irrespective of any small print, as this may be unreasonable and therefore invalid in law. **All insurance companies require you to report any loss (or any incident for which you intend to make a claim) to the local police or carriers within 24 hours and to obtain a report. Failure to do this will mean that your claim usually won't be considered.**

6.

EDUCATION

The quality and variety of schools in a particular country or region is an important consideration for families with school-age children. Education standards vary considerably from country to country and even from school to school. There are good private and international (usually English language) schools in most of the EU capitals and in some major cities, although the standard of state-funded education may leave a lot to be desired, particularly in run-down neighbourhoods. Education is compulsory in EU countries between the ages of 5 to 7 and 15 or 16, although students are often encouraged to remain at school until the age of 18 and go on to university.

State education (from nursery to secondary school) is usually free, although parents may be required to pay for certain items such as text books, writing materials, art supplies, musical instruments and sports equipment. Many schools have a school uniform, which may be compulsory (particularly in private schools) and expensive. Schools may provide a canteen or restaurant, although this is rare in most countries, and transport to and from school may also be provided (there's usually a fee for these services). University (tertiary) education may be free or subsidised for residents, while non-resident students may have to pay hefty fees, which may include education in your home country if a child's parents are non-residents. Some countries provide grants or loans for university students, which are repaid out of future income.

State schools in most EU countries are co-educational (mixed) day schools, although some may accept boarders, particularly secondary schools in those areas where students must travel long distances to school. In many countries, private schools usually include both day and boarding schools, and are mostly single-sex, although this is changing in some countries. Admission to a state school for foreign children may be dependent on the type and duration of the residence permit granted to their parents. In any country, your choice of state and private schools will vary considerably according to where you live.

Your children's education is one of the most important decisions facing families when considering a move abroad. The choice of school and education regime should be made only after consideration of all the options and obtaining independent expert advice. You should think long-term and consider your child's interests, particularly regarding their education when your period abroad ends and you return home. If your child has any special educational needs (see page 163), particularly concerning learning difficulties, you should seriously consider whether relocation is in the family's best interests, as it's unlikely that you will find the right sort of help and support abroad. Any help you find will probably be limited, particularly if you move to a country where lessons will be conducted in a foreign language (other than your child's mother tongue).

One of the most important decisions facing parents abroad is whether to send their children to a state or private school. In some countries, state schools are equal to the best private schools (or better), while in others, particularly in neglected inner city areas, they lack resources and may achieve poor results. However, many parents prefer to send their children to a private school, even when this involves considerable financial sacrifice. There are virtually no private schools in Scandinavian countries. In most EU countries, there's no legal obligation for parents to educate their children at school and they may educate them themselves or employ private tutors. Parents educating their children at home don't usually require a teaching qualification, although they must satisfy the education authorities that a child is receiving full-time education appropriate for his or her age, abilities and aptitude (they will check and may test your child).

In some EU countries, both state and private schools publish brochures and there are also independent guides to both state and private schools, published by local councils, newspapers and publishers. In many EU countries, there are also independent education advisers who can provide advice and information on any aspect of education. You can also obtain information from embassies and consulates, many of which have an education section or officer, and there are other official organisations in many countries. For example, the British Council, which has offices in around 80 countries (🖥 www.britishcouncil.org), provides foreign students with information concerning all aspects of education in the UK.

In most EU countries, the Ministry of Education has a website (possibly with an English language version) and individual education authorities or even schools (particularly private schools) often have their own websites. Other useful websites include the European Council of International Schools (🖥 www.ecis.org), which publishes an *International Schools Directory*; International Schools Services (🖥 www.iss.edu), which serves international schools around the world and produces *The Directory of International Schools* for Americans, published annually; the US State Department (🖥 www.state.gov/m/a/os), which contains information about American-sponsored elementary and secondary schools overseas; the Council of British Independent Schools in the European Communities (🖥 www.cobisec.org); the International Baccalaureate Organisation (🖥 www.ibo.org), which has four regional offices and representatives in several countries; and Ibiblio – the Public's Library (🖥 www.ibiblio.org/cisco/schools/international) which contains a list of American international schools.

In addition to a detailed look at state and private education, this chapter contains information about higher and further education and language schools.

CHOOSING A SCHOOL

If you're able to choose the country where your child is educated or can choose between state and private education, the following checklist will help you:

● How long are you planning to remain abroad? If you're uncertain, then it's probably better to assume a long stay. Owing to language and other integration problems, enrolling a child in a foreign school with a foreign syllabus (state or private) is advisable only for a minimum of two to three years, particularly for teenage children.

● The area in which you choose to live may affect your choice of local school(s). Although it may be unnecessary to send your children to the state school nearest your home, you may have difficulty obtaining admission to a state school if you don't live within its catchment area. If you choose a private day school, it must be within a reasonable travelling distance of your home.

- If you will be living abroad for a limited period, do you know where you're going to live afterwards? This may be an important consideration with regard to your children's schooling. How old are your children and what age will they be when you plan to leave the country? What future plans do you have for their education and in which country?

- What age are your children and how will they fit into a private school or the state school system abroad? The younger they are, the easier it will be to place them in a suitable school.

- If your children are English-speaking, how do they view the thought of studying in a foreign language? Will they be able to communicate with their teachers? Is teaching available in English?

- Will your children require your help with their studies? Will you be able to help them, particularly with a foreign language?

- What are the school hours? What are the holiday periods? How will the hours and holidays influence your work and leisure activities? State schools in some countries (e.g. France) have classes on Saturday mornings.

- Is religion an important consideration in your choice of school? In state schools in some countries, religion is a compulsory subject. Parents can, however, usually have their children excused religious instruction, although some schools are maintained by religious organisations and may make stipulations as to religious observance.

- Do you want your children to attend a co-educational (mixed) school? State schools in most countries are co-educational.

- Should you send your children to a boarding school? If so, in which country?

- What are the secondary and further education prospects for your children abroad or in another country? Are foreign educational qualifications recognised in your home country or the country where you plan to live next?

- Does the school have a good academic record? Most schools must provide exam pass rate statistics and a prospectus, which they may post to you or which may be available on the school website.

- What are the facilities for art and science subjects, for example arts and crafts, music, computer studies (how many computers?), sciences, hobbies, drama, cookery and photography? Does the school have an extensive library of up-to-date books (a good library is usually an excellent sign)? These should be listed in a school's prospectus.

- How large are the classes? What is the teacher/pupil ratio?

Obtain the opinions and advice of others who have been faced with similar decisions and problems, and collect as much information from as many different sources as possible before making a decision. Speak to teachers and the parents of children attending schools on your shortlist. If possible, interview the head teacher before making a decision. Most parents find that it's desirable to discuss the alternatives with their children before making a decision.

In many EU countries there are separate state schools for children with special educational needs (see page 163), including those with emotional and behavioural difficulties, moderate and severe learning difficulties, communication problems, hearing or sight impairment, or physical disabilities. There may also be special schools or facilities for gifted children.

See also **Choosing A Private School** on page 161.

Language

There are many considerations to take into account when choosing an appropriate school abroad, not least the language of study. In most EU countries, the only schools that use English as the teaching language may be foreign (e.g. American or British) and international private schools. In some countries there are multi-lingual schools, which teach students in both English and the local language (but not simultaneously!). If your children attend any other school, they must study all subjects in the local language. Many state schools also teach regional languages, although these may be optional or taught outside normal school hours. However, in some countries, state schools in certain autonomous regions may teach most or all lessons in a local language or dialect (e.g. Basque or Catalan in Spain). This may leave you no option but to pay for a private school (or move to another region).

For most children, studying in a major foreign language such as French, German, Italian, Portuguese or Spanish isn't such a handicap as it may at first appear, particularly for those aged under ten. The majority of children adapt reasonably quickly and most become reasonably fluent within three to six months (if only it were so easy for adults!), although you shouldn't underestimate the difficulties they will initially face. Not all children adapt equally well to a change of language and culture, particularly teenagers (at around 10 to 12 years of age children begin to learn languages more slowly), many of whom encounter great difficulties during their first year or so.

State school systems in most EU countries make little or no concession to children who don't speak the local language fluently, for example by providing intensive language lessons. This can make the first few months quite an ordeal for foreign children. On the other hand, foreign children in some countries, particularly children of secondary school age, are placed in a 'reception' or special class, depending on the degree of language assistance necessary. This allows them more time to concentrate on learning the language (with extra language tuition), as they will usually have covered the syllabus already. They integrate into the normal stream only when they've learnt the language and can follow the lessons. It's worthwhile inquiring about the availability of extra classes before choosing where to live.

While undergoing extra language study, children may fall behind in other subjects. In some EU countries, children who don't make the grade must repeat a year (or even two) and there's usually a fairly wide age range in the higher school classes. There's usually no stigma attached to the repetition of classes (except among some children), as children learn at different speeds and many school systems simply recognise this fact. However, if a child fails to maintain the required standard in a higher grade secondary school, e.g. a high school, he may be required to join another school with a less demanding curriculum.

If your local state school doesn't provide extra language classes, your only choice will be to pay for private lessons or send your child to another (possibly private) school, where extra tuition is provided. Some parents send a child to an English-speaking school for a year, followed by a move to a bilingual or local language school. Other parents believe that it's better to throw their children in at the deep end, rather than introduce them gradually. Given the choice (and with hindsight!), many children prefer to attend a local school which allows them to become fully integrated into the local community, language and culture. It depends on the character, ability and wishes of the child. Whatever you decide, it will help if your child has some intensive language lessons before you move abroad. It may also be possible to organise an educational or cultural exchange with a school or family abroad before you make the move, which is a considerable help in integrating a child into the local language and culture. **Parents should also learn the local language!**

If English is your mother tongue or a second or additional language, then you're probably already aware of its importance and growing influence throughout the world. It's a big advantage to your children if they can speak it at home every day, particularly if it isn't taught at school. Children may not start learning English in state schools until they reach secondary level, and even then it may be voluntary (although in many EU countries children now start learning English in primary school). English may become compulsory only when a child is studying modern languages, for example in a high school, or when a specialist subject is studied requiring English language proficiency. In some countries, English-speaking parents organise private English classes for their children or teach them themselves.

STATE SCHOOLS

The quality of schools, their teaching staff and the education they provide, varies considerably according to the country, region, city and even the particular neighbourhood of a city. If you want your children to have a good education, it's essential to get them into a good school, even if it means moving house and changing your job. You may have the right to express a preference for a particular state school, but priority is often given to children living in a school's catchment area, families with a child already at a particular school and children with special family or medical circumstances.

It's vital to research the best schools in a given area and to ensure that your child will be accepted at your chosen school, **before** buying or renting a home. Admission to state schools is usually decided largely on the local catchment area and if you live outside a school's area your child may not be admitted. Not surprisingly, homes near the best state schools are at a premium and prices in some areas are driven up by the high demand. Schools are sometimes forced to reduce their catchment area, thus excluding many children whose parents may have moved home specifically so their offspring could attend a particular school. In some areas, children can be denied the right to attend a particular school simply because they live on the wrong side of a street.

Enrolment

To enrol in a state school, you should enquire at the local town hall or the local schools information service. You may also be able to obtain information by post or via the internet. When enrolling, you need to provide details of a child's age, previous schooling and knowledge of the local language. You must also provide certain documents which may include a child's birth certificate or passport, with an official translation (if necessary), proof of residence and possibly proof of immunisation (see **Children's Health** on page 118). In most EU countries, immunisations are recorded in a child's health book, which is issued to parents when a child is born.

PRIVATE SCHOOLS

Private fee-paying schools are usually termed private schools, although they may be called independent schools or public schools, for example in the UK. What they all have in common is that all or part of their funding comes from private sources rather than the state. However, in some countries, private schools are largely funded from state funds and follow the same curriculum as state schools. Private schools may be owned by an individual, an institution or a company and, although traditionally the preserve of the wealthy, in many countries they attract an increasing number of pupils from less privileged backgrounds.

In many countries, private schools take pupils from the ages of 2 or 3 to 19 and include boarding and day schools (some are both), single-sex and co-educational schools. Some schools cater for special education needs (see page 163) and there are also private schools for children gifted in art, music, theatre or dance in some countries. Some private schools follow special or unorthodox methods of teaching, for example Montessori nursery schools and Rudolf Steiner schools, although all schools must usually meet certain minimum criteria and be registered with the local Ministry of Education. Although fee-paying, private schools aren't always run for private profit and all surplus income is often reinvested in the running of schools (many private schools are run by charitable foundations).

In many countries, private schools include American, British, international and other foreign schools. Students at **American schools** are prepared for entry to an American college or university through Advanced Placement (AP) courses or follow the International Baccalaureate (IB) pre-university curriculum, which provides an international university entry qualification. American and British schools usually accept students of all nationalities and religious backgrounds, although they may give priority to American or British citizens. Non-English students receive intensive tuition in English, where necessary. The fees at American schools may be considerably higher than those at other private schools, particularly for boarders.

International schools usually prepare students for the local university entrance examination plus the two-year International Baccalaureate (IB) pre-university course. The IB diploma is recognised as an entry qualification by universities throughout the world and many North American universities grant students with an IB diploma up to one year's credit. Some international schools offer an American curriculum in addition to the IB curriculum. For information, contact the International Baccalaureate Organisation (🖳 www.ibo.org), which has a European regional office. Like some American and British schools, many international schools have a comprehensive English-as-a-Second Language (ESL) programme and attract students from many countries. International schools generally provide a better standard of education than state schools, although the regime may be tougher and children should be prepared for this. Many international schools are heavily oversubscribed and most classes have waiting lists. If you can, plan well in advance and enrol your child as soon as possible. A complete list of international schools in 75 countries worldwide is contained in the *International Schools Directory*, published annually by the European Council of International Schools (ECIS), 21B Lavant Street, Petersfield, Hants. GU32 3EL, UK (☎ 01730-268244, 🖳 www.ecis.org).

There are foreign schools in many EU countries (usually located in or near the capital city) which may include Canadian, Chinese, Dutch, French, German, Greek, Japanese, Norwegian, Spanish and Swedish schools. For further information contact the appropriate embassy. Children who wish to be taught in certain languages, such as Dutch, French, German or Italian may be able to gain admittance to a special European School (🖳 www.eursc.org) in a number of European Union countries, although entry is strictly limited if parents aren't employed by the EU. European Schools are located in Alicante (Spain), Bergen (the Netherlands), Brussels (3 schools) and Mol (Belgium), Culham (UK), Frankfurt, Karlsruhe and Munich (Germany), Luxembourg and Varese (Italy).

Private school fees vary considerably according to a variety of factors, including the country, the age of pupils, the reputation and quality of the school, and its location (schools in major cities are generally much more expensive than those situated in rural areas). Day school fees vary from as little as a few thousand euros (or GB£) a year or term for primary schools up to tens of thousands of euros (or GB£) a year or term for a senior boarding school. Fees aren't usually all-inclusive and additional obligatory charges are made in addition to optional extra services. There are also commercial tutorial colleges or 'crammers' in many countries, providing a one-term or one-year re-sit course for students who have failed their university entrance exams. Many schools provide scholarships for bright or talented pupils, usually awarded as a result of competitive examination, which vary in value from full fees to a proportion only.

Private schools range from nursery (kindergarten), to day and boarding schools, and include both experimental schools and traditional institutions. There are also private schools for religious and ethnic minorities, for example schools for Muslims in non-Muslim countries, where there's a strict code regarding the segregation of boys and girls. In some countries, most private schools are single-sex, although there are also usually mixed schools (co-educational). Entrance to schools is by examination, report or assessment, interview or a combination of these. In most countries, private schools follow a similar curriculum to state schools, although foreign schools may follow the curriculum (and examinations) of their mother country and may also offer the International Baccalaureate (IB) examination.

Don't assume that all private schools are excellent or that they offer a better education than state schools. In many countries, the vast majority of parents choose to send their children to a state school, even when the cost of private education isn't an important consideration. However, private schools may provide a more broad-based education and offer a more varied approach to sport, music, drama, art and a wider choice of academic subjects, than a state school. Their aim is usually the development of the child as an individual and the encouragement of his unique talents, which is made possible by small classes that allow teachers to provide pupils with individually-tailored lessons and tuition. Some private schools cater for special needs, including gifted children and slow learners or those who suffer from dyslexia.

Make applications to private schools as far in advance as possible. Obviously if you're coming from abroad, you won't usually be able to apply one or two years in advance, which is usually considered to be the best time to book a place. It isn't simply a matter of selecting a school. Although many nursery and junior schools accept pupils on a first-come, first-served basis, the best and most exclusive schools have waiting lists or a demanding selection procedure. Most popular schools, particularly day schools in major cities, have long waiting lists. Don't rely on enrolling your child in a particular school and neglect other alternatives, particularly if your chosen school has a rigorous entrance examination. When applying, you're usually requested to send previous school reports, exam results and records. Before enrolling your child in a private school, ensure that you understand the withdrawal conditions.

Choosing A Private School

The following checklist is designed to help you choose an appropriate and reputable private school in the EU:

- Does the school have a good reputation? Does it belong to a recognised national body for private schools? How long has it been established? Is it financially stable?

- Does the school have a good academic record? For example, what percentage of pupils gain good examination passes or go on to good universities? What subjects do pupils do best in? All schools provide exam pass-rate statistics. On the other hand, if your child isn't exceptionally bright, you may prefer to send him to a school with less academic pressure.

● What does the curriculum include (a broad and well-balanced one is best)? Ask to see a typical timetable to check the ratio of academic to non-academic subjects. Check the number of free study periods and supervision.

● Do you wish to send your children to a single-sex or a co-educational school? Many children, particularly girls, make better progress without the distractions of the opposite sex.

● Day or boarding school? If you're considering a day school, what are the hours? Does the school provide transport? Some schools offer weekly boarding, which allows pupils to return home at weekends.

● If you've decided on a boarding school, what standard and type of accommodation is provided? What is the quality and variety of food provided? What is the dining room like? Does the school have a dietician?

● Do you intend to send your children to a junior or senior private school only or both?

● How many children attend the school and what is the average class size? What is the ratio of teachers to pupils? Are pupil numbers increasing or decreasing? Check that class sizes are in fact what it says they are in the prospectus. Has the number of pupils increased dramatically in the last few years (which could be a good or a bad sign)?

● What are the qualification requirements for teachers? What nationality is the majority of teachers? What is the teacher turnover? A high teacher turnover is a bad sign and usually suggests under-paid teachers and poor working conditions.

● What extras will you have to pay? For example, optional lessons (e.g. music, dancing and sports), lunches, art supplies, sports equipment, school trips, phone calls, clothing (most schools have obligatory uniforms, which can be expensive), insurance, textbooks and stationery. Most schools charge parents for every little thing.

● Which countries do most students come from?

● Is religion an important consideration in your choice of school? What is the religious bias of the school, if any?

● Are special English classes provided for children whose English doesn't meet the required standard? Usually if a child is under ten years of age it doesn't matter if his English is weak. However, children over this age may not be accepted unless they can read English fluently (as printed in textbooks for their age). Some schools provide intensive language tuition for foreign students.

● What languages does the school teach as obligatory or optional subjects? Does the school have a language laboratory?

- What is the student turnover?
- What are the school terms and holiday periods? Private school holidays are much longer than state schools in some countries, e.g. four weeks at Easter and Christmas and ten weeks in the summer, and they often don't coincide with state school holiday periods.
- What are the withdrawal conditions, should you wish to remove your child? A term's notice is usual.
- What examinations are set? In which subjects? How do they fit in with future education plans?
- What sports instruction and facilities are provided?
- What are the facilities for art and science subjects, for example arts and crafts, music, computer studies (how many computers?), science, hobbies, drama, cookery and photography?
- What sort of outings and holidays does the school organise?
- What medical facilities does the school provide, e.g. infirmary, resident doctor or nurse? Is health and accident insurance included in the fees?
- What sort of discipline and punishments are imposed and are restrictions relaxed as children get older?
- What reports are provided for parents and how often? How much contact does the school have with parents?
- Last, but not least, unless someone else is paying, what are the fees?

Draw up a shortlist of possible schools and obtain a prospectus (some schools provide a video). If applicable, also obtain a copy of the school magazine. Before making a final choice, it's important to visit the schools on your shortlist during term time and talk to teachers and students. **Where possible, check the answers to the above questions in person and don't rely on a school's prospectus to provide the information.** If you're unhappy with the answers, look elsewhere. Having made your choice, maintain a check on your child's progress, listen to his complaints and compare notes with other parents. If something doesn't seem right, try to establish whether a complaint is founded or not, and if it is, take action to have the problem resolved. See also **Choosing A School** on page 155.

SPECIAL EDUCATION

The provision of special education for children with special needs varies considerably from country to country and is poor or non-existent in some EU countries. Special education includes that for children with moderate or severe learning difficulties (e.g. a hearing, speech, or sight impediment, a physical disability, dyslexia or autism) or a behavioural problem, which either prevents or hinders them from attending a mainstream school for their age group. Some countries provide dedicated schools, while others prefer (whenever possible) to educate children with special education needs in mainstream schools, in order to give them the same education as other children.

In most countries there are too few special schools and it's estimated that many pupils with special education needs are educated in mainstream schools (although there are often educational and social reasons for this). Some special schools are run privately by voluntary bodies, which may receive a grant from central government for capital expenditure and equipment, and some private schools provide education wholly or mainly for children with special education needs. Most education systems provide an educational psychological service for children with behavioural problems.

In some countries, the state education system also provides special teaching and facilities for gifted children (those with very high IQs), although generally the only avenue open to most parents is to pay for private tuition or apply for a scholarship. Some organisations, such as Mensa (🖳 www.mensa.org), provide help to develop the potential of gifted children through special schools and individual counselling. It's as important to choose the best possible school for a talented or gifted child as it is for a child with learning difficulties.

In many EU countries there are schools for children with special needs, which may include both day and boarding schools. Contact a country's local embassy, Ministry of Education or the local education authority for information.

HIGHER & FURTHER EDUCATION

Post-school education is generally divided into higher and further education, although the distinction is often blurred. Higher education is usually defined as advanced courses of a standard higher than a secondary school-leaving certificate (such as the International Baccalaureate) and usually refers only to first degree courses. Further education generally embraces everything except first degree courses. Courses may be full-time, part-time or sandwich courses (ones that combine full-time study, with training and paid work in industry and commerce). As at all levels of education, the quality and value varies considerably according to the country and, more importantly, the educational establishment. Each year thousands of foreign students study in EU countries, particularly the UK, where teaching foreign students is a lucrative business.

The minimum age of admission to university in most countries is 18, although some universities admit exceptional students at a younger age, and first degree courses usually last for a minimum of three or four years. In contrast, in some EU countries, courses have no set length and many students take as long as seven to nine years to attain their degree.

Foreign students may also need a student visa or residence permit. A foreign national over 18 years of age who wishes to study full-time in the EU on a course lasting longer than three or six months (and which will lead to a professional or educational qualification) must provide evidence of his educational qualifications and his financial means. Evidence must be provided to both the educational establishment and the immigration authorities.

Fees

Most EU countries set different fee levels for local students, e.g. those from local schools or the local county or state, students from other counties or states within the same country (who may be termed 'home' students), and foreign students. There are no fees for local students in many countries or nominal fees only, which may also apply to foreign students who have lived in a country for a number of years, e.g. those who have attended a local secondary school. Students whose parents are resident in the same country may also pay the same fees as local students. In many countries, grants, scholarships and student loans are available to foreign students.

Grants & Scholarships

In most EU countries there are grants (e.g. from governments, professional bodies, educational trusts, universities and colleges), public and private scholarships and award schemes available to overseas students, particularly at postgraduate level. In some countries, students can apply for financial help from special funds and scholarships, which colleges and universities distribute at their discretion to their most needy students. It's advisable to apply as early as possible for a grant or scholarship. In many EU countries, companies and professional organisations (plus the military) also sponsor higher education, in return for a number of years' service. However, even with a grant you must be able to support yourself during your studies.

EU Students

Grants covering fees and living expenses that are available to local nationals in EU countries are also available to the children of other EU nationals working in the country, and to officially recognised refugees and their children. EU nationals who are normally resident within the EU are eligible for grants (covering university fees only) on the same basis as local residents, but must pay their own living expenses. With the exception of these grants, authorities can give grants covering fees and living expenses only to students who have been resident in an EU country for the three years immediately prior to the first year of their course. The factors determining the size of a grant are complex (as is anything devised by civil servants), but it usually depends on a student's financial resources and those of his parents. EU students can obtain a booklet, *Investing in the Future: Help with tuition fees for European Union (EU) Students* (available in a number of languages).

Non-EU Nationals

Non-EU students must usually pay the full cost of their courses and living expenses. This includes non-EU European Economic Area (EEA) nationals unless they've been migrant workers in an EU country or are the child or spouse of an EEA migrant worker. However, a variety of grants and scholarships is available to foreign students (see above).

Cost Of Living

The cost of living (excluding course fees) varies considerably according to the country, region and particular city or town. In many countries, students are forced to choose their university not on course preference, but on where they can more easily survive or where they can get a part-time job. The cost of living, particularly accommodation, is generally much lower in a provincial town than in a major or capital city. Many universities have 'job clubs' or agencies to help students supplement their income and in some countries students work their way through university. Overseas students studying in an EU country for longer than six months are entitled to free health care from the public health service. Financial hardship is a major cause of student drop-outs in many countries.

Entrance Qualifications

The minimum qualification for entrance to a university in most countries is the examinations that students take before leaving high school at the age of 17 or 18, e.g. A-levels in England, the baccalaureate in many European countries or the International Baccalaureate. Generally, the better the university (or the better the reputation) and the more popular the course, the higher the entrance qualifications. Minimum entrance requirements are set by individual universities and colleges and may vary considerably. However, universities and other institutions may be flexible in their entrance requirements, particularly with regard to mature students (e.g. those aged 21 or over) and those with qualifications other than standard school-leaving diplomas.

Generally, overseas students' qualifications which would admit them to a university in their home country are taken into consideration, although passes in certain subjects may be mandatory, depending on the particular course. Whatever your qualifications, all applications are considered on their merits. All foreign students require a thorough knowledge of English or the language of study, which will usually be tested unless a certificate is provided. Most universities accept the International Baccalaureate certificate as an entrance qualification, but an American high school diploma isn't usually accepted. Contact individual universities for detailed information.

Applications

To apply for a place at university you should begin by writing to the Admissions Officer of selected universities, giving your personal details and asking for information. If you're encouraged by the reply, you must then apply formally. Applicants can apply for a number of courses (which may be at different universities), for which there may be a nominal fee. The number of applicants per university place varies considerably from university to university. You'd be wise not to make all your applications at universities where competition for places is at its fiercest (unless you're a genius).

If you plan to study a full-time first degree course at a university in the UK, you must apply to the Universities and Colleges Admissions Services (UCAS), PO Box 28, Cheltenham, Gloucestershire GL52 3LZ, UK (☎ 0870-112 2211, 🖳 www.ucas.co.uk). You can apply by post or online for a maximum of six courses, for which there's a fee of around £15. UCAS publishes the comprehensive *UCAS University and College Entrance Official Guide*.

The university year begins in October in many countries and you usually need to make an application in autumn of the year before you plan to start your course, i.e. one year in advance.

Accommodation

The cost of accommodation is a major factor for many students when choosing a university, and in many countries most students live at home and study locally to reduce costs. Following acceptance by a college or university, students are advised to apply for a place in a hall of residence ('in hall') or other college accommodation, such as self-catering houses and apartments. Such accommodation is usually limited, although many universities accommodate all first year students and may give priority to foreign students. You should write as soon as possible after acceptance to accommodation or welfare officers, whose job is to help students find suitable accommodation (both college and private). In some countries, many students rent privately-owned apartments or houses, which are shared with other students, although this kind of accommodation may be difficult to find and expensive. Another alternative is to find lodgings where you rent a room in a private house with meals included.

Student Bodies

In most EU countries, universities have a huge variety of societies and clubs, many of which are organised by a students union or council, which is the centre of social activities. Most universities have excellent sports facilities and many offer sports scholarships. Wherever you're studying, take at least a dozen passport-size photographs for student identity cards, hall and travel cards.

Further Information

There are many books for anyone planning to continue higher or further education abroad, including the *ECIS Higher Education Directory* (🖳 www. ecis.org), *Making the Most of Higher Education, Which Subject?* (Which?, UK), *The Student Book 2005* by Klaus Boehm (Macmillan, UK), which contains everything you need to know about how to get into and survive university, and *The Times Good University Guide* (UK).

LEARNING THE LANGUAGE

If you don't speak the local language fluently, you may wish to take a language course. Obtaining a working knowledge of the local language in many countries is relatively easy, as you will be constantly immersed in the language and will have the maximum opportunity to practise. However, if you wish to speak or write it fluently, you will probably need to attend a language school or find a private tutor (see below). It's usually necessary to have a recognised qualification in a language in order to be accepted at a college of university.

It isn't essential for temporary residents and those who live and work among the expatriate community to learn the local language, although it certainly makes life easier and less frustrating. **However, for anyone living abroad permanently, learning the local language should be seen as a necessity.** It's vital to start studying as soon as possible after you arrive and to avoid foreign 'ghettos' if you really want to learn the language. **Most foreigners living abroad find that their business and social enjoyment and success is directly related to the degree to which they master the local language.**

If you don't learn the language, you will be continually frustrated and will be constantly calling on people to assist you, or even paying people to do jobs you could easily do yourself. **However, the most important and serious purpose of learning the local language is that, in an emergency, it could save your life or that of a loved one.** Learning the language also helps you appreciate the local way of life and make the most of your time abroad, and opens many doors that remain firmly closed to resident 'tourists'.

A big handicap for English-speakers is that in most countries there's usually someone around who speaks English, particularly when you want to speak the local language! One of the penalties of being a native English speaker is that you may receive little or no encouragement to learn the local language, but will be condemned as a lazy foreigner if you don't. Don't get caught in the trap of seeking refuge in the English language or allowing others to practise their English at your expense. You must persist in speaking the local language: give in too easily and you will never learn.

Information about language courses in most countries can be obtained from embassies and consulates, Chambers of Commerce, trade organisations, universities and colleges, via the internet, and direct from language schools.

Methods

Most people can teach themselves a great deal through the use of books, tapes, videos or computer-based courses. However, even the best students require some help. Teaching languages is a big business in most EU countries, with classes offered by language schools; local and foreign colleges and universities; private and international schools; foreign and international organisations; local associations and clubs; chambers of commerce and town halls; and private teachers. In some countries, there's an ethnic minority language service providing information and counselling in a variety of languages. These may organise a wide range of classes, including home tuition, open learning and small classes, at beginner and intermediate levels.

Most universities offer courses all year round, including special summer courses; these are often cheaper than language schools, although classes may be larger. Free language courses are available for foreigners in some EU countries. Classes range from courses for complete beginners, through specialised business and cultural courses, to university-level seminars leading to recognised diplomas. If you already speak the language but need conversational practice, you may wish to enrol in an art or craft course at a local institute or club.

Language Schools

There are language schools in most large towns and cities in EU countries, offering a wide range of classes. Most schools run various classes depending on ability, how many hours you wish to study a week, how much money you're prepared to pay, and how quickly you wish to learn. Some employers provide free in-house classes or may pay an employee's course fees (corporate courses are big business in many countries).

Language classes generally fall into the following categories: extensive (four hours per week), intensive (15 hours) and total immersion (20 to 40 hours). Don't expect to become fluent in a short period. Unless you need to learn a language quickly, it's probably better to arrange lessons over a long period. However, don't commit yourself to a long expensive course before ensuring that it's the right one. Most schools offer free tests to help you find your correct level, a free introductory lesson and small classes or private lessons. **It's important to choose the right course, particularly if you're want to continue with full-time education (or get a job) and need to reach a minimum standard or gain a particular qualification.**

Some schools offer combined courses where language study is linked with other subjects, including business language; art and culture; local history; and traditions and folklore. Some schools combine language courses with a range of social and sports activities such as horse riding, tennis, windsurfing, golf, skiing, hang-gliding and scuba diving.

Private Lessons

You may prefer private lessons, which offer a quicker, if more expensive, way of learning. The main advantage is that you learn at your own speed. If private lessons are too expensive, you can try to find a partner wishing to learn English (or your mother tongue); this is called a 'language exchange'. You can advertise for a private teacher or partner in local newspapers and on bulletin and notice boards (in shopping centres, supermarkets, universities, clubs, etc.). Don't forget to ask your friends, neighbours and colleagues if they can recommend a private teacher. Private teachers often advertise in local English language publications. See also **English Teachers & Translators** on page 59.

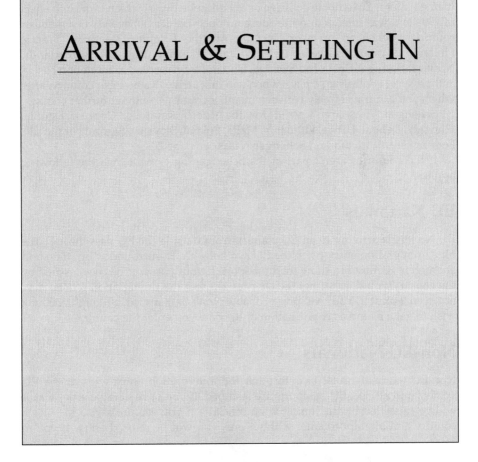

7.

ARRIVAL & SETTLING IN

On arrival in the EU, your first task will be to negotiate immigration and customs. For people moving from one EU country to another, this presents few problems but, for those arriving in the EU from outside, there are more formalities. You may require a visa to enter, particularly if you plan to work. You may also be required to enter via a particular airport, port or land border.

In addition to information about immigration and customs, this chapter contains checklists of tasks to be completed before or soon after arrival and when moving house, plus suggestions for finding local help and information.

IMMIGRATION

When you arrive in an EU country, you must pass through immigration, unless the country you've come from and the country you're travelling to are both signatories to the Schengen agreement (see **Schengen Agreement** on page 20) in which case there are no immigration controls. Thirteen members of the EU plus Norway and Iceland in the EEA are signatories to the Schengen agreement (named after a Luxembourg village on the Moselle River) which came into effect in 1994 and was intended to introduce an open-border policy between member countries. Schengen members include Austria, Belgium, Denmark, France, Finland, Germany, Greece, Iceland, Italy, Luxembourg, the Netherlands, Norway, Portugal, Spain and Sweden. Under the agreement, immigration checks and passport controls take place when you first arrive in a member country, after which you can travel freely between member countries without further checks.

Schengen visas aren't valid for the Czech Republic, Cyprus, Estonia, Hungary, Ireland, Latvia, Lithuania, Malta, Poland, Slovakia, Slovenia or the UK. For further information on **Schengen Visas** see page 20.

If the countries aren't part of the Schengen agreement then the following applies:

EU Nationals

EU Nationals arriving in an EU country from outside the EU pass through the blue immigration entry (with the EU symbol – an 'E' surrounded by stars) and are merely required to show their passport. If your passport has been issued by the country you're entering, the chances are that the immigration official may not even look at it. Your passport probably won't be stamped, although you may wish to get a stamp as confirmation of the date you enter the country.

Non-EU Nationals

Non-EU nationals must pass through the immigration entry without the EU symbol and all non-EU passports are stamped. If you have a single-entry visa it will be cancelled by the immigration official – if you require a visa to enter a country and attempt to enter without one, you will be refused entry. If you're entering the EU to work, study or live, you may be asked to show documentary evidence. Immigration officials may also ask visitors to produce a return ticket, proof of accommodation, health insurance and financial resources, e.g. cash, travellers' cheques and credit cards. The onus is on visitors to prove that they're genuine and won't violate immigration laws. Immigration officials aren't required to prove that you will break the law and can refuse you entry on the grounds of suspicion. Immigration officials in most countries are usually polite and efficient, although they're occasionally a little over-zealous in their attempts to exclude illegal immigrants, and certain nationalities or racial groups may experience harassment or even persecution.

CUSTOMS

Customs regulations in the EU vary according to the country you're travelling from and whether you're travelling from one Schengen country to another.

Arrivals From Within The EU

There are generally no customs formalities for EU nationals travelling from one EU country to another and if your plane or ferry comes from another EU country, you should go through the blue EU customs entry (indicated by the EU flag – an 'E' surrounded by stars). There are generally few customs checks and inspections here, but customs officers can (and do) inspect anyone they regard as suspicious. However, those arriving in an EU country (including EU citizens) are still subject to limitations on what may be imported duty-free (for information on duty-free allowances see **Shopping Abroad** on page 202. There are no restrictions on the import or export of local or foreign banknotes or securities within the EU, although if you enter or leave a country with more than a certain amount in cash (e.g. more than €6,000 in Spain) or negotiable instruments (see **Importing & Exporting Money** on page 129), you must make a declaration.

Arrivals From Outside The EU

On arrival at your destination and after passing through immigration control, you must go through customs. There are two customs lanes for arrivals from a non-EU country: 'Nothing to Declare' (green) and 'Goods to Declare' (black). If you have no goods requiring a customs declaration and you're within the permitted duty-free allowances (see **Shopping** on page 202 for a list), you should pass through the 'Nothing to Declare' entry. Otherwise you must go through the 'Goods to Declare'. If you're in any doubt, it's better to go through the 'Goods to Declare' entry. Customs inspections are frequent in both these entries.

Personal Effects

The rules regarding the importation of furniture and personal effects usually vary according to your nationality and whether you will be a temporary or permanent resident. Before making any plans to ship goods to any country, check the latest regulations with a local embassy or consulate in your home country. You may need a special application form (available from local embassies), plus a detailed inventory of the items to be imported and their estimated value in local currency. All items to be imported should be included on the list, even if some are to be imported at a later date.

If you use a shipping company to transport your belongings, they will usually provide all the necessary forms and complete the paperwork. Always keep copies of all forms and communications with customs officials, both with those abroad and in your home country. If the paperwork isn't in order, your belongings may end up incarcerated in a customs storage depot for a number of weeks or months. If you personally import your belongings, you may need to employ a customs agent at the point of entry to clear them. You should have an official record of the import of valuables in case you wish to export them later.

Shipments Within The EU

The shipment of personal (household) effects from one EU country to another isn't subject to customs formalities, although an inventory must be provided on request. EU nationals planning to take up residence in another EU country are permitted to import their household and personal effects free of duty or taxes, provided they were purchased tax-paid within the EU or have been owned and used for at least six months.

Shipments From Outside The EU

Personal effects imported from outside the EU generally require customs documents, which must usually be signed and presented to an embassy or consulate abroad with your passport.

- **EU Nationals** – EU nationals taking up residence in an EU country are permitted to import their household and personal effects free of duty or taxes, provided they were purchased tax-paid within the EU or have been owned and used for at least six-months.

- **Non-EU Nationals** – Non-EU nationals must have owned and used their personal effects for at least six months to qualify for duty-free import into an EU country. It's usually necessary to show proof of having rented or purchased a home and, in some countries, you may need to pay a deposit or obtain a bank guarantee equal to the value (or a percentage) of the personal effects to be imported. The deposit is returned after a specified period, e.g. one or two years, or when the goods are exported or you've obtained a residence permit. Belongings imported duty-free mustn't be sold within a certain period, e.g. one or two years of their importation, and, if you leave the country within this period, everything imported duty-free must be exported or duty paid.

Prohibited & Restricted Goods

Certain goods are subject to special regulations in all EU countries and in some cases their import and export is prohibited or restricted. These may include the following:

- Animal products;
- Plants;
- Wild fauna and flora and products derived from them;
- Live animals;
- Medicines and medical products (except for prescribed drugs and medicines);
- Firearms and ammunition;
- Certain goods and technologies with a dual civil/military purpose;
- Works of art and collectors' items.

If you're unsure whether anything you're importing falls into one of the above categories, check with the local customs authorities. If you're planning to import sporting guns, you may require a certificate from an embassy or consulate abroad, which is usually issued on production of a local firearms licence. Those travelling to the EU from 'exotic' regions, e.g. Africa, South America, and the Middle and Far East, may find themselves under close scrutiny from customs and security officials searching for illegal drugs.

Car Importation

Car importation is a popular topic among expatriates in many EU countries, where importing a car often entails a long, drawn out battle with local bureaucracy. The process is relatively simple for European Union (EU) citizens moving between EU countries, although it still involves completing a mountain of forms and can take a number of weeks. In most EU countries, a permanent resident isn't permitted to use a car on foreign registration plates and must import it and use it on local plates or return the car to its country of origin. The registration of a right-hand drive vehicle in a country where traffic drives on the right may be prohibited (the same applies to left-hand drive vehicles in countries that drive on the left). Car importation in general is often a costly (and time-consuming) business and, before importing your car, it's worth doing some calculations to find out whether it's actually cheaper to buy a new or second-hand car.

Most EU countries allow residents to import a car that has been owned for a limited period, e.g. six months. After you import and register a car in a new country, you must de-register it in its original country. A vehicle that's imported tax and duty-free mustn't usually be sold, rented or transferred within one year of its registration. In many countries (e.g. the UK) you can buy a tax-free car and operate it for six months before exporting it, which may help reduce your tax liability.

An imported vehicle must comply with certain safety and other requirements (called homologation) before it can be registered, although this isn't necessary when taking a locally-registered car from one EU country to another. When necessary, homologation can be prohibitively expensive in some countries, particularly if the car is an unusual make. Local taxes must usually be paid when importing a car, depending on its year of manufacture, where it was manufactured and its current registration. These may include VAT, registration or car tax, and import duty. The amount payable is usually based on the vehicle's original price with a reduction for its age. The procedure for the importation of a boat, caravan or motorcycle (with an engine capacity above 49cc) is usually the same as for a car. Mopeds with engines below 49cc can be freely imported into many EU countries as part of your personal possessions and require no special paperwork

EU Nationals

EU nationals who have bought their car in the EU and paid VAT and have owned it for more than six months may import their car into any EU country with no restrictions. The importation of new cars is not restricted either, but you will have to pay registration tax in most countries (e.g. 7 or 12 per cent in Spain).

Non-EU Nationals

Cars imported by non-EU nationals must undergo homologation (see above) and be certified by the manufacturer. This process can be lengthy and cost up to €500 or more. VAT, registration tax and import duty are usually payable – rates vary from country to country. Before you import your car (especially if it's an unusual make), check that spare parts and repair services are available in the country you're moving to.

Non-Residents

Non-residents can operate a foreign-registered vehicle in most EU countries for up to six months in a calendar year without paying local taxes and may be permitted to keep a foreign-registered vehicle permanently at a holiday home abroad. The vehicle must be road-legal in its home country, meaning that it must be inspected (for roadworthiness) and taxed each year in its country of registration (which may entail taking it home each year to have it tested!), and must be insured for local use. Non-residents can operate a car on tax-free (or 'tourist') plates in some countries (e.g. Spain). **Anyone who illegally uses a vehicle on foreign or tax-free plates can be fined and the vehicle confiscated.**

RESIDENCE

Foreigners (legally) residing in a country for longer than 90 or 180 days must usually either obtain a visa extension as a visitor or apply to become a resident. If you don't have a regular income or adequate financial resources, your application may be refused. Failure to apply for a residence permit within the specified time is a serious offence and can result in a heavy fine or even deportation, although this is unusual if you're an EU national. For further information on residence permits in individual EU countries see **Residence Permits** in the **Miscellaneous** section of **Country Profiles in Chapter 9**.

EMBASSY REGISTRATION

Nationals of some countries are required to register with their local embassy or consulate after taking up residence abroad. Registration isn't usually mandatory, although most embassies like to keep a record of their country's citizens abroad. Many countries maintain a number of consulates in certain countries, e.g. most EU countries maintain consulates in areas in other EU countries where their nationals reside. This also applies to American and Canadian consulates in European countries. Consulates are an important source of local information and can often provide useful contacts.

FINDING HELP

One of the major problems facing new arrivals in a foreign country is where to get help with day-to-day problems. How successful you are at finding local help depends on the town or area where you live (e.g. those in cities and resort areas are far better served than those living in rural areas), your nationality, your language proficiency and your sex (women are usually better catered for than men, through women's clubs). There's often an abundance of information available in the local language, but little in English and other foreign languages. An additional problem is that much of the available information isn't designed for foreigners and their particular needs. You may find that your friends, neighbours and colleagues can help as they can often offer advice based on their own experiences and mistakes. **But take care!** Although they mean well, you're likely to receive as much false and conflicting information as accurate (it may not necessarily be wrong, but often it won't apply to your particular situation).

If a woman lives in or near a major town she's able to turn to many English-speaking women's clubs and organisations for help. The single foreign male (who, of course, cannot possibly have any problems) must usually fend for himself, although there are men's expatriate clubs in some areas and mixed social clubs in most countries.

Among the best sources of information and help for women are the American Women's Clubs (AWC) located in major cities. AWC clubs provide comprehensive information in English about both local matters and topics of more general interest, and many provide data sheets, booklets and orientation programmes for newcomers. Membership in the organisation is sometimes limited to Americans or those with active links to the US, e.g. through study, work or a spouse who works for a US company or the US government, but most publications and orientation programmes are available to others for a fee. AWC clubs are part of the Federation of American Women's Clubs Overseas (FAWCO), which can be contacted via their website (💻 www.fawco.org).

Ask the embassy or consulate in your new country about expat associations in your area. For example, in countries where there are large British populations there may be branches of the British Association. These not only offer help to newcomers, but also provide support to members in hospital, lend wheelchairs, arrange events etc. The British Association is active in parts of France and may be contacted on their website 💻 www.angloinfo. com/online/ba. Dutch nationals may also find there are Dutch clubs offering similar support.

In addition to the above, there are many social clubs and expatriate organisations for foreigners in most countries, whose members can help you find your way around. They may, however, be difficult to locate, as most clubs are run by volunteers and operate out of the president's or secretary's home, and they rarely bother to advertise or take out a phone listing. If you ask around among your neighbours or colleagues, it's possible to find various Anglo 'friendship' clubs or English-speaking organisations. Finally, don't neglect to check the internet, where local newspapers, government offices, clubs and organisations often have their own websites. Contacts can also be found through expatriate magazines and newspapers.

Your town hall may be a good source of information, but you usually need to speak the local language to benefit and may still be sent on a wild goose chase from department to department. However, town halls in some countries where there are many foreign residents sometimes have a foreigners department, where staff may speak English and other foreign languages such as Dutch, French, German and Swedish – an advantage of living somewhere where there are lots of other foreigners!

Many businesses (particularly large multi-national companies) produce booklets and leaflets containing useful information about clubs or activities in the area. Bookshops may have some interesting publications about the local region, and tourist and information offices are also good sources of information. Most embassies and consulates also provide their nationals with local information, which may include the names of local lawyers, interpreters/translators, doctors, dentists, schools, and social and expatriate organisations and clubs.

Home Help

If you spend long periods at a home abroad or live abroad permanently, you may wish to employ someone to help around the home such as a cleaner, housekeeper, maid, nanny, cook, gardener, chauffeur, nurse or baby-sitter. If you have young children you may wish to consider employing an au pair (see page 56). If you need or wish to hire a full-time employee, there are a number of important points to take into consideration. These may include work and residence permits; employment contracts; working conditions; minimum wages; holidays and time off; income tax and social security; meals, room and board; dismissal; redundancy payments; and accident and health insurance.

In most EU countries there are strict regulations concerning the employment of full-time domestic staff, including minimum salaries, time off and paid holidays. Minimum salaries may vary considerably according to nationality, age and experience. You may need to apply for a work or residence permit and pay for a pension, accident and health insurance (or part). It may also be necessary to deduct tax at source from your employee's income (including lodging and meals, if part of his salary) and complete all the associated official paper work. In many countries, an employer and a domestic employee must have a written contract of employment and, if there's no written contract, the law may assume that there's a verbal agreement for a minimum period, e.g. one year. If you break the law regarding the hiring and firing of employees, an employee may have redress to a labour court, which can result in a substantial compensation award.

Most regulations apply to full-time staff only and not to temporary staff employed for less than a specified number of hours per week, e.g. 15 or 20. In most EU countries you should ensure that employees are covered by social security, as you can be held responsible should they have an accident on your property. Always ask to see an employee's social security card and obtain legal advice if you're unsure of your obligations under the law. If you're found to be employing someone who isn't paying social security (and income tax), you can be heavily fined and may have to pay any unpaid social security payments.

In some countries you should ask for a written quotation from temporary staff stating the work to be done and the cost, as this will then make them legally responsible for their own insurance and social security. Although there are statutory minimum wages in many countries for full-time employees, you may need to pay a higher rate for a temporary employee who's employed by the hour, half-day or day. Enquire among your neighbours and friends to find out the going rate as, if you pay too much, you could find yourself unpopular. If you need to hire someone who speaks English or another 'foreign' (non-local) language, you may need to pay a premium.

CULTURE SHOCK

'Culture shock' is the term used to describe the psychological and physical state felt by foreigners when they relocate abroad. Culture shock can also be regarded as the period of adjustment to the new country. The symptoms are essentially psychological and are caused by the tremendous sense of alienation you feel when you're bombarded on a daily basis with cultural differences in an environment where there are few, if any, familiar references. However, there are also physical symptoms that may manifest themselves in the form of an increased incidence of minor illnesses (e.g. colds and headaches) or more serious psychosomatic illnesses brought on by depression. Culture shock takes a number of forms, but is typically as follows:

1. The first stage is known by expatriates as the 'honeymoon stage' and usually lasts from a few days to a few weeks after arrival. This stage is essentially a positive one, when a newly-arrived expatriate finds everything is an exciting and interesting novelty. This feeling is similar to that of being on holiday.

2. The second stage is usually completely opposite to the first and is essentially negative and a period of crisis, as the initial excitement and holiday feeling wears off and the expatriate starts daily life – except, of course, that this daily life is nothing like any he has previously experienced. This crisis is characterised by a general feeling of disorientation and confusion as well as loneliness. Physical exhaustion brought on by jet lag, extremes of hot or cold, and the strain of having hundreds of settling-in tasks to do is an important physical symptom of this stage.

3. The third stage is sometimes known as the 'flight' stage (because of the overwhelming desire to escape) and is usually the one that lasts the longest and is the most difficult to cope with. During this period the expatriate feels depressed and angry, as well as resentful towards the new country and its people. He may also feel resentment towards whoever is responsible for the relocation (this is particularly true of expatriate spouses). Depression is worsened by the fact that at this stage you can see nothing positive or good about the new country and focus exclusively on the negative aspects of the relocation, refusing to acknowledge any positive points.

It's generally agreed that the period of readjustment lasts around six months, although there are expatriates who adjust earlier and those who never get over the 'flight' stage and are forced to return home.

Experts agree that all expatriates suffer from culture shock and there's no escaping the phenomenon, although its effects can be reduced. Non-working spouses and teenage children would appear to be the ones most affected, simply because they rarely have any choice about a relocation and therefore feel most resentment when they find themselves in a situation in which they've little control or any familiar references. These two groups may also feel alone and isolated – the expatriate wife left behind in the new home while the husband goes to his new office to meet new people who all speak his language; or the expatriate teenager at a new school trying desperately to be accepted by a new peer group. Younger children are also victims of culture shock, although they will probably suffer its effects for a shorter time than their older siblings and parents.

Although culture shock is to a greater or lesser extent unavoidable, its negative effects can be reduced considerably and there are certain things you can do about it before you relocate:

- The key to reducing the negative effects of culture shock is a positive attitude towards your relocation and its country. If you can approach a forthcoming relocation with confidence and convince yourself that the new experience isn't going to be 'bad' but certainly 'different', this will go a long way towards helping you feel less negative and resentful.

- Obviously, in order to feel positive about a relocation, you need to feel confident that it's a good move for you (or your spouse). To help convince yourself you need to have as much information as possible about the new country. Prepare yourself thoroughly before you go. There are literally hundreds of publications about relocation, different countries, culture, etc., as well as numerous websites designed for expatriates (see **Appendices A** to **C**). Discover as much as possible about your new location before you go, so that your arrival and settling in period aren't quite as much of a surprise as they might be. Many expatriate websites provide access to expatriates already living in a country who can answer questions and provide useful help and advice. There are also 'notice boards' on some websites where you can post a message or question. Before you go, try to find someone in your local area who has visited the country and talk to them about it. Some companies organise briefings for families before departure.

- Learn the language. As well as a positive attitude, overcoming the language barrier will probably be the most decisive factor in your time abroad. The ability to speak the local language isn't just a practical and useful tool (the one that will allow you to buy what you need, find your way around, etc.), but it's also the key to understanding a country and its culture. If you can speak the local language, even at a low level, your scope for possible friends and acquaintances is immediately widened beyond the usual limited expatriate circle. Obviously not everyone is a linguist and learning a language can take time and requires motivation. However, with sufficient motivation and perseverance, virtually anyone can learn enough of another language to participate in the local culture. Certainly the effort pays off and expatriates who manage to overcome the language barrier find their experience abroad decidedly richer and more exciting than those who don't. If you make an effort at communicating with the local people in their own language, the chances are that you will also find them far more receptive to you and your needs. See also **Language Schools** on page 169.

- Make a conscious effort to get involved in the new culture. There are usually plenty of local clubs where you can practise sport or keep fit, join an arts club, learn to cook local dishes, taste wine, etc. Not only will this fill some of your spare time, giving you less time to miss home, but you will also meet new people and make friends. If you feel you cannot join a local club, perhaps because the language barrier is too great, then you can always participate in activities for expatriates of which there are usually many in the most popular destinations.

- Get out and see the country and visit the tourist sites and attractions. If possible, make sure your family has plenty of weekend tourist breaks – you may never get the chance again!

- Talk to other expatriates. Although they may deny it, they've all been through exactly what you have and faced the same feeling of disorientation. Even if they may not be able to provide you with advice, it helps to know that you aren't alone and that it gets better in the end.

Culture shock is an unavoidable part of relocation, but if you're aware of it and take steps to lessen its effects before you go and while you're abroad, the chances are that the period of adjustment will be shortened and its negative and depressing consequences reduced.

There are books designed to help you understand and overcome culture shock, including *Breaking Through Culture Shock* by Dr. Elizabeth Marx (Nicolas Brealey) and many expatriate websites also offer advice and help, including many of those listed in **Appendix C**.

CHILDREN

Once you've arrived in your new country, try to establish a routine for your children as soon as possible. Children need routine, which is essentially their point of reference in life and their way of keeping a grip on reality. Whatever circumstances you find yourself in, develop a daily routine so that your children feel more stable and secure (this will also be beneficial for parents!).

Although families may be given relatively short notice before a relocation and you often don't have a lot of choice about when you can arrive in a new country, you should try to arrive a few weeks before the start of a new term or school year. This will give your children time to settle into their new home and surroundings, possibly time to visit their new school, but not so much time that they will become bored without school (and their friends). They will also quickly get back into the school routine, albeit a different one. Be aware that your children's school(s), as well as being totally new, may also have a different educational system or curriculum from what they're used to. They may therefore find themselves immersed in two new cultures, that of the country and the school – to say nothing of possibly having to learn another language!

You should ensure that your children have plenty of contact with home and their friends. It may be possible for them to communicate by email with their friends and previous school class. It also helps to encourage letter writing to friends and relatives. When you first arrive, ensure that your children have plenty of photos and reminders of life back home in their new home, particularly in their bedrooms. However, be aware that your children may quickly consider the new country to be 'home' – probably well before you do!

Encourage your children to learn a new language (see page 157), a task younger children find astonishingly easy compared to adults. Pre-teenage children quickly pick up a foreign tongue and, if they're at a local school rather than an international establishment (where English is the main teaching language), they will usually quickly become fluent. You should encourage this as it has been proved that bilingual children are generally more intelligent, culturally aware and tolerant. However, you should take care that your children aren't bilingual to the detriment of their mother tongue. It's advisable to speak to them in your own language, have a ready supply of books and videos in their native tongue, and to encourage visits to their home country. When children attend a local school where they're taught in a foreign language, expatriate parents often arrange for private English lessons (or lessons in their mother tongue) during school holidays, if possible with other expatriate children.

Expatriates in many countries tend to live their lives in sanitised 'expatriate bubble', within which everything is orientated towards expatriate needs and demands, and where there's little or no contact with the host country's culture or people. You should encourage your children to experience the new culture so that they can understand the real country, rather than seeing it through (rose-tinted?) expatriate spectacles. This will undoubtedly mean greater effort on your part as you will need to find extra motivation to learn the language, to travel, and take part in local customs and traditions. However, if you endeavour to integrate (even to a small extent), it will be much easier for your children to experience the new culture. It's worth bearing in mind that research has shown that expatriate children who are actively exposed to another culture benefit far more than those who are constrained by the 'expatriate bubble'.

With teenagers, you need to take care that they don't feel their lives are too sheltered in their new home. Teenagers, especially older ones, will be used to the freedom afforded them at home, where they probably hung out with their friends at weekends, went shopping at the local mall on their own or with friends, and popped down to the local sports centre for a swim or a game of tennis. The ground rules may be very different abroad and need to be established from the start. If you've moved to a country where teenage children cannot feasibly go on a shopping trip by themselves, then you need to provide some sort of acceptable alternative, preferably one that you've discussed and agreed upon beforehand. Depending on the country and the situation there, you may also need to discuss with your children the potential dangers of drugs, alcohol, prostitution and crime (etc.) in the context of the new culture.

While health and safety issues are of paramount importance for any expatriate, they're even more important when you have children, and they should be planned for thoroughly before leaving your home country. They may include the following:

- **Vaccinations** – Find out well in advance of your departure the vaccinations your family will need and, if there are any optional recommended vaccinations, it's advisable to have those also. Check how long the vaccinations are valid and keep them up to date. Many schools in EU countries require children to have an up to date vaccination card.

- **Medicines & Drugs** – Take useful medicines and a first-aid kit with you. In some EU countries some medicines aren't always available or are difficult to find. Therefore it's advisable to take a good supply of infant analgesic and anti-fever medicines with you. You may also wish to take a supply of anti-diarrhoea and other general drugs for your children.

- **Hygiene** – Scrupulous hygiene often provides the solution to not being ill, particularly in warm countries. Unless the tap water is 100 per cent safe to drink, consume bottled water – but make sure that it's from a reliable source. Wash all fresh produce (fruit and vegetables) thoroughly, and don't use ice made from tap water in drinks unless you're certain it's drinkable. Teach your children not to drink from public water supplies unless it is stated that the water is fit for drinking.

- **Insurance** – Make sure that your health insurance covers your family for all eventualities and that it includes evacuation when treatment isn't available locally (see page 120).

- **Medical Services** – When you arrive at your destination, one of your first priorities should be to find out where the nearest local doctor and hospital are and how to get there. It's advisable to register with a doctor soon after arrival. Children are accident-prone and you never know when you may need medical help. Therefore you should keep a list of emergency numbers by the telephone. Embassies can usually provide the names and addresses of reputable local doctors and clinics, and other expatriates may be able to make recommendations.

- **Local Dangers** – Prepare your children for the possible dangers of their new environment, which may include people, animals and road traffic. Inform them about no-go areas and teach them what to do in threatening situations.

- **Unwelcome Attention** – If your children are fair-haired and you're moving to a southern European country, prepare them for the fact that they (particularly teenager girls) may receive unsolicited attention, although this will be probably be limited to cat calls and wolf whistles. Teach them what to do if they find themselves the centre of unwelcome attention and how to deal with it.

CHECKLISTS

Before Arrival

The checklists on the following pages list tasks which you need (or may need) to complete before and after arrival abroad. They also offer a reminder of the many people whom you may need to inform when moving abroad.

- Check that your family's passports are valid!

- Obtain a visa, if necessary, for all your family members. Obviously this **must** be done **before** travelling abroad.

- Arrange health and travel insurance for your family (see pages 119 and 149 respectively). This is essential if you aren't already covered by a private insurance policy and won't be covered by a country's national health service.

- Open a local bank account and transfer funds – you can open an account with many banks from abroad or even via the internet.

- It's best to obtain some local currency (if possible) before your arrival, which will save you having to change money immediately on arrival. Failing this, take some euros or GB£, which are readily accepted in most countries.

- Obtain an international driver's licence, if necessary.

- If you don't already have one, it's advisable to obtain an international credit card, which will prove invaluable during your first few months abroad.

- If you plan to become a permanent resident, you may also need to do the following:

  - Arrange schooling for your children.

  - Organise the shipment of your personal and household effects.

  - Obtain as many credit references as possible, for example from banks, mortgage companies, credit card companies, credit agencies, companies with which you have had accounts, and references from professionals such as lawyers and accountants. These will help you establish a credit rating abroad.

- Inform:

  - Your landlord, if you live on rented accommodation.

  - Your employer (e.g. give notice or arrange leave of absence).

  - Your local town hall or municipality (you may be entitles to a refund of property or other taxes).

  - The police, if it was necessary to register with them.

  - Your electricity, gas, water and telephone companies (well in advance if you need to have a deposit refunded).

  - Your insurance companies, banks, post office, stockbroker and other financial institutions'; credit card, charge card and hire purchase companies; lawyer and accountant; and local businesses where you have accounts.

  - Your local tax and social security offices.

  - Your family doctor, dentist and other health practitioners (your records should be transferred to your new doctor and dentist abroad).

- Your family's schools (try to give a term's notice and obtain copies of any relevant reports or records).
- All regular correspondents, subscriptions, social and sports clubs, professional and trade journals, friends and relatives. Give them your new address and telephone number and arrange to have your post redirected (by the post office, a friend or a property management company if you are letting your former home).

- Return all library books or anything borrowed.

- Arrange shipment of your furniture and belongings, by booking a shipping company well in advance (see page 102). International shipping companies can provide a wealth of information about relocation. Find out the procedure for shipping your belongings from a local embassy or consulate.

- Arrange to sell anything you aren't taking with you (e.g.. house, car, furniture). If you're selling a hoe or business, obtain legal advice, as you may be able to save tax by establishing a trust or other legal vehicle. If you own more than one property, you may have to pay capital gains tax on the profits from selling all but your principal home.

- If you are exporting a car, complete the paperwork for doing so and re-register on arrival. You may also have to return the registration plates. Contact a local embassy or consulate for information.

- Arrange inoculations, documentation and shipment for any pets you're taking with you (see page 199);

- It's advisable to arrange health, dental and optical tests for your family before leaving (see **Chapter 4**) and have any necessary or recommended inoculations. Obtain copies of health records and a statement from your private health insurance company of your present level of cover.

- Check if you qualify for rebates on tax and/or social security contributions. You may also have the option to continue making contributions to qualify for a full, or larger, pension when you retire. Contact your company personnel department for information on your company pension.

- Terminate any outstanding loan, lease of hire purchase contracts and pay bills (allow plenty of time, as some companies may be slow to respond).

- Check whether you're entitled to a rebate on your road tax, car or other insurance. Obtain statements of no-claims discounts.

- Check whether you nee an international driving permit or a translation of your driving licence(s). Some non-EU residents may be required to take a driving test (see page 36).

- If you will be living abroad for an extended period (but not permanently), you may wish to give someone a power of attorney so that they can handle your financial affairs in your home country while you are away. This can be for a fixed period, open-ended or limited to specific purposes. **You should seek legal advice before doing this!**

- Allow plenty of time to get to your port or airport of departure, check in your luggage and clear security and immigration.

After Arrival

The following checklist contains a summary of tasks to be completed after arrival (if not already done before):

- On arrival at an airport, port or land border post, have your visa cancelled and your passport stamped, as applicable.
- If you're not taking a car with you, you may wish to hire one (see page 35) or buy one locally. It's difficult to get around in many countries without a car, unless you live in a major city. In rural areas, it's practically impossible.
- Open a bank account (see page 132) at a local bank and give details to your employer and any companies you plan to pay by direct debit or standing order;
- Arrange any necessary insurances (e.g. health, car, home).
- Contact offices and organisations to obtain local information;
- It's advisable to make courtesy calls on your neighbours and the local mayor soon after arrival. This is particularly important in villages and rural areas if you want to be accepted and to integrate into the local community.
- If you plan to become resident abroad, you may need to do the following within the next few weeks (if not done already):
  - Apply for a residence permit.
  - Register for membership of the state health service.
  - Register with a local doctor and dentist.
  - Apply for a local driving licence (see page 36).
  - Arrange schooling for your children.

Have a good trip!

8.

MISCELLANEOUS MATTERS

This chapter covers important miscellaneous considerations and includes information about climate, crime, pets, safety, shopping abroad, social customs, television and radio, and time difference.

CLIMATE

For most people the climate is one of the most important factors when deciding where (or whether) to live in the EU, particularly if you have a choice of countries or are planning to retire. When choosing where to live, you should consider the climate in both winter and summer, the average daily sunshine, plus the rainfall and wind conditions. You may also wish to check whether an area is noted for fog, which can make driving conditions hazardous.

The best climate in which to live is generally considered to be one without big extremes of cold and heat, and where the average temperature over the year has the smallest swings between the coldest and hottest days. Examples are such places as the Algarve in Portugal, Cyprus, the Greek island of Crete and the Canary Islands, the Costa Blanca and Costa del Sol in Spain. You may also wish to avoid the coldest countries such as those in Northern Europe, where winters can be severe, lasting five months or longer, and driving conditions can be very bad. On the other hand, you may also want to avoid countries that experience extremely hot conditions in the summer (most of Europe in summer 2003!).

In winter in northern Europe and some central European locations, such as southern Germany and Austria, it's cold or freezing everywhere and snowfalls may be frequent as well as chilling winds and occasional ice storms, when 'snow' instantly freezes forming a thick coat of ice on everything. Temperatures are often reduced considerably by the wind speed, which creates what's known as the wind chill factor. A temperature of 10°F (-12°C) combined with a wind speed of 25mph (40kph) results in a wind chill factor of -29°F (-34°C). If you're a keen skier you will welcome some snow, but won't perhaps be so enthusiastic when snowdrifts make the roads impassable, engulf your home and cut you off from the outside world!

It's important to check whether an area is prone to natural disasters such as floods (which are common in many EU countries – Germany is still counting the cost of the terrible floods in 2002), storms (sometimes with hurricanes or tornadoes), forest fires, landslides or earthquakes. Forest fires are a danger in summer in many EU countries, particularly those in the south (the south of France and Portugal were affected badly in summer 2003), while earthquakes are a constant threat in some southern European countries, particularly parts of Italy.

Many countries have experienced severe flooding in recent years, including the UK, France, Germany and Italy. Every year there is flooding somewhere in the EU and flash floods can be dangerous in some countries, particularly in mountainous areas. If you live near a coast or waterway it can be expensive to insure against floods. The good news is that your chances of experiencing a hurricane, tornado, flood, earthquake or forest fire are rare in most areas. On the other hand, in regions with little rainfall (e.g. much of southern Europe) there are often droughts and severe water restrictions (plus high water bills).

In some countries people overreact to extremes of climate with freezing air-conditioning in summer and sweltering heating in winter. Because most buildings are either too hot or too cold, it's often a problem knowing what to wear and people dress in layers that they take off or put on, depending on the indoor or outdoor temperature. Many people use humidifiers to counteract the dry air caused by powerful heating or air-conditioning.

Weather forecasts are given in newspapers and broadcast on radio and TV stations, and European weather conditions are also available via many websites, including ⌨ www.worldclimate.com (average statistics for most European cities), ⌨ http://asp.wn.com/worldweather/europe, ⌨ http://weather.yahoo.com/regional/EUROPEX and ⌨ www.bbc.co.uk/weather/world/europe.

CRIME

The crime rate (and what constitutes a crime) varies considerably from country to country. Therefore it's important to investigate the level in a particular country, region or city before deciding where to live. Most EU countries are very safe places to live and several (e.g. Austria, Cyprus, Denmark, Finland, Greece, Malta and Sweden) are among the safest places to live in the world. However, the crime rate in some EU cities, particularly drug-related crime, can be high. Major cities have the highest crime rates and some areas are best avoided at night. Many cities, particularly those in Eastern European countries, are notorious for petty crime such as handbag snatching, pickpockets and thefts of (and from) vehicles. In contrast, crime in villages and rural areas (away from tourist areas) is virtually unknown in most EU countries and windows and doors are often left unlocked.

The most common crime is theft, which embraces a multitude of forms. One of the most common in southern European countries is the bag snatcher, possibly on a motorbike or moped, grabbing a hand or shoulder bag (or a camera) and riding off with it, sometimes with the owner still attached (occasionally causing serious injuries). It's advisable to carry bags on the inside of the pavement and to wear shoulder bags diagonally across your chest, although it's better not to carry a bag at all (the strap can be cut) but to wear a wrist pouch or money belt. You should also be wary of bag snatchers in airport and other car parks, and never wear valuable jewellery and watches in high-risk areas. Motorcycle thieves may smash car windows at traffic lights to steal articles left on seats, so bags should be stowed on the floor or behind seats.

Tourists and travellers are the targets of many of the world's most enterprising criminals, including highwaymen, who pose as accident or breakdown victims and rob motorists who stop to help them. Don't leave cash or valuables unattended when swimming or leave your bags, cameras, mobile phones or jackets lying around on chairs in cafés or bars (always keep an eye on your belongings in public places). Beware of gangs of child thieves in cities, pickpockets and over-friendly strangers. Always remain vigilant in tourist haunts, queues and anywhere there are large crowds, and never tempt fate with an exposed wallet or purse or by flashing your money around. One of the most effective ways of protecting your passport, money, travellers cheques and credit cards is with an old-fashioned money belt.

Foreigners (particularly holiday home owners) are often victims of housebreaking and burglary, which are rife in resort areas in most EU countries. Always ensure that your home is secure (see page 104) and that your belongings are well insured, and never leave valuables lying around. It's advisable to install a safe if you keep valuables (e.g. jewellery) or cash in your home. In some EU countries, property developments (particularly luxury ones in resort areas or major cities) may be patrolled by security guards, although they often have little influence on crime rates and may instil a false sense of security. It's advisable to arrange for someone to check a property periodically when it's left unoccupied.

Fortunately, violent crime is still relatively rare in EU countries, although muggings, murders, rapes and armed robbery have increased considerably in the last decade or so in many countries. There are also dangers for women travelling alone and hitchhiking isn't recommended anywhere. Sexual harassment is also a problem in some countries (Greece in particular), where women (especially blondes) are often subjected to unwanted attention. It's advisable for lone women to use taxis rather than public transport late at night.

Drug addiction is the main impetus for crime in many EU countries, where in some major cities the bulk of crime may be drug-related. Drug addiction is a huge and growing problem throughout the EU (and the world) and drug addicts (and prostitutes) are a common sight in many major towns and cities. It's an offence to possess soft drugs such as hashish in many EU countries, while in some (e.g. the Netherlands and Spain) it's legal for personal use or the law tends to turn a blind eye to its use. However, the possession and use of hard drugs such as heroin and cocaine is strictly prohibited in all EU countries and the penalties for trafficking are high. You should also be wary of giving strangers lifts and **never** transport anyone across an international border.

In some EU countries 'petty' laws (such as illegal parking and jaywalking) may be widely ignored, while in others they're strictly enforced, therefore it's important to know the local ropes.

One of the biggest financial threats to foreigners abroad isn't from the locals, but from your own countrymen and other foreigners. It's common for expatriate 'businessmen' in some countries to run up huge debts, either through dishonesty or incompetence, and cut and run owing their clients and suppliers a fortune. In many resort areas, confidence tricksters, swindlers, cheats and fraudsters lie in wait and newcomers must constantly be on their guard (particularly when buying a business). Fraud of every conceivable kind is a fine art in many countries. Always be wary of someone who offers to do you a favour or show you the ropes, or anyone claiming to know how to 'beat the system'. **If anything sounds too good to be true, you can bet it almost certainly is.** It's a sad fact of life, but you should generally be more wary of doing business with your fellow countrymen abroad than with the local populace.

Despite the foregoing catalogue of disasters, in most EU countries you can usually safely walk almost anywhere at any time of the day or night, and there's absolutely no need for anxiety or paranoia about crime. However, you should be 'street-wise' and take certain elementary precautions, including learning the 'ground rules' (which vary from country to country). If you follow the rules, your chances of being a victim of crime are usually low – but break the rules and they rise dramatically. These include avoiding high-risk areas, particularly those frequented by drug addicts, prostitutes and pickpockets. When you're in an unfamiliar city, ask a tourist office official, policeman, taxi driver or other local person about any unsafe neighbourhoods – and avoid them! As with most things in life, prevention is better than cure. This is particularly true when it comes to crime prevention, as only a relatively small percentage of crimes are solved and the legal process in some EU countries is agonisingly slow. It's also important to have adequate insurance for your possessions.

Crime Prevention & Safety

Staying safe in a large city is largely a matter of common sense (plus a little luck), although you need to develop survival skills in some cities. Most areas are safe most of the time, particularly when there are a lot of people about. At night, stick to brightly lit main streets and avoid secluded areas (best of all, take a taxi). Walk in the opposite direction to the traffic so no one can curb-crawl (drive alongside) you at night. Walk on the outside of the pavement (sidewalk), so you're less likely to be mugged from a doorway. Avoid parks at night and keep to a park's main paths or where there are other people during the day.

If you find yourself in a deserted area late at night, remain calm and look as though you know where you're going by walking briskly. If you need to wait for a train or bus at night, do so in the main waiting room, a well-lit area, or where there's a guard or policeman. If possible, avoid using subways in the late evening or after midnight. Most major cities have 'no-go' areas at night and some have areas that are to be avoided at any time. Women should take particular care and should never hitchhike alone; rape statistics are extremely high in some countries and most go unreported.

It's advisable to carry the bare minimum of cash on you, say €20 to €50, referred to as 'mugger's money' in the US. This is because in the event that you're mugged, it's usually sufficient to satisfy a mugger and prevent him from becoming violent (or searching further). In some countries, parents give their children mugger's money as a matter of course whenever they leave home. You should warn your children about the dangers of street life, particularly if you've been living in a country where it's taken for granted that you can safely go anywhere at any time of the day or night. It may be necessary to re-educate your family regarding all aspects of public life. Wherever you live and whatever the age of your children, you should warn them against taking unnecessary risks and discourage them from frequenting remote or high-risk areas, talking to strangers or attracting unwanted attention.

Some experts advise you to keep your cash in at least two separate places and to split cash and credit cards. Don't keep your ID card or passport, driver's licence and other important documents in your wallet or purse where they can be stolen. Never resist a mugger. It's far better to lose your wallet and jewellery than your life! Many muggers are desperate and irrational people under the influence of drugs, and they may turn violent if resisted. Anaesthetic sprays sold in drugstores or ordinary hair or insect sprays are carried by some people to deter assailants (as are pepper sprays and mace, although usually illegal). These are, however, of little use against an armed assailant and may increase the likelihood of violence.

Don't leave cash, cheques, credit cards, passports, jewellery and other valuables lying around or even hidden in your home. Good quality door and window locks and an alarm will help, but may not deter a determined thief. In many cities, triple door locks, metal bars and steel bars on windows are standard fittings. If you live in a city, you should be wary of anyone hanging around outside your home or apartment block. Have your keys ready and enter your home as quickly as possible. Most city dwellers always lock their doors and windows, even when going out for a few minutes only.

Often apartments are fitted with a security system, so that you can speak to visitors before allowing them access to your building. Luxury apartment buildings may have (armed) guards in the lobby with closed-circuit TV and voice identification security systems. In addition, most apartment doors have a peephole and security chain, so you can check a caller's identity before opening the door. Be careful whom you allow into your home and check the identity of anyone claiming to be an official inspector or an employee of a utility company. Ask for ID and confirm it with their office before opening the door. Also beware of bogus policemen (who may flash an imitation badge), who may stop you in the street and ask to see your money and passport – and then run off with them!

Store anything of value in a home safe or a bank safety deposit box and ensure that you have adequate insurance. Never make it obvious that no one is at home by leaving tell-tale signs such as a pile of newspapers or post. Many people leave lights, a radio or a TV on (activated by random timers) when they aren't at home. Ask your neighbours to keep an eye on your home when you're on holiday. Many towns have crime watch areas, where residents keep an eye open for suspicious characters and report them to the local police.

If you're driving, keep to the main highways and avoid high-risk areas. Never drive in cities with your windows or doors open or valuables (such as handbags or wallets) on the seats. Take extra care at night in car parks and when returning to your car, and never sleep in your car. If you have an accident in a dangerous or hostile area (any inner-city area), police often advise you not to stop, but to drive to the nearest police station to report it. In remote areas, accidents are sometimes staged to rob unsuspecting drivers (called 'highway hold-ups') and cars are deliberately bumped to get drivers to stop (again, seek out the nearest police station). If you stop at an accident in a remote area or are flagged down, keep the engine running and in gear and your doors locked (ready to make a fast getaway), and only open your window a fraction to speak to someone. In some countries, hire cars are targeted by muggers and you should be wary of collecting a hire car from an airport at night.

In most EU countries, police forces, governments, local communities and security companies all publish information and advice regarding crime prevention. Your local police station may also carry out a free home security check. See also **Car Security** on page 39 and **Home Security** on page 104.

THE EUROPEAN UNION

The European Union (EU) is a trade organisation providing a single market among member states, which on 1st May 2004 (when it increased from 15 to 25 members) included: Austria, Belgium, Cyprus, the Czech Republic, Denmark, Estonia, Finland, France, Germany, Greece, Hungary, Ireland, Italy, Latvia, Lithuania, Luxembourg, Malta, the Netherlands, Poland, Portugal, Slovakia, Slovenia, Spain, Sweden and the UK. The *raison d'etre* of the EU and the philosophy behind its creation was to provide a 'single' European market for goods, services, capital and labour, free of restrictions such as work permits, customs duties and tariffs. Similar 'unions' exist between other countries including Canada, Mexico and the US (which comprise the North American Free Trade Association or NAFTA) and Argentina, Brazil, Paraguay and Uruguay (which make up Mercosur), although the EU is by far the most diverse and influential organisation.

Over the years, however, the EU has developed into much more than a free-trade organisation with far-reaching policies and laws that apply to all members, and its own parliament, commission, courts and council. Individual member states do, however, retain national sovereignty and have considerable autonomy over domestic affairs (although less than some people would like). The EU is represented in many international political and economic bodies and contributes to numerous projects in developing and underdeveloped countries. Currently there's no single EU military body, although there's a 'rapid-response' force comprising troops from the major EU countries and most member states are also members of NATO. However, a 'European' army is planned along with an EU police force. The euro is the EU's single currency, although not all EU countries have adopted it (see **Currency** on page 129).

The EU is, in general, a united group and referendums on accession have been approved in most candidate countries (old and new), usually by a comfortable majority. It's not all smooth running, however, and frequent disagreements crop up, such as Ireland's rejection of the enlargement of the EU in a referendum in 2001 (the country later accepted enlargement in a second referendum) and more recently, the acrimonious split over the decision to invade Iraq in 2003 between (mainly) France and Germany on the one hand and Italy, Spain and the UK on the other.

The first attempts at some sort of European union were made in 1948 by the Benelux countries (Belgium, the Netherlands and Luxembourg), who formed the Benelux Customs Union while most of Europe was still suffering from the crippling aftermath of the Second World War. The Benelux Customs Union laid the foundations for a larger European union and in 1951 France, Germany and Italy joined the Benelux countries to form the European Coal and Steel

Community (ECSC), which then became the European Economic Community (EEC) in 1957. Denmark, Ireland and the UK joined in 1973, followed by Greece in 1981, Portugal and Spain in 1986, and Austria, Finland and Sweden in 1995. (See the **Map** in **Appendix E**) Under the Maastricht Treaty of 1991, the EEC was renamed the European Union (EU).

The EU's next enlargement, and greatest economic and political challenge, came in May 2004 when ten new states joined: Cyprus, the Czech Republic, Estonia, Hungary, Latvia, Lithuania, Malta, Poland, Slovakia and Slovenia. This increased the EU's population by some 20 per cent to almost 450 million, although its GDP grew by a mere 4.4 per cent (GDP per capita actually fell by 13 per cent). The enlargement came at a time when economies throughout the world had slumped; several EU countries officially went into recession in 2003 and GDP growth in the euro zone was zero.

The long-term benefits of enlargement aren't expected to be felt for at least five years and for some new members it could take much longer. There will inevitably be teething problems as the new members get to grips with EU laws, policies and red tape, although most have already done the groundwork. Some of the existing (prior to 1st May 2004) member states lost valuable EU funds in favour of the new states, although enlargement is expected to lead to an increase in the gap between the richest and poorest members, accentuating the impression of a two-speed union. However, the biggest challenge facing the EU will be producing a European Constitution, on which members failed to agree in 2003.

EU Institutions

Below is a brief guide to the main EU institutions and fundamental aspects underlying the concept of the EU. Further and more comprehensive information is provided in numerous books (see **Appendix B** for details) and from EU offices and the official EU website (🖳 http://europa.eu.int).

Acquis Communautaire: This is the term (which can be translated as 'the Community Patrimony') used to denote the principles, policies, laws, practices, obligations and objectives that have been agreed or developed within the EU. In short, everything the EU stands for! The term is particularly important when a new member state joins the EU, as it must accept the *acquis communautaire* in its entirety in order to join.

EU Capitals

Brussels and Luxembourg. Brussels is the main capital and as such houses many EU institutions and bodies including: the Council of Ministers (the main decision-making body in the EU); the European Commission (essentially the EU's civil service, employing some 21,000 people); the Economic and Social Committee; and the Committee of Regions. The European Parliament (based in Strasbourg) also has many staff in Brussels and national representatives from the member states are also based there – Brussels has the world's second-largest press corps after Washington. Luxembourg is home to part of the European Parliament and the European Court of Justice.

European Constitution

This presents one of the main challenges facing the 'new' EU and the one currently causing most problems, mainly concerning the allocation of power and voting rights within the enlarged EU. Smaller countries are worried that they may lose power in important decision-making in favour of the large countries such as France and Germany, which between them comprise 60 per cent of the EU's GDP. At present an agreement on the European constitution seems unlikely despite frantic diplomacy by politicians – the Italian premier, Silvio Berlusconi, claimed he was so stressed by his own efforts at consensus that he was forced to retire briefly to a Swiss spa centre! Whether diplomacy and consensus manage to iron out many of the discrepancies remains to be seen.

European Council

This is the name given to the meetings (often known as 'summits') held by the leaders of the EU member states and the president of the European Commission (currently Romano Prodi). The Council usually meets four times a year and many of the EU's most important decisions are made at these meetings.

European Courts

The European Court of Justice in Luxembourg deals with disputes arising from the interpretation of applications of EU treaties or legislation based on them. The European Court of Humans Rights in Strasbourg deals with claims of violations of human rights within the EU.

European Elections

Elections to the European Parliament are held every five years (the next elections are due in June 2004) and are the world's only international elections. In the new EU there will be 732 European Members of Parliament (MEPs). The number for each EU member state depends on its population, e.g. Germany has 99 MEPs, Ireland 13 and Estonia 6. National and European parties are represented and in the 1999 elections some 16 parties had seats in the European Parliament. These included conservatives, socialists and liberals, as well as more unusual parties such as the 'Anti-Maastricht Danes', the Austrian Freedom Party and the 'French Defenders of Rural Traditions' – a mixture that would seem to put pay to worries that the EU removes individual states' identities!

The turnout for European elections ranges from poor (little more than 30 per cent in some member states) to high in others, although EU nationals generally appear to have little interest in who represents them at the EU level. All EU nationals are entitled to vote in European elections irrespective of where they live in the EU, although they must cast their vote in the country where they are resident – so if you're Danish but live in Spain, you must vote for a Spanish MEP.

European Parliament

The European Parliament is made up of the MEPs (see **European Elections** above) elected by EU nationals in European elections. Its headquarters are in Strasbourg, although committees also meet in Brussels and Luxembourg. The European Parliament has four main powers: legislative, budget, international agreements and supervisory, and as such, is the EU's most powerful body.

Four Freedoms

There are 'four freedoms' that encapsulate the essence of the EU single market, which are described below:

- **Freedom Of Movement Of Capital** – Under EU legislation, all restrictions on the free movement of capital between member states have been removed. However, you may have to declare the movement of capital or the origin of funds from one EU state to another, and some EU countries require you to make a customs declaration if you import or export capital above a certain amount (a measure designed to prevent money laundering).

- **Freedom Of Movement Of Goods** – A fundamental part of the single market concept under which there are no customs duties on imports and exports between member states. However, there are still limits on duty-free purchases between member states.

- **Freedom Of Movement Of People** – This is probably the most important 'freedom' and the one that affects most EU nationals. This freedom gives EU nationals the right to travel and live or work anywhere within the EU. This also applies to EEA member countries (which include the EU countries plus Iceland, Liechtenstein and Norway). Freedom of movement also includes the right to practise a trade or profession (as an employee or self-employed) anywhere in the EU, and all member states are obliged to recognise qualifications awarded in another member state. There are certain limitations to the freedom of movement, e.g. in order to reside in another EU country you must prove that you have sufficient funds, and employment in the public service is usually open to nationals only.

- **Freedom To Provide Services** – EU nationals are permitted to provide services (commercial, industrial and professional) anywhere in the EU without the necessity of being established (i.e. maintain an office) in the country where the service is provided. This also applies to the EEA.

Further Information

Certain 'Euro Facts' are included in **Chapter 8 – Miscellaneous Matters**, and further information about the EU is available from numerous books on the subject (see **Appendix B**) including the excellent *Penguin Companion to the European Union* by Timothy Bainbridge (Penguin). The EU also provides a wealth of information from its offices in member states and its website (🖳 http://europa.eu.int), where most information is provided in the languages of the 15 member states prior to 1st May 2004. It contains excellent 'factsheets' on numerous aspects of life in each member state, as well as vast sources of additional information. The EU also provides a useful freephone information service from anywhere within the EU (☎ 00-800 6789 1011) and the Europe Direct website (🖳 http://europedirect-cc-cec.eu.int) where you can make enquiries 'live' (rather like a chatroom), which is particularly useful if you can't find your way around the main website.

PETS

If you plan to take a pet to the EU or to another country within the EU, it's important to check the latest regulations. Make sure that you have the correct papers, not only for your country of destination, but for all the countries you will pass through to reach it, e.g. when travelling overland. Particular consideration must be given before exporting a pet from a country with strict quarantine regulations. If you need to return prematurely, even after a few hours or days abroad, your pet may need to go into quarantine.

Several EU countries in addition to the UK operate a quarantine period (e.g. Cyprus, Ireland, Malta and Sweden), which may be in the owner's own home (e.g. Cyprus and Ireland), and some (such as Sweden and the UK) have a pet's passport scheme. All EU countries require pets to have a health certificate issued by an approved veterinary surgeon and practically all EU countries require vaccination certificates for rabies and possibly other diseases. Even if a rabies vaccination isn't required to import an animal, it's worth getting your pet vaccinated against rabies since the disease exists in many parts of eastern Europe, although it's close to being eradicated within the original 15 member countries of the EU. A rabies vaccination must usually be given not less than 20 days or more than 11 months prior to the date of issue of the health certificate. Pets aged under 12 weeks are usually exempt, but must have a health certificate and a certificate stating that no cases of rabies have occurred for at least six months in the local area. There's no quarantine period (or a much- reduced one) in Ireland, Malta and Sweden when pets are exported from countries without rabies.

If you're transporting a pet by ship or ferry, you should notify the shipping company. Some companies insist that pets are left in vehicles (if applicable), while others allow pets to be kept in cabins. If your pet is of nervous disposition or unused to travelling, it's best to tranquillise it on a long sea crossing. Pets can also be transported by air: contact airlines for information. Animals may be examined at the port of entry by a veterinary officer in the country of destination, as is the case of Slovakia.

In some EU countries, such as Belgium, France, Italy and Spain, pets must be registered and may be issued with a disc to be worn on a collar around their neck, while others require dogs to be tattooed on their body or in an ear as a means of registration. In recent years, many countries have introduced a microchip identification system (replacing tattooing) for dogs, whereby a microchip is inserted under the skin. Registration can be expensive, particularly if you have more than one dog. Regardless of whether your dog is tattooed or microchipped, it's advisable to have it fitted with a collar and tag with your name and telephone number on it, and the magic word 'reward'. Most countries have rules regarding the keeping of dogs, which may require a health card if they're older than three months. In public areas, a dog may need to be kept on a lead (and muzzled if it's dangerous) and wear a health disc on its collar. Dogs are usually prohibited from entering places where food is manufactured, stored or sold, and may also be barred from sports and cultural events, and banned from beaches. Some EU countries (e.g. Austria, Germany and the Netherlands) levy an annual dog tax on dog owners and amounts range from €45 to €105 depending on the size of the dog.

If you intend to live abroad permanently, dogs should also be vaccinated against certain other diseases in addition to rabies, which may include hepatitis, distemper and kennel cough. Cats should be immunised against feline gastroenteritis and typhus. Pets should also be checked frequently for ticks and tapeworm. There are diseases and dangers for pets in some countries that aren't found in North America and Northern Europe. These include the fatal leishmaniasis (also called Mediterranean or sandfly disease), that can be prevented by using sprays or collars, as well as processionary caterpillars, leeches, heartworm, ticks (a tick collar can prevent these), feline leukemia virus and feline enteritis. Obtain advice about these and other diseases from a vet in your home country or on arrival abroad. Take extra care when walking your dog in country areas, as hunters sometimes put down poisoned food to control natural predators. Don't let your dog far out of your sight or let it roam free, as dogs may be stolen (pedigree dogs are particular targets) or mistakenly shot by hunters.

Health insurance for pets is available in most EU countries (vet fees can be astronomical) and it's advisable to have third party insurance in case your pet bites someone or causes an accident. In areas where there are poisonous snakes, some owners keep anti-venom (which must be changed annually) in a refrigerator. In some countries the keeping of dogs may be restricted or banned from long-term rental or holiday accommodation (so check in advance). Some countries also have strict laws regarding cleaning up after pets in public places (so called 'poop-scoop' laws) and you can be heavily fined for not doing so.

Veterinary surgeons are well-trained in EU countries, where there are also kennels, catteries and animal hospitals and clinics (which may provide a 24-hour emergency service), and even pet cemeteries. There are also animal welfare organisations in many countries, operating shelters for stray and abused animals and inexpensive pet hospitals.

EU Pet Passport

In 2003, members of the EU Parliament approved legislation for an EU Pet Passport, designed to facilitate the transit of pets within the EU. The passport will be issued by vets to pets within the EU and will include details of all vaccinations, including rabies, and the animal's microchip number. The passport is expected to be introduced during 2004, but there will be a five-year transitional period for Ireland, Sweden and the UK, which will maintain present quarantine regulations until then.

British Pet Owners

In 2000, the UK introduced a pilot Pet Travel Scheme (PETS), which replaced quarantine for qualifying cats and dogs. Under the scheme, pets must be microchipped (they have a microchip inserted in their neck), vaccinated against rabies, undergo a blood test and be issued with a health certificate. **The PETS certificate isn't issued until six months after these treatments have been carried out.** Pets must also be checked for ticks and tapeworm 24 to 48 hours before embarkation on a plane or ship.

The scheme is restricted to animals imported from rabies-free countries and countries where rabies is under control, namely 26 European countries (the 15 original EU countries plus Andorra, Cyprus, Gibraltar, Iceland, Liechtenstein, Malta, Monaco, Norway, San Marino, Switzerland and the Vatican), and Canada, Bahrain and the US. The current quarantine law will remain in place for pets coming from Eastern Europe, Africa, Asia and South America. The new regulations cost pet owners around €300/GB£200 (for a microchip, rabies vaccination and blood test), plus €90/GB£60 per year for annual booster vaccinations and around €30/GB£20 for a border check. Shop around and compare fees from a number of veterinary surgeons. To qualify, pets must travel by sea via Dover or Portsmouth, by train via the Channel Tunnel or via Gatwick or Heathrow airports (only certain carriers are licensed to carry animals and they can usually take only one animal per flight). Additional information is available from Department for Environment, Food and Rural Affairs (DEFRA), Animal Health (International Trade) Area 201, 1A Page Street, London SW1P 4PQ, UK (☎ 0870-241 1710, 💻 www.defra.gov.uk/animalh/quarantine).

British owners must complete an Application for a Ministry Export Certificate for dogs, cats and rabies-susceptible animals (form EXA1), available from DEFRA at the above address. DEFRA will contact a vet you've named on the form and he will perform a health inspection. You will then receive an export health certificate, which must be issued no more than 30 days before your entry into another EU country with your pet.

Further information is available from DEFRA (☎ UK 020-7904 6000 or 020-7238 6951, ✉ pets.helpline@defra.gsi.gov.uk).

SAFETY

Although most countries in the EU are generally very stable, it's important to be aware of anything that's happening in a country where you're planning to live or work that could affect your personal safety, such as riots, terrorism, kidnappings and general civil unrest, to name but a few. You also need to be aware of crime and drugs (see page 191), health (see **Chapter 4**), motoring problems (see page 34), and how to deal with local officials and matters such as bribery and corruption – which is a way of life in parts of some countries. If you have any problems concerning safety while abroad, you should contact your local consulate or embassy for advice. If you register with your local embassy (see page 177) they will contact you in times of serious civil unrest and may assist you in returning home (if necessary).

Most governments post warnings for their nationals on official websites. In many cases, these will apply to all travellers and can, of course, be referred to by anyone. It's rare to find any EU countries on these listings, but it may be worth checking. Websites include the US Department of State (🖳 http://travel.state.gov/travel_warnings and http://travel.state.gov/warnings_list); this website also contains warnings about drugs (🖳 http://travel.state.gov/drug_warning) and a list of useful travel publications (🖳 http://travel.state.gov/travel_pubs). Other useful websites include the British Foreign and Commonwealth Office (🖳 www.fco.gov.uk/travel), SaveWealth Travel (🖳 www.savewealth.com/travel/warnings) and the Australian Department of Foreign Affairs and Trade (🖳 www.dfat.gov.au/travel).

There are also many books about safety for travellers, including *Your Passport to Safer Travel* edited by Mark Hodson (Thomas Cook) and *Safety and Security for Women Who Travel* by Sheila Swan (Travelers' Tales). Safety information may also be available via your local television teletext service, e.g. BBC Ceefax in the UK.

Where applicable, warnings are also included under **Political Stability** or **Crime Rate** in the **Country Profiles** in **Chapter 9**, although these aren't comprehensive and are intended only as a guide.

SHOPPING ABROAD

Shopping by mail order, phone, fax or via the internet is popular among expatriates in many countries, particularly those where it's difficult or impossible to buy many western goods (or they're prohibitively expensive). Direct retailing by companies (cutting out the middle man) has becoming much more widespread in recent years and many companies sell goods and services by post, often via their own websites.

Many major stores publish catalogues and will send goods anywhere in the world, particularly American and British stores. Many companies provide account facilities or payment can be made by credit card. Although some foreign mail order companies won't send goods abroad, there's nothing to prevent your obtaining catalogues via friends or relatives and ordering through them. Buying goods mail order from the US can result in huge savings, even after paying postage and local taxes. One company of interest to avid mail order shoppers is Shop the World by Mail (💻 www.shoptheworldbymail) which publishes a catalogue of catalogues of US mail order companies.

Internet Shopping

Retailers and manufacturers in most countries offer internet shopping, but the real benefit comes when shopping abroad, when savings can be made on a wide range of products (you can buy virtually anything via the internet). However, when comparing prices, take into account shipping costs, insurance, duty and VAT. Shopping on the internet is very secure (secure servers, with addresses beginning https://rather than http://, are almost impossible to crack) and in most cases safer than shopping by phone or mail order. **However, it isn't foolproof and credit card fraud is a growing problem.**

To find companies or products via the internet, simply use a search engine such as Altavista, Google or Yahoo. Useful sites include 💻 www.allucanbuy (includes a useful directory of internet shopping); 💻 www.myprimetime.com; 💻 www.pricewatch.com, 💻 www.mytaxi.co.uk (which contains internet addresses of 2,500 retail and information sites); 💻 www.amazingemporium.co.uk (furniture); 💻 www.buy.com (which also publishes an e-zine, *BuyMagazine*); 💻 www.eurooffice.co.uk (office supplies); 💻 www.usecolor.com; and 💻 www. virgin.net (which has a good directory of British shopping sites). Many websites offer online auctions, including 💻 www.qxl.com; 💻 www.ebay.com (and 💻 www.ebay.co.uk as well as sites in France, Germany, Ireland, Italy and Spain); 💻 www.auctions.yahoo.com; and 💻 www.loot.com. Many websites also provide useful advice about shopping abroad.

With internet shopping, the world is your oyster and savings can be made on a wide range of goods, including CDs, clothes, sports equipment, electronic gadgets, jewellery, books, wine and computer software, and services such as insurance, pensions and mortgages. Savings can also be made on holidays. Small high-price, high-tech items (e.g. cameras, watches and computers) can usually be purchased more cheaply somewhere abroad, particularly in the US, with delivery by courier worldwide within as little as three days.

When buying goods overseas you should ensure that you're dealing with a bona fide company and that the goods will work in your country of residence (e.g. electrical equipment or video games). You should also check the vendor's returns policy. You may not be protected by consumer protection legislation when shopping abroad and, should anything go wrong, it can take ages to get it resolved. If possible, always pay by credit card when buying by mail order or over the internet, as you have more security and the credit card issuer may be jointly liable with the supplier. **When you buy expensive goods abroad, always have them insured for their full value.**

When you purchase a large item abroad, it's advisable to have it shipped by air freight to the nearest international airport. The receiving freight company will notify you when it has arrived and you must usually provide them with details of the contents and cost so that they can clear it through customs. They will deliver the goods to you with the bill for taxes, duty and freight, payable on the spot, unless you make alternative arrangements.

Taxes & Duty

When buying overseas, take into account shipping costs, duty, VAT and other taxes. Carefully calculate the total cost in local currency or the currency in which you're paying – you can do this with the universal currency converter (🖥 www.xe.com). There's no duty or tax on goods purchased within the EU. Most countries levy no taxes on goods imported from abroad below a certain nominal value (e.g. GB£18 in the UK). Don't buy alcohol or cigarettes abroad, as the duty is often too high to make it pay (and it may be illegal!). When VAT or duty is payable, the payment is usually collected by the post office or courier company on delivery.

Duty-Free Allowances

Travellers going from one EU country to another are permitted to enter with the following:

- 800 cigarettes;
- 400 cigarillos;
- 200 cigars;
- 1kg tobacco;
- 10 litres of spirits;
- 20 litres of fortified wine (e.g. port or sherry);
- 90 litres of wine (of which a maximum of 60 litres may be sparkling wine);
- 110 litres of beer.

The above allowances are issued as guidelines only and the goods are considered to be for your own use.

If you enter the EU from a non-EU country, including the Canary Islands, the Channel Islands, and Gibraltar, you may bring the following:

- 200 cigarettes (100 cigarettes for Danish residents who have spent less than 24 hours in another country).
- 100 cigarillos or 50 cigars or 250g of tobacco.
- 1 litre of spirits over 22 per cent volume (Danish residents who have spent less than 24 hours in another country cannot bring in spirits).
- 2 litres of fortified or sparkling wine.
- 2 litres of still wine.

- 50g of perfume.
- 250ml eau de toilette.
- Other goods up to the value of €175 (€90 for travellers under 15, except for entry to Denmark, Germany, the Netherlands and the UK).

SOCIAL CUSTOMS

All countries have their own particular social customs, standards of behaviour and social rules, which may be based on class, tradition, race or religion. Be aware that people are much more formal in some countries than in others – particularly more so than most English-speaking countries – and newcomers should tread carefully to avoid offending anyone. Good manners, politeness and consideration for others are important in all countries. Some pointers are listed below:

- When introduced to someone, you generally follow the cue of the person performing the introduction – i.e. if someone is introduced as Tom, you can usually call him Tom. Most people will usually say 'Please call me Tom', after a short time (unless his name happens to be Montague). In some EU countries (particularly those in Eastern Europe), it's customary to use a person's title (e.g. doctor, reverend, professor, general or president) when addressing or writing to them, particularly when the title-holder is elderly.

- After you've been introduced to someone, you usually say something (in the local language, if you can) such as 'How do you do?', 'Pleased to meet you', 'My pleasure' or 'Delighted' and shake hands. When saying goodbye, it's customary in some countries to shake hands again. In formal circles, gentlemen may be expected to bow and kiss the back of a lady's hand while, in informal gatherings, strangers are more inclined simply to shake hands. In many countries it's traditional for men to kiss ladies on the cheek (or once on either cheek) and women may also follow this custom when greeting other women. Men may also kiss and embrace each other in some countries, particularly in southern European countries, although in others this isn't usual.

- When talking to a stranger, in many languages (e.g. French, German, Italian, Spanish, etc.) you should use the formal form of address and not use the familiar form or call someone by their first name until you're invited to do so. Generally, the older or more important person will invite the other to use the familiar form of address and first names. The familiar form is used with children, animals and God, but almost never with your elders or work superiors. However, people in many countries are becoming less formal and younger people often use the familiar form and first names with colleagues, unless they're of the opposite sex, when it may imply a special intimacy! It's customary to use the formal form of address in conversations with shopkeepers, servants, business associates and figures of authority (the local mayor), or those with whom you have a business relationship, e.g. your bank manager, tax officials and policemen.

- If you're invited to dinner, it's customary in most countries to take a small present of flowers, a plant, chocolates or a bottle of wine. Flowers can be tricky as, to some people, carnations mean bad luck, chrysanthemums are for cemeteries and roses signify love. Wine can also be a problem, particularly if your hosts are wine connoisseurs. It's customary in some countries to serve wine brought by guests at the meal, although don't expect your hosts to serve your cheap red. If you stay with someone as a guest for a few days, it may also be usual to give your host or hostess a small gift when you leave.

- Many Europeans say 'good appetite' before starting a meal. If you're offered a glass of wine, you should wait until your host has made a toast before taking a drink. If you aren't offered a/another drink, it's time to go home.

- When planning a party, it's polite to notify your neighbours (and perhaps invite them if they're particularly attractive/interesting).

- In many EU countries people dress well and formally, and presentation and impression are all-important. They may judge people by their dress, the style and quality being as important as the correctness for the occasion. Bathing costumes, skimpy tops and flip-flops or sandals without socks are considered strictly for the beach or swimming pool in most EU countries, and not, for example, the streets, restaurants or shops (although foreigners and their 'eccentric' behaviour are usually tolerated). Locals may also carefully choose the occasions when they wear jeans, which aren't usually considered appropriate for a classy restaurant or church (even if they're the latest designer fashion). When going anywhere that may be remotely formal (or particularly informal), it's wise to ask in advance what you're expected to wear. Usually when dress is formal, such as evening dress or dinner jacket, it's stated in the invitation and you will be unlikely to be admitted if you turn up in the wrong attire. If you're invited to a wedding, enquire about the dress. In some EU countries, black or dark dress is usually worn at funerals, although this tradition is no longer adhered to as much.

- In most countries, guests are expected to be punctual with the exception of certain society parties when late arrival is *de rigueur* (unless you arrive after the celebrity guest!) and at weddings (when the bride is often late). Dinner invitations may be phrased as 8pm for 8.30pm, which means arrive at 8pm for drinks and dinner will be served (usually promptly) at 8.30pm. Anyone who arrives very late for dinner (unless his house has burnt down) or, horror of horrors, doesn't turn up at all (when death is a good excuse), should expect to be excluded from future guest lists. If you're confused by a multitude of knives, forks and spoons (the rule is to start at the outside and work in), don't panic but just copy what your neighbour is doing. If he's another ignorant foreigner, you will at least have some company in the social wilderness to which you will both be consigned.

- You should introduce yourself before asking to speak to someone on the telephone. In southern European countries, local people have a siesta in the afternoon and it isn't advisable to telephone during the siesta hours (e.g. 2 to

4pm). If you call between these times it's polite to apologise for disturbing the household if you know people are likely to be having a siesta (particularly very young children and elderly people).

● If you have a business appointment with a foreigner, he'll usually expect you to be on time, although he may be five or ten minutes late. However, if **you're** going to be more than five minutes late, it's advisable to telephone and apologise. Business people in most EU countries usually exchange business cards on business and social occasions.

TELEVISION & RADIO

Although most people complain endlessly about the poor quality of television (TV) programmes in their home countries, many find they cannot live without a TV when they're abroad. Fortunately, the growth of satellite TV in the last few decades has enabled people to enjoy TV programmes in English and a variety of other languages almost anywhere in the world. Cable TV is also available in many countries, and often includes English-language stations such as CNN and BBC World News.

The quality of local radio (including expatriate stations in some countries) is generally excellent, and if you have a high quality receiver (or a satellite TV system) it's possible to receive radio stations from around the globe. A TV licence is required in several EU countries and a separate radio licence is necessary in Denmark and Germany.

Television

The standards for TV reception **aren't the same in all countries**. Most western European countries use the PAL B/G standard, except for the UK which uses a modified PAL-I system that's incompatible with other European countries. France has its own standard called SECAM-L, which is different from the SECAM standard used elsewhere in the world, e.g. SECAM B/G in the Middle East and North African countries, and SECAM D/K in some eastern European and many African countries. Most televisions and video cassette recorders (VCRs) operating on the North American NTSC system won't function in Europe.

If you want a TV that will operate in the UK, France or another European country, and a VCR that will play NTSC, PAL and SECAM videos, you must buy a multistandard unit. These are widely available in some countries and contain automatic circuitry that switches from PAL-I (UK), to PAL-B/G (rest of Europe) to SECAM-L (France). If you have a PAL TV, it's also possible to buy a SECAM to PAL transcoder that converts SECAM signals to PAL. Some people opt for two TVs, one to receive local programmes or satellite TV and another to play their favourite videos. A British or US video recorder won't work with a French TV unless it's dual standard (with SECAM), and although you can play back a SECAM video on a PAL VCR, the picture will be in black and white.

Cable TV

Cable TV is available in many EU countries, some of which (such as Belgium, Holland and Switzerland) have around 90 per cent coverage. However, some countries (e.g. Italy) don't have cable TV. There are a number of cable TV companies in most countries, although if you live in an apartment or townhouse with a communal aerial you will usually be billed automatically for the services of the communal cable (or satellite) TV service (unless you have no TV); all you need to do to receive the service is connect your TV aerial to a wall socket.

Cable TV consists of cable relays of local and foreign TV stations, dedicated cable-only stations and satellite stations. The number of stations available varies and may run from 20 to over 100, according to the package you (or your community/development) choose. In the EU, English-language cable TV stations are widely available and include BBC World News, Bloomberg, CNBC, CNN, Eurosport, ITN News, MTV and Sky News. In addition to unscrambled TV channels, scrambled TV channels are available in many areas. Like some satellite TV stations (see below), you require a decoder (which can be hired from and installed by most TV shops) to receive some stations and must pay a monthly subscription. Cable companies also offer pay-per-view services, where you pay to watch a particular live event, such as a sporting event or concert.

Satellite TV

Wherever you live in the EU, it's likely that you will be able to receive satellite TV, although the signal strength and number of stations that can be received will depend on your equipment and your location. Europe is served by a number of geo-stationary satellites carrying over 100 TV channels broadcasting in a variety of languages. Satellites include the following (the most popular are marked with an asterisk):

- Arabsat fleet – 26° east (Arabic – covers most of Europe);
- Astra 1 fleet – 19.2° east (European – covers all Europe)*;
- Astra 2 fleet – 28.2° east (Sky digital UK and most of EU)*;
- Eutelsat W2 – 16° east (European – covers most of Europe);
- Hispasat fleet – 30° west (Spanish – covers most of Europe)*;
- Hotbird fleet – 13° east (European – covers all Europe)*;
- Nilesat fleet – 7° west (Arabic – covers most of Europe);
- PAS 3R/6/6B – 43° west (American – covers most of Europe);
- Sirius/Thor fleet – 1° west (European – covers most of Europe);
- Turksat – 42° east (Turkish – covers most of Europe).

Most of the above transmit in both digital and analogue formats, although some now transmit only digital signals, as analogue is being phased out.

Astra: The Astra satellites offer TV addicts a huge choice of English- and foreign-language channels. Among the many English-language channels available on Astra are Channel 5, The Discovery Channels, The Disney Channel Eurosport, Film Four, Plus, Sky Cinema 1 & 2, Sky Movies 1-9, Sky News, Sky One, Sky Sports (three channels), TCM, UK Gold and UKTV Gold. Other channels are broadcast in Dutch, German, Japanese, Swedish and various Indian languages. The signal for many channels is scrambled (the decoder is usually built into the receiver) and viewers must pay a monthly subscription to receive programmes. The best served by unscrambled (clear) channels are German-speakers (many German channels on Astra are clear). Further information can be found on Astra's website (⌨ www.astra.lu).

A bonus of Astra is the availability of radio stations, including all the national BBC stations (see **Satellite Radio** on page 212).

Sky Television: You need a Sky Digital receiver and dish, which is provided free by Sky television, provided that you agree to Sky's terms and conditions. You don't need to subscribe to Sky television, but you must have the system installed by Sky. For non-subscribers the installation cost is GB£120; if you take out a subscription, the installation cost is GB£60.00 if you opt for the comprehensive Sky World package or GB£100 if you choose any other Sky package. If you choose the Sky World package, many retailers offer a deal, sometimes including free installation, although you may pay as much as GB£40 per month for the subscription. (Note that Sky packages are flexible and you can alter your package after the first month's viewing without penalty.)

If you don't wish to be bound by Sky's terms and conditions, you may find a retailer who will sell you a new Sky Digibox for between GB£170 and GB£200. Second-hand Digiboxes can be bought for around GB£75.

If you don't wish to subscribe to Sky, you will still have access to around 100 channels. However, these won't include ITV1, CH4 or CH5, even though these channels are free-to-view (FTV, also called free-to-air/FTA). To receive these channels, you must currently subscribe to Sky (their minimum package includes all three channels), although it's likely that free-to-view cards will become available in the near future.

You must subscribe to Sky to receive one or more of the many channel packages available, other than Sky News, which isn't scrambled. To receive scrambled channels such as Sky Movies and Sky Sports you need an address in the UK. Subscribers are sent a coded card 'smart' card (like a credit card) that must be inserted in the Digibox (cards are updated every few years to thwart counterfeiters). Sky won't send smart cards to overseas viewers, as they have the copyright for a British-based audience only, so overseas homeowners need to obtain a card through someone in the UK. However, a number of satellite companies in France (some advertise in the expatriate press) supply Sky cards.

Various packages are available from Sky, costing from around GB£14.00 for the basic package to GB£40.00 for Sky World, which offers over 100 channels, including the Movie and Sports channels, along with many interactive services such as Sky News Active.

A common misconception regarding Sky is that a Digibox must be connected to a telephone line to ensure that the Digibox's software can be automatically updated. In fact, update information is sent to the Digibox via the satellite and is received by your dish; the telephone connection is used only if you want to use online services such as sending emails from your Digibox, which you can only do from the UK. Therefore, for viewing channels and ordinary operation, a telephone connection isn't required. Further information can be found on Sky's website (🖥 www.sky.com).

Digital TV: The benefits of digital TV, which was launched in 1998 by Sky in the UK, include a superior picture, CD quality sound, including Dolby Digital 5.1, widescreen format and access to many more channels. To watch digital satellite TV, you require a Sky Digibox (see above). Digital satellite television has become very popular, and distributors offer a range of interactive services in addition to television programming, including home banking, games, and software downloads and buying products related to your favourite television programmes, such as mugs, sweatshirts, video tapes and DVDs.

Eutelsat: Eutelsat runs a fleet of communications satellites carrying TV channels to over 50 million homes, although its channels are mostly non-English. The English-language channels on Eutelsat include BBC World, CNBC Europe and Eurosport. Other channels are broadcast in Arabic, French, German, Hungarian, Italian, Polish, Portuguese, Spanish and Turkish. Further information can be found on Eutelsat's website (🖥 www.eutelsat.org).

BBC: The BBC has recently stopped encrypting (scrambling) its channels coming from the Astra satellite that it shares with Sky, which means that you don't need a Sky Digibox to receive the BBC channels, including BBC interactive services. (However, a Sky satellite receiver won't allow you to receive ITV1, CH4 or CH5 – see above.)

The BBC's commercial subsidiary, BBC World Television (formerly BBC Worldwide Television) broadcasts two 24-hour channels: BBC World (24-hour news and information) and BBC Prime (general entertainment). BBC World is free-to-view, while BBC Prime is encrypted. BBC World is normally included as part of the 'international' offering with basic cable or digital satellite services in France. BBC Prime costs GB£88, and there's a one-time charge of GB£14 for a smart card.

For more information and a programming guide contact BBC World Television, PO Box 5054, London W12 0ZY, UK (☎ 020-8433 2221). The BBC publishes a monthly magazine, BBC On Air, giving comprehensive information about BBC World Television programmes. A programme guide is also listed on the internet (🖥 www.bbc.co.uk/worldservice/programmes) and both BBC World and BBC Prime have their own websites (🖥 www.bbcworld.com and www.bbcprime.com). When accessing them, you need to enter the name of the country (e.g. France) so that schedules appear in local time.

Equipment: The dish size required to receive the above satellites varies according to where you are in Europe. In most cases an 80cm dish will do the job, although you may need up to a 2m dish (for which you may need special permission) or you could obtain a good signal with just a 35cm dish. Always check with a local installer.

The signal from many stations is scrambled and viewers must pay a monthly subscription fee to receive programmes. The best served by clear (unscrambled) stations are German-speakers (most German stations on Astra are clear). To receive scrambled stations, a satellite receiver should have a built-in Videocrypt decoder (and others such as Eurocrypt, Syster or SECAM if required) and be capable of receiving satellite stereo radio. A system with an 85cm dish (to receive Astra stations) costs from around €300, plus installation, which may be included in the price. A digital system is more expensive, for example, a BskyB system costs around €1,000 in most European countries (excluding the UK and Ireland). Shop around, as prices can vary considerably. There are satellite sales and installation companies in many EU countries, some of which advertise in the expatriate press. Alternatively, you can import your own satellite dish and receiver and install it yourself. **Before buying a system, ensure that it can receive programmes from all existing and planned satellites.**

Location: To receive programmes from any satellite, there must be no obstacles between the satellite and your dish, i.e. no trees, buildings or mountains must obstruct the signal, therefore check before renting or buying a home. Before buying or erecting a satellite dish, check whether you need permission from your landlord, development or local municipality. Some towns and buildings (such as apartment blocks) have regulations regarding the positioning of antennae, although in some countries owners can mount a dish almost anywhere without receiving any complaints. Dishes can usually be mounted in a variety of unobtrusive positions and can also be painted or patterned to blend in with the background. However, in some countries, private dishes in apartment blocks are prohibited and have been replaced by a single communal antenna with a cable connection to individual homes.

Programme Guides: Many satellite stations provide teletext information and most broadcast in stereo. Sky satellite programme listings are provided in a number of British publications such as *What Satellite, Satellite Times* and *Satellite TV Europe* (the best), which are available on subscription and from local newsagents in some countries. Satellite TV programmes are also listed in expatriate newspapers and magazines in many EU countries. The annual *World Radio TV Handbook* edited by David G. Bobbett (Watson-Guptill Publications) contains over 600 pages of information and the frequencies of all radio and TV stations worldwide.

Radio

Radio flourishes in EU countries, where it's often more popular than TV with a much larger audience. Numerous public and private, local, regional, national and foreign radio stations can be received in most countries, with programme standards varying from excellent to agonisingly amateurish. There's a wealth of excellent FM (VHF stereo) and AM (medium waveband) stations in the major cities and resort areas in most countries, although in remote rural areas (particularly mountainous areas) you may be unable to receive any FM stations clearly. The long wave (LW) band is little used in most countries, although LW stations are common in the UK and Ireland. A short wave (SW) radio is useful for receiving international stations.

English-Language Stations

There are English-language and other foreign language commercial radio stations in the major cities and resort areas in some EU countries, where the emphasis is usually on music and chat with some news. Some expatriate stations broadcast in a variety of languages (not simultaneously), including English, Dutch, German and various Scandinavian languages, at different times of the day. Unfortunately (or inevitably), expat radio tries to be all things to everyone and, not surprisingly, usually falls short, particularly with regard to music, where it tries to cater for all tastes. However, it generally provides a good service and is particularly popular among retirees. The main drawback of expatriate radio (and most commercial radio) is its agonising, amateurish advertisements, which are obtrusive and repetitive, and make listening a chore. English-language radio and other foreign radio programmes are published in the expatriate press in many countries.

BBC & Other Foreign Stations

The BBC World Service is broadcast on short wave on several frequencies (e.g. 12095, 9760, 9410, 7325, 6195, 5975 and 3955 kHz) simultaneously. The signal strength varies according to where you live, the time of day and year, the power and positioning of your receiver, and atmospheric conditions. The BBC World Service plus BBC Radio 1, 2, 3, 4 and 5 are also available via the Astra 2A satellite. For a free guide and frequency information, write to BBC World Service (BBC Worldwide, 4PH, Woodlands, 80 Wood Lane, London, W12 0TT, UK, ☎ 020-8433 2000). The BBC publishes a monthly magazine, *BBC On Air*, containing comprehensive information for BBC World Service radio, BBC Prime TV and BBC World TV. It's available on subscription from the BBC (BBC On Air Magazine, Room 310 NW, Bush House, Strand, London WC2B 4PH, UK, ☎ 020-7557 2803, ✉ bbc onair.@bbc.co.uk) and from news stands in some countries.

Many other foreign stations also publish programme listings and frequency charts for expatriates keen for news from home, including Radio Australia, Radio Canada, Denmark Radio, Radio Nederland, Radio Sweden International and the Voice of America. Don't forget to check for websites, where you can often download and hear broadcast material as well as view schedules.

Cable & Satellite Radio

If you have cable or satellite TV, you can also receive many radio stations via your cable or satellite link. For example, BBC Radio 1, 2, 3, 4 and 5, BBC World

Service, Sky Radio, Virgin 1215 and many foreign language stations are broadcast via the Astra satellites. Satellite radio stations are listed in British satellite TV magazines such as *Satellite Times*. If you're interested in receiving radio stations from further afield, you should obtain a copy of the *World Radio TV Handbook* edited by David G. Bobbett (Watson-Guptill Publications).

TIME DIFFERENCE

When living in the EU, it's important to be aware of the differences between local time and the time in countries where you have friends or family or do business. World time is calculated as the difference (plus or minus) between Greenwich Mean Time (GMT), which is the time at Greenwich in England from where world time is calculated. EU countries change to 'summer' time in the spring (usually on the last Sunday in March), when people put their clocks forward one hour, and back to 'winter' time in autumn (usually on the last Sunday in October), when clocks are put back one hour. Time changes are announced in local newspapers and on radio and TV, and usually officially take place at 2 or 3am.

In most EU countries, times in timetables are written using the 24-hour clock, when 10am is written as 10h and 10pm as 22h. Midday is 1200 and midnight is 2400, while 7.30am is written as 07.30. However, the 24-hour clock is rarely referred to in speech. In some countries, times are given using the 12-hour clock ('am' and 'pm'), in which case they may be printed in timetables in light type to indicate before noon (am) and in **bold** type to indicate after noon (pm).

When making international telephone calls or travelling long distance by air, you should check the local time difference (one sure way to upset most people is to wake them at 3am). This is usually shown in the 'International Dialling' section of telephone books and can also be found on numerous websites, including ▣ www.worldtimeserver.com/country.asp, ▣ www.timeanddate.com/world clock, ▣ www.worldtime.com and ▣ www.worldtimezone.com. No EU country has more than one time zone.

Most EU countries are one hour ahead of GMT except for the Canary Islands, Ireland, Portugal and the UK on GMT, and some, namely the Baltic States, Cyprus, Finland, Greece and Malta (during the summer only), which are two hours ahead.

The time difference between the UK (when it's noon GMT) and some major international cities is shown below:

LONDON	CAPE TOWN	BOMBAY	TOKYO	LOS ANGELES	NEW YORK
Noon	2pm	5.30pm	9pm	4am	7am

9.

COUNTRY PROFILES

This chapter contains profiles of the 25 countries covered by this book, summarising information detailed elsewhere in the book and including additional details.

AUSTRIA

General Information

Capital: Vienna.

Population: 8.1 million.

Foreign Community: Vienna is home to OPEC and the UN Industrial Development Organisation, but there isn't a large western expatriate community, although the country is home to quite a large number of refugees from Eastern Europe.

Area: 83,850km^2 (32,374mi^2).

Geography: Austria is a mountainous, landlocked country located in southern central Europe with two-thirds of its territory situated in the Alps, a third of which is forested. It has a strategic position at the crossroads of central Europe with easily crossed Alpine passes and valleys. The Danube basin in the east, where the capital Vienna is situated and most of the population lives, provides excellent communication with Eastern Europe.

Climate: Austria is found in the central European climatic zone and can be divided into three areas: the east of the country has warm summers and low rainfall; the central Alpine region has long cold winters and short summers; and the west of the country high precipitation and a temperate climate. Average temperatures for Vienna are 0°C (32°F) in January and 20°C (68°F) in July.

Language: The official language is German.

Government: Federal, multiparty republic where individual regions have considerable autonomy.

Political Stability: Austria has a long history of political and territorial instability although, since World War II, the country has been relatively stable politically and declared neutrality in 1955. It has been a member of EFTA since 1960 and joined the EU in 1995. The general election of 2000 resulted in a majority for the extreme right with racist and xenophobic policies, which led to diplomatic sanctions from the EU. Sanctions were lifted after reassurances of moderation from the Austrian government and in 2003 the social democrats returned to the government.

EU Accession: 1995.

Economy

Overview: Austria's economy is generally very stable and has experienced steady growth over the last decade. The economy is heavily reliant on the German market both for imports and exports, and benefits strongly from its good strategic position in central Europe. These benefits are set to increase further once the EU accepts central and eastern European countries as members in 2004.

GDP Per Head: US$33,360.

Growth (2003): 0.9 per cent.

Forecast Growth For 2004: 1.9 per cent.

Main Industries: automotive, chemicals, food and beverages, and mechanical and structural engineering.

UK Trade Partner Ranking: 26.

US Trade Partner Ranking: 35.

Working

Overview: Austria has one of the EU's healthiest employment markets with consistently low unemployment. Employment practices in the country are highly considered and include extensive apprenticeship programmes. Around 57 per cent of the population is employed in services industries.

Unemployment Rate (2003): 4.5 per cent.

Work Permits: Nationals from the original EU member states don't require a work permit. EU citizens from new member states must obtain a work permit in order to start work, but may visit the country and seek work for up to six months under the same conditions as other EU nationals. Regulations are expected to change in May 2006 and you should check with the authorities for the latest information. Non-EU nationals must obtain a firm offer of employment before arrival and apply for work and residence permits at an Austrian consulate or embassy in their home country **before** arrival.

Labour Relations: Labour relations are generally excellent and based on a strong social partnership between the unions and management. Austria enjoys the EU's lowest strike rate. In 2003, however, there were two general strikes against proposed pension reforms

Employment Conditions: Conditions are similar to those in most western European countries with similar rights. The economy is buoyant and unemployment is low. There's a 40-hour working week and most professionals are allowed up to 30 days paid holiday annually.

Business Hours: Businesses generally open from 7.30am to 6.30pm from Monday to Thursday and from 7.30am to noon or 1pm on Friday. Banks open from 8am to 12.30pm and from 1.30 to 3pm on Monday, Tuesday, Wednesday and Friday and from 8am to 12,30pm and 1.30to 5.30pm on Thursday.

Public Holidays: 13 per year:

- 1st January
- 6th January
- Easter Monday
- 1st May

- Ascension Day
- Whit Monday (May/June)
- 15th August
- 26th October
- 1st November
- 8th, 25th & 26th December

Business Etiquette: Business is conducted in a formal manner and you should shake hands at the beginning and end of meetings, where business cards are usually exchanged. Punctuality is of great importance.

Finance

Currency: Euro (€).
    Exchange Rate: €1 = US$1.26.
    Exchange Controls: None.
    Banks: The banking system is highly efficient and modern, and banks offer a comprehensive range of services. The Austrian National Bank controls banking activity and there are several large Austrian banks and a limited number of branches of foreign banks, mainly in Vienna. The banking industry is expected to expand significantly into central and Eastern Europe once the EU opens its doors to additional members.
    Cost/Standard Of Living: Owing to a stable and thriving economy, Austrians generally enjoy a high standard of living and salaries are high, particularly for executives. However, taxes and social security payments are also high.
    Loans: Banks provide a range of loans to both residents and non-residents.
    Interest Rate (Early 2004): 2 per cent (European Central Bank).

Taxation

All professionals and businesses must register with the Tax Office.
    Corporate Tax: Corporate income and capital gains taxes are levied at 34 per cent. Non-resident companies are taxed on Austrian-source income only.
    Personal Income Tax: Income is taxed at source through a PAYE system and rates are progressive from 21 per cent (on taxable income over €3,640) to 50 per cent (on taxable income over €50,870). There are numerous allowances and deductions. Expatriates who fulfil certain conditions are entitled to a tax-free relocation allowance, including expenses for moving, double households, home leaves and education of children.
    Capital Gains Tax: Capital gains are taxed at the same rates as income tax when the purchase and sale take place within a year (10 years for real estate). Up to €440 gains are tax-exempt. Principal residences are exempt after five years of ownership.

Wealth Tax: None.

Inheritance & Gift Tax: Inheritance tax is levied at between 14 and 60 per cent, depending on the relationship between the donor and recipient, and the amount.

Value Added Tax: Value added tax rates are 10 per cent on food, agricultural products and property rents, 20 per cent on most other items and 34 per cent on cars.

Withholding Taxes: Dividends and interest are subject to 25 per cent withholding tax. Non-residents are liable only for withholding tax on interest if the underlying loan is secured by Austrian real estate.

Tax Filing: Taxpayers must file a tax return if they earn over the basic minimum (€8,720 a year for employees and €6,975 for the self-employed). The annual declaration is either for income tax or employee assessment. Returns must usually be filed before 15th May of the following year.

Accommodation

Building Standards: Excellent. Property is built to very high specifications.

Restrictions On Foreign Ownership: Because of a housing shortage and speculation on property prices, all provinces impose strict regulations on property purchase by non-Austrians. Purchases must be approved by provincial governments. In some areas it's virtually impossible for foreigners to buy property, although this may change for EU nationals once Austria fully adopts EU laws.

Cost Of Housing: Prices vary according to the area, but you can expect to pay from €120,000 for a two-bedroom apartment and from €175,000 for three bedrooms.

Fees: Purchase fees total around 10 per cent of the price and include purchase tax levied at 8 per cent of a property's value.

Local Mortgages: Local mortgages (for both residents and non-residents) are available from Austrian banks.

Property Taxes: Property tax is 0.5 per cent and real estate tax around 0.8 per cent of the assessed value of a property. Both are payable annually.

Renting: Monthly rental costs in Vienna and other major cities are from €500 to €2,000 per month for a two-bedroom apartment and from €2,200 for a three-bedroom townhouse. Rental accommodation is generally let unfurnished, which means empty! Monthly maintenance and service charges are usually added to the rent and you must usually pay three months deposit in advance.

Personal Effects: Household and personal effects may be imported into Austria tax-free, although they must be accompanied by an inventory.

Utilities: The electricity supply (220V) is reliable and charges are reasonable. Water charges are quite high, although the quality is excellent. Mains gas is available in most cities and large towns. Utility fees (e.g. water, heating) for rental accommodation are based on the previous year's usage and included in the service charges.

Services

Getting There: There are six international airports, with frequent flights to all major world capitals. There is also quick and easy access from neighbouring countries by rail and road.

Public Transport: A highly developed and efficient public transport system includes Austrian Federal Railways, which cover most of the country and provide rail links with all major european cities, and comprehensive domestic air setvices, mainly operated by Tyrolean Airways. Mountain routes may be impassable in winter. Within cities, trams and bicycles are widely used.

Motoring: The excellent road network includes over 1,000km (625mi) of well-maintained motorways, for which a toll label (*vignette*) is necessary. These may be obtained from border posts and petrol stations. Speed limitd are 50kph in built-up areas, 100kph outside such areas (including dual carriageways) and 130kph on motorways. Maximum permitted alcohol level is 50mg per 100ml of blood. A warning triangle and first aid kit must be carried by all vehicles. No leaded petrol is available. EEA driving licences are valid indefinitely. All others must be exchanged for an Austrian licence within six months of arrival.

Medical Facilities: The health service is generally very good, operated by each of the nine provinces. Medical treatment is free for everyone, although foreigners are advised to have private health insurance.

Education: Free and compulsory for children aged from 6 to 15. Standards are high, with good facilioties for secondary and technical education. There are very few private schools, apart from two international schools in Vienna and Salzburg.

Postal Services: The postal service is very efficient and also provides a banking service called Postsparkassen, which is one of Austria's largest banks.

Telephone: The telephone service is highly developed and efficient. It is operated by Telekom Austria (once a state monopoly) and several other companies. Call charges are competitive and prices are continually being reduced. There are also four mobile phone operators.

Internet: The internet is popular in Austria and most companies have their own websites. There are numerous ISPs offering both subscription and free services.

English TV & Radio: Austrian TV and Radio broadcasts exclusively in German, but English language programmes are available via cable and satellite TV. An annual TV licence is payable.

Miscellaneous

Crime Rate: Austria has a low crime rate and is one of the safest countries in the world.

Visas: Nationals from many countries including the EU, Canada, Japan and the US don't require a visa to visit Austria for any purpose for up to three months. Business visas for visits up to three months are available for many non-

EU countries under the same conditions as the Schengen Visa (see page 20).For further visa information see page 19.

Residence Permits: EU nationals don't need residence permits, but must register their place of residence with the local Residents Registration Service within three days of arrival and re-register if they move. Non-EU citizens must apply for a residence permit **before** arriving.

International Dialling Code: 43.

Time Difference: GMT +1.

Weights & Measures: Metric.

Reference

Useful Addresses

Austrian Employment Service (Arbeitsmarktservice), Weihburggasse 30, 1011 Vienna (☎ 01-515250, 🖳 www.ams.or.at) – Includes job search and job posting facility.

British Embassy, Jauresgasse 12, A-1030 Vienna (☎ 01-716130, 🖳 www.british embassy.at).

US Embassy, Boltzmanngasse 16, A-1090 Vienna (☎ 01-313390, 🖳 www. usembassy.at).

Austrian Embassy, 18 Belgrave Mews West, London SW1X 8HU, UK (☎ 020-7235 3731, 🖳 www.austria.org.uk).

Austrian Embassy, 3524 International Court, NW, Washington DC 20008, USA (☎ 202-895 6700, 🖳 www.austria.org).

Further Reading

Austrian Taxbook – A useful booklet with comprehensive information about personal income tax, available in pdf format from the Ministry of Finance (🖳 www.bmf.gv.at).

Useful Websites

Austrian Business Agency (🖳 www.aba.gv.at) – The website includes several useful downloadable documents on doing business and working in Austria.

Government Help (🖳 www.help.gv.at) – Comprehensive information for foreign citizens provided by the Austrian government.

Virtual Vienna (🖳 www.virtualvienna.net) – Useful information about life in Austria's capital city).

BELGIUM

General Information

Capital: Brussels.

Population: 10.2 million.

Foreign Community: Brussels is home to many EU institutions and consequently the city has a large European expatriate population, plus a substantial number of African and Turkish immigrants. Official estimates claim Belgium has an expatriate population of around 9 per cent, although the real figure is probably considerably higher.

Area: 30,510km^2 (11,780mi^2).

Geography: Belgium is a relatively small country situated in the west of Europe with borders with France, Germany and the Netherlands. The country has a particularly strategic position with all western European capitals within a 1,000km (621mi) radius. The country can be divided into the Ardennes uplands in the north, home to Belgium's coalfields and the textile industry, and the lowland plains in the south, which are farmed extensively. Brussels and the main towns in the north form a densely populated urbanised area.

Climate: Belgium has a temperate climate, consisting of mild winters and cool summers, although it's often rainy and cloudy. Average temperatures for Brussels are 4°C (39°F) in January and 180°C (64°F) in July.

Language: The official languages are Flemish (akin to Dutch), French and German, while English is widely spoken, particularly in Brussels.

Government: Constitutional monarchy with a bicameral legislature.

Political Stability: Belgium is politically stable although there's a long-standing discord between the Flemish and French populations, occasionally leading to government instability. The country has three governments: the national government in Brussels, and regional assemblies for Flanders and Wallonia, both of which have comprehensive autonomy in matters of education, transport and economy.

Accession EU: Founder member.

Economy

Overview: Belgium generally has a stable economy, although growth has been slow over the last few years. Budget deficits and large government debt are perennial problems that successive governments have failed to solve. High unemployment is also a problem.

GDP Per Head: US$22,401.

Growth (2003): 0.9 per cent.

Forecast Growth For 2004: 1.8 per cent.

Main Industries: The main industries in northern Belgium are: agriculture, biotechnology, car manufacture, food, horticulture and textiles. In southern

Belgium they are: banking, financial services, hospitality, IT and metallurgy. In Brussels they are: banking and business.
UK Trade Partner Ranking: 5.
US Trade Partner Ranking: 50+.

Working

Overview: Belgium has one of the highest unemployment rates in the EU, although rates vary widely throughout the country with low unemployment in Flanders and high rates in Wallonia. Some 66 per cent of the workforce is employed in the services sector and the country has one of the highest productivity rates in the world.
Unemployment Rate (2003): 8.1 per cent.
Employment Opportunities: Most job opportunities are found in Brussels, where there's a shortage of administrative and clerical staff and translators within the European Commission and NATO, as well as in banking and IT sectors. Throughout the country there are opportunities in financial management, IT and tourism. Competence in the appropriate language (French or Flemish) is essential.
Work Permits: Nationals from the original EU member states don't require a work permit. Those from new member states must have work permits, at least until May 2006, but may visit to seek work for up to six months under the same conditions as other EU citizens. Non-EU nationals must have a firm offer of employment and obtain work and residence permits **before** arrival.
Labour Relations: Generally good, with an efficient conciliation service established in 1999. Collective bargaining is commonplace and the strike rate is among the lowest in the EU.
Employment Conditions: Good, given extensive legislation favouring the employee. The working week is 40 hours and workers are generally entitles to four weeks paid holiday. A 13th month salary payment is common and productivity bonuses are widely offered.
Salaries: Generally about the EU average and similar to those in Ireland, the Netherlands and Spain. An accountant can expect to earn around €49,000 a year and a graphic designer €42,000.
Minimum Monthly Wage (2003): €1,163.
Social Security: Employees and the self-employed make compulsory monthly payments to an insurance fund (*Mutuelle/Ziekenfond*) which provides heathcare, pensions, unemployment and sick pay benefits. The rate of contribution is around 13 per cent of gross monthly salary. Employers pay around 39 per cent for blue-collar workers and around 33 per cent for white-collar employees.
Business Hours: Offices open from 8.30am to 5.30pm Monday to Friday. Banking hours are from 9am to noon and from 2 to 4pm Monday to Friday. Some banks open from 9am to noon on Saturday.
Public Holidays: Ten per year nationally, plus three regional holidays:

- 1st January
- Easter Monday
- 1st May
- Ascension Day
- Whitsun (May/June)
- 1st July (Flemish Community)
- 21st July
- 15th August
- 27th September (French Community)
- 1st & 11th November
- 15th November (German Community)
- 25th December

Business Etiquette: Business is conducted in a formal manner and punctuality is of the utmost importance. Belgians like to get to know the people they deal with. In Flanders, the official business language is English, which is on the increase, but in Wallonia French should be used.

Finance

Currency: Euro (€).
  Exchange Rate: €1 = US$1.26.
  Exchange Controls: None.
  Banks: Belgian financial institutions are subject to strict control by the Banking Commission and have a reliable reputation. There are several Belgian banks such as BACOB, BBL and Kredietbank, and many international banks have branches in Brussels. Belgian banks provide advice on the management of finances, although they take no responsibility for this, which is undertaken by 'private banking' practised by stockbrokers, fund managers and financial brokers, and carefully regulated and controlled by the authorities. When choosing a bank, shop around for the best deal because rates and bank charges vary greatly. However, it can be difficult to change banks once you have opened an account with one.
  Cost/Standard Of Living: The standard of living in Belgium is high and is reflected in generally high wages. The cost of living is reasonable and only slightly higher than the UK and France.
  Loans: Loans are available from banks in Belgium for both residents and non-residents. **Interest Rate (Early 2004):** 2 per cent (European Central Bank).

Taxation

Corporate Tax: Corporate income rates are 33 per cent. Small and medium companies whose taxable profit does not exceed €323,750 are subject to income tax at rates from 24.25 to 34.5 per cent. Companies with their central management or principal address in Belgium are considered resident and as such are subject to income tax on their worldwide income. Corporate capital gains is also levied at 33.99 per cent, but capital gains on shares bought or sold by a Belgium resident company are exempt.

Personal Income Tax: Salaries, fees, profits, etc. are subject to income tax on a progressive, no-ceiling basis. Belgium has one of the highest income tax rates in the EU ranging from 0 per cent (on annual earnings under €5,570) to 50 per cent (on annual earnings over €29,740). Communal and regional income tax is also payable at rates from 0 to 8.5 per cent (6 per cent is the most common rate). Numerous allowances exist. There are substantial tax concessions for expatriates who aren't permanent residents in the country, officials of the European Union and employees working for foreign companies in Belgium, although there are strict qualifying conditions.

Capital Gains Tax: None. In this respect Belgium is regarded as a tax haven for those holding capital.

Wealth Tax: None.

Inheritance & Gift Tax: None.

Value Added Tax: Value added tax (known as TVA or BWT) is levied on almost all goods and services sold in Belgium at the rate of 21 per cent. There is a reduced rate of 6 per cent for daily necessities (e.g. foodstuffs), and 12 per cent for tobacco and fuel.

Withholding Taxes: 15 per cent on interest and 25 per cent on dividends.

Tax Filing: All individuals are required to file tax returns, which are usually sent by the Tax Office in April and should be filed before the end of June.

Accommodation

Building Standards: New developments are built to very high standards but the quality of older buildings varies greatly.

Restrictions On Foreign Ownership: None.

Cost Of Housing: A two-bedroom apartment costs from €50,000 to €90,000 and an average three-bedroom house in the region of €100,000 to €150,000, although property in Brussels costs at least 40 per cent more.

Fees: The fees associated with buying property in Belgium are high and registration and notary fees add between 15 and 20 per cent to the price of a property. However, the payment of transfer tax of 12.5 per cent of the price can be made up to four months after a purchase. Transfer tax is lower in Flanders and Brussels.

Local Mortgages: Local mortgages are available from Belgian banks and lenders, although banks insist on additional security from non-residents.

Property Taxes: An annual property tax is calculated on the rateable value of a property and the amount is from 20 to 50 per cent of the rateable value depending on the area. An annual occupation tax is payable to the local commune.

Renting: The monthly rent for an apartment for a single person costs in the region of €350 to €500. The equivalent for a three-bedroom house is around €1,250 to €1,500 per month. Rental prices in Brussels are at least twice this amount, e.g. from €1,000 to €2,000 for a two-bedroom apartment. There are two types of rental contract: a three-year lease, under which you cannot leave before three years without paying high penalties; and a nine-year lease which is more flexible and penalties are lower. Most expatriates take out a nine-year lease.

Personal Effects: Household and personal effects can be imported tax-free.

Utilities: Electricity (220V) and mains gas are available countrywide, and prices are reasonable. Bottled gas is also widely available. Water quality is very good and rates are low.

Services

Getting There: Because of its geographical position, Belgium has excellent communications, particularly with the rest of Western Europe. Brussels international airport has frequent flights to most of the world's major cities. The northern ports of Ostend and Zeebrugge offer extensive ferry services to the UK and Scandinavia.

Public Transport: In a small country distances are short and communications by both road and rail are good, though often crowded around the capital. The main port of Antwerp is one of the world's busiest and more than 2000km (1250mi) of ship canals are mostly in regular commercial use.

Motoring: There is a good network of roads and motorways, though driving can be chaotic. Speed limits are 50kph in built-up areas, 90 or 100kph outside such areas (including dual carriageways) and 120kph on motorways. Maximum permitted alcohol level is 50mg per 100ml of blood. A warning triangle must be carried by all vehicles. No leaded petrol is available. All foreign driving licences must be exchanged for Belgian licences. Licences from the EEA and some other countries, including Canada and the US, can be changed automatically; licence holders from other countries must take both theoretical and practical exams to obtain a Belgian licence.

Medical Facilities: Health facilities are generally of a high standard and offer a comprehensive service with over 380 hospitals and 30,000 doctors. All residents must belong to a sickness insurance fund (*mutuelle/Ziekenfond*), to which employees contribute monthly. You must pay a fee when you visit a family doctor and for prescriptions, although most *mutuelles/Ziekenfonds* reimburse around 75 per cent of the bill

Education: Education is free and compulsory for all children from 6 to18, although from the age of 15 pupils can combine study with part-time employment. Standards are generally high. As well as state schools, there are numerous private schools throughout the country and several European and international schools, particularly in Brussels.

Postal Services: The Belgian postal service is generally good and post offices offer limited banking services.

Telephone: Belgium has an excellent telephone service that's provided by three main companies and call charges are highly competitive. There are also three mobile phone operators.

Internet: Internet services are available throughout Belgium from a large number of ISPs.

English TV & Radio: English-language programmes are broadcast only on cable and satellite channels in Belgium. Reception is excellent.

Miscellaneous

Crime Rate: Belgium has an average crime rate and is a relatively safe place to live. Drug and unemployment-related crime is, however, on the increase.

Pets: Cats and dogs require a certificate of good health dated no more than two days before departure from your home country and an anti-rabies vaccination certificate dated at least 30 days before the animal's arrival in Belgium. Dogs must be identified and registered with a local vet.

Visas: Nationals from many countries, including the EU, Canada, Japan and the US, don't need a visa to visit Belgium for any purpose for up to three months. Business visas for up to three months are available for many non-EU countries under the same terms as for a Schengen Visa (see page 20). For further visa information see page 19.

Residence Permits: EU nationals must register at the local town hall (*maison communale/gemeentehuis*) within three months of arrival, when a temporary residence permit (valid for five months) is issued. This is extended for a further year if you have a job or can prove you have the financial means to maintain yourself. Dependent children must also be registered at the local town hall. Non-EU nationals wishing to remain in Belgium for longer than three months must apply for a temporary residence permit (ASP or VVV) from a Belgian consulate or embassy in their home country **before** they arrive. Once you arrive in Belgium, you should report to your local town hall within three days (non-EU) or eight days (EU) and apply for a Certificate of Registration in the Register of Aliens (CIRE). A one-year extension is possible on a non-EU national's residence certificate. If you change address within Belgium you must re-register.

International Dialling Code: 32.

Time Difference: GMT +1.

Weights & Measures: Metric.

Reference

Useful Addresses

British Embassy, Rue d'Arlon 85, 1040 Brussels (☎ 02-287 6211, 🖳 www.british-embassy.be).

US Embassy, 27 Boulevard du Régent, 1000 Brussels (☎ 02-508 2111, 🖳 http://brussels.usembassy.gov).

Belgian Embassy, 103 Eaton Square, London SW1W 9AB, UK (☎ 020-7470 3700, 🖳 www.diplobel.org/uk).

Belgian Embassy, 3330 Garfield Street, NW, Washington DC 20008, USA (☎ 202-333 6900, 🖳 www.diplobel.us – provides useful downloadable booklets).

Further Reading

Living & Working in Holland, Belgium and Luxembourg, Beverly Laflamme (Survival Books Ltd, 🖳 www.survivalbooks.net).

Made in Belgium – annual business and trade publication (Made In Belgium, 🖳 www.madeinbelgium.be).

Useful Websites

British Chamber of Commerce (🖳 www.britcham.be).

Expatica (🖳 www.expatica.com/belgium) – An excellent expat website with the latest news, job opportunities and features on life in Belgium.

Expats in Brussels (🖳 www.expatsinbrussels.com) – Excellent website for foreigners in the capital including a city guide.

Invest in Belgium (🖳 www.invest.belgium.be) – Official foreign investment agency.

CYPRUS

General Information

Capital: Nicosia.

Population: 755,000.

Foreign Community: There's a sizeable expatriate population in Cyprus made up mainly of British retirees and concentrated primarily in resort areas.

Area: 9,250km² (3,571mi²).

Geography: Cyprus is Europe's southernmost point and the Mediterranean's third-largest island and, although politically part of Europe, geographically it's closer to the Middle East. Cyprus has two mountain ranges: the Troodos in the west, snow-covered for much of the winter, and the Kyrenia range in the north. The central plain is home to the capital Nicosia and extensive agriculture. The coastline consists of long, sandy beaches and spectacular white cliffs.

Climate: Excellent. With an average of 340 days of sunshine per year, Cyprus is one of Europe's warmest places in winter. Summers are long, hot and dry with average temperatures on the coast of 30°C (90°F) in July, though temperatures are much higher inland. Winters are short and generally mild with an average temperature of 16°C (62°F) but much colder in the Troodos mountains. Rainfall is generally low throughout the year.

Language: The official language is Cypriot Greek, although English is widely spoken and is the main language for international business.

Government: Parliamentary democracy.

Political Stability: Cyprus remained a united island until 1974, when the northern region was invaded by Turkish troops. Some 40 per cent of the island now comprises the 'Turkish Republic of Northern Cyprus', recognised only by Turkey. The southern part of Cyprus (known as the Republic of Cyprus) is prosperous and a member of the UN. Although there are Turkish troops in the north, UN peacekeeping forces along the border (the 'green line'), and British troops in the south, Cyprus is politically stable. Attempts at unification of the two regions have resulted in failure, although the Turkish government has recently shown more willingness to discuss the island's future. The Greek Cypriots, however, aren't so keen: in the April 2004 referendum organised under the auspices of the EU and UN they voted overwhelmingly against unification.

Cyprus has so far achieved a high level of EU targets in its legislation and is one of only two new member states that will apply freedom of movement for employment to original EU nationals once it joins. Cyprus is also the only new member state not to have held a referendum on joining the EU. Accession is seen by the authorities as highly beneficial to the island, although they recognise there will be short-term disadvantages such as a rise in the cost of living. Most Cypriots reportedly share this view.

EU Accession: 2004.

Economy

Overview: Cyprus generally has a buoyant economy (one of the highest in the Mediterranean) based mainly on tourism. Growth is solid and unemployment rates are very low, although the economy is somewhat volatile because of the dependence on tourism.

GDP Per Head: US$12,999.

Growth (2003): 2 per cent.

Forecast Growth For 2004: 3.4 per cent.

Main Industries: Consumer products, finance and banking, food and drink, hotel and catering, IT and tourism.

UK Trade Partner Ranking: 50+.

US Trade Partner Ranking: 50+.

Working

Overview: The workforce is well educated. Most Cypriots prefer to work in the public sector where wages are higher and benefits greater.

Unemployment Rate (2003): Low: it has remained below 5 per cent for several years and was 4.4 per cent in 2004.

Employment Opportunities: Most opportunities are found in tourism, IT and the financial sector.

Work Permits: There is no transitional period for employment in accession to the EU and citizens from the original member states don't need work permits. They are, however, required for all others, although citizens of new member states may visit to seek work for up to six months under the same conditions as other EU nationals. Non-EU nationals will be granted work permits only if no Cypriot can be found to fill a post, though foreigners in executive or managerial positions seem to be able to obtain them fairly easily. Even so, a contract of employment must be produced and a work permit obtained **before** arrival. Illegal employment is not tolerated and you should not accept promises from prospective employers that they will arrange your work permit after you arrive.

Labour Relations: Free collective bargaining is the norm, unions are strong and labour relations are generally good. Although strikes are rare, there have lately been several over Cost of Living Allowance (COLA) payments.

Employment Conditions: There is a statutory minimum monthly wage, and a 40-hour week with 15 days paid holiday is usual.

Salaries: Both salaries and the cost of living are considerably lower than the EU average.

Minimum Monthly Wage (2003): CY£292.

Social Security: Social insurance contributions are paid by both employer and employee at the rate of 6.3 per cent and the self-employed pay 11.6 per cent on annual incomes, up to an income ceiling of CY£22,104.

Business Hours: Normally from 8am to 5pm Monday to Friday. Banks open from 8.15am to 12.30pm Monday to Friday, with some central branches open on weekday afternoons except Tuesday.

Public Holidays: 15 per year, of which the ten most common are:

- 1st & 6th January
- 25th March
- Easter Monday
- 1st May
- 15th August
- 1st & 28th October
- 25th & 26th December

Business Etiquette: Cypriot business expects punctuality and business dress should be smart. The use of business cards is important and exchanges are always made on first meeting.

Finance

Currency: Cyprus Pound (CY£).

Exchange Rate: Pegged to the euro at CY£1 = €1.71. The Cyprus pound isn't traded internationally.

Exchange Controls: Residents are subject to certain exchange control restrictions on capital transfers, although these are currently being phased out in line with EU regulations. Check with the Central Bank of Cyprus for up-to-date information. Non-residents aren't subject to any exchange controls. You're permitted to import or export only CY£50 in hard currency.

Banks: The Cypriot banking system closely follows the British model and Cypriot banks are modern, efficient and equipped with the latest technology. There are nine commercial banks and some 30 foreign banks represented on the island. Residents and non-residents can open bank accounts, although residents living and working in Cyprus must open a Local Disbursement Credit (LDC) account with a local bank, which must be used for living expenses and can be credited only with amounts transferred from convertible accounts held in Cyprus or abroad. Upon departure from Cyprus, any residual balance in an LDC account can be transferred to any convertible account either in Cyprus or abroad.

Cost/Standard Of Living: Cyprus is generally considered to be one of the least expensive countries in Europe, with prices around 25 to 50 per cent lower than most northern European cities and extensive tax incentives for expatriates. However, the cost of living is rising (and expected to rise still further once Cyprus joins the EU) and imported goods can be expensive.

Loans: Loans are available from banks, but they are generally restricted to permanent residents or Cypriot nationals.

Interest Rate (Early 2004): 4.5 per cent.

Taxation

Corporate Tax: Corporate tax is levied at the rate of 25 per cent on semi-government organisations and at 10 per cent on all others. Profits in excess of CY£1 million are taxed at an additional 5 per cent.

Personal Income Tax: Income tax is deducted at source (PAYE) at 0 per cent (on annual income under CY£9,000), 20 per cent (income up to CY£12,000), 25 per cent (up to CY£15,000) and at 30 per cent on annual income in excess of CY£15,000. Foreign pension income is taxed at the flat rate of 5 per cent and there's an annual exemption of CY£2,000. Salary earned by an individual not resident in Cyprus for three years before the commencement of employment on the island is taxed at the flat rate of 20 per cent with a maximum of CY£5,000 annual exemption. Deductions for certain items (e.g. rental income) are available and there are grants for dependent children and full-time education costs.

Special Contribution For Defence: This extra tax is levied at the rate of 15 per cent on all tax-resident individuals.

Capital Gains Tax: CGT at 20 per cent is payable on gains made from immovable property. If the property is a gift between first or second degree relatives, profits are exempt from CGT. There's a once in a lifetime exemption of CY£50,000 per individual on CGT from property.

Wealth Tax: None.

Inheritance & Gift Tax: None.

Value Added Tax: VAT is levied on most goods and services at the standard rate of 15 per cent. There's a reduced rate of 5 per cent for hotel accommodation and catering, and a zero rating for goods such as exports, food, printed matter, medicines and children's clothes and shoes.

Withholding Taxes: Amounts payable depend on the tax treaty between Cyprus and the country in question. Dividends are generally subject to rates between 0 and 15 per cent, and interest to rates from 0 to 20 per cent.

Tax Filing: The tax year is the calendar year and most employees are not required to present a tax return unless they have chargeable income, in which case they must notify the tax office by 30th April. Businesses must file tax returns – an estimate of tax due must be made by 1st August and provisional tax paid in three instalments (1st August, 30th September and 31st December).

Accommodation

Building Standards: Variable, although new developments and villas are built to a high standard.

Restrictions On Foreign Ownership: Non-Cypriot citizens are permitted to own only one building plot or property and permission for ownership by non-EU nationals must be sought from the Council of Ministers. This permission is usually granted automatically.

Cost Of Housing: Property prices in Cyprus have risen in recent years (by 30 per cent in 2002 alone) and are expected to rise considerably once Cyprus joins the EU, although property is currently still inexpensive by North American and northern European standards. Prices vary considerably according to the location, with a two-bedroom apartment costing from CY£50,000 and a three-bedroom villa from CY£130,000.

Fees: Fees total up to 11 per cent of the purchase price and include stamp duty (1.5 to 2 per cent), transfer tax (from 3 to 8 per cent on properties costing over CY£100,000) and legal fees (usually 1 per cent). If you have a mortgage, the arrangement fees are included in the lawyer's fees.

Local Mortgages: Mortgages are available from local banks, although the loan will be in foreign currency and Cypriot banks rarely lend to non-residents. The amount ranges from 60 to 80 per cent of the value of the property with a repayment period from 5 to 15 years. The minimum amount for a mortgage is usually CY£25,000.

Property Taxes: All property owners in Cyprus, whether resident or not, are liable for rates and an Immovable Property Tax, both payable annually. Rates range from CY£50 to CY£150 per year depending on the locality and the Immovable Property Tax calculated according to the market value as of 1st January 1980. Tax rates are from 2.5 per cent (on properties valued at between

CY£100,001 and CY£250,000), 3.5 per cent (on properties valued at between CY£250,001 and CY£500,000) to 4 per cent (on properties valued at over CY£500,001). Properties valued below CY£100,000 are exempt from this tax, which is payable on 30th September every year.

Renting: Rental properties are readily available in Cyprus, particularly in coastal and resort areas. In the high season, prices are considerably higher and properties more difficult to find. Rental properties are usually let furnished and a two-bedroom apartment costs between CY£250 to CY£500 a month.

Personal Effects: Personal effects can be imported duty-free, provided the goods are for your personal use, have been owned and used for at least one year, and you intend to settle permanently in Cyprus. You can also import a car duty-free.

Utilities: Electricity (220–240V) is provided by the Electricity Authority of Cyprus (EAC). Charges are reasonable and billed every two months. Mains gas isn't available in Cyprus but bottled gas is widely used and costs around CY£3 for a 10kg bottle. Water is a precious commodity in Cyprus and droughts and water shortages are commonplace, particularly in the long summer months. Tap water is safe to drink.

Services

Getting There: Cyprus has two international airports, at Larnac and Paphos, and is well served by worldwide flights. There are also ferry services from Greece and the Middle East,

Public Transport: Limited to buses with infrequent services.

Motoring: Roads are generally good with excellent dual carriageways lonking the main towns. However, driving standards are poor and some rural roads are unsurfaced. Cars are inexpensive – about half the price in most Western European countries. Vehicles drive on the left. Speed limits are 50kph in built-up areas, 80kph outside these areas, including dual carriageways, and 100kph on motorways. Speed cameras operate permanently. Alcohol tolerance is zero. All vehicles must carry warning triangles. No leaded petrol is available. International and EU driving licences are valid up to six months, after which a Cypriot licence must be obtained by passing both theoretical and practical exams.

Medical Facilities: The quality of healthcare copmpares favourably with most western countries. After six months residence, social security contributors enjoy free or low cost healthcare. Otherwise, private medical insurance is essential. All emergency treatment is provided free.

Education: Recent investment has sharply raised education standards. Education is free and compulsory for children aged from 5 to 16 years. There are several private schools and international schools in main towns.

Postal Services: The Cypriot postal service is generally very efficient and there are post offices in most towns and villages. Post offices also provide limited financial transactions, such as transfers and currency exchange.

Telephone: Telecommunications in Cyprus are operated exclusively by the Cyprus Telecommunications Authority (CTA) and are very reliable. Charges are reasonable. There's also a mobile phone service.

Internet: Cyprus is well served with internet facilities as a result of huge investment by CTA in internet facilities, including ISDN lines. Most companies have websites and email, and there's a number of ISPs.

English TV & Radio: Cyprus Broadcasting (CyBC) broadcasts news bulletins in English and films are usually shown in English with Greek subtitles. Satellite reception is good throughout the island. CyBC radio also broadcasts frequently in English and the British Forces stations broadcast in English 24 hours a day.

Miscellaneous

Crime rate: Extremely low, far below the EU average, although thefts from hotels and car thefts have increased in recent years.

Pets: Dogs are subject to six months quarantine on arrival in Cyprus at either government premises or your home if approved by the authorities. Pets require a health certificate showing internal and external parasitation and an import permit available from the Director of Veterinary Services.

Visas: Nationals from many countries, including the EU, Canada, Japan and the US, don't need visas to visit for any purpose for up to three months. For other visa information, see page 19. **Visitors whose passports have a stamp from North Cyprus may be refused a visa and/or entry to the south.**

Residence Permits: All foreigners staying for longer than 90 days in Cyprus require a residence permit. The type of permit depends on your status: retirees must prove they have sufficient means to live on (annual income of at least CY£5,600) and obtain an immigration permit. Retirees cannot undertake any form of employment. Foreigners coming to live and work in Cyprus should obtain a permit from the Migration Department (Ministry of the Interior, 1457 Nicosia, ☎ 22-804502). EU nationals may apply for the permit from within Cyprus, but non-EU nationals must apply for a permit **before** arrival on the island.

International Dialling Code: 357.

Time Difference: GMT +2.

Weights & Measures: Metric.

Reference

Useful Addresses

British Embassy, Alexandrer Pallis Street, PO Box 21978, 1587 Nicosia (☎ 22-861100, 🖳 www.britain.org.cy).

Cyprus High Commission, 93 Park Street, London W1Y 4ET, UK (☎ 020-7499 8272).

Cyprus Embassy, 2211 R St., NW, Washington, DC 20008, USA (☎ 202-462 5772, 💻 http://cyprus.usembassy.org).

US Embassy, Gonia Metochiou & Ploutarchou, Engomi, 2407 Nicosia (☎ 22-776400, 💻 www.americanembassy.org.cy).

Useful Websites

Cyprus Chamber of Commerce and Industry (💻 www.ccci.org.cy) – Useful point of contact for business information.

Cyprus in the EU (💻 www.cyprus-eu.org.cy) – The official website for the island's accession to the EU.

Living Cyprus (💻 www.living-cyprus.com) – Property company website including information on property purchase, working and setting up a business in Cyprus.

CZECH REPUBLIC

General Information

Capital: Prague.

Population: 10.3 million.

Foreign Community: There's quite a large foreign community, particularly in the capital, mainly comprised of Germans, although there's also a significant American and British presence.

Area: 78,864km² (30,451mi²).

Geography: The Czech Republic is a landlocked country situated in central Europe bordering on Germany to the west, Poland to the north, Slovakia to the east and Austria to the south. The country can be roughly divided into two: Bohemia, a mountainous region in the west, and Moravia, a rich agricultural plain in the east. The capital lies in the centre of the two regions.

Climate: The Czech Republic has a typically continental climate with cold winters and warm summers. Average temperatures are 0°C (32°F) in January and 20°C (68°F) in July.

Language: The official language is Czech. German is widely spoken as well as some English.

Government: Parliamentary democracy.

Political Stability: Excellent. The Czech Republic, formed in 1993 after the break up of former Czechoslovakia, is now an established democracy and a member of NATO and the OECD. The Czechs are keen Europeans and one of the wealthiest nations to join (the Czech GDP is nearly 60 per cent of the EU average). The Czech Republic has fulfilled many of the EU criteria, although there are several outstanding issues including competition (particularly in steel restructuring), transport and mutual recognition of qualifications, particularly in the healthcare sector. When the country joins the EU, in 2004, it will need to address the problems of implementation of laws and systems and the budget crisis, where the issues of pensions, healthcare and education need to be resolved. **EU Accession:** 2004.

Economy

Overview: The Czech economy suffered a severe recession during 1997-98 caused by political instability, a currency crisis and widespread flooding. Recovery has been consistent but slow and there are still significant pending reforms such as the restructuring of the energy sector. However, the economy is considered to be one of good potential and the country has a particularly strong manufacturing sector and well-developed infrastructure.

GDP Per Head: US$8,880.

Growth (2003): 3.4 per cent.

Forecast Growth For 2004: 2.8 per cent.

Main Industries: Automotive, electronics, financial services, food and food processing, and IT.

UK Trade Partner Ranking: 34.

US Trade Partner Ranking: 48.

Working

Overview: The workforce is generally well trained and well qualified.

Unemployment Rate (2003): Following the 1997-98 recession, unemployment rose sharply and has remained at around 9 per cent for the last few years. Hidden unemployment is also high.

Employment Opportunities: Mainly in electronics, environment, finance, food, IT, security, safety equipment, telecommunications and tourism.

Work Permits: These are required for all workers but EU citizens may visit to seek work for up to six months. Regulations are expected to change in May 2006 and you should check for the latest information. For non-EU citizens, it is up to the employer to obtain a work permit, which must then accompany your visa application. Permits are required even for employment lasting less than 90 days. If you find a job while visiting the country, you must still obtain a visa, which must be applied for from **outside** the country. Visa processing can take at least two months.

Labour Relations: Trade union membership is no longer compulsory and the level has declined to around 30 per cent of the workforce. Relations are generally good with few private sector strikes and increasingly fewer in the public sector.

Employment Conditions: There's a national minimum wage, a 40-hour week and employees are entitled to three to four weeks annual paid holiday.

Minimum Monthly Wage (2003): €199.

Social Security: All employees make monthly contributions to five social funds, covering health, social insurance, pensions, sickness and unemployment benefits. Employees pay 12.5 per cent of gross salary and employers 35 per cent. Expatriate workers whose contracts are not subject to Czech labour law are exempt from these payments.

Business Hours: Offices and businesses generally open from 8am to 5pm, and banks from 9am to 3pm, Monday to Friday.

Public Holidays: 12 per year:

- 1st January
- Easter Monday
- 1st & 8th May
- 5th & 6th July
- 28th September
- 28th October
- 17th November
- 24th, 25th & 26th December

Business Etiquette: The Czechs are proud of having once been one of the world's leading manufacturing economies and resent being treated as a developing country. Business is generally formal and punctuality expected. Meetings can be lengthy and interpreters may be needed as, although many Czechs speak English, misunderstandings easily occur.

Finance

Currency: Koruna (CZK).

Exchange Rate: €1 = CZK33.23 (February 2004).

Exchange Controls: These were liberalised in 1999 and permission isn't generally required to import or export funds.

Banks: Restructuring followed a banking sector crisis in the '90s. Most state banks have been privatised and smaller ones closed or merged into larger banks. Almost all the 40-odd banks are foreign-backed. However, Czech banking remains unstable and it's advisable to use foreign banks, although some demand high initial deposits.

Cost/Standard Of Living: Prices have risen lately to levels comparable with those in Western Europe and the standard of living is generally high. However, most salaries have failed to keep pace with the cost of living. Imported goods aren't generally expensive.

Loans: All banks offer loans but, given the instability of Czech banks, those from foreign banks may be preferable.

Interest Rate (Early 2004): 2 per cent.

Taxation

The Czech taxation system underwent profound reform during the '90s to bring it in line with EU directives. However, the system still has many idiosyncrasies and expatriates are strongly advised to take expert legal advice regarding their finances. Tax compliance is important and there are severe fines for tax evasion. There is no longer a favourable tax regime for expatriates.

Corporate Tax: Corporate income and capital gains taxes are levied at 31 per cent. Resident companies are subject to tax on their worldwide income and non-resident on Czech source income only.

Personal Income Tax: Income tax is deducted at source (PAYE) by employers and tax rates are from 15 per cent (on annual earnings below CZK109,200) to 32 per cent on annual earnings over CZK331,200. There are tax allowances for individuals and their dependants.

Capital Gains Tax: Profits from shares and dividends are taxed at the same rates as income tax (see above).

Wealth Tax: None.

Inheritance & Gift Tax: Inheritance tax is levied at rates from 0.5 to 20 per cent and gift tax at rates from 1 to 40 per cent on any immovable or movable property in the Czech Republic. Close relatives of the deceased or donor are exempt.

Value Added Tax: The standard rate of value added tax is 22 per cent, which is levied on most goods, with a reduced rate of 5 per cent on foodstuffs, medicines, printed material and most services. Post office, banking and insurance services are exempt, as are education and healthcare.

Withholding Taxes: Both residents and non-residents are subject to 15 per cent withholding taxes on dividends and interest.

Tax Filing: The tax period for companies is twelve calendar months and for individual taxpayers, the calendar year. Tax returns must be filed by the end of March. Expatriates employed by a foreign employer established in the Czech Republic are required to make advance tax payments depending on their tax liability of the previous year.

Accommodation

Building Standards: Extremely variable.

Restrictions On Foreign Ownership: Only 'foreign exchange residents' (residents with a fixed domicile in the Czech Republic) and companies registered in the Czech Republic are permitted to buy property. Many expatriates buy property through a company or create one specifically for property purchase. This situation is not expected to change even for EU nationals for sometime.

Cost Of Housing: Property prices have risen dramatically in recent years in response to the country's imminent entry into the EU and rising demand from foreigners. Prices vary greatly according to the region or suburb of a city. A two-bedroom apartment costs from CZK3 million and a three-bedroom house from CZK 4.5 million upwards. Prices in some areas of Prague can be much higher, particularly in a desirable area such as postal districts 1 and 2.

Fees: Fees include transfer tax of 5 per cent, usually paid by the seller.

Local Mortgages: Local mortgages are available but, given the current instability in the banking system (see **Banks** above), it's advisable to take out a mortgage with a foreign bank (if possible).

Property Taxes: Property taxes are levied annually by local authorities and based on the location, size and quality of a property. Charges vary from CZK1.3 or CZK4 per m² multiplied by a coefficient of between 0.3 and 5 per cent (the highest charges are in Prague).

Renting: Rental accommodation isn't difficult to find, with the exception of Prague, where there's high demand and short supply, particularly for family houses. Accommodation is expensive and available furnished or unfurnished. Monthly costs for a two-bedroom apartment are around CZK40,000 and around CZK80,000 for a three-bedroom house.

Personal Effects: No duty is payable on the importation of personal effects if you're going to live in the Czech Republic. Cars are subject to 18 per cent duty.

Utilities: The electricity supply (220V) is reliable and charges aren't high; there are two tariffs, peak and off-peak. Mains gas is available in some areas but bottled gas can be difficult to obtain. Mains water is generally safe to drink.

Services

Getting There: Prague has the only international airport, well served by flights from most European cities and North America. The country can also be easily reached by road and rail from Westwern Europe.

Public Transport: There are domestic airports with limited flights at Ostrava and Brno. Train and bus services are comprehensive and efficient.

Motoring: Road conditions are good and currently in process of modernisation and upgrading. To use the motorways you must buy a *vignette* (an annual toll ticket), available at borders and petrol stations. Driving standards are poor and alcohol tolerance is zero. Speed limits are 50kph in built-up areas, 100kph outside built-up areas, including dual carriageways, and 130kph on motorways. A warning triangle and first aid kit must be carried in all vehicles. No leaded petrol is available. Foreigners with a Czech residence permit must exchange their driving licence for a Czech one within three months. For non-EU licence holders this may involve taking a theoretical and/or practical test.

Medical Facilities: Medical treatment is generally of a good standard, although markedly better in the private sector. If you contribute to the Czech social security system you can benefit from state medical care, but most foreigners prefer to have private medical insurance. **Health warning: if you plan to visit any forested areas, you should be vaccinated against tick-borne encephalitis.**

Education: Standards are high and education is free and compulsory for children aged from 6 to 16. There are several international schools in Prague.

Postal Services: There are post offices in most towns and the postal service is reasonably efficient, although parcels and valuable items are best sent by courier, since packages are often 'lost'.

Telephone: The telephone service is reasonable and has improved greatly in recent years, although lines are frequently saturated and call charges are high. Mobile phones are very popular.

Internet: The internet has been slow to take off, mainly owing to lack of investment and problems with telephone lines. However, most Czech companies now have websites and email addresses, although private uptake remains low (around 10 per cent in 2002). There are several service providers.

English TV & Radio: Cable and satellite are the only options if you wish to watch English-language broadcasts. Many rental apartments in Prague have cable TV and satellite TV installation is readily available and reception generally good.

Miscellaneous

Crime Rate: Petty crime in the Czech Republic, particularly against tourists, is commonplace, as is theft from hotels. You should take particular care over valuables and avoid crowded places. You should take official taxis only and beware of bogus plain-clothes policeman, who may ask to see your foreign currency and passport, only to disappear with them. Violent crime is rare.

Pets: Pets being imported into the Czech Republic require an up-to-date health certificate and must have been vaccinated against rabies at least 30 days before entry.

Visas: Many foreign nationals may visit for business or pleasure for up to 90 days without a visa. US nationals may visit for 30 days without a visa and extend their stay to 90 days by application to the Foreigners Police once in the country. Under these provisions you may not undertake any gainful employment and extension beyond 90 days is not permitted. Visa processing can take at least two months. For further visa information, see page 19.

Residence Permits: All foreign nationals staying for longer than 90 days require a residence permit, which must be obtained before entry into the country by applying for a long-term visa. The visa is valid for one year. After arrival in the country, foreigners should go to the nearest office of the Czech Immigration Police to obtain a Czech ID card (cost CZK1,000). Regulations for EU nationals are likely to change in the near future.

International Dialling Code: 420.

Time Difference: GMT +1.

Weights & Measures: Metric.

Reference

Useful Addresses

British Embassy, Thunovska 14, 11800 Prague 1 (☎ 2-5740 2111, 🖳 www.britain.cz).

Czech Embassy, 26 Kensington Palace Gardens, London W8 4QY, UK (☎ 020-7243 1115, 🖳 www.czech.org.uk).

Czech Embassy, 3900 Spring of Freedom St, NW, Washington DC 20008, USA (☎ 202-274 9100, 🖳 www.mzv.cz/washington).

US Embassy, Trziste 15, 11801 Prague 1 (☎ 2-5753 0663, 🖳 http://prague.usembassy.gov).

Further Reading

The Prague Post – Weekly English-language publication (also available online: 🖳 www.praguepost.com) including useful small ads section.

Useful Websites

Czech Information (🖳 www.czech.cz) – Official country website including tourist and business information.

Czech Invest (🖳 www.czechinvest.org) – Official foreign investment portal.
Prague Guide (🖳 www.prague.cz) – Excellent guide to the capital city.

DENMARK

General Information

Capital: Copenhagen.
 Population: 5.4 million.
 Foreign Community: There isn't a large expatriate community in Denmark.
 Area: 43,070km² (16,629mi²).
 Geography: Denmark is the smallest of the Scandinavian countries although it's the second largest in population. The country consists of the Jutland peninsula bordering Germany and an archipelago of 406 islands, of which 89 are inhabited. The largest and most densely populated of the islands is Zealand, site of the capital, which is now connected to Sweden by a modern bridge. Denmark also retains connections with its ex-colonies, Greenland and the Faroe Islands, although neither of these countries belongs to the EU. The country is essentially an agricultural nation (mainly dairy and pig farming), although it's also a prosperous industrial centre.
 Climate: Denmark has a cold climate, although it isn't as cold as other countries on the same latitude. Winters tend to be long, cold and damp, and summers dry and reasonably warm, while spring and autumn are short. Average temperatures for Copenhagen are 0°C (32°F) in January and 23°C (73°F) in July.
 Language: The official language is Danish. English is widely spoken.
 Government: Parliamentary monarchy with unicameral legislature. Denmark was the first Scandinavian country to join the EU, although it still co-

operates closely with the five other Scandinavian countries on the Nordic Council. Allegiance to the EU isn't total, however: in a 1992 referendum the people rejected the Maastricht treaty and in a 2000 referendum chose not to join the euro group of countries.

Political Stability: Excellent.

EU Accession: 1973.

Economy

Overview: Denmark has a prosperous economy with strong and steady growth, although in recent years its highly specialised industry has become less competitive and the country has high foreign debt. The economy's base is formed by small and medium companies (around 75 per cent of Danish companies employ fewer than 50 people), which act as a buffer against economic recession but also reduce competitiveness.

GDP Per Head: US$39,050.

Growth (2003): 1.4 per cent.

Forecast Growth For 2004: 1.8 per cent.

Main Industries: Healthcare, software and service industries such as finance, tourism and transport.

UK Trading Partner Ranking: 20.

US Trading Partner Ranking: 30.

Working

Overview: The workforce is well educated and highly competitive. Around 67 per cent is employed in the service sector, although agriculture and fishing are also important. Labour mobility is high, as is the proportion – 75 per cent – of women working. Salaries are competitive and labour costs mostly low, with virtually no employer contributions to social security.

Unemployment Rate (2003): 6 per cent.

Employment Opportunities: Currently there are shortages of biologists, biophysicists, chemists, doctors, engineers, geologists, IT specialists, mathematicians, nurses, pharmacists, physicists, radiographers, and statisticians. Up-to-date lists are available from the Danish Immigration Service (🖳 www.udlst.dk/english). Doctors and nurses require authorisation from the National Board of Health to work in Denmark.

Work Permits: Nationals of the original EU member states don't need work permits. Those from new member states must obtain permits before starting work, but may visit for up to six months to seek work. Regulations may change in May 2006 and you should check for the latest information. Non-EU nationals must obtain work permits from Danish embassies or consulates in their home countries before arriving. Permits for jobs in fields where staff is short (see **Employment Opportunities** above) are easier and quicker to obtain under the 'job-card' scheme. All nationals need permits to work in Greenland or the Faroe Islands and must obtain them **before** arrival.

Labour Relations: There's generally a high degree of cooperation between managements and employees. Trade unions are active in most industries, although labour regulations, including hiring and firing, are flexible. Strikes are infrequent.

Employment Conditions: Generally excellent with generous employee protection legislation. There is a 37-hour working week and employees are usually entitles to 30 days annual paid leave. The ability to speak Danish is usually essential for finding employment and there's strong local competition for most jobs. Most job opportunities are to be found in Copenhagen.

Salaries: Gross salaries are amongst the highest in the EU but after deductions compare with those of Belgium, the Netherlands and Sweden.

Minimum Monthly Wage (2003): Not applicable.

Social Security: Social security contributions – known as Labour Market Contributions (*ATP-bidrag*) – are compulsory for all employees, unless their home countries have reciprocal agreements. They amount to 9 per cent of gross monthly pay and are tax-deductible. Generous benefits are available to all residents, regardless of nationality. Registering as a resident enrols you in the national health insurance scheme. Medical treatment by doctors and in hospitals is free but you must pay a small percentage of prescription charges. Employers are not obliged to make social security contributions and pay only part of the supplementary pensions scheme (ATP), about DK1,790 a year per employee.

Business Hours: Most factories and offices work from 8 or 9am to 4 or 5pm Monday to Thursday, and from 8 or 9am to 2pm on Friday. Banking hours are 9.30am to 4pm on weekdays, with an extension to 6pm on Thursday.

Public Holidays: Ten per year:

- 1st January
- Maundy Thursday
- Good Friday & Easter Monday
- 1st, 16th & 29th May
- 5th June
- 25th & 26th December

Business Etiquette: Danes favour a formal approach to business and punctuality. Business talk is generally direct and to the point, and communication tends to be easy and straightforward, even over money matters.

Finance

Currency: Krone (DK).
Exchange Rate: €1= DK7.45 (February 2004).
Exchange Controls: None.

Banks: Danish banking is currently undergoing large-scale restructuring and consolidation, with the result that there are now fewer medium and small banks, and five main large banks led by Den Danske Bank and Unibank, which now dominate the banking market. Some foreign banks also operate in Denmark. Danish banking is efficient and offers a wide range of services, including internet banking. To open a bank account, you require a fiscal number obtainable from the local town hall.

Cost/Standard Of Living: The Danish enjoy a high standard of living and salaries are considerably higher than in many other western European countries, although deductions are also high. The cost of living in Denmark is among the highest in Western Europe and on a par with other Scandinavian countries.

Loans: Loans are available from Danish banks.

Interest Rate (Early 2004): 2 per cent.

Taxation

Corporate Tax: Corporate income and capital gains taxes are levied at 30 per cent, although shares that have been owned for longer than three years are exempt from CGT.

Personal Income Tax: Income tax is payable to both central and local governments on a PAYE basis, with combined rates up to 59 per cent less deductions and a depreciation allowance. Foreign residents paid by a foreign employer who fulfil certain strict conditions – e.g. if their employment is temporary and lasts for a maximum of three years and who earn more than DK 54,300 (2003) after deduction of social security contributions – are taxed at a reduced rate of 25 per cent. The self-employed may choose a special tax system, whereby all business income is taxed at a flat rate of 30 per cent, provided that the income is kept in the business. Income tax rates are set to be reduced over a three-year period from 2004 to 2007.

Capital Gains Tax: CGT is payable on assets at the same rates as income tax. Primary residences are exempt if situated on an area of less than 1,400m².

Wealth Tax: None.

Inheritance & Gift Tax: Inheritance and gift taxes start at 15 per cent and depend on the relationship between the donor and the beneficiary. In both cases the first DK191,000 is exempt.

Value Added Tax: Value added tax (MOMS) is charged at a rate of 25 per cent on all services and goods. Certain domestic transactions are exempt, such as most banking and insurance transactions and the sale of land and buildings.

Withholding Taxes: Withholding taxes on dividends are refundable if your home country of has a treaty with Denmark.

Tax Filing: A tax card (*skattekort*) with your fiscal number is required and available from the local town hall. The Danish tax year is the calendar year and final settlements are made in the year following the tax return lodged by 1st May each year.

Accommodation

Building Standards: Generally excellent, as might be expected in a country with a reputation for craftsmanship. More than half of the housing stock has been built since 1960 and many houses are very large. The quality of some older properties may vary.

Restrictions On Foreign Ownership: Non-residents aren't allowed to own property in Denmark and foreign residents must obtain permission from the Minister of Justice. Permission is usually given, provided there's evidence that the property is for permanent residence. EEA citizens may purchase property for all-year residence without permission from the Ministry of Justice, but must provide evidence that the property is for permanent residence. Permission is generally refused for holiday or second homes unless the foreigner has special ties with Denmark.

Cost Of Housing: Housing is quite expensive and there's a shortage of small properties, although the cost is relatively low considering the high standard of living. In Copenhagen an average two-bedroom apartment costs from DK1.2 million and a three-bedroom town house costs from DK2.6 million.

Fees: The purchase of real estate incurs the payment of transfer duty at 1.2 per cent of the purchase price.

Local Mortgages: Mortgages are tied to the property not to the purchaser and it's common practice to buy a house and take over (assume) the mortgage on it. Building societies (*kreditforeninger*) compete with banks for the mortgage market. The maximum loan allowed by law is 80 per cent of a property's value and mortgage rates and terms are fixed at the outset. Danish mortgages are unique in that the capital is raised not by the loan of money, but from the purchase of bonds on the real-estate bond market.

Property Taxes: Property tax is a point of contention in Denmark, where owners are subject to a high annual rate based on a percentage of around two-thirds of the rateable value. There are reductions for pensioners and those in a lower tax band, but the average earner can expect to pay between 16 and 46 per cent of the land value in property taxes, depending on the area, e.g. in Copenhagen the rate is 34 per cent. Property tax is levied either twice a year in January and July or quarterly. There's also a fee for refuse collection and water.

Renting: Although some 40 per cent of Danes live in rented accommodation, there's a shortage and it's difficult to find, particularly in Copenhagen: it's advisable to secure accommodation before your arrival if you plan to live there. In order to rent a property you need to fulfil certain conditions, such as you must occupy the property for at least 180 days a year or 4 days a week and you must have a residence certificate or a work permit. There are a large number of purpose built homes in housing associations (*boligselskaber*), which provide cheap rental accommodation, although there are usually long waiting lists. Typical rents for a small apartment range from DK4,000 to 6,000, and a three-bedroom house costs around DK8,500 a month.

Personal Effects: Personal and household effects can be imported duty-free. If you're on a short-term assignment to Denmark (i.e. less than three years), there's a substantially reduced duty on car importation.

Utilities: Electricity (220/240V) is reliable and charges are around the EU average. Denmark is one of the few European countries where larger electrical appliances (such as washing machines, dryers and heaters) require a 3-phase, 380V supply provided by special 5-pin plugs and sockets. Mains gas is available in most urban areas and most rural areas also have access to gas for home use. Water charges are included in annual property bills and are reasonable. Danish water pressure is higher than in most other countries, therefore it's advisable to have insurance covering damage caused by leaking or burst pipes!

Services

Getting There: Copenhagen is the main airport for international flights and has good connections. It's also easy to reach Denmark by road from mainland Europe and there are frequent ferry services to other Scandinavian countries, Iceland, Poland and the UK.

Public Transport: The public transport system is reliable and inexpensive. There are several small domestic airports served by flights from the capital. The rail network is extensive and good. All populated islands are linked by a comprehensive ferry network.

Motoring: Road conditions are excellent, although car prices are very high. Speed limits are 50kph in built-up areas, 80kph elsewhere, including dual carriageways, and 120kph on motorways. Maximum permitted alcohol level is 50mg per 100ml of blood. All vehicles must carry warning triangles, No leaded petrol is available. Holders of EU driving licences are not required to exchange their licence for a Danish one. Non-EU licence holders must exchange their licence for a Danish one within 14 days of obtaining a residence permit.

Medical Facilities: Standards are high. Treatment by doctors and in hospitals is free to resident who must, however, pay a proportion of prescription charges. EU nationals are immediately eligible for treatment under the public health scheme but others must wait six weeks after arrival to become eligible. All foreigners must pay a proportion of the costs of essential dental treatment.

Education: Compulsory for children aged from 5 or 6 to 15 or 16 years. Most children are educated in state schools and it's common for a child to have the same teacher throughout his schooling. There are many private schools and several English and European schools, mainly in or near Copenhagen, some catering for special ethnic or religious requirements.

Postal Services: The Danish postal service is reliable and fast, and also provides banking services.

Telephone: Telephone installation and services are provided by Tele Danmark, which currently has a monopoly – therefore call charges are high. Mobile phones are popular, but if you wish to buy and operate a mobile phone locally, you can do so only if you have an address in the country.

Internet: Denmark's companies are among Europe's leaders in the use of e-commerce, but use of the internet isn't high, although personal use is increasing. There are numerous ISP's with competitive rates.

English TV & Radio: English-language programmes are shown with Danish subtitles and all films are shown in their original language. There are also several radio stations providing English-language programmes. An annual radio and TV licence is necessary and is available from post offices.

Miscellaneous

Crime Rate: Low – violent crime is virtually unknown.

Pets: Dogs and cats with up-to-date health certificates and a rabies vaccine applied between 30 days and twelve months before arrival may be imported into Denmark.

Visas: Nationals from many countries, including the EU, Canada, Japan and the US, don't need a visa for visits for any purpose up to three months. Business visas for visits up to three months are available for many non-EU countries under the same conditions as for the Schengen Visa (see page 20). For further visa information, see page 19.

Residence Permits: EU nationals must apply at their local police station for a residence permit within three months of entering the country (six months if you're looking for a job). They must provide proof of either employment or income. After obtaining a residence permit, EU nationals must register at their local town hall. Non-EU nationals must obtain a residence and work permit **before** arriving in Denmark. It's worth noting that residence laws are strict and obtaining a permit can often be a long, seemingly arbitrary process, even for EU nationals. It's particularly difficult for dependent spouses to obtain residence permits (even when it's a legal entitlement!).

International Dialling Code: 45.

Time Difference: GMT +1.

Weights & Measures: Metric.

Reference

Useful Addresses

British Embassy, Kastelsvej 38/40, 2100 Copenhagen (☎ 3544-5293, 💻 www.britishembassy.dk).

Royal Danish Embassy, 55 Sloane St., London SW1X 9SR, UK (☎ 020-7333 0200, 💻 www.denmark.org.uk).

Royal Danish Embassy, 3200 Whitehaven St., NW, Washington DC 20008, USA (☎ 202-234 4300, 💻 www.denmarkemb.org).

US Embassy, Dag Hammerskjölds Allé 24, 2100 Copenhagen (☎ 3555-3144, 💻 http://denmark.usembassy.gov).

Useful Websites

Danish Internet Expat Club (🖳 www.foreignhelp.dk) – A wealth of useful advice about relocating to Denmark as well as a meeting point for expats from all over the world.

Invest in Denmark (🖳 www.investindk.com) – Official foreign investment site with useful information about doing business and working in the country.

Work in Denmark (🖳 www.workindenmark.dk) – Excellent website about living and working in Denmark.

ESTONIA

General Information

Capital: Tallinn.
  Population: 1.5 million.
  Foreign Community: There's a sizeable population of Russians and people from other neighbouring countries, but relatively few westerners.
  Area: 45,227km² (17,463mi²).
  Geography: Estonia is the northernmost of the three Baltic States and has borders with the Russian Federation to the east, Latvia to the south and the Baltic Sea to the west and north. It is the smallest Baltic state and is comprised largely of forests and lakes. Over a third of the population lives in the capital, Tallinn, situated on the north coast at the head of the Gulf of Finland.
  Climate: Estonia has a mixture of continental and maritime climates, and the westerly wind usually ensures temperatures don't fall much below freezing. Winters are generally long and cold, and summers warm and pleasant, although August is the wettest month in the region. Average temperatures are -2°C (29°F) in January and 20°C (68°F) in July.
  Language: The official language is Estonian (similar to Finnish). English, German, Polish and Russian are also spoken, although English now dominates as the second language.
  Government: Parliamentary democracy.
  Political Stability: Very good and democracy is now firmly established in Estonia, which is a member of the UN. Estonia joins NATO in May 2004. The Estonians have a somewhat ambivalent view of EU membership since many regard it as a step backward in sovereignty, especially after decades of Soviet domination. Estonian's leading politicians, however, have pushed negotiations forward and the country is well set to fulfil most criteria. The country is poor by EU standards (GDP per capita is a mere 38 per cent of the EU average), but Estonia has opened itself up to trade, is highly integrated in the European economy and information technology is readily available. Challenges facing the country once it joins the EU include liberalisation of the

energy sector, the eradication of duty-free shopping, labour law and sexual equality, particularly in the workplace.
EU Accession: 2004.

Economy

Overview: Of the three Baltic states, Estonia has made the best transition to a free market economy and privatisation of small and medium companies is practically completed. The economy grew rapidly during the mid-'90s and since then growth has been steady. Although the Estonian economy relies to some extent on the Russian, the country has now begun to look towards the EU as its main trading partner. Foreign investment is currently high.
GDP Per Head: US$5,162.
Growth (2003): 4.3 per cent.
Forecast Growth For 2004: 5.2 per cent.
Main Industries: Construction, export management, hotels and restaurants, infrastructure, IT and sales and marketing.
UK Trade Partner Ranking: 50+.
US Trade Partner Ranking: 50+.

Working

Overview: The labour market has changed considerably in recent years and most new jobs are being created in education and the financial and real estate sectors. Employees are generally skilled and well trained, particularly in IT.
Unemployment Rate (2003): 9.7 per cent.
Employment Opportunities: Most skilled workers (except accountants, economists and lawyers) and project managers are in short supply. TEFL is currently a boom area, but salaries are low and contracts short-term. There's also great scope for entrepreneurs.
Work Permits: EU citizens must obtain permits to start work but may visit for up to six months to seek work. Regulations may change in May 2006 and you are advised to seek the latest information. New regulations require that jobs must be offered through employment agencies and employers must establish that no Estonian with suitable qualifications is available before employing a foreigner. Hence non-EU nationals may find it hard to obtain work permits.
Labour Relations: Generally good: unions and employer associations are encouraging collective bargaining and agreements, which are currently negotiated in relatively few sectors. Strikes are rare.
Employment Conditions: Employees work a 40-hour Monday to Friday week and have 28 days paid annual leave under labour legislation. There's a countrywide minimum wage and unusually generous (by EU standards) maternity leave.

Salaries: Much lower than in Western Europe, though higher than in some other new member states. The average annual wage in Tallinn is about €7,300 and on Tartu around €5,600. Financial sector workers have the highest salaries. **Minimum Monthly Wage (2003):** €138.

Social Security: Employers contribute 33 per cent of employees' gross monthly pay to social security and employees 1 per cent towards unemployment insurance and 2 per cent to the pension scheme. The system is comprehensive, covering illness and disability allowances, retirement and disability pensions and subsidised medical care.

Business Hours: Offices and businesses open from 9am to 5pm and banks from 8.30am to 5pm Monday to Friday.

Public Holidays: 12 per year:

- 1st January
- 24th February
- Good Friday & Easter Sunday
- 1st May
- 8th, 23rd & 24th June
- 25th & 26th December

Business Etiquette: Business is conducted formally and you should shake hands with all contacts. Dress is formal and business cards are usually exchanged. English is widely spoken and Estonian, but speaking Russian may cause offence.

Finance

Currency: Kroon (EEK).

Exchange Rate: Pegged to the euro at €1= 15.65 kroon.

Exchange Controls: None.

Banks: The Estonian banking system is stable and well developed. Banking processes are efficient and highly computerised, although some procedures such as clearing cheques take a lot longer (up to three weeks) than in Western banks.

Cost/Standard Of Living: Although Estonia has the highest average monthly wages in the Baltic States, the cost of living is generally much lower than in the rest of the EU. Imported goods are expensive.

Loans: Local banks can provide loans but they are probably best avoided since 18 months is considered a long-term loan! There are also specialised financial institutions.

Interest Rate (Early 2004): 3 per cent.

Taxation

Corporate Tax: Corporate tax on profits was abolished in 2000. Income tax is, however, payable on dividends and other profit distributions, fringe benefits and expenses and payments not related to the business. Corporate CGT is levied at 26 per cent.

Personal Income Tax: Income tax is levied at a flat rate of 26 per cent.

Capital Gains Tax: CGT is levied at the same rate as income tax. Principal residences and summer houses owned for longer than two years and with under 0.25 hectares are exempt.

Wealth Tax: None.

Inheritance & Gift Tax: None.

Value Added Tax: The standard rate for VAT is 18 per cent and there are two reduced rates of 0 and 5 per cent.

Withholding Taxes: Dividends are subject to 26 per cent withholding tax.

Tax Filing: The tax year is the calendar year and individuals must file an annual return by 31st March. The company tax year must be 12 months long but the entity can choose to end its tax year on 31stMarch, 30thJune, 30th September or 31st December. Tax must be paid monthly.

Accommodation

Building Standards: Variable and poor in many apartment blocks in cities and main towns.

Restrictions On Foreign Ownership: None:

Cost Of Housing: Typical prices for a two-bedroom apartment are from EEK750,000 and from EEK1.1 million for a house.

Fees: Fees for property purchase include notary and land registry fees, estate agent's commission (2 to 4 per cent) and state duty from between EEK260 and 40,000 on properties costing up to EEK1 million and 0.4 per cent above this.

Local Mortgages: Mortgages are available from local banks for up to 30 years for maximum amounts of 85 per cent of the property's price.

Property Taxes: Land tax is levied at rates between 0.1 and 0.25 per cent of the property's market value.

Renting: Rental property is widely available, although foreigners will find the standards lower than they are used to. Prices are also often inflated for 'rich' foreigners who may have to pay twice as much as locals for the same accommodation. It's best to consult a reputable local agency specialising in rentals before committing yourself. A two-bedroom apartment costs from EEK20,000 a month.

Personal Effects: Residents in Estonia may import belongings and effects free of import duty and tax.

Utilities: The electricity supply (220V) is generally reliable. Tap water is safe to drink.

Services

Getting There: Tallinn International Airport, renovated in 1999, has frequent flights from most European cities and particularly Scandinavia. There are also good rail connections, notably to Moscow and St Petersburg. and ferries across the Baltic and to Finland, Germany and Sweeden.

Public Transport: The rail network was privatised in 2001 and offers a good service countrywide. The main cities have adequate tram and bus services.

Motoring: The road network is undergoing ambitious reconstruction: priority routes are those linking the capital to Narva, Pärnu and Tartu. The Via Baltica, connecting Scandinavia with Central and Southern Europe via Poland and the Baltic States will also pass through Estonia. Driving standards are poor and the accident rate high. Conditions in winter are poor with snow tyres mandatory. Speed limits are 50kph in built-up area, 90kph elsewhere and 120kph on motorways. Alcohol tolerance is zero, All vehicles must carry a warning triangle, fire extinguisher and first aid kit. No leaded petrol is available. Residents with EU driving licences need not exchange them. Others must exchange their licences after 12 months of residence. Some foreigners may have to take theoretical and practical exams to obtain an Estonian licence. Anyone committing a motoring offence that leads to a licence suspension must take the Estonian driving test to regain it.

Medical Facilities: Healthcare facilities are fair but below standards that westerners expect. Standards are higher in the private sector. Emergency and much minor treatment is free; otherwise you must pay. A comprehensive international health insurance policy is essential.

Education: Generally of a high standard with lessons conducted in the local language and Russian. Schooling is free and compulsory for children aged from 7 to 15 or 16. The majority of children attend state schools. There are very few private schools and no international ones.

Postal Services: The postal service is generally reliable and post from Western Europe takes up to a week to arrive.

Telephone: The telephone service is operated by Estonian Telephone, at present the monopoly holder. International charges are high, although discounts are available at night and weekends. Three mobile phone companies operate within the country.

Internet: Internet is increasingly popular both in business and at home. Some 20 per cent of the population have a pc at home. Several companies offer internet subscription services.

English TV & Radio: Cable and satellite TV channels are available in Estonia, as is the BBC World Service.

Miscellaneous

Crime Rate: Unlike many Eastern Euripean countrties, Estonia's crime rate is not particularly high, though petty crime is common, mostly in crowded places.

Pets: Pets can be imported if they have an international veterinary certificate showing they are in good health.

Visas: Nationals from many countries, including the EU, Australia, Japan, New Zealand and the US (but not Canada) don't need a visa for visits of up to six months. Others must obtain a visa **before** arrival. Business visas were abolished in May 2003. For further visa information, see page 19.

Residence Permits: All foreigners wishing to stay in Estonia for more than 90 days during a period of six months must apply for a residence permit. EU nationals may apply within Estonia, but non-EU nationals must apply for a work permit before arrival and then for a residence permit once they have entered Estonia.

International Dialling Code: 372.

Time Difference: GMT +2.

Weights & Measures: Metric.

Reference

Useful Addresses

British Embassy, Wismari 6, Tallinn 10136 (☎ 667-4756, ☐ www.british embassy.ee).

Estonian Embassy, 16 Hyde Park Gate, London SW7 5DG, UK (☎ 020-7589 7690, ☐ www.estonia.gov.uk).

Estonian Embassy, 2131 Massachusetts Ave NW, Washington DC, USA (☎ 202-588 0101, ☐ www.estemb.org).

US Embassy, Kentmanni 20, Tallinn 15099 (☎ 668-8100, ☐ www.usemb.ee).

Useful Websites

Estonian Investment Agency (☐ www.eia.ee) – The website provides comprehensive downloadable factsheets about doing business and working in the country.

Estonian Ministry of Foreign Affairs (☐ www.vm.ee/eng) – A wealth of useful information about Estonia.

Enterprise Estonia (☐ www.eas.ee) – Information about setting up a business in Estonia.

Official State Web Centre (☐ www.riik.ee/en) – Links to most Estonian ministries and public offices. Not all the links are in English.

Visit Estonia (☐ www.visitestonia.com) – The official tourist site.

FINLAND

General Information

Capital: Helsinki.

Population: 5.2 million.

Foreign Community: There isn't a large expatriate community in Finland apart from people from the Baltic states, although there has been an huge influx of immigrants from Asia and Africa in recent years. Relatively few westerners work in Finland.

Area: 338,130km² (130,552mi²).

Geography: Finland is the most northerly country in mainland Europe and one-third of its territory lies within the Arctic Circle. The country is essentially flat except for Lapland in the north where there are several peaks over 1,000m (3,280ft). There are thousands of long, narrow lakes in the southern half of Finland, while some 60 per cent of the country is covered in forest. This accounts for the fact that forest-based products constitute almost half Finland's exports, although the engineering and metallurgical industries are also of prime importance. Some localities on the south and west coasts have a majority of Swedish-speaking inhabitants, a legacy of the time when Finland was under Swedish rule (until 1809).

Climate: Winters with very short days are long and cold, and it's common for the sea to freeze across a substantial distance, although snowfall isn't generally heavy. Summers are short and warm and the days are extremely long, particularly in the north where, during the month of June, there's practically no night. Average temperatures for Helsinki are -6°C (21°F) in January and 17°C (63°F) in July, although in the north temperatures of -30°C (-22°F) are common in winter.

Language: The official languages are Finnish and Swedish. English is widely spoken.

Government: Multiparty parliamentary republic with a unicameral legislature. Finland is a member of EFTA and joined the EU in 1995.

Political Stability: Excellent.

EU Accession: 1995.

Economy

Overview: Over recent years Finland has successfully closed the wealth gap with other Scandinavian nations and is now at the forefront of EU economies with steady growth and strong competitiveness in the world market. GDP growth over the last few years has been one of the strongest in the EU. Finland is strategically placed and a major gateway to the vast markets opening up in Russia and the Baltic States, which account for around 80 million consumers.

GDP Per Head: US$31,090.

Growth (2003): 1.6 per cent.

Forecast Growth For 2004: 3 per cent.

Main Industries: Chemicals, electronics, forestry and forestry products, industrial design, manufacture of machinery and equipment, shipbuilding and telecommunications.

UK Trade Partner Ranking: 18.

US Trade Partner Ranking: 28.

Working

Overview: Two recent surveys place Finland among the top countries for business environment. The workforce, 60 per cent of which is engaged in the services sector, is generally well educated and skilled but a potential crisis is looming over the next decade when many Finns reach retirement age; hence a government priority is to restructure retirement provisions. Unemployment, traditionally high, has reduced in recent years.

Unemployment Rate (2003): 8.9 per cent.

Employment Opportunities: There are opportunities in all the main industries, although foreign employees tend to be concentrated in accountancy, finance, international marketing, IT, TEFL and tourism.

Work Permits: Not required for nationals of the original EU member states, but necessary for all others. Nationals of new member states may visit for up to six months to seek work, but regulations are expected to change in May 2006 and should be checked for the latest information. Non-EU nationals must secure a work permit **before** arrival, supported by a statement from the Department of Labour obtained by the prospective employer.

Labour Relations: Trade unions are strong and most employees are members, so collective bargaining is commonplace. Employment contracts, written or oral, are subject to legislation and foreign potential employers should seek legal advice.

Employment Conditions: Generally very good, with a 35-day paid holiday allowance and many benefits for employees. A working knowledge of Swedish is recommended.

Salaries: Around the EU average and similar to those in Belgium, France and the Netherlands.

Minimum Monthly Wage (2003): Not applicable.

Social Security: Contributions – 4.8 per cent of gross monthly pay for pensions and 1.5 per cent for sickness benefit – are compulsory for all employees unless their home country has a reciprocal agreement. Benefits are generous.

Business Hours: Businesses operate from 8am to 5pm in winter and to 4pm in summer. Banks open from 9.15am to 4.15pm Monday to Friday. During the summer holiday period – late-June to mid-August – it is difficult to do business.

Public Holidays: 12 per year:

- 1st & 6th January
- Good Friday & Easter Monday
- 1st & 29th May
- 19th & 30th June
- 31st October
- 24th, 25th & 26th December

Business Etiquette: Finns have a strong work ethic and value conscientiousness and punctuality. Their business manner is direct and to the point and they tend to be quality conscious and to expect punctual deliveries.

Finance

Currency: Euro (€).
    Exchange Controls: None.
    Banks: The Finnish banking system is highly developed and secure. There are numerous banks in Finland (including several foreign banks), offering a full range of modern and efficient banking services. The largest bank is MeritaNordbanken, which has branches in a number of European capitals.
    Cost/Standard Of Living: The Finns enjoy a high standard of living with salaries to match, although income tax and social security deductions are high, as is the cost of living.
    Loans: Loans are available from Finnish banks.
    Interest Rate (Early 2004): 2 per cent (European Central Bank).

Taxation

Corporate Tax: Corporate income and capital gains taxes are levied at 29 per cent.
    Personal Income Tax: Income tax is deducted at source (PAYE). State income tax is levied at rates ranging from 13 per cent (on annual income up to €14,300) to 36 per cent on amounts over €54,700. There are numerous allowances and deductions. Local income tax is from 15 to 18 per cent. Church tax of 1 to 2 per cent is also payable. Non-residents are subject to a flat rate on income earned in Finland. Residents are taxed on their worldwide income. An expatriate may qualify for a special tax at a flat rate of 35% for two years if certain conditions are fulfilled. This rule is currently effective only if the employment started in 2003 or earlier, but check for recent up-to-date information.
    Capital Gains Tax: CGT is levied on assets and gains at a flat rate of 29 per cent. Principal residences are exempt provided that the owner has owned and lived in the property for at least two years.
    Wealth Tax: Wealth tax is assessed on assets in Finland exceeding €135,000 at a rate of 0.9%.
    Inheritance & Gift Tax: Rates depend on the relationship between the deceased or donor and the heir or recipient of a gift. For relationships of the first degree, rates range from 10 to 16 per cent. Tax is levied on the individual not the estate.
    Value Added Tax: The standard rate of value added tax (known as *arvonlisavero*) is 22 per cent, while there are reduced rates of 17 per cent on food and 8 per cent on hotel services, most medicine and books.
    Withholding Taxes: Dividends are subject to 28 per cent withholding tax and residents only are subject to 28 per cent on interest.
    Tax Filing: You require a tax card number provided by the tax authorities. The Finnish tax year is the calendar year and annual tax returns must be completed by the end of January of the following year. Joint filing is not possible. Corporate entities must file a tax return within 4 months from the end of their accounting period.

Accommodation

Building Standards: Excellent.

Restrictions On Foreign Ownership: None,

Cost Of Housing: Accommodation is quite expensive in Finland where a two-bedroom apartment in Helsinki costs from €175,000 and a three-bedroom house from €225,000.

Fees: Fees for property purchase include a 4 per cent transfer tax plus legal fees (purchases made by first-home buyers aged between 18 and 39 years are exempt from transfer tax).

Local Mortgages: Mortgages are available from local banks if you can provide a guarantor and have had a fixed salary in Finland for at least three years. Banks will provide up to 100 per cent finance, although 70 to 80 per cent is more usual. Lengths of loans vary from 10 to 25 years.

Property Taxes: Property tax is calculated on the taxable value of the property and ranges from 0.5 to 1 per cent according to the community. Permanent residences are taxed at rates of from 0.22 to 0.5 per cent, with the latter being the average.

Renting: There's a shortage of rental accommodation in most population centres, and the situation is particularly difficult in the capital. Houses are almost impossible to rent. A two-bedroom apartment costs from €1,000 per month and a three-bedroom apartment from €1,500 per month.

Personal Effects: Personal and household effects can be imported duty-free provided they have been owned for at least six months.

Utilities: The electricity supply (230V) is reliable and available in all but the most remote parts of the north. Rates are below the EU average. Water rates are generally low and the quality is good. Mains gas isn't available, although bottled gas is widely available. Many households use oil for heating.

Services

Getting There: Helsinki has a busy international airport with services to worldwide destinations provided by most major carriers. There's an extensive range of international ferry services to countries such as Estonia, Germany, Norway and Sweden.

Public Transport: There are some 20 domestic airports and the main carrier, Finnair, operates one of the cheapest services in Europe. Public transport is generally excellent and covers the whole country apart from remote areas of Lapland. Rail services are efficient and economic and domestic ferries serve destinations on the Baltic Sea and inland lakes.

Motoring: Road conditions are good and cars reasonably priced. Speed limits are 50kph in built-up areas, 80 or 100kph elsewhere and 120kph on motorways, but all are reduced in winter (October to February). Maximum permitted alcohol level is 50mg per 100ml of blood. All vehicles must carry a warning triangle. No leaded petrol is available. EU and international driving licences may be used for up to a year but, if a foreigner is living permanently or studying for over six months, his licence must be exchanged for a Finnish one. EEA licences are directly exchanged but other foreigners may have to take a Finnish driving test.

Medical Facilities: Healthcare standards are high and the facilities modern. The national health system, which foreigners may join after 12 months residence, covers most requirements, with patients paying 10 per cent of costs. Private healthcare supplements the national system in most towns and cities, with a proportion of costs reimbursed by the state.

Education: Free, co-educational and compulsory for children aged from 7 to 16 years. Most children attend state schools; there are hardly any private schools but a few international ones around Helsinki.

Postal Services: The Finnish postal service is highly efficient and also provides a comprehensive banking system, which is particularly useful in rural areas where there are no banks.

Telephone: The telephone service is excellent and since the state monopoly was abolished in the '90s, there are several companies competing and call charges have been greatly reduced. Finland is **the** mobile phone country (Nokia is a Finnish company) and has more mobile phones per head than any country in the world and very competitive prices.

Internet: Finland has the highest number of internet connections per capita in the world and there are numerous ISPs offering competitive or free services.

English TV & Radio: Finnish TV and radio broadcast exclusively in Finnish or Swedish, but English-language cable and satellite TV is available.

Miscellaneous

Crime Rate: Low. Violent crime is virtually unknown.

Pets: Regulations regarding the importation of pets are complex and depend on whether your country of origin is rabies-free and within the EU. Dogs and cats from the UK and Ireland with no symptoms of infectious diseases may be imported without specific import documentation. Animals from other countries need vaccination and health certificates. Check with a Finnish representation abroad for up-to-date requirements.

Visas: Nationals from many countries, including the EU, Canada, Japan and the US, don't need visas for visits up to three months. Business visas for up to three months are available for many non-EU citizens under the same conditions as for the Schengen Visa (see page 20).

Residence Permits: Non-EU nationals must apply for a residence permit at the same time as a work permit after they have entered Finland. Residence permits are a formality for EU nationals, who should report to the local police station within 15 days of their arrival, but must also register with the local Register Office and notify them every time they move house.

International Dialling Code: 358.

Time Difference: GMT +2.

Weights & Measures: Metric.

Reference

Useful Addresses

British Embassy, Itäinen Puistotie 17, FIN 00140 Helsinki (☎ 09-2286 5100, 🖳 www.ukembassy.fi).

Finnish Embassy, 38 Chesham Place, London SW1X 8HW, UK (☎ 020-7838 6200, 🖳 www.finemb.org.uk).

Finnish Embassy, 3301 Massachusetts Avenue, NW, Washington DC 20008, USA (☎ 202-298 5800, 🖳 www.finland.org).

US Embassy, Itäinen Puistotie 14B, FIN 00140 Helsinki (☎ 09-616250, 🖳 www. usembassy.fi).

Further Reading

Guide to Moving to Finland (for immigrants) published in pdf by the Finnish Labour Administration (🖳 www.mol.fi/migration)

Useful Websites

Finn Facts (🖳 www.finnfacts.com) – Provides a wealth of interesting mainly economic statistics.

Information for Expats (🖳 www.suomi.fi/english) – Plenty of useful information for expats.

Invest in Finland Bureau (🖳 www.investinfinland.fi) – Official foreign investment body with offices in several countries including the UK.

Labour Administration (🖳 www.mol.fi) – Website includes many job vacancies.

FRANCE

General Information

Capital: Paris.
 Population: 59.2 million.
 Foreign Community: France has a sizeable foreign community in its major cities and some rural areas (e.g. Dordogne and Provence) have a large number of British and other foreign residents.
 Area: 551,500km² (212,934mi²).
 Geography: France is the largest countries in Europe, bordered by Andorra, Belgium, Germany, Italy, Luxembourg, Spain and Switzerland. The opening of the channel tunnel in 1994 connected it with the UK (albeit by rail only). There are a variety of landscapes, including the high Alpine and Pyrenean mountain

ranges, the vast Massif Central and several important river valleys. France also incorporates the Mediterranean island of Corsica (*Corse*) situated 160km (99mi) from France and 80km (50mi) from Italy.

Climate: France is the only country in Europe that experiences three distinct climates: continental, maritime and Mediterranean. The west and north-west (e.g. Brittany and Normandy) have a maritime climate with mild winters and warm summers, and most rainfall in spring and autumn. The Massif and eastern France have a moderate continental climate with cold winters and hot and stormy summers. However, the centre and eastern upland areas have an extreme continental climate, with freezing winters and sweltering summers. The south of France enjoys a Mediterranean climate of mild winters (daytime temperatures rarely drop below 10°C (50°F)) and humid, hot summers, with temperatures often above 30°C (86°F). Paris has an average temperature of 5°C (41°F) in January and of 23°C (73°F) in July, and the capital is quite wet.

Language: The official language is French. France also has a number of regional languages and local dialects are also common in many areas. English is spoken by many people.

Government: Republic with bicameral legislature.

Political Stability: Excellent, although periodically shaken by national strikes and riots. In 2002, the far right-wing leader, Jean Marie Le Pen, reached the second round of the presidential election, although a massive campaign by all other parties against his party, the FN, ensured that he was beaten by Jacques Chirac.

EU Accession: Founder member.

Economy

Overview: France, the world's fourth largest economy, is the strongest of the EU economies and has maintained steady growth over recent years, although it entered recession in the first half of 2003 and GDP growth for the year was just 0.4 per cent. Government spending is one of the highest in the developed world (over 50 per cent of GDP) and state intervention in industry is also very high. France ranks among the top host countries in Europe for multi-national firms and from 2000 to 2002 more than 60,000 jobs were created by international investors.

GDP Per Head: US$21,857.

Growth (2003): 0.4 per cent.

Forecast Growth For 2004: 1.75 per cent.

Main Industries: Agriculture and foodstuffs, banking, insurance, pharmaceuticals, telecommunications, tourism and transport.

UK Trade Partner Ranking: 3.

US Trade Partner Ranking: 11.

Working

Overview: Unemployment has decreased in recent years but remains uncomfortably high. The workforce, 68 per cent of which is engaged in the services sector, is generally well educated and trained. Labour laws permit the temporary employment of extra staff and France has the world's second largest temporary employment market after the US.

Unemployment Rate (2003): 9.5 per cent.

Employment Opportunities: TEFL and language assistants, IT, management (there is currently a shortage of graduates) and tourism. Most foreign employees tend to work for multinational or large national firms. Good qualifications and fluent French are essential.

Work Permits: Not required for nationals of original EU member states. Nationals of new member states must obtain permits before starting work but may visit for up to six months to seek employment. Work permits are difficult for non-EU nationals to obtain since France has for several years had a virtual freeze on employment of non-EU citizens.

Labour Relations: Traditionally difficult where union membership is high and workers often protest by striking. In 2003, government plans to reform the pension system sparked off a nationwide strike and numerous huge demonstrations. There's a minimum wage and collective bargaining is commonplace.

Employment Conditions: Good: a 35-hour week has been successfully introduced on a large scale. Paid annual holidays usually amount to five weeks and a 13th month salary payment is common practice. Employers must contribute to housing and welfare schemes and employees enjoy many fringe benefits.

Salaries: Around the EU average, although professionals generally earn less than in Belgium, Greece or Ireland. In 2003, the average gross annual salary was €16,000.

Minimum Monthly Wage: €1,036.

Social Security: Contributions are high for both employer (around 35 per cent of the employee's gross salary) and employee (about 25 per cent) but benefits are generous. The self-employed make contributions as they earn, the amount depending on total earnings. Contributions are paid on 1st April and 1st October.

Business Hours: Businesses operate from 9am to noon and 2 to 6pm Monday to Friday. Banks open from 9.30am to noon and 2 to 6pm although provincial branches often close on Monday.

Public Holidays: 13 per year:

- 1st January
- Good Friday & Easter Monday
- 1st May
- Ascension Day
- Whitsun (May/June)
- 14th July
- 15th August
- 1st & 11th November
- 25th & 26th December

Note that it's advisable to avoid doing business in July and August, when most of the country is on holiday.

Business Etiquette: Business is conducted very formally and first names are rarely used in business relationships. You should shake hands on greeting and leaving and smart dress is expected. The French appreciate efforts to speak their language and it's worth learning a few phrases beforehand.

Finance

Currency: Euro (€).

Exchange Controls: None.

Banks: Banks in France are either commercial or cooperative and most have branches in all towns and cities. Many foreign banks, particularly British, are present in France, although branches tend to be concentrated in Paris. Both residents and non-residents may open a bank account, although current accounts receive no interest. It's illegal to be overdrawn even by one euro and transgressors are heavily penalised

Cost/Standard Of Living: Salaries are generally high in France and the French enjoy a high standard of living. With the exception of Paris, where the higher cost of living is offset by higher salaries, the cost of living in France is lower than the EU average, particularly in rural areas.

Loans: Loans are available from French banks, although terms and conditions are more conservative than in many other European countries and business loans to foreigners can be difficult to obtain.

Interest Rate (Early 2004): 2 per cent (European Central Bank).

Taxation

Corporate Tax: Corporate income and capital gains taxes are levied at 33.3 per cent, although there are substantial reductions for reinvestment of profits and long-term capital gains and certain small companies qualify for a reduced rate of 19 per cent. Capital gains taxes are levied at 33.3 per cent, but smaller companies are subject to a rate of 15 per cent for the portion of profit below €38,112, and to the standard rate for amounts above this.

Personal Income Tax: Income tax for most people in France is below the average for EU countries, particularly for large families. However, when income tax is added to the high social security contributions and other taxes, then French taxes are among the highest in the EU. Income Tax isn't deducted at source. Most taxpayers pay their tax a year in arrears in three instalments. Tax returns must be filed by the end of February and are for the previous calendar year. Tax rates range from 0 per cent (on annual income under €4,191) to 49.58 per cent (on annual income in excess of €47,131), although there are numerous allowances that reduce the amount payable. Non-residents' French-source income is generally subject to withholding tax at lower rates than residents' income tax of between 15 and 25 per cent.

Capital Gains Tax: Gains on profits made on the sale of real estate in France are taxable but the base is reduced according to the holding period. Principal residences are exempt from CGT, but second homes are liable at different rates depending on the length of ownership. CGT on securities and shares is levied at 16 per cent (plus 10 per cent social surcharges).

Wealth Tax: A wealth tax of between 0.5 and 1.8 per cent is levied on French residents and is based on the value of worldwide assets exceeding €720,000.

Inheritance & Gift Tax: Inheritance tax in France is paid by individual beneficiaries, irrespective of where they are domiciled, and not by the estate. The rate of tax and allowances vary according to the relationship between the beneficiary and the deceased. There are allowances for close relatives, after which inheritance tax is levied on a sliding scale of from 5 to 40 per cent. Gift tax is levied at the same rates, although there are allowances for gifts between spouses and to children or grandchildren.

Value Added Tax: The standard rate of value added tax (TVA) in France of 19.6 per cent applies to the vast majority of goods and services. There is a reduced rate of 5.5 per cent and a super-reduced rate of 2.1 per cent. Certain items such as food, children's clothes and insurance are exempt from VAT.

Withholding Taxes: Withholding tax is payable on dividends and interest.

Tax Filing: The French tax year is the calendar year and all individuals and businesses must file tax returns. Employees must file by late March and the self-employed by late April.

Accommodation

Building Standards: Variable.

Restrictions On Foreign Ownership: None.

Cost Of Housing: Properties in France are considerably more expensive in the south and the capital than in the north. Similarly, the closer you are to the coast or Paris, the more expensive property is, with properties on the French Riviera the most expensive of all (and among the most expensive in Europe). Modern two-bedroom apartments cost from €175,000, although in the provinces €80,000 will buy a small detached house.

Fees: The total fees payable when buying a house in France are between 10 and 15 per cent of the price for a small to medium sized property over five years old. Fees for properties less than five years old are 3 or 4 per cent, but VAT at 19.6 per cent is included in the purchase price. Fees comprise the notary's fee (around 5 per cent), stamp duty (from €150 to €250), registration fees (around 5 per cent), land registry fees (around 0.6 per cent) and agent's fees. Prices may be quoted inclusive or exclusive of agent's fees, therefore you should check whether they are included in the price quoted and who is going to pay them.

Local Mortgages: Mortgages are available from all major French banks (both for residents and non-residents) and many foreign banks. Crédit Agricole is the largest French lender with around 25 per cent of the market. Mortgages can be obtained for any period from 2 to 20 years, although the usual term is 15 years. French mortgages are usually limited to 70 or 80 per cent of a property's value.

Property Taxes: There are two property-based taxes in France. Real estate tax (*taxe foncière*) is paid by owners and is similar to the property tax (or rates) levied in most countries. Residential tax (*taxe d'habitation*) is payable by anyone who resides in a property, whether as an owner, tenant or rent-free. Both taxes are based on the average (notional) rental value of property in the previous year, adjusted for inflation (as calculated by the land registry), although rates vary widely from one region to another.

Renting: In Paris and other major cities, rental accommodation is in high demand and short supply, and rents are among the highest in Europe. Monthly rent for a small apartment costs from €800 and €1,600 although rents in a fashionable area can be much higher. Detached houses are almost impossible to rent in Paris and prohibitively expensive. Outside Paris and in provincial cities such as Lyon and Bordeaux, a small apartment rents for around €500 per month and a three-bedroom house from around €750 a month.

Personal Effects: Personal effects can be imported into France tax and duty-free although you must provide an inventory and, if you're a non-EU national, all imported goods must have be owned for at least six months prior to importation and cannot be sold for a year afterwards.

Utilities: Electricity is provided by EDF throughout the country and the consumer must choose the maximum power supply they require for domestic use. In rural areas, the power supply may be frequently interrupted. Mains gas is available in most large towns and cities, and the consumer can choose between four tariffs to suit his requirements. In rural areas and smaller towns, bottled gas or a tank are the only options available. Water is metered in France and the cost varies from region to region, with the most expensive tariffs in towns. Water is a scarce commodity in some regions of the country, particularly in the south-east where droughts are common. In rural areas there may also be shortages.

Services

Getting There: Paris has two international airports and there are numerous airports around the country. Flights to Paris are frequent and available from practically all major worldwide destinations. France is easily reached by road and rail from mainland Europe and there are frequent ferry services across the Channel to the UK and Ireland, as well as the Eurotunnel car train service.

Public Transport: Communications in France are excellent and one of the country's investment priorities. There are numerous domestic airports and a good flight service. Public transport in the cities is generally excellent and Paris has one of the cheapest and most efficient public transport systems in the world. French railways are the jewel in the French communications crown and France has Europe's most extensive rail network and the world's fastest passenger trains (*TGV*), which serve the main routes and a number of European destinations. Fares are reasonable.

Motoring: Roads are excellent with toll motorways connecting most major cities, although toll charges are high. The heavily congested roads around Paris and in the city itself are one of Europe's motoring nightmares. Speed limits are 50kph in built-up areas, 90kph or 110kph outside built-up areas including dual carriageways, and 130kph on motorways. Holders of EU driving licences exceeding speed limits by more than 25kph may have their licences confiscated on the spot by the police. Maximum permitted alcohol level is 50mg per 100ml of blood. A warning triangle must be carried in all vehicles. No leaded petrol is available. You can drive in France for up to a year with an international or most foreign licences. After a year non-EU licence holders must exchange their licence for a French one. EU holders don't have to exchange theirs unless they commit a driving offence involving loss of points.

Medical Facilities: Excellent. French doctors are highly trained and general hospitals are superbly equipped, although they are few and far between in some rural areas. France has an excellent national health service for those contributing to social security and for retirees, under which around 75 per cent of the cost of medical treatment is reimbursed. However, the doctor or hospital offering the treatment must be part of the social security system (*conventionné*). Prescriptions are also subject to a refund of 40 to 70 per cent depending on the type of medication. If you aren't covered by the national health scheme, private health insurance is essential and often obligatory for residents.

Education: Education is free and compulsory for children aged from 6 to 16 and standards are generally very high. For pre-school children, there are many day nurseries and crèches, many of which are state-subsidised. Although the majority of French children attend state schools, there are also many private schools, mostly Catholic and largely state-funded. International schools (e.g. American and British) are found mainly around Paris and on the French Riviera.

Postal Services: Most towns and villages have a post office, which provides a wide range of services, including money transfers and the payment of utility bills. The French postal service is reputably among the slowest in Europe, although services have improved in recent years.

Telephone: The telephone service is operated by numerous companies in France, the three main ones being France Télécom (the largest and previous monopoly holder), Cegetel and Omnicom. France has one of the most modern and efficient telephone systems in the world and tariffs are reasonable by European standards. There are three mobile phone operators.

Internet: France was slow off the mark with the internet, mainly because it had pioneered Minitel and lacked widespread computer ownership. However, massive government investment has meant that many businesses and households are now on-line. There are many ISPs and, with increasing competition, prices are competitive. ADSL connections, however, remain expensive and broad band technology is available only in large towns and cities.

English TV & Radio: Most television stations broadcast all programmes in French, although some films and news programmes are in English with French subtitles. There's a mandatory television licence a year costing around €120. Satellite television reception is good throughout France and cable TV is available in the major towns and cities. Some French radio stations broadcast news bulletins in English and in the south of France there are several English-language stations.

Miscellaneous

Crime Rate: France has a similar crime rate to most European countries, with quite a high rate in the cities and relatively little crime in rural areas.

Pets: Cats, dogs, parrot-like birds and other small pets may be imported into France provided they have a health certificate issued no more than five days before departure. Cats and dogs under three months cannot be imported. Rabies vaccinations are compulsory in many parts of France and all animals should have an up-to-date vaccination certificate. Dogs must be registered and tattooed with an identity number in one of their ears.

Visas: Nationals of many countries, including the EU, Canada and the US, don't require visas for visits up to three months. Business visas for up to three months are available for many non-EU countries under the same conditions as for the Schengen Visa (see page 20). For further visa information see page 19.

Residence Permits: All foreigners remaining in France for more than 90 days require a residence permit available from police stations or town halls. EU nationals must apply within three months of arrival and those who are employed are issued with renewable ten-year residence permits. Unemployed EU nationals are issued with a one-year temporary residence permit. It's expected that the residence permit requirement for EU nationals will be abolished in the near future. Non-EU nationals must apply for a temporary residence permit within two months of arrival

International Dialling Code: 33.

Time Difference: GMT +1.

Weights & Measures: Metric.

Reference

Useful Addresses

British Embassy, 35 rue de Faubourg St Honoré, 75383 Paris (☎ 01 44 51 31 00, 🖳 www.amb-grandebretagne.fr).

French Embassy, 58 Knightsbridge, London SW1X 7JT, UK (☎ 020-7073 1000, 🖳 www.ambafrance-uk.org).

French Embassy, 4101 Reservoir Rd., NW, Washington DC 20007, USA (☎ 202-944 6000, 🖳 www.info-france-usa.org).

US Embassy, 2 Avenue Gabriel, 75008 Paris (☎ 01 43 12 22 22, 💻 www.amb-usa.fr).

Further Reading

Living and Working in France, David Hampshire (Survival Books Ltd, 💻 www.survivalbooks.net).

Useful Websites

All For France (💻 www.all4france.com) – Information about living and working in France.

AngloFrance (💻 www.anglofrance.net) – Comprehensive expatriate site.

Expatica (💻 www.expatica.com) – Good expatriate site.

Franco-British Chamber of Commerce and Industry (💻 www.francobritishchambers.com).

Invest in France Agency (💻 www.afii.fr/France) – Official foreign investment site with offices in a number of countries, including the UK and US.

Paris Anglo (💻 www.paris-anglo.com) – A good expatriate site for foreigners based in the capital.

GERMANY

General Information

Capital: Berlin.
Population: 82.4 million.
Foreign Community: Germany has a large foreign community of over 4 million foreign workers, mostly Italians, Turks and Yugoslavs. There is also a sizeable number of Americans and Britons working there.
Area: 356,910km² (137,803mi²).
Geography: Germany is situated at the heart of Europe and has borders with Austria, Belgium, the Czech Republic, Denmark, France, Luxembourg, the Netherlands, Poland and Switzerland. It extends from the North Sea and Baltic coasts in the north to the flanks of the central Alps in the south. The country is comprised of three main regions: in the south, the terrain is mountainous, extending into the Bavarian Alps and the foothills of the Swiss Alpine mountain range; the Central German Uplands consist of forested black mountains and intermediate plateaux (part of the same formation as the Massif Central in France), which continue east into Poland; and the north of the country is part of the North European Lowlands, consisting of marshes and mud flats extending to the coast and into Denmark.

Climate: Germany has a predominantly mild, temperate climate, with occasional continental influences from the south creating periods of extreme heat or cold. Rainfall is evenly distributed throughout the year, with April and October the driest months. Summers are usually warm with average temperatures of 17°C (63°F), although temperatures can rise to over 30°C (86°F) in Berlin. Winters are cold throughout the country and can be severe in mountainous regions. The average winter temperature is 0°C (32°F).

Language: The official language is German with regional dialects. English is widely spoken, although less so in the former East German states.

Government: Federal, multiparty republic with bicameral legislature.

Political Stability: Excellent. Germany, particularly the former West Germany, has been one of the most politically stable countries in Europe since the Second World War. It's divided into 16 self-governing states with a large degree of autonomy. The reunification of Germany in 1990 created enormous economic and social problems, and has led to some political unrest in the east. Relatively high unemployment has created friction between Germans and foreign workers and refugees in some areas.

EU Accession: Founder member.

Economy

Overview: Germany's economy has traditionally been one of the world's giants, ranking third in the world. Germany has Europe's largest consumer market with an extensive import market; the UK, for example, exports just about something of everything to Germany. The economy is generally stable, although it slowed down significantly in 2001 and 2002, managing annual growth of a mere 0.6 and 0.2 per cent respectively. There were few signs of recovery in 2003 when the German economy entered recession. The now faltering economy faces several problems including budget deficit; rigid labour laws and bureaucratic regulations; and high taxes as well as huge injections of funds (around €20 billion) needed to repair damage from the 2002 floods. Unification problems remain far from solved and it's expected to take another decade before the former East Germany will be able to exist without substantial subsidies from the West. In late 2003, Germany adopted Agenda 2010, far-reaching and drastic economic measures designed to halt recession and rising unemployment.

GDP Per Head: US$29,210.

Growth (2003): 0 per cent.

Forecast Growth For 2004: 1 per cent.

Main Industries: Automobile industry, civil aircraft, creative design, electonic components, gardening equipment and supplies, health and safety, home interiors, ICT and railways.

UK Trade Partner Ranking: 2.

US Trade Partner Ranking: 5.

Working

Overview: The workforce is generally highly skilled, well educated and productive, and the government runs extensive apprenticeship programmes, combining on-the-job experience with academic training. The employment market has strict regulations, with substantial worker protection. Wages and fringe benefits are among the highest in the world.

Unemployment Rate (2003): High, but with significant differences between Easy Germany (around 17 per cent) and West Germany (about 8 per cent).

Employment Opportunities: Mostly in the automotive, catering, chemical, construction, hotel, TEFL and tourism industries, as well as in engineering. There is currently a shortage (estimated at 150,000) of workers in the high technology sector, for which an immigration programme has been introduced to attract foreign specialists. Fluency in German is recommende for all jobs.

Work Permits: Not required for nationals of original EU member states, but needed by all others. Those from new member states may visit to seek work for up to six months until at least May 2006 (check the latet information). Non-EU nationals must obtain a permit **before** arrival, though these are dificult except for IT and computer specialists.

Labour Relations: Generally good with a high degree of cooperation between workers and management. Colective bargaining is common, and union membership is high, often resulting in high minimum wages.

Employment Conditions: Generally excellent: there is a strong work ethic and good employee protection. The standard working week is 36-40 hours, though unions are lobbying for a 35-hour week, and employees have a minimum of 20 paid days leave, in addition to public holidays. Fringe benefits are usually generous and often include a 13th month pay at Christmas.

Salaries: These are determined collectively for each industry and are higher than other EU countries apart from Luxembourg. A marketing manager can expect to earn about €83,000 a year and an accountant €72,000. Salaries in the former East Germany are around 75 per cent of those in the west.

Minimum Monthly Wage: Not applicable.

Social Security: Employers and employees each pay about 20 per cent of gross monthly salary into the social security scheme, which covers healthcare, sick and accident pay, unemployment benefit, pensions and long-term care insurance. Only foreign employees working in Germany for a limited time for foreign companies, and those earning over €40,500 annually, are exempt, provided the employer contributes to private health and insurance plans. The self-employed contribute 42.3 per cent.

Business Hours: These vary by region but most businesses open from 8am to 4.30pm Monday to Thursday and from 8am to 12.30pm on Friday. Banks generally open from 9am to noon Monday to Friday and from 2.30 to 4pm with an extension to 5.30pm on Thursday.

Public Holidays: Nine per year:

- 1st January
- Good Friday & Easter Monday
- 1st May
- Ascension Day
- Whitsun (May/June)
- 3rd October
- 25th & 26th December

There are several other, mostly religious, holidays observed in certain states.

Business Etiquette: Germans are extremely punctual – 'time is money' – and use formal titles. Small talk should be avoided unless you know your business contact well. English is widely spoken, but less so in the east, All documentation should be in German.

Finance

Currency: Euro (€).

Exchange Controls: None.

Banks: The banking industry is one of Germany's most important and the many banks offer a comprehensive range of services, including 24-hour telephone and internet banking. Numerous foreign banks also have branches around the country. Residents and non-residents can open bank accounts in Germany and obtain loans and mortgages – although German banks aren't as free with their money as some of their European counterparts.

Cost/Standard Of Living: Germany enjoys a high standard of living with low inflation. The cost of living is relatively high, but only slightly higher than in the UK and France, although in the former East Germany living standards are generally much lower and unemployment is a major problem.

Loans: Loans are generally available from German banks, although they tend to make them only where there's adequate collateral or the borrower is making major investment from personal resources. Foreigners may find German bankers reluctant to make business loans.

Interest Rate (Early 2004): 2 per cent (European Central Bank).

Taxation

Germany's tax system was largely reformed in 2002 and taxes on businesses and employers reduced. Residents are taxed on their worldwide income and non-residents on German-source income only, when a minimum tax rate of 25 per cent generally applies. A solidarity surcharge (*Solidaritätszuschlag*) of 5.5 per cent, introduced to finance the unification of East and West Germany, is also levied on both individual and corporate income tax as well as withholding taxes.

Corporate Tax: Corporate income tax is levied at a flat rate of 25 per cent. Entities resident in Germany are subject to tax on their worldwide income and non-resident entities on German-source income only. Companies are also subject to Trade Tax levied by local communities at rates from around 15 to 20 per cent, although some localities have a zero rate in order to promote business in their area.

Personal Income Tax: Germany has a PAYE system with rates from 17 per cent (15 per cent in 2005) on annual income above €7,426 to 47 per cent (42 per cent in 2005) on income above €52,293. Tax-free allowances are doubled for married taxpayers.

Capital Gains Tax: Capital gains from the sale of non-business assets (including second homes) are generally exempt from tax unless they're considered to be speculative. In the case of a second home, the gains are regarded as speculative if the property is sold within ten years of purchase. Speculative gains are calculated as income and taxed at normal rates. Property sold two years after purchase is exempt from CGT.

Wealth Tax: None.

Inheritance & Gift Tax: Inheritance tax is paid by the beneficiary and gift tax is paid by both the donor and the recipient. For non-residents, tax is limited to property situated in Germany. Exemptions and tax rates vary according to the relationship of the donor and recipient, and the value of the property inherited or received as a gift. Inheritance tax ranges from 7 to 30 per cent for relatives of the first degree and from 17 to 50 per cent for non-related people.

Other Taxes: Members of Christian churches or Judaism pay around 9 per cent of their income tax liability as church tax (pensioners are exempt). A solidarity surcharge (to finance the reunification of the two Germanys) is also levied at 5.5 per cent of your income tax due.

Value Added Tax: The standard rate of value added tax is 16 per cent, which is applied to most goods and services. There's a reduced rate of 7 per cent for certain items of food and 'necessary' social services.

Withholding Taxes: Interest is subject to 30 per cent withholding tax and dividends to 20 per cent. The 5.5 per cent solidarity tax is also levied.

Tax Filing: The tax year in Germany is the calendar year and tax returns must filed annually usually by 31st May following the calendar year under assessment. Employees don't usually need to file a tax return unless they need to claim a tax adjustment. The self-employed and business owners must file if their income from all sources exceeds €7,426.

Accommodation

Building Standards: Among the best in the world, although housing stock in the easy is poor, particularly in the ubiquitous high-rise apartment blocks.

Restrictions On Foreign Ownership: None.

Cost Of Housing: German property is among the most expensive in Europe, although the property market has stabilised over the last few years. Latest estimates claim that, relative to disposable income, prices are at their lowest level since 1987 and property is considered an excellent long-term investment. Prices vary considerably according to the city and region, with the cost of a townhouse ranging from €130,000 to well over €350,000, and detached family houses costing from €180,000 to over €900,000. Prices are highest in Munich where prime apartments cost between €8,650 and €11,000 per m². Property is cheaper in the former East German states, although prices have risen here as well in recent years.

Fees: Transfer tax (*Grundwerbesteuer*) on land and buildings is 3.5 per cent of the assessed tax value and the notary's fee is between 1 and 1.5 per cent.

Local Mortgages: The maximum mortgage (*Hypothek*) available in Germany is 60 per cent, which means that buyers must make a 30 or 40 per cent down payment or secure a second mortgage. Bank mortgages are usually over a maximum of 30 years with a low fixed rate of interest for the whole period of the loan. Many buyers have a combination of a building society loan and a mortgage from a bank. Despite the high down payment and low rates of interest, Germany has the highest average mortgage repayments in the EU. Mortgages are often paid by a whole family and assumed by the next generation. Most lenders require that all mortgages be repaid before normal retirement age.

Property Taxes: These taxes are levied by local communities and the amount payable is the basic rate (usually around 0.35 per cent of a property's rentable value) multiplied by a percentage determined annually by each community.

Renting: Rents vary considerably according to the location of the property, with the highest rents found in city-centres and areas with good public transport. For a two-bedroom apartment in a major city such as Frankfurt you should expect to pay in the region of €500 to €900, and at least twice as much in Munich. Quoted rents don't usually include extra costs (*Nebenkosten*) which add another 10 to 20 per cent and include such things as heating (when included), cable TV, water, taxes, rubbish disposal, and maintenance costs for the building and grounds.

Personal Effects: Goods purchased within the EU can be imported duty-free and don't need to be retained for a minimum period. However, goods purchased outside the EU must have been owned for at least six months and cannot be sold for one year after importation.

Utilities: Electricity (220V to 250V) is supplied by a number of companies and the consumer is free to choose his supplier. Electricity rates are among the highest in Europe although, because of strong competition, they are now lower. Mains gas isn't widely available in Germany and few properties have gas cooking facilities, although in rural areas households may use bottled gas. Water costs in Germany are around the European average and are included in the monthly 'extra costs' bill (*Nebenkosten*).

Services

Getting There: There are numerous international airports with an extensive network if international flights. Germany can also be easily reached from other European countries by road, rail and, in some cases, ferry.

Public Transport: Communications are generally excellent, particularly in towns, but standards are lower in the east and rural transport throughout the country can be patchy. Domestic air and high-speed rail services link most major cities. The train service is good and fares reasonable.

Motoring: The road system is excellent and all major cities are linked by motorways (*Autobahn*), though road congestion is a major problem in some areas. Speed limits are 50kph in built-up areas and 100kph elsewhere, including dual carriageways. There is no speed limit on motorways, although a maximum speed of 130kph is advised. Maximum permitted alcohol level is 50mg per 100ml of blood. All vehicles must carry warning triangles. No leaded petrol is available. EU driving licences are valid, even for residents. Others must be exchanged for German ones after six months. While some non-EU countries (e.g. Switzerland and some US states) have reciprocal arrangements allowing automatic licence exchange, most non-EU drivers must take the theoretical and practical driving test.

Medical Facilities: German hospitals and clinics are staffed and equipped to the highest standards and the country has the highest ratio of hospital beds to population in the EU. There is a compulsory national health insurance fund (*Krankencasse*) supported by obligatory contributions, and most treatments and medicines are free at the point of delivery. Pensioners must continue to contribute after retirement. For those not covered by social security private health insurance is essential.

Education: Free and compulsory for at least nine years, starting at the age of five or six. Academic standards are high and the system is hihgly competitive and selective from the age of ten. Private schools are mostly run by the Catholic Church or Waldorf schools. The relatively few international schools are to be found in cities with high concentrations of diplomats or international companies. e.g. Berlin and Munich.

Postal Services: Deutsche Post provides one of the best postal services in Europe and is very efficient. It has recently been privatised and, although you can still pay bills and open a savings account at a post office, banking transactions have been considerably reduced.

Telephone: Since privatisation in 1996, telephone services in Germany have been provided by many telephone companies, although Deutsche Telekom remains the largest and most popular. Standards of service are high and the cost of calls has fallen considerably owing to the increased competition, making it worthwhile shopping around for the best deal.

Internet: The internet is extremely popular in Germany and many servers provide a free or inexpensive service. Deutsche Telekom provides the most widely used service, T-Online.

English TV & Radio: German television broadcasts some English-language programmes with German subtitles, although the majority of programmes are dubbed into German. There's a mandatory annual TV licence. Cable TV is common in cities and satellite TV reception is good throughout the country. Radio programmes tend to broadcast exclusively in German, although in the areas around US and British military bases you can receive English-language forces stations. A radio licence is necessary.

Miscellaneous

Crime Rate: Relatively low, though it has increased markedly since unification and the rise in unemployment, particularly in the east. Burglaries and car crime are high in the major cities. Violent crime is low, although muggings have increased in the last decade.

Pets: Dogs and cats require a vaccination certificate including rabies, which must have been applied at least 30 days and no longer than a year before arrival. The certificate must be issued by a licensed vet. Dogs must be licensed annually (costing from €70 to €100).

Visas: Foreigners from countries such as Australia, Canada, Japan and the US don't need visas for visits up to three months, and may not undertake any employment (although some business activity is permitted). For longer visits, visas are required and may be extended within limits. Business visas for visits up to three months are available for many non-EU countries under the same conditions as for the Schengen Visa (see page 20). For further visa information, see page 19.

Residence Permits: Nationals from the EU, Australia, Canada, Israel, Japan, New Zealand, Switzerland and the US must apply for a residence permit within three months of arrival in Germany. Residence permits are issued by the local residents registration office (*Einwohnermeldeamt*) and you are usually required to provide proof of accommodation, health insurance and means of support. You also have to provide a certificate of health, obtainable from registered doctors or local health offices. Residence permits for EU nationals are valid for five years and renewable. For other nationals, permits are usually for one year. If you are from a country other than those listed above you must apply for a residence permit **before** arrival.

International Dialling Code: 49.
Time Difference: GMT +1.
Weights & Measures: Metric.

Reference

Useful Addresses

British Embassy, Unter den Linden 32-34, 10117 Berlin (☎ 030-204570, 🖳 www.britischebotschaft.de).

German Embassy, 23 Belgrave Square, London SW1X 8QB, UK (☎ 020-7824 1300, 🖳 www.german-embassy.org.uk).

German Embassy, 4645 Reservoir Rd., NW, Washington DC 20007, USA (☎ 202-298 4000, 🖳 www.germany-info.org).

US Embassy, Wilhemstrasse 70, 10117 Berlin (☎ 030-204507, 🖳 http://berlin.usembassy.gov).

Further Reading

Living & Working in Germany, David Hampshire (Survival Books Ltd, 🖳 www.survivalbooks.net).

Useful Websites

Berlin (🖳 www.berlin.de) – Website about all aspects of life in Germany's capital.

Expatica (🖳 www.expatica.com/germany) – A useful site for expatriates.

German Desk (🖳 www.germandesk.com) – A useful business and trade website, including job opportunities.

Germany Info (🖳 www.germany-info.org) – Comprehensive information about many aspects of Germany in English.

Government Employment Office (Zentralstelle fur Arbeitsvermittlung/ZAV, 🖳 www.arbeitsamt.de) – The website includes details of job vacancies throughout Germany).

Invest in Germany (🖳 www.invest-in-germany.com) – Official guide to doing business in the German federal states, including useful information about state investment agencies.

GREECE

General Information

Capital: Athens.

Population: 10.9 million.

Foreign Community: Although it's becoming more popular with foreigners from Northern Europe, particularly retirees, Greece doesn't have a large foreign community. However, there is a sizeable number of Britons and other EU nationals resident on islands such as Corfu, Crete and Rhodes.

Area: 131,990km^2 (50,961mi^2).

Geography: Mainland Greece consists of a mountainous peninsula extending some 500km (310mi) into the Mediterranean from the south-west corner of the Balkans bordering on Albania, Bulgaria, Turkey and Macedonia, with the Aegean Sea to the east, the Ionian Sea to the west and the Mediterranean Sea to the south. In addition to the mainland, Greece encompasses some 3,000 islands, around 150 of which are inhabited, comprising around 20 per cent of its territory. The principal structural feature of Greece is the Pindos Mountains extending south-east from the Albanian border and covering most of the peninsula. Some 80 per cent of the mainland is mountainous and woodland covers around half the country (almost 90 million hectares).

Climate: Greece has a Mediterranean climate with long, hot, dry summers and mild sunny winters in the south, although winters can be cold inland in northern areas. It enjoys some 3,000 hours of sunshine a year and average temperatures well above 25°C (77°F) in summer, when the oppressive heat is often tempered by cooling breezes. Athens is notorious for its high air pollution in summer and is the most polluted city in Western Europe, with choking smog and temperatures above 35°C (95°F).

Language: The official language is Greek. English and other languages are widely spoken in tourist areas.

Government: Unitary multiparty republic.

Political Stability: Greece is traditionally one of the least politically stable countries in the EU (only Italy provides any competition), although it has been reasonably stable in recent years. The March 2004 elections returned a centre-right government after 10 years of socialist rule. Economic strength and performance remain relatively weak and the lowest in the EU. However, Greece fulfilled the economic criteria to join the euro and the 2004 Olympic games in Athens have boosted the economy to the extent that Greece was one of the fastest growing economies in the EU in 2003. The country has historically bad relations with its neighbour Turkey, which are exacerbated by Turkey's continuing military occupation of northern Cyprus. Diplomats from both countries have been recently making concerted efforts to resolve the situation as Cyprus joins the EU, although efforts have so far had little effect.

EU Accession: 1981.

Economy

Overview: The Greek economy is largely dependent on tourism and industry, although the traditional backbone of agriculture and shipping continues to be important. The economy is now generally stable and significant progress has been made with problems such as a large public sector, persistently high inflation, reform-resistant labour unions and massive public debt. Greece remains the poorest country in the original 15-member EU, although the GDP is considerably higher than that in neighbouring countries. The underground or hidden economy continues to be a major problem – estimated at almost 30 per cent of total economic activity – and is the largest in OECD countries. Reform of the underfunded public pension and welfare system is one of the greatest challenges currently facing the Greek economy. Greece has enjoyed higher economic growth than other EU countries over the past five years and improved relations with Turkey, together with 2004 Olympic Games to be held in Athens, mean the economy will continue to grow. Benefits from the Olympics are expected to last at least until 2010.

GDP Per Head: US$15,060.

Growth (2003): 4 per cent.

Forecast Growth For 2004: 4.2 per cent.

Main Industries: Airport equipment and services, clothing, energy, healthcare, IT (the country's fastest growing industry), sports and leisure, telecommunications and tourism.

UK Trade Partner Ranking: 46.

US Trade Partner Ranking: 50+.

Working

Overview: The employment market is dominated by rigid working practices and influential public sector unions (covering some 15 per cent of the workforce). Timid attempts to counter these forces have had little effect on unemployment, despite high economic growth. The Olympic Games are expected to create some 65,000 jobs over the next two years. There's no shortage of skilled, semi-skilled or unskilled labour, the latter group largely made up of illegal immigrant workers from Eastern Europe and the Balkans. Competition for jobs is strong, particularly among graduates.

Unemployment Rate (2003): 9 per cent.

Employment Opportunities: Mainly in TEFL and tourism, particularly for non-Greek speakers. The Olympic Games have created business opportunities in related sectors. Most expatriates work in Athens for multinational companies.

Work Permits: Not required for nationals of original EU countries, but for all others. Citizens of new member states may visit to seek work for up to six months until at least May 2006 (but check for the latest information). Non-EU nationals must obtain a work permit before starting work, though getting one can be difficult, if not impossible.

Labour Relations: Generally good in the private sector but strikes are common in the public sector.

Employment Conditions: Below average with labour legislation leaving a lot to be desired. The working week is 44 hours and employees usually have 21 days annual paid holiday. There are 14 annual salary payments per year (so employing someone can be expensive). Job opportunities for foreigners are scarce.

Salaries: Mostly below the EU average, although those for professionals in management, engineering and IT are higher than in Finland, France and Italy.

Minimum Monthly Wage (2003): €605.

Social Security: All working residents must contribute to a social security fund, usually the state-run IKA although some collectives have their own insurance funds. Contributions vary according to the region and type of occupation. In Athens, for example, employers pay 28 per cent and employees about 16 per cent of gross monthly salary, to a maximum of €1,820, Benefits include healthcare and pensions. Greece has reciprocal agreements with several countries, including the EU, Canada, New Zealand, Switzerland and the US. Nationals from these countries may be exempt from participation in IKA for periods up to one year.

Business Hours: Offices generally open from 8 or 9am to 6pm Monday to Friday, but government offices may be open to the public only from 11am to 1pm. Banks mostly open from 8am to 2pm Monday to Thursday and from 8am to 1.30pm on Friday.

Public Holidays: 15 per year, including local and regional holidays:

- 1st & 6th January
- 23rd February
- 25th March
- Good Friday & Easter Monday
- 3rd, 28th & 31st May
- 30th August
- 28th October
- 25th, 26th, 27th & 28th December

Business Etiquette: Greeks are formal and appreciate personal contact. Business meetings often start with coffee or fruit juice and some social conversation. Handshakes and formal address are used. If a non-Greek speaker is present, meetings will often be conducted in English, as is correspondence. Company brochures are often published in English as well as Greek.

Finance

Currency: Euro (€).

Exchange Controls: None. However, funds imported to buy a property should be officially documented so that the proceeds can be repatriated when it's sold.

Banks: Greece generally had good banking facilities, which are safe and reasonably efficient, although foreigners used to northern European banking practices will find the service somewhat 'leisurely'. There are some 50 domestic banks as well as around 20 foreign-owned banks (based almost exclusively in Athens) in Greece and there are no restrictions on the opening of bank accounts.

Cost/Standard Of Living: Greece has a lower living standard and cost of living than most other EU countries, although cars and luxury items are expensive, and it has a relatively high rate of inflation. Athens is much more expensive than the rest of the country.

Loans: Loans are available from Greek banks, although they are reluctant to lend to non-residents.

Interest Rate (Early 2004): 2 per cent (European Central Bank).

Taxation

Greek tax policy changes frequently (usually annually) and you are advised to seek up-to-date information from a professional expert. Expatriates arriving in

Greece under secondment agreements may be required to register with the tax authorities and obtain a personal tax identity number.

Corporate Tax: The corporate income tax rate is 35 percent. Companies incorporated in Greece are subject to tax on their worldwide income and non-resident companies are subject to tax on Greek-source income only.

Personal Income Tax: The income tax rate in Greece is around the European average although, when it's added to the high social security contributions, Greek taxes are among the highest in Europe. Income tax is deducted at source (PAYE) and rates (2004) range from 15 per cent (annual income below €10,000 is exempt for employees and pensioners) to 40 per cent (on annual income over €23,400). There are many allowances and deductions, particularly for families.

Capital Gains Tax: CGT is payable on business transactions only, such as transfers of business-related rights (30 per cent), gains from business transfer (20 per cent) and transactions on the stock exchange (0.3 per cent).

Wealth Tax: None.

Inheritance & Gift Tax: Inheritance and gift tax are based on the value of the bequest and the relationship between the donor and recipient. Rates are between 5 and 25 per cent for relatives of the first degree (spouses and children) and from 10 to 60 per cent for others.

Value Added Tax: VAT is 4 per cent on books and other printed materials; 8 per cent on food products, public transport, homes, and cafeteria and restaurant services; and 18 per cent (standard rate) on all other goods and services. Certain goods and services are exempt from VAT, including medical and legal services, and exports. On certain island groups, such as the Dodecanese and the Sporades, VAT rates are reduced.

Withholding Taxes: Withholding tax on interest is levied at 15 or 20 per cent for individuals and at 40 per cent on non-resident legal entities. Dividends are exempt from withholding tax.

Tax Filing: The Greek tax year is the calendar year and individuals under the PAYE scheme are not required to file a tax return. The company tax year is also generally the calendar year, although the accounting year may differ. Annual tax returns should be filed by the tenth day of the fifth month following the end of the accounting year.

Accommodation

Building Standards: New homes and properties are generally well designed and built. The quality of older property is variable.

Restrictions On Foreign Ownership: Some restrictions on security grounds, e.g. in some border areas or islands close to Turkey. Foreign ownership is restricted on some islands, e.g. Corfu and Rhodes, although foreigners may get around them by buying through a Greek company. EU citizens have the same rights as Greeks in most of the country.

Cost Of Housing: Costs vary considerably according to the location and whether you buy a new or an old property – Athens is expensive and prices have risen sharply in recent years because of the Olympics. A two-bedroom apartment costs from €175,000 and a house from €450,000. New apartments on the islands cost from around €120,000 for two bedrooms and a new two-bedroom townhouse or villa costs from around €175,000.

Fees: Fees associated with a purchase in Greece are high and total around 15 to 20 per cent of the purchase price, including purchase tax of 11 to 13 per cent, 1.5 per cent lawyer's fees, 1 to 2 per cent notary's fees and 0.3 per cent land registry fees.

Local Mortgages: Both Greek and foreign banks provide mortgages, although it's extremely difficult for non-residents to take out a mortgage in Greece. Mortgages are usually available for a maximum of 70 per cent of a property's value over a term of 5 to 15 years, although longer terms are obtainable. Mortgage rates have traditionally been high in Greece, but are now in line with other Euro countries.

Property Taxes: A small annual property tax is levied at a rate of 0.25 and 0.35 per cent on the market value of the property. Other property fees are levied by local communities to pay for local services.

Renting: Rentals in resort areas and Athens, particularly long-term rentals, are in high demand and short supply. A small two-bedroom apartment costs between €750 to €1,500 per month in an average Athens suburb. In a resort area, rentals can be much more expensive in high season, although relatively cheap outside the main tourist season.

Personal Effects: Personal effects can be imported tax and duty-free, provided they've been owned for at least six months and an inventory is provided.

Utilities: Electricity (220-240V) is provided by the DEH and is subject to frequent cuts in some areas, where it may be necessary to install a diesel generator. In remote rural areas there's often no mains electricity and installation of a generator is mandatory. Mains gas is available only in Athens, although bottled gas is available throughout Greece. Water is an expensive commodity in Greece, where drought is often a serious problem. In drought-affected areas, water supplies may be restricted or cut for lengthy periods. Tap water is safe to drink in all urban areas, although because of its poor quality, many people prefer to drink bottled water. Water in rural areas isn't always safe to drink.

Services

Getting There: Greece is generally well served by international flights, mainly to Athens. In the high season there are competitively priced charter flights to the main islands. There are also ferries from the neighbouring countries,

Public Transport: Communications within Greece are generally reasonable, although the quality and quantity vary considerably according to the region. Athens and some resorts have a good network but, outside the main towns and cities, public transport is scarce. Major investment in the Athens public transport including an underground metro service is currently underway in preparation for the 2004 Olympics. Greece has a comprehensive domestic flight service, although fares are high. Trains are limited to the mainland and services are generally slow. There's an extensive ferry network linking islands and the mainland. Services are considerably reduced out of season and often cancelled in bad weather.

Motoring: Road conditions vary greatly and although the limited network of motorways (mainly toll) is good, great care must be exercised when using other roads. Greece has some of the worst traffic problems in Europe (traffic congestion in Athens is legendary) and the second highest accident rate after Portugal among the original EU states. Cars are expensive but petrol is among the EU's cheapest and some islands such as Hydra are car-free. Speed limits are 50kph in built-up areas, 90kph or 110kph outside built-up areas, including dual carriageways, and 120kph on motorways. Maximum permitted alcohol level is 50mg per 100ml of blood. A warning triangle must be carried in all vehicles. No leaded petrol is available. Foreign residents who don't hold an EU driving licence have to exchange their licence for a Greek one once they have a residence permit.

Medical Facilities: Although much improved, the Greek public health system is one of the worst in Europe, with overcrowded hospitals and standards well below Northern Europe. Free or low cost healthcare is provided for those who contribute to the social security fund, as well as their dependants. Contributors pay 25 per cent of the cost of prescriptions. However, even if you contribute to social security system, the inadequacies of the public health system make private health insurance mandatory for those who can afford it.

Education: Free and compulsory for children aged from 6 to 15. Standards are reasonable although, for language reasons, expatriates may prefer to send their children to an international school, of which there are several around Athens.

Postal Services: The Greek postal service is one of the slowest in Europe, although services have improved recently. Post to islands without an airport can be particularly slow. Post offices are provided in most towns and villages, and offer a wide range of services, including cash transfers and currency exchange.

Telephone: The Greek telephone service is run by OTE (in the process of partial privatisation), which has invested heavily in the modernisation of services that are now on a par with the rest of Europe. Calls are expensive although they are expected to fall once much-needed competition is introduced.

Internet: The internet has been slow to take off in Greece, mainly because of the shortage of lines from providers. However, improvements are being made almost daily and most large Greek companies now have websites.

English TV & Radio: The majority of channels broadcast most English-language programmes and films in the original language with Greek subtitles. Satellite television reception is good throughout most of the country.

Miscellaneous

Crime Rate: Greece is one of Europe's safest countries with a low crime rate and a well-deserved reputation for honesty. However, sexual harrassment is quite common and women should take particular care late at night.

Pets: Dogs and cats may be imported provided they have a health certificate including proof of a rabies vaccine dated no more than six days before departure.

Visas: Nationals from many countries, including the EU, Canada, Japan and the US, don't need a visa for visits up to three months. EU business visas for up to three months are available for many non-EU countries under the same conditions as for the Schengen Visa (see page 20). For further visa information, see page 19.

Residence Permits: Residence permits are a formality for EU nationals who must apply for a temporary residence permit from the local police or Aliens Bureau within three months of their arrival. Permits are usually valid for one year and renewable for up to five years. Non-EU nationals must apply for a residence permit within one week of arrival.

International Dialling Code: 30.

Time Difference: GMT +2.

Weights & Measures: Metric.

Reference

Useful Addresses

British Embassy, 1 Ploutarchou Street, 10675 Athens (☎ 21-727 2600, ⌨ www.british-embassy.gr).

Embassy of Greece, 1A Holland Park, London W11 3TP, UK (☎ 020-7229 3850, ⌨ www.greekembassy.org.uk).

Embassy of Greece, 2221 Massachusetts Avenue, NW, Washington DC 20008, USA (☎ 202-939 1300, ⌨ www.greekembassy.org).

US Embassy, 91 Vas. Sophias Ave, 10160 Athens (☎ 21-721 2951, ⌨ www.usembassy.gr).

Useful Websites

Athens Chamber of Commerce and Industry (⌨ www.acci.gr).

British-Hellenic Chamber of Commerce (⌨ www.bhcc.gr).

Expatriate information (⌨ www.geocities.com/Athens/7243).

The Hellenic Centre for Investment/ELKE (⌨ www.elke.gr) – The investment site provides comprehensive information in English.

HUNGARY

General Information

Capital: Budapest.

Population: 10 million.

Foreign Community: There's a large American expatriate community in Budapest, as well as a sizeable German community. Outside the capital, there are few foreigners.

Area: 93,030km² (35,921mi²).

Geography: Hungary is a landlocked country in central Europe bordering on Slovakia and Austria to the north and west, Croatia and Serbia to the south, and Romania and the Ukraine to the east. The country is essentially flat with fertile agriculture plains covering much of its area. The Danube River divides the country in two from north to south and there are thousands of lakes, of which Lake Balaton is the largest in Europe.

Climate: Hungary has a typical continental climate with long, hot summers and cold winters. Spring is usually wet, particularly in the west. Average temperatures in Budapest are -1°C (30°F) in January and 22°C (72°F) in July.

Language: The official language is Hungarian. Slovakian and German are also widely spoken, plus English to a lesser extent.

Government: Parliamentary republic.

Political Stability: Very good. Hungary broke away from the Soviet bloc in 1989, since when it has established a constitutional democracy. It's a member of NATO.

EU Accession: Of the ten new members joining in 2004, Hungary was the first to apply for EU membership and is currently one of the most reformed candidates, having implemented many EU laws and regulations. Fiscal reform is still needed, however, and several aspects of agriculture still don't meet EU criteria. Accession should bring many immediate advantages, particularly the injection of structural funds and the country should encounter no major problems.

Economy

Overview: Hungary's economy has undergone major restructuring and stabilisation since 1994 and this, together with substantial foreign investment, has produced a stable economy with steady annual growth. EU accession has been one of the country's main priorities and to date Hungary has fulfilled a large part of the requirements. It occupies a strategic trading position in central Europe as a border country between the EU and the former USSR.

GDP Per Head: US$7,690.

Growth (2003): 2.7 per cent.

Forecast Growth For 2004: 3.1 per cent.

Main Industries: Agriculture (although less dominant than in the past), chemicals, engineering and machine tool manufacture.

UK Trade Partner Ranking: 39.

US Trade Partner Ranking: 25.

Working

Overview: The workforce is generally skilled and well educated, although there are shortages in sectors such as telecommunications and IT.

Unemployment Rate (2003): Nationally 5.7 per cent, but variable across the country, from zero in the capital to relatively high in the north and east.

Employment Opportunities: TEFL is the main area, although opportunities are increasingly opening up in such fields as advertising, marketing and public relations. Managerial staff is also required. A good knowledge of Hungarian is essential for most jobs.

Work Permits: All foreigners must have a permit to start work, but EU nationals may visit for up to six months to seek a job. For non-EU nationals, prospective employers with firm job offers must apply for a work permit and send you a work visa application; this must be returned to the Hungarian embassy or consulate in your home country.

Labour Relations: Generally good with collective bargaining commonplace. Union membership is high, particularly in the public sector.

Employment Conditions: Regulated by the Labour Code and negotiated by workers councils. A 42-hour week is the norm and employees are entitled to 20-30 days paid annual leave.

Salaries: Generally low in comparison with those in Western Europe, although those of top managers are similar. Pay for executives and top professionals is increasingly linked to performance targets and fringe benefits are generous. However, there are complaints that the rise in the cost of living has not been matched by equivalent pay rises.

Minimum Monthly Wage (2003): €212.

Social Security: All employers and employees (except foreigners working for companies with more than one foreign shareholder) make obligatory payments into two funds, for pensions and health and for unemployment benefits. Foreigners must contribute 1.5 per cent of gross pay to the latter. Employees contribute 12.5 per cent of gross monthly salary and employers 32 per cent. Currently reciprocal treaties exist only with neighbouring countries, but more are expected following EU accession.

Business Hours: Most businesses open from 8am to 4.30pm Monday to Friday. Banks open from 8am to 3pm Monday to Thursday and from 8am to 1pm on Friday.

Public Holidays: Ten per year:

- 1st January
- 15th March
- Easter Monday
- 1st May
- Whitsun (May/June)
- 20th August

- 23rd October
- 1st November
- 25th & 26th December

Business Etiquette: Very formal with professional and academic titles still used. Handshakes and exchanges of business cards are expected.

Finance

Currency: Forint (HUF).
 Exchange Rate: €1= HUF264.55 (February 2004).
 Exchange Controls: Virtually none, although the Bank of Hungary retains control of large movements of capital and the Hungarian authorities recommend that, to avoid problems when leaving Hungary, it's advisable to declare convertible currency over HUF100,000.
 Banks: There are 45 banks in Hungary of which over half have assets owned by foreign banks. The central Bank of Hungary controls all banking activity. Banks offer a wide range of sophisticated banking activities and foreigners are free to open bank accounts.
 Cost/Standard Of Living: Although not as cheap as it was, the cost of living in Hungary is still well below that in Western Europe and you can live reasonably inexpensively. Imported goods and luxury items are expensive.
 Loans: Both local and foreign banks offer financing and competition is fierce, particularly for medium and large scale foreign investments. Personal loans are also available, although banks tend to lend to residents only and interest rates are by far the highest in the EU.
 Interest Rate (2004): (A very high) 12.5 per cent.

Taxation

Corporate Tax: Corporate income and capital gains taxes are levied at 18 per cent, although companies that are completely foreign-owned and provide services outside Hungary are subject to corporate tax at 3 per cent.
 Personal Income Tax: Income tax rates range from 20 per cent on earnings up to HUF600,000 to a maximum of 40 per cent on earnings above HUF1,200,000. Gains from transactions other than those listed in CGT below, are included in taxable income and must be declared. There are various allowances, which include pension contributions and a monthly child allowance.
 Capital Gains Tax: Gains are usually taxed as income at the applicable income tax rate. Sales of real estate, investments and certain high-value items are subject to CGT of 20 per cent.
 Wealth Tax: None.
 Inheritance & Gift Tax: Inheritance tax rates are from 2.5 to 21 per cent, depending on the relationship between the deceased and beneficiaries. Property

is taxed at lower rates and applies only to property situated in Hungary. Gift tax is levied only on gifts valued in excess of HUF150,000.

Value Added Tax: Value added tax (*AFA*) is levied at a standard rate of 25 per cent, affecting most goods and services, with a reduced rate of 12 per cent on certain items.

Withholding Taxes: Dividends paid to foreign companies or individuals are subject to 20 or 35 per cent withholding tax. Hungarian companies are exempt.

Tax Filing: The tax year is the calendar year and returns must be filed by 20th March. If an individual's only taxable income is from one Hungarian employer, he need not file a tax return. Businesses and the self-employed must file annual returns and must make quarterly estimated tax payments.

Accommodation

Building Standards: Variable.

Restrictions On Foreign Ownership: Ownership of Hungarian property by foreigners is subject to approval from the public administration office in Budapest, and foreigners must have either an immigration permit or have lived in Hungary for employment purposes for at least five years.

Cost Of Housing: Land and property prices have risen greatly in recent years in anticipation of Hungary's EU membership, and high quality housing is expensive. In Budapest, the property market is currently booming and there's high demand for good quality housing and many new developments currently under construction. A small apartment costs from €100,000 and houses outside the capital are available from €120,000.

Fees: Transfer tax is levied on property purchases and rates for houses and apartments are 2 per cent on the first HUF4 million of the purchase price and 6 per cent on the remainder. All other properties are subject to a flat rate of 10 per cent.

Local Mortgages: Local mortgages are available but, given the current instability in the banking system and the high interest rates, it's advisable to take out a loan with a foreign bank (if possible).

Property Taxes: Buildings are subject to 3 per cent of the market price or HUF900 per m^2.

Renting: Rental property can be difficult to find in the capital, where apartments in good residential areas cost from €700 per month and small houses from €1,000 per month.

Personal Effects: Personal effects up to the value of HUF8,000 may be brought into Hungary duty-free on your first entry and up to HUF500 on each subsequent entry. Above these values, duty of 15 per cent is payable.

Utilities: The electricity supply (220V) is reliable and charges are reasonable. Mains gas is available in the main population centres. Tap water is safe to drink in the capital, although many people prefer bottled water.

Services

Getting There: Budapest has the country's only international airport, with flights to and from most European cities and the US. Fares are high. There are also road and rail links to many European cities.

Public Transport: Generally good with buses and trains serving most of the country. Budapest's network of metro, trams and trolley buses is efficient and one of the cheapest in Europe.

Motoring: Roads are generally good. Car headlights must be used at all times. An annual toll ticket (*vignette*) is required for the use of motorways and is obtainable from border posts and petrol stations. Speed limits are 50kph in built-up areas, 90kph elsewhere, 110kph on dual carriageways and 130kph on motorways. Alcohol tolerance is zero. All vehicles must carry a warning triangle and first aid kit. No leaded petrol is available. New residents and holders of EU driving liences must exchange them for Hungarian licences within six months. Non-EU licences must be surrendered after six months and their holders must take a Hungarian driving test.

Medical Facilities: Emergency medical treatment is free but all other treatment must be paid for, usually immediately and in cash. Comprehensive medical insurance is essential. **If you plan to visit any forested areas, you should be inoculated against tick-borne encephalitis.**

Education: Standards are high. There are numerous international schools – American, British, French and German – in the Budapest area.

Postal Services: The postal service in Hungary is fairly efficient and there are post offices in most cities and towns. International post, however, is slow. Anything urgent should be sent by courier. Post offices provide currency exchange services, but no banking facilities are available.

Telephone: The telephone service has been privatised (most of it is owned by Deutsche Telekom) and approaches western standards but some services, such as the installation of telephones, are slow. Call prices are high, particularly international, although they are expected to fall over the next few years. There are three mobile phone operators.

Internet: The internet is very popular in Hungary, which has the second highest proportion of homes connected to the internet in Eastern Europe after Estonia. Access is generally excellent and cheap. There are numerous internet service providers.

English TV & Radio: Hungarian TV and radio broadcasts nothing in English, therefore satellite TV is necessary to receive English-language programmes. Reception is good in the capital but varies in other parts of the country.

Miscellaneous

Crime Rate: About average for Europe though petty crime, particularly on crowded public transport, and car theft are common. Violent crime is rare. The crime rate is low outside towns and cities. In the capital you should beware of being forced to pay exorbitant prices (possibly accompanied by threats) in restaurants and hotels. This can be avoided by choosing establishments carefully and refusing to accompany anyone who 'knows a good place' to eat or stay.

Pets: Dogs and cats require a valid veterinary certificate in order to enter Hungary.

Visas: European (except Albanian and Turkish), Canadian and US nationals don't need a visa for visits up to 90 days (180 days in the case of British nationals). All other nationals and EU nationals wanting to stay for longer periods must obtain visa from their home country Hungarian embassy or consulate. For further visa information, see page 19.

Residence Permits: All foreign nationals require a residence permit to live in Hungary. It should be applied for from the local police within 15 days of arrival in the country. Some nationalities require a residence visa from a Hungarian embassy or consulate **before** arrival in the country.

International Dialling Code: 36.

Time Difference: GMT +1.

Weights & Measures: Metric.

Reference

Useful Addresses

British Embassy, Harmincad Utca 6, 1051 Budapest (☎ 1-266 2888, 🖳 www. britishembassy.hu).

Hungarian Embassy, 35 Eaton Place, London SW1X 8BY, UK (☎ 020-7235 5218, 🖳 www.huemblon.org.uk).

Hungarian Embassy, 3910 Shoemaker St, NW, Washington DC 20008, USA (☎ 202-362 6730, 🖳 www.hungaryemb.org).

US Embassy, Unit 1320, Szabadságtér 12, 1054 Budapest (☎ 1-475 4400, 🖳 www. usembassy.hu).

Further Reading

Budapest Business Journal – published every Monday (🖳 www.bbj.hu).

Budapest Sun – English-language newspaper published every Thursday (🖳 www.budapestsun.hu). The paper also publishes a monthly visitors guide and the @ *Home in Budapest* series for expats.

The Essential Guide To Living in Hungary – Good guide to Budapest and advice for the newcomer downloadable (in pdf) from Inter Relocation (🖳 www.interrelo.com).

Useful Websites

British Chamber of Commerce (💻 www.bcch.hu) – Useful information and advice on setting up in Hungary.

Hungarian Home Page (💻 www.fsz.bme.hu/hungary/homepage) – Comprehensive information on the country.

Hungarian Investment and Trade Development Agency (💻 www.itd.hu) – A wealth of information about doing business and working.

Hungary Tourism (💻 www.hungarytourism.hu) – The official tourism site.

IRELAND

General Information

Capital: Dublin.

Population: 3.8 million.

Foreign Community: Only 7 per cent of the population was born outside Ireland. Britons make up the largest expatriate community and there's a sizeable American community in Dublin.

Area: 70,280km² (27,135mi²).

Geography: Ireland is the large island situated to the west of the UK in the North Atlantic and is part of the British Isles. However, the Republic of Ireland, with which this section deals, comprises only some 80 per cent of the island of Ireland (or 26 of the 32 counties). Ireland is separated from mainland Britain by the Irish Sea. The Irish landscape consists mostly of rich farmland interspersed with rolling hills, bleak moors and lakes, surrounded by a rocky coastline. The country is largely unspoilt and has little industry and no real cities apart from Dublin.

Climate: Ireland is wet at most times of the year, particularly in the west, hence its green countryside and popular name, the 'Emerald Isle'. It has cold winters and warm summers, when July and August are the hottest months. The climate is similar to that of the UK, i.e. cold, damp and changeable for most of the year, with average temperatures 4°C to 7°C (39°F to 45°F) in January and 14°C to 24°C (57°F to 75°F) in July.

Language: Ireland has two official languages: Irish (or Gaelic) and English. It's mandatory for many government employees to speak Irish, although relatively few people speak it fluently and these live mainly in the *Gaeltacht* (designated Irish-speaking areas mostly in the north and west). The everyday language is English, which is spoken by virtually everybody.

Government: Unitary, multiparty republic with a bicameral legislature.

Political Stability: The Republic of Ireland consists of the 26 counties of Ireland governed from Dublin, occupying some 80 per cent of the island. The information in this section refers mainly to the Irish Republic and excludes the six counties in Northern Ireland that remained part of the United Kingdom when the Republic of Ireland was formed in 1921. Ireland is very stable despite the problems created by the IRA in Northern Ireland which have rarely caused much unrest in the Republic. It has a weak coalition government which, although it makes long-term policy-making difficult, hasn't damaged the country's economy – Ireland has one of the highest growth rates in the EU. Relations with the UK government have improved in recent years following the IRA ceasefire. Ireland is a member of the European Union, which it joined with the UK and Denmark in 1973. In 2001, Ireland rejected the Treaty of Nice by referendum thereby blocking further expansion of the EU and raising doubts about Ireland's commitment to the EU. In a second referendum in 2002, however, the Treaty of Nice was ratified.

EU Accession: 1973.

Economy

Overview: Ireland's economy is relatively small by EU standards, but the growth of its economy during the '90s was spectacular and is generally referred to as a 'miracle'. Ireland has succeeded in reversing its high unemployment and emigration trends, and now enjoys record immigration figures as well as labour growth. Ireland is also the biggest per capita exporter in the world. Inflation, however, remains one of the highest in the EU and growth slowed down in 2002 and 2003.

GDP Per Head: US$18,473.

Growth (2003): 2.75 per cent.

Forecast Growth For 2004: 4 per cent.

Main Industries: Chemicals, engineering, finance, global investment services, pharmaceuticals, science and technology and software (Ireland is the second largest exporter of software in the world after the US).

UK Trade Partner Ranking: 8.

US Trade Partner Ranking: 10.

Working

Overview: The Irish government has invested heavily in recent years in education and, as a consequence, the workforce is one of the most skilled in the developed world and second only to Japan.

Unemployment Rate (2003): Traditionally very high in Ireland, it reached record lows in 2001, although it has since risen slightly to 4.6per cent.

Employment Opportunities: Customer service, engineering, finance, IT, marketing and purchasing. Candidates with a combination of business, linguistic and technology skills are in high demand.

Work Permits: Nationals from the original EU member states don't require a work permit. Those from new member states must obtain a work permit in order to start work, but may visit the country and seek work for up to six months under the same conditions as other EU nationals. Regulations are expected to change in May 2006 and you should check with the authorities for the latest information. Work permits are difficult to obtain for non-EU nationals, who must apply **before** arriving in the country – except in certain sectors where there's a shortage of skilled staff. Examples are architecture, construction engineering, IT, nursing, surveying (quantity and building) and town planning, for which the government has created a special 'fast track' visa procedure. Applicants under this scheme are given priority and work permits are usually provided quickly and easily.

Labour Relations: Generally very good and there's a system of collective bargaining as well as periodic agreements between government, industry and unions designed to advance economic development. The Programme for Prosperity and Fairness, introduced in 2000, mainly provided for pay rises over the next two years.

Employment Conditions: The average working week is 39 hours (the maximum is 48 hours) and the paid holiday entitlement 20 days a year, although many employees receive more. A working knowledge of English is essential for most jobs and there are plenty of short-term job opportunities in the cities, particularly Dublin.

Salaries: Salaries are higher than the EU average and professionals can expect to earn more here than in Belgium, France and the Netherlands.

Minimum Monthly Wage (2003): €1,073.

Social Security: All employees must contribute to the Pay Related Social Insurance (PRSI) scheme, which provides a wide range of benefits. Employees pay 4 per cent on all earnings (the first €127 a week is exempt) up to a maximum of €40,420 and an additional health levy of 2 per cent. Employees who earn more than €40,420 pay the health levy only; employers contribute 8.5 per cent on employees' earnings up to €356 and 10.75 per cent on higher amounts. The self-employed pay 3 per cent PRSI and 2 per cent health levy on all income above €18,512. If they earn less than €18,512 they are exempt from the health levy.

Business Hours: Normally 9am to 5pm Monday to Friday. Banks open from 10am to 4pm Mondayto Wednesday and unto 5pm Thursday and Friday.

Public Holidays: Ten per year:

- 1st January
- 17th March
- Easter Monday
- May bank holiday (first Monday)
- June bank holiday (first Monday)
- August bank holiday (first Monday)
- October bank holiday (last Monday)
- 25th & 26th December

Business Etiquette: Business culture is open and friendly and it is common to be on first name terms with contacts from early in a business relationship.

Finance

Currency: Euro (€).

Exchange Controls: None.

Banks: The banking system is well developed and there are eight local banks in Ireland, plus branches of several foreign banks in Dublin, all of which offer a full range of banking products and services. Ireland also has a number of merchant banks available for corporate finances.

Cost/Standard Of Living: The cost of living is high in relation to salaries, which are relatively low in rural areas. Cars, petrol and luxury goods are particularly expensive, although the country also has a rapidly rising standard of living. An increasing number of Britons retire to Ireland, often to take advantage of the high level of benefits paid to pensioners, which include free public transport, free TV licences, free phone rental (plus a number of free calls), free healthcare, and allowances for clothing, fuel, electricity and gas. Ireland is the second most expensive country in the eurozone.

Loans: Loans are available from Irish banks which are used to dealing with both international and domestic customers.

Interest Rate (Early 2004): 2 per cent (European Central Bank).

Taxation

Corporate Tax: This tax was further reduced in 2003 to 12.5 per cent for companies with trading income, one of the lowest rates in non-tax haven countries. Companies with non-trading income are subject to 25 per cent corporate income tax. Small and medium enterprises (SMEs) with annual trade below €253,948 qualify for the 12.5 per cent rate. Corporate CGT is levied at 20 per cent.

Personal Income Tax: Income tax is relatively high owing to the small workforce, although it has been reduced in recent years. It's progressive and deducted on a PAYE system with single person rates at 20 per cent on income up to €28,000 and 42 per cent on the excess. There are personal tax credits and allowances, although some of these, such as mortgage interest, are dealt with at source. Foreign workers classed as resident but not domiciled in Ireland are taxed only on income from Irish sources.

Capital Gains Tax: CGT is levied at 20 per cent (except on development land, which attracts CGT at 40 per cent). Gains made on the sale of a principal residence are exempt.

Wealth Tax: None.

Inheritance & Gift Tax: Inheritance and gift tax is called Capital Acquisition Tax (CAT) and is levied at 20 to 40 per cent above certain thresholds. The wife and children of a donor are granted exemptions of up to €381,000 each. CAT is payable by the recipient and not the estate.

Value Added Tax: The standard rate of VAT is 21 per cent. There's a reduced rate of 13.5 per cent on certain goods and services, including adult clothing, footwear and theatre tickets. Most food, children's clothing, medicines and books are zero-rated, and services such as education, finance, health and insurance are exempt.

Withholding Taxes: 20 per cent is levied on dividends and other profit distributions made by an Irish tax resident individual or company.

Tax Filing: The Irish tax year is now the calendar year (since 2002) and individuals must file tax returns by 31st October of the year following the tax year. For businesses, a self-assessment basis operates whereby the company determines its tax liability. 90 per cent of the estimated tax liability must be paid within 6 months after the company year-end and the corporation tax return filed within nine months after year-end. Businesses may determine their own tax years.

Accommodation

Building Standards: Generally very good.

Restrictions On Foreign Ownership: None.

Cost Of Housing: Property is expensive in Dublin, where a two-bedroom apartment can cost at least €250,000. In September 2003, the average property price was €296,454 in the capital where prices rose by nearly 18 per cent in 2003. Outside Dublin, the average property cost €195,449 and prices rose by 14 per cent in 2003. Property in rural areas is generally better value and a modern semi-detached three-bedroom house costs from around €175,000 and a detached three-bedroom house from around €200,000.

Fees: The fees associated with buying a property in Ireland range from around 2 to 12 per cent of the price. Legal fees are 1 or 1.5 per cent of the purchase price plus VAT (20 per cent) and there are small fees for land registration and a surveyor (if necessary). VAT is included in the price of new properties. The main fee is stamp duty, which ranges from zero per cent on properties costing up to €150,000 to 9 per cent on properties costing more and all properties purchased for investment. Stamp duty is waived for first-time buyers and isn't payable on new properties.

Local Mortgages: Mortgages are available from Irish banks. The maximum loan is usually 90 per cent, payable over a period of 15 years.

Property Taxes: There's no longer a residential property tax, 'rates' or 'poll tax' in Ireland. The only charge normally made to householders is for refuse collection, which varies between nothing and €650 per year or more, according to the location of a property. The refuse tax is extremely controversial and there have been protests in recent months.

Renting: A two-bedroom apartment in the capital costs upwards of €1,000 per month and a small house from €1,300, whereas prices are considerably lower in small towns.

Personal Effects: Personal effects (including a motor vehicle) can be imported duty-free, provided they've been owned and used for six months.

Importation must take place within six months of your arrival or 12 months after the date of the transfer of your normal residence. VAT is payable on vehicles imported into Ireland from outside the European Union.

Utilities: Electricity (230V/50Hz) is provided by the Irish Electricity Supply Board (ESB). The service is reliable and relatively inexpensive. Mains gas (supplied by *Bord Gáis*) is available in most parts of the country and bottled gas is also available. Domestic water is free and safe to drink, although many people prefer bottled water.

Services

Getting There: Ireland is well connected by ointernational flights and those from theUK are very competitively priced. There are regular ferry services from France and the UK.

Public Transport: There are good domestic airline services, though fares are high. Other public transport varies from good in Dublin to limited in rural areas, where private transport is virtually essential. Comprehensive bus services and a limited rail network connect other parts of Ireland to the capital.

Motoring: Main roads are good but minor roads often poor. Cars are expensive to buy or hire. Driving standards are generally poor. Speed limits are 48kph (30mph) in built-up areas, 96kph (60mph) elsewhere, including dual cattiageways, and 112kph (70mph) on motorways. Maximum permitted alcohol level is 80mg per 100ml of blood. No leaded petrol is available. International driving licences may be used for up to a year. EU nationals may maintain their existing licences but others must exchange theirs for an Irish one, which may entail taking a test. Drivers must always have their driving licences with them.

Medical Facilities: Generally excellent though limited in some rural areas. There are around 1,650 general practitioners (GPs) and the ratio of people per doctor (680 on average) is much the same as in the UK, though higher than in most of the rest of Europe. The number of public hospitals is limited, though all have highly trained staff and the latest equipment, but there are several private and voluntary (semi-private) hospitals. Healthcare is free only to Medical Card holders (about 30 per cent of the population, generally those on low incomes). Most other people have private medical insurance through either the Voluntary Health Insurance Board (VHI) or the UK-based BUPA.

Education: Free for all children aged 6 to 16 and generally of a high standard. Teaching is in English but the study of Irish is compulsory. There's a wide range of types of school, including single-sex, private and a few international ones (American, French, German and Japanese) in the Dublin area.

Postal Services: The Irish postal service is operated by the state-controlled *An Post*, although the recent liberalisation of the postal market means that around a quarter of postal services has been privatised. *An Post*'s service is as efficient, reliable and inexpensive as any in Europe.

Telephone: Irish telephone services began to be deregulated in 1994, but the semi-state company *Eircom* still provides all domestic services. The telephone system is generally excellent and Ireland is at the forefront of telecommunications technology. The number of mobile phones recently outstripped the number of fixed phones in use.

Internet: Internet usage in Ireland has grown spectacularly in recent years and is now on a par with countries such as the UK and Finland. Most large companies have websites and email. The Irish government has invested heavily in internet technology and Ireland is one of the few EU countries with 100 per cent internet access in primary schools.

English TV & Radio: Irish TV and radio services are operated by RTÉ (*Radio Telefís Éireann*), the public broadcasting company, which transmits nationally on three channels: RTÉ 1, Network 2 and TG4, the Gaelic station. There's also an independent Irish TV station, TV3. British TV stations can also be received, as well as dozens of cable and satellite stations. An annual TV licence is payable, which partly finances RTÉ. Irish national radio services are also operated by RTÉ, which transmits in English on four channels and there are numerous local radio stations.

Miscellaneous

Crime Rate: Low, except in parts of Dublin, where there's a significant amount of drug-related crime.

Pets: Ireland has strict regulations regarding the importation of pets. Dogs and cats from all countries except the UK require an import licence. To obtain the licence the animal must be put in approved quarantine in Ireland for six months or in approved quarantine for one month and approved private arrangements for five months. The latter option is available only to animals from certain countries, with a rabies vaccination and certificate, and if the animal meets certain conditions after one month's quarantine. There's only one approved quarantine premises in Ireland and places are in short supply.

Visas: Nationals from many countries, including the EU, Canada, Japan and the US, don't need visas for visits up to three months. Business visas for visits up to three months are available for many non-EU countries under the same conditions as for the Schengen Visa (see page 20). For further visa information, see page 19.

Residence Permits: All foreign nationals except British must have either a work or residence permit for visits longer than 90 days. All foreign visitors (except British) must register with the local police in Ireland if they plan to stay for longer than 90 days and obtain a police registration certificate.

International Dialling Code: 353.

Time Difference: GMT.

Weights & Measures: Metric.

Reference

Useful Addresses

British Embassy, 31 Merrion Road, Dublin 4 (☎ 01-205 3700, ☐ www.british embassy.ie).

Irish Embassy, 17 Grosvenor Place, London SW1X 7HR, UK (☎ 020-7235 2171).

Irish Embassy, 2234 Massachusetts Ave., NW, Washington, DC 20008, USA (☎ 202-462 3939, ☐ www.irelandemb.org).

US Embassy, 42 Elgin Road, Dublin 4 (☎ 01-668 8777, ☐ http://dublin. usembassy.gov).

Further Reading

Living & Working in Ireland, Joe Laredo (Survival Books Ltd, ☐ www. survivalbooks.net).

Useful Websites

Irish Development Agency (☐ www.idaireland.com) – Useful information about doing business and working in Ireland.

Move to Ireland (☐ http://movetoireland.com) – A comprehensive site on moving to Ireland with information on most aspects of living there.

ITALY

General Information

Capital: Rome.
  Population: 57.8 million.
  Foreign Community: There are many foreigners in the major Italian cities and also foreign communities in many resorts and rural areas, particularly in central (e.g. Rome) and northern Italy (e.g. Tuscany), including some 40,000 Britons.
  Area: 301,270km² (116,320mi²).
  Geography: Italy, which is shaped like a boot, has a vast coastline and borders with Austria, France, Slovenia and Switzerland. There's a wide variety of landscape and vegetation, characterised by its two mountain ranges, the Alps and the Apennines (almost 80 per cent of the country is covered by hills and mountains). The Alps extend across northern Italy in a longitudinal direction and include a number of peaks over 4,000m (13,000ft) and the lakes of Como, Garda and Maggiore. The Apennines form the backbone of the peninsula and extend the length of the country. Northern Italy has large areas of woods and

farmland, while the south is mostly scrubland. Italy's principal islands are Sicily and Sardinia, plus Elba, Capri and Ischia.

Climate: Italy has a temperate climate influenced by the Mediterranean and Adriatic Seas. Summers are generally very hot everywhere, with average temperatures in July and August around 24°C (75°F). Winters are cold and dry in the Alps (average temperature -2°C (29°F) and mild in Rome, on the Italian Riviera and in Sicily and the south (average temperature 8°C (46°F).

Language: The official language is Italian. Minorities speak German (Alto Adige), French (Valle d'Aosta), Slovene and Ladino, and there are also numerous regional dialects. French is widely understood and English is spoken in the major cities and tourist centres.

Government: Democratic republic with bicameral legislature.

Political Stability: Italy is one of the most politically unstable countries in the EU, although this appears to have little outward effect on the country's economy or daily life. There have been numerous changes of government since World War II, largely because Italy's system of proportional representation almost guarantees fragmented and shaky coalitions (an attempt at electoral reform in recent years doesn't appear to have had much effect). In April 2001, the country held its 59th general election since 1945 when the right-wing Silvio Berlusconi was elected president.

EU Accession: Founder member.

Economy

Overview: Italy's economy has shown very slow growth in recent years and there are several serious problems facing the country's economic situation, including chronic public debt, political fragmentation and serious wealth divides between regions. Although privatisation has boosted the state coffers, successive governments have failed to make the most of the profits. Small and medium enterprises are the backbone of the Italian economy and the government is establishing high-tech areas (mainly in Sicily)

with some success in an attempt to modernise the economy. In 2002, Fiat, one of Italy's insignia companies, ran into serious financial difficulties with widespread redundancies. In 2003, Italy officially entered a recession recording negative growth over the first nine months of the year, but the outlook for 2004 is considerably better.

GDP Per Head: US$24,700.

Growth (2003): 0.5 per cent.

Forecast Growth For 2004: 1.75 per cent.

Main Industries: Aerospace, communication, clothing, design, financial and insurance sectors, food and drink, healthcare, IT, oil and gas, railways and security.

UK Trade Partner Ranking: 6.

US Trade Partner Ranking: 50+.

Working

Overview: Although unemployment has recently reached record lows, the overall figure conceals vast differences: in southern Italy the rate is over 20 per cent, while the Veneto regions has full employment. Thus employers in the north contract immigrants to meet the labour shortage while as much as 50 per cent of young adults are unemployed in the south.

Unemployment Rate (2003): 8.4 per cent.

Employment Opportunities: Most foreign personnel work for multinational organisations. TEFL is a growth area and casual employment is usually available in tourism. Most opportunities for expatriates are in the north and a good knowledge of Italian is essential.

Work Permits: Not required for nationals of original EU member nations, but for all others. Citizens of new EU states may visit to seek work for up to six months until at least May 2006 (check the latest information). Non-EU nationals may have difficulty in obtaining work permits, as employers must prove that there are no suitable Italian workers available before employing a foreigner.

Labour Relations: Traditionally unstable with strikes commonplace, particularly in the public sector. The last general strike was in October 2002.

Employment Conditions: There's a 40-hour working week and a minimum annual paid holiday allowance of 20 days. Most employees receive 14 months' salary and other benefits, such as housing and childcare allowances. Minimum salary rates are mandatory for most job categories, although there isn't a national minimum wage.

Salaries: Around the EU average, except for academics and Italian MEPs, whose salaries are far higher than in other EU countries.

Monthly Minimum Wage: Not applicable.

Business Hours: Offices generally open from 8 or 9am to noon or 1pm and from 2 or 3pm to 6 or 7pm Monday to Friday. Banks open from 8am to 2pm Monday to Friday.

Public Holidays: Ten per year:

- 1st & 6th January
- Easter Monday
- 25th April
- 1st May
- 15th August
- 1st November
- 8th, 25th & 26th December

Business Etiquette: Business is conducted in a formal manner. Personal contact is extremely important and an intrinsic part of business culture. Most Italians in the north speak English, but civil servants rarely do so.

Finance

Currency: Euro (€).

Exchange Controls: None.

Banks: The Italian banking and financial system is undergoing fundamental changes. There are hundreds of Italian banks, although many are localised and small, but all operate under the authority of the Italian Central Bank. Many smaller banks are now rationalising services and forming alliances with larger banks. Banking isn't very efficient in Italy, although services are improving, and charges are high. To open a resident's account you require a fiscal number.

Cost/Standard Of Living: There's a huge disparity between the prosperous north and central regions of Italy, where there are some of Europe's richest areas, and the relatively poor south of the country. In the north the standard and cost of living are high and on a par with other EU countries, while in the south living costs and standards are much lower and below the EU average. Taxation in Italy is one of the highest in the EU and luxury and quality products are particularly expensive, as are cars. Italy, along with Portugal and Spain, is rated one of the cheapest countries in the eurozone.

Loans: Loans are available from Italian banks, but you should shop around for rates since Italian banks have traditionally levied some of the highest charges in the world.

Interest Rate (Early 2004): 2 per cent (European Central Bank).

Taxation

Corporate Tax: Corporate income and capital gains taxes are levied at 37 per cent and in some regions there's an additional corporate income tax known as IRAP fixed at 4.25 per cent.

Personal Income Tax: Income tax (IRPEF) is high in Italy and ranges from 18 (up to €10,339) to 45 per cent (over €69,722), although there are numerous allowances and credits. Income tax for employees is usually taxed at source (PAYE). Residents require a fiscal number (*codice fiscale*) which must be used in all communications with the tax authorities and an annual tax return must be filed. There are tax allowances for dependants, mortgage interest payments, pension funds and medical expenses. Individuals also qualify for tax credits. There are also regional additional taxes (from 0.9 to 1.4 per cent) and municipal additional taxes (up to 0.5 per cent).

Capital Gains Tax: None for property used as a primary residence. CGT is levied on gains made on stocks and shares at two rates: 12.5 and 27 per cent, depending on the gain.

Wealth Tax: None.

Inheritance & Gift Tax: Inheritance and gift taxes have been practically abolished in Italy (from October 2001). Inheritance tax has been abolished completely and gift tax is levied only on gifts made to relatives beyond the fourth degree. Mortgage and cadastral taxes are, however, still levied.

Value Added Tax: The standard rate of value added tax is 20 per cent and there are reduced rates of 4 and 10 per cent. VAT is payable on new properties at 4 per cent and 20 per cent for luxury property

Withholding Taxes: Dividends and interest are subject to 12.5 per cent withholding tax if received by resident individuals and to 27 per cent if non-resident.

Tax Filing: All individuals (unless they are employees and have no other source of income) and companies must file annual tax returns. The Italian tax year is the calendar year and employee returns must be filed by 30th June and self-employed returns by 31st July.

Accommodation

Building Standards: Excellent to poor. Most new buildings are of good quality.

Restrictions On Foreign Ownership: None.

Cost Of Housing: Property prices in Italy vary considerably and are generally high in cities and towns (e.g. from €250,000 in Rome for a two-bedroom apartment) and relatively low in rural areas (e.g. from €100,000 for a three-bedroom country house), except in areas where high demand from foreign buyers has driven up prices.

Fees: Total fees when buying a property in Italy are usually between 10 and 18 per cent of the purchase price, including registration tax (3 per cent of the fiscal value for residents and 7 per cent for non-residents), land registry tax (1 per cent of the fiscal value for second home buyers and non-residents, a fixed price of €130 for first home resident buyers), notary, legal fees (1 or 2 per cent) and estate agent's fees (between 3 and 8 per cent).

Local Mortgages: Mortgages are available from Italian banks, and maximum loans are generally 50 or 60 per cent for second homes and 85 per cent for principal homes. The usual term is 5 to 15 years.

Property Taxes: A local community tax or rates (*Imposta Comunale sugli Immobili*/ICI) is paid by all property and landowners in Italy, whether they're residents or non-residents. It's levied at between 0.4 to 0.7 per cent of a property's fiscal value (*valore catastale*), the actual rate being decided by the local municipality depending on a property's size, location, class and category. It's paid in two instalments in June and December.

Renting: Rental accommodation is usually easy to find in Italy, with the exception of the major cities, where it's in high demand and short supply. Properties are usually let unfurnished and without kitchen appliances. A two-bedroom apartment costs from €750 to €2,000 a month to rent and a three-bedroom apartment from €1,100 to €2,000 a month. Prices in central Rome and in major northern cities can be up to three times higher.

Personal Effects: Personal effects (including a motor vehicle) can be imported duty-free provided they've been owned and used for six months (an inventory should be provided and approved by an Italian consulate in your home country). A certificate of residence or proof of having purchased a home is required, and belongings must be imported within six months of taking up residence.

Utilities: The electricity supply (220V) is provided by *Ente Nazionale per l'Energie Elettrica* and is generally reliable, although power cuts are commonplace in some rural areas and charges are higher than in other EU countries. Mains gas is available only in the north of the country, although bottled gas is widely available. Water charges are among the most expensive in Europe and water shortages and cuts are common in central and southern parts of the country.

Services

Getting There: Italy has some 15 international airports with frequent flights to worldwide destinations. It can also be reached by rail and road from most of Europe. Ferries operate across the Adriatic to Croatia and Greece.

Public Transport: The north has excellent communications, particularly for commuters, but in the south they vary greatly and are poor in some parts. There are good domestic flights linking all major cities and a comprehensive rail network with excellent services in the north. Regular ferry services link all islands (particularly Sardinia and Sicily) to various points on the mainland.

Motoring: Roads are generally good and there's an excellent motorway system (mostly toll). Italian driving leaves a lot to be desired and anarchy and chaos are widespread. Speed limits are 50kph in built-up areas, 90 or 100kph elsewhere, including dual carriageways, and 130kph on motorways. Maximum permitted alcohol level is 80mg per 100ml of blood. All vehicles must carry warning triangles. No leaded petrol is available. EU driving licences need not be changed for Italian ones but residents should have theirs stamped at the local motor registry. Non-EU drivers may use their existing licences for up to a year (they must be accompanied by an Italian translation) after which they must be exchanged. Many countries in South America and Asia have reciprocal driving licence agreements but many others, e.g. Australia, Canada, New Zealand and the US, don't.

Medical Facilities: These vary from poor to excellent. The public health service is overstretched and underfunded and quality of service varies according to region and hospital. There are many private hospitals, often run by the Catholic Church, and private health insurance is highly recommended.

Education: Free and compulsory for children aged from 6 to 16 and standards are reasonably high. There are many private schools, mostly run by the Catholic Church, and several international schools in Milan and Rome.

Postal Services: The postal service isn't very efficient (it's easily the worst in Western Europe), although modernisation and investment are slowly improving services. There are post offices in most areas, which also provide banking services.

Telephone: Several companies provide telephone services in Italy, of which Telecom Italia is the main provider with a monopoly on local calls and the installation of phone lines. Competition between the various companies means call charges are continually being reduced.

Internet: Italy was slow to take to the internet, but is now catching up fast with Northern Europe and most companies now use email and many also have websites. There are numerous ISPs in Italy, both free and subscription.

English TV & Radio: There are various state and privately owned TV and radio stations in Italy but, apart from the occasional news broadcast and some expatriate radio stations, there's little in English. There's no cable TV, but satellite reception is good in most regions. There's an annual TV and radio licence.

Miscellaneous

Crime Rate: The rate varies considerably from region to region. Violent crime is rare but muggings occur in resort areas and there are armed (and dangerous) bandits in parts of the south. Housebreaking and burglary are a problem in most areas and car crime is widespread. Organised crime isn't generally a threat to foreigners, although kidnappings aren't uncommon in the south.

Pets: Cats and dogs require a health certificate that must include proof of a rabies vaccination given more than 20 days and less than 11 months before the certificate is issued. You must also provide an export health certificate (bilingual, English/Italian), obtainable from Italian consulates abroad. Dogs in Italy must be registered with the local authorities and identified either by tattoo or microchip.

Visas: Nationals from many countries, including the EU, Canada, Japan and the US, don't require a visa to visit Italy for any purpose for up to three months. Business visas for visits up to three months are available for many non-EU countries under the same conditions as the Schengen Visa (see page 20). For further visa information see page 19.

Residence Permits: All foreigners staying for more than 90 days must apply for a 'permit to stay' at the local police station within eight days of arrival. There are several categories of permit depending on your purpose. If you wish to apply for a residence permit (there are many advantages in doing so) you should apply to the register office of the local town hall.

International Dialling Code: 39.

Time Difference: GMT +1.

Weights & Measures: Metric.

Reference

Useful Addresses

British Embassy, Via XX Settembre 80A, 00187 Rome (☎ 06-4220 0001, 💻 www. britain.it).

Italian Embassy, 14 Three Kings Yard, London W1Y 2EH, UK (☎ 020-7312 2200, 💻 www.embitaly.org.uk).

Italian Embassy, 3000 Whitehaven Street, NW, Washington, DC 20008, USA
(☎ 202-612 4400, 🖳 www.italyemb.org).

US Embassy, Via Vittorio Veneto 119A, 00187 Rome (☎ 06-46741, 🖳 www.
usembassy.it)

Further Reading

Living & Working in Italy, Nick Daws (Survival Books Ltd, 🖳 www.
survivalbooks.net).

Useful Websites

The Informer (🖳 www.informer.it) – Online subscription magazine with
comprehensive expatriate information.

In Italy Online (🖳 www.initaly.com) – Extensive information about many
aspects of Italy and daily life there.

Italy Trade (🖳 www.italtrade.com) – Provides assistance with import and
export of products as well as trade information.

Milan (🖳 www.hellomilano.it) – Information on just about everything to do
with Milan.

Rome Buddy (🖳 www.romebuddy.com) – A general guide to all aspects of
living in Rome and Italy.

LATVIA

General Information

Capital: Riga.
   Population: 2.4 million.
   Foreign Community: There's a sizeable population of Russians and
people from other neighbouring countries in the Baltic States, but relatively
few westerners.
   Area: 63,700km² (24,596mi²).
   Geography: Latvia is the middle Baltic State and has borders with Estonia in
the north, the Russian Federation and Belarus in the east, Lithuania in the south
and the Baltic Sea in the west. Latvia has flat coastal plains, although inland it's
forested and hilly.
   Climate: Latvia has a mixture of continental and maritime climates, and the
westerly wind usually ensures temperatures don't fall much below freezing.
Winters are generally long and cold, and summers warm and pleasant, although
August is the wettest month in the region. Average temperatures are -2°C (29°F)
in January and 20°C (68°F) in July.

Language: The official language is Latvian (similar in some aspects to German). English, German, Polish and Russian are also spoken.

Government: Parliamentary democracy.

Political Stability: Very good. Democracy is well established in Latvia, which is a member of the UN. Latvia joins NATO in May 2004 at the same time as joining the EU.

EU Accession: Latvia is the poorest member of the ten new candidates (GDP per capita is 30 per cent of the EU average), but has been quick to fulfil criteria and has made excellent progress in negotiations, although taxation reforms (particularly VAT administration), customs and agricultural issues are as yet unresolved. Despite the benefits of EU accession, medium-term forecasts predict that Latvia will remain poor for at least another two decades before reaching 75 per cent of the EU average GDP.

Economy

Overview: Latvia has the highest foreign direct investment in the Baltic states, but the country is the most dependent on the Russian economy. Growth in the aftermath of the Russian crisis in 1998 was very low. However, the economy has since recovered substantially and in 2003 Latvia was one of Europe's fastest growing countries.

GDP Per Head: US$3,801.

Growth (2003): 6.2 per cent.

Forecast Growth For 2004: 6.4 per cent.

Main Industries: Chemicals, financial services, food processing, IT and electronics, mechanical engineering and metal processing, metals and minerals, textiles industry, transportation and distribution, and travel and tourism.

UK Trade Partner Ranking: 49.

US Trade Partner Ranking: 50+.

Working

Overview: The workforce is generally well trained and motivated. Employment is now concentrated in business administration, legal services and telecommunications, with a fast-growing market in engineering and IT. Latvia expects to become one of the EU's main exporters of software in the near future.

Unemployment Rate (2003): 11.5 per cent.

Employment Opportunities: Agriculture, IT (a major growth area), legal work, management consultancy, manufacturing and service industries.

Work Permits: EU citizens must obtain a permit before starting work at least until May 2006 (but check the latest information), although they may visit to seek work for up to six months. Non-EU citizens must apply for a permit **before** coming to Latvia. Applications must normally be supported by a firm offer of employment from an established enterprise. To work in Latvia you must also have a residence permit.

Labour Relations: Generally very good. There are few strikes.

Employment Conditions: The Labour Code was revised in 2002 to provide better conditions for employees. The working week is 40 hours Monday to Friday and there's a minimum paid holiday allowance of 28 days per year.

Salaries: Low compared with those in Western Europe,

Minimum Monthly Wage (2003): €116.

Social Security: Contributions vary according to the resident status of employer and employee and are up to a maximum of LVL17,300. For companies registered in Latvia, the contributions are 26.09 per cent for employers and 9 per cent for employees. Non-resident company employers pay nothing and their employees 8.52 per cent. Contributions are paid quarterly. Foreigners working in Latvia for less that 12 months, who regularly contribute to their home country's social security system, are exempt.

Business Hours: Office and business hours are 8.30am to 5.30pm and banks open from 9am to 5pm Monday to Friday.

Public Holidays: 11 per year:

- 1st January
- Good Friday, Easter Sunday & Easter Monday
- 1st May
- 23rd & 24th June
- 18th November
- 25th, 26th & 31st December

Business Etiquette: Business conduct and attire are formal, as are forms of address. Business cards are usually exchanged.

Finance

Currency: Lat (LVL).

Exchange Rate: €1= LVL0.66 (February 2004).

Exchange Controls: None.

Banks: The local banking system is well developed and there are several foreign banks present in Latvia. Some local banks offer international services, although the range of services is much more limited than westerners are used to, but the situation is improving. Internet banking is increasingly popular.

Cost/Standard Of Living: The cost of living is generally lower than in Western Europe, but imported goods are very expensive, although multinational companies tend to pay their employees higher salaries to compensate for this. In general, the standard of living is good, although much lower than in Western Europe.

Loans: Loans are somewhat difficult to obtain from Latvian banks, particularly for non-residents.

Interest Rate (Early 2004): 3.7 per cent.

Taxation

Corporate Tax: Latvia levies corporate income and capital gains taxes at 22 per cent.

Personal Income Tax: There's a flat rate of 25 per cent. Tax is payable after deductions and a personal allowance of LVL21 per month (2003 figure).

Capital Gains Tax: Latvian residents are exempt from CGT unless the gains are on immovable property held for less than 12 months. Non-residents are subject to CGT at the same rate as income tax.

Wealth Tax: None.

Inheritance & Gift Tax: None.

Value Added Tax: VAT (PVN) is levied at the standard rate of 18 per cent on most goods and services, except for certain goods and services such as medical goods, media, tourist accommodation services and water supply, which are subject to the reduced rate of 9 per cent.

Withholding Taxes: Dividends and interest for non-residents are taxed at the same rate as income tax.

Tax Filing: The tax year is the calendar year and individuals must file an annual tax return by 1st April.

Accommodation

Building Standards: Variable and poor in many town and city apartment blocks.

Restrictions On Foreign Ownership: None.

Cost Of Housing: An apartment in Riga costs from €800 to €1,500 per m².

Fees: Fees include notary and registration fees plus 2 per cent of the property's cadastral value (up a maximum of LVL30,000).

Local Mortgages: Mortgages are available from local banks for up to 20 years and maximum amounts are up to 85 per cent of the property's price.

Property Taxes: Real estate tax is levied at 1 per cent of the property's registered value.

Renting: Rental property is widely available, although foreigners will find the standards lower than they are used to. Prices are also often inflated for 'rich' foreigners who may have to pay twice as much as locals for the same accommodation. It's best to consult a reputable local agency specialising in rentals before committing yourself. A two-bedroom apartment costs from €2,000 a month. Apartments are particularly spacious in Riga.

Personal Effects: Personal effects can be imported and exported from Latvia, usually without paying duty. However, you must sign an 'entry declaration' on arrival or departure, which must be accompanied by an inventory (which cannot be modified), and duty may be payable on certain items.

Utilities: Electricity (220V) is widely available throughout Latvia. The service is generally reliable, and charges are considerably lower than in western European countries. Mains gas is available for cooking and heating in most towns and cities. Water is officially safe to drink in all towns and cities, but bottled water tastes much better.

Services

Getting There: Riga International Airport is served by several international flights daily. Ferries run from other Baltic States and Scandinavia, amd trains run to and from Russia.

Public Transport: Generally good and reasonable. An extensive rail network links the main cities, although journeys can be slow. Riga has an efficient electric commuter train service. Countrywide bus services are quicker and cheaper than trains.

Motoring: The well-developed road network will form part of the ambitious Via Baltica connecting Scandinavia with Central and Southern Europe via the Baltic States and Poland. Minor roads may be in poor condition and queues at borders can be long. Speed limits are 50kph in built-up areas, 90kph elsewhere, including dual carriageways, and 100kph on motorways. Maximum permitted alcohol level is 50mg per 100ml of blood. All vehicles must carry a warning triangle, first aid kit and fire extinguisher. No leaded petrol is available. All foreign residents must exchange their driving licences for Latvian ones after six months. The exchange is automatic for EU nationals but others may be required to take a theoretical test.

Medical Facilities: Facilities are reasonable, though below the standards expected by westerners. Standards are higher in the private sector. Emergency and much minor treatment is free but everything else must be paid for. A comprehensive international health insurance policy is essential.

Education: Generally of a high standard with teaching in the local language and Russian. Schooling is free and compulsory for children aged 7 to 15 or 16 and most children attend state schools. There are few private schools and only one international school.

Postal Services: The postal service is reasonably efficient and quick. Post between Latvia and the rest of Europe takes a few days and local post one or two.

Telephone: The telephone service is reliable, although call charges are high. Two mobile phone companies operate within the country.

Internet: Internet is increasingly popular and the country is investing heavily in new technology. Service providers are available.

English TV & Radio: Cable and satellite TV channels are available in Latvia, as is the BBC World Service.

Miscellaneous

Crime Rate: Unlike many other Eastern European countries, Latvia doesn't have a particularly high crime rate, although petty crime is common, particularly in crowded places.

Pets: Dogs and cats require a veterinary certificate of good health and vaccination from an authorised vet in their home country.

Visas: Nationals of many countries, including the EEA, Australia, Canada and the US, may visit Latvia for up to 90 days without a visa, although the 90 days must be within one half-calendar year, ie. from January to June or from July to December. Other nationals require a visa, which is usually also valid for the other Baltic States. Foreign nationals remaining in Latvia for more than 90 days must apply for a temporary residence permit. For further visa information see page 19.

Residence Permits: Foreigners planning to spend more than 90 consecutive days in Latvia must have residence permits.

International Dialling Code: 371.

Time Difference: GMT +2.

Weights & Measures: Metric.

Reference

Useful Addresses

British Embassy, 5J Alunana iela, LV-1010 Riga (☎ 777-4700, 🖥 www.britain.lv).

Latvian Embassy, 45 Nottingham Place, London 1M 3FE, UK (☎ 020-7312 0040).

Latvian Embassy, 4325 17th Street, NW, 20011 Washington DC, USA (☎ 202-726 6785, 🖥 www.latvia-usa.org).

US Embassy, Raina Bulvaris 7, LV-1510 Riga (☎ 703-6200, 🖥 www.usembassy.lv).

Further Reading

Latvian Business Guide (published by the Latvian Development Agency, Perses 2, Riga, LV-1042 ☎ 703-9400, 🖥 www.lda.gov.lv).

Useful Websites

Baltics Worldwide (🖥 www.balticsww.com) – A useful guide to many aspects of the Baltic States.

Baltic Trade (🖥 www.baltictrade.lv) – Comprehensive information about doing business and some aspects of living in Latvia.

Latvian Development Agency (🖥 www.lda.gov.lv) – Useful business information.

LITHUANIA

General Information

Capital: Vilna.

Population: 3.7 million.

Foreign Community: There's a sizeable population of Russians and people from other neighbouring countries in the Baltic States, but relatively few westerners.

Area: 65,300km² (25,214mi²).

Geography: Lithuania is the southernmost and largest of the Baltic States, and borders with Latvia in the north, Belarus in the east, Poland in the south and the Baltic Sea in the west. It has a mainly flat landscape dotted with lakes.

Climate: A mixture of continental and maritime climates. The westerly wind usually ensures temperatures don't fall much below freezing. Winters are generally long and cold, and summers warm and pleasant, although August is the wettest month in the region. Average temperatures are -5°C (23°F) in January and 17°C (63°F) in July.

Language: The official language is Lithuanian (similar in some aspects to German). English, German, Polish and Russian are also spoken, although English now dominates as the second language.

Government: Parliamentary democracy.

Political Stability: Poor – the country has seen six governments since 1999, although the political parties have made successful attempts to overcome their differences in a bid to speed up EU accession. Lithuania joins NATO in May 2004.

EU Accession: Lithuania is one of the poorest new members (GDP is around 33 per cent of the EU average), but the country has made good progress on EU demands and reforms. The price has been high, however, for many Lithuanians who have seen unemployment rise and social security spending reduced. These are expected to continue together with a general rise in prices for the short term once Lithuania joins the EU in May 2004. Obstacles also remain in the energy sector, particularly regarding privatisation and the status of the Russian enclave of Kaliningrad, between Lithuania and Poland, which will become isolated and its inhabitants will require visas to travel to Russia after EU enlargement. Lithuania also needs to make more progress on fiscal and pension reform to meet EU criteria.

Economy

Overview: There's now a generally stable economy and growth is steady. Despite the country's few natural resources, economic expansion and foreign investment in the country are both on the increase and GDP growth in 2003 was one of the highest in the world.

GDP Per Head: US$4,482.

Growth (2003): 8.1 per cent (the highest in the EU).

Forecast Growth For 2004: 6.5 per cent.

Main Industries: Chemicals, electrical goods, electronics, manufacture of electrical equipment and machinery, energy, furniture manufacture, light industry, metal processing, optical goods, telecommunications, textiles and timber processing.

UK Trade Partner Ranking: 50+.
US Trade Partner Ranking: 50+.

Working

Overview: The workforce is well trained and educated, with a high number of graduates. Productivity is high and labour costs among the lowest in Central and Eastern Europe – which accounts for the high level of foreign investment.

Unemployment Rate (2003): 12.2 per cent.

Employment Opportunities: Openings may be found in household goods, manufacturing, postal services and communications, recreation and leisure (including tourism), TEFL and transport, particularly ports.

Work Permits: EU nationals require permits before starting work at least until May 2006 (check the latest information), but may visit for up to six months to seek work. Others must obtain permits **before** arriving in the country, although they are occasionally issued to foreigners already there. There are strict annual quotas and permits are usually granted only to those with a firm employment offer.

Labour Relations: Generally very good. Unions, now independent of government, are active in collective bargaining. Strikes are infrequent.

Employment Conditions: Good. Employment contracts are heavily regulated by law. The working week is 40 hours Monday to Friday and employees are entitled to 28 days paid annual leave.

Salaries: Very low by Western European standards, Average monthly salaries in administration are €770 and €750 in the financial sector. Those in manufacturing are much lower.

Minimum Monthly Wage (2003): €130.

Social Security: Contributions – employers 31 per cent and employees 3 per cent of gross monthly salary – are compulsory. The self-employed pay 50 per cent of the basic pension per month and are exempt from obligatory health insurance. Companies are liable for a further 3 per cent of employee salaries for health insurance. Voluntary health insurance is also available and employers may contribute up to 10 per cent of the official average monthly salary.

Business Hours: Offices and business open from 8am to 5pm and banks from 8am to 3pm Monday to Friday, though some branches open at weekends.

Public Holidays: Ten per year:

- 1st January
- 16th February
- 11th March
- Easter Monday
- 1st May

- 6th July
- 15th August
- 1st November
- 25th & 26th December

Business Etiquette: Business is conducted formally and dress should be smart, Handshakes are the accepted form for starting and ending a meeting. Business cards are always exchanged.

Finance

Currency: Litas. It is planned to adopt the euro by 2008.

Exchange Rate: Linked to the euro at a fixed exchange rate of LTL3.45 = €1.

Exchange Controls: None.

Banks: The banking sector has developed rapidly over recent years and commercial banks have expanded their range of services, which is now comparable to those offered in Western Europe.

Cost/Standard Of Living: The cost of living is generally lower than in Western Europe, but imported goods are very expensive, although multinational companies tend to pay their employees higher salaries to compensate for this. In general, the standard of living is good, although much lower than in Western Europe.

Loans: Lithuanian banks offer personal loans, although terms may not be as generous as those in Western Europe.

Interest Rate (Early 2004): 3 per cent.

Taxation

All taxpayers must register with the tax authorities and acquire a tax number.

Corporate Tax: Corporate income and capital gains tax rates are 15 per cent and all companies engaging in business in Lithuania are subject to tax on their worldwide income.

Personal Income Tax: Income tax is levied at the flat rate of 33 per cent and there's a monthly tax-exempt minimum (TEM – LTL250 in 2003). Employment income from foreign companies is taxed at 20 per cent.

Capital Gains Tax: CGT is levied on 10 per cent on gains other than the sale of a principal residence.

Wealth Tax: None.

Inheritance Tax: Inheritance tax is levied at 5 per cent on estates valued up to LTL0.5 million and at 10 per cent on higher amounts. Relatives of the first and second degree are exempt.

Value Added Tax: The standard rate of VAT is 18 per cent and there are two reduced rates of 9 per cent (heating services) and 5 per cent (domestic airline services). Certain goods and services such as education and medicines are exempt.

Withholding Taxes: Dividends are subject to 15 per cent withholding tax and the rates for interest vary according to the existence of a tax treaty.

Tax Filing: The tax year is the calendar year and all individuals and businesses are required to file an annual tax return. Individuals must file by 1st February.

Accommodation

Building Standards: Variable and poor in many town and city apartment blocks.

Restrictions On Foreign Ownership: None for individuals but companies must obtain a permit from the government.

Cost Of Housing: Apartments with two bedrooms cost from LTL150,000 to 250,000.

Fees: Fees include a registration fee.

Local Mortgages: Mortgages are available from local banks for up to 40 years for maximum amounts of up to 85 per cent of the property's price.

Property Taxes: None.

Renting: Rental property is widely available, although foreigners will find the standards lower than they are used to. Prices are also often inflated for 'rich' foreigners who may have to pay twice as much as locals for the same accommodation. It's best to consult a reputable local agency specialising in rentals before committing yourself. A two-bedroom apartment costs from LTL3,000 a month.

Personal Effects: Personal effects can be imported and exported from Lithuania, usually without paying duty. However, you must sign an 'entry declaration' on arrival or departure, which must be accompanied by an inventory, and duty may be payable on certain items.

Utilities: Electricity (220V) is widely available throughout Lithuania and the service is generally reliable with charges are lower than in other western European countries. Mains gas is available for cooking and heating in most towns and cities. Water is officially safe to drink in all towns and cities, but bottled water tastes much better.

Services

Getting There: The capital has four international airports, the main one at Vilna just outside the city centre with flights to most major European cities and some Middle East destinations. There are ferry services to Vilna from Scandinavia.

Public Transport: Communications are reasonable and Lithuania claims to be the prime transport centre linking Western and Eastern Europe. There are four international airports, excellent roads and the only ice-free port in the Eastern Baltic at Klaipeda, which has recently received vast funds for expansion.

In winter, transport services are considerably reduced. There's a limited rail service and most regions are served by buses and coaches.

Motoring: Road standards vary enormously. Main roads are excellent and will form part of the ambirious Via Baltica, linking Scandinavia with Central and Southern Europe via the Baltic States and Poland. Minor road surfaces are generally poor and the region has the highest road accident rate in the world! Speed limits are 60kph in built-up areas. 90kph elsewhere, including dual carriageways, and 110kph on motorways. Maximum permitted alcohol level is 40mg per 100m, of blood. All vehicles must carry a warning triangle, first aid kit and fire extinguisher. Leaded petrol is available. All foreign residents must exchange driving licences for Lithuanian ones after six months. EU licence holders receive them automatically but others may have to take a theoretical and/or driving test.

Medical Facilities: Reasonable but below the standard expected by westerners. Standards are higher in private hospitals. Emergency and much minor treatment is free but anything else must be paid for. A comprehensive international health insurance policy is essential.

Education: Generally of a high standard with teaching in the local language and Russian. Education is free and compulsory for children aged 7 to 15 or 16. Most children attend state schools. There are very few private schools and no international schools,

Postal Services: The postal service is reliable and efficient.

Telephone: The telephone service is provided principally by Lithuanian Telecom (owned mainly by a Finnish and Swedish consortium) and is modern, offering a good service. Mobile phone facilities are offered by several companies and most Lithuanians have a mobile.

Internet: The internet has expanded rapidly in Lithuania and there are several service providers.

English TV & Radio: Cable and satellite TV channels are available in Lithuania, as is the BBC World Service.

Miscellaneous

Crime Rate: Unlike many other Eastern European countries, Lithuania does not have a particularly high crime rate, although petty crime is common, particularly in crowded places.

Pets: Pets require an up-to-date health certificate, which must be presented at the border.

Visas: Nationals of many countries, including the EEA, Australia, Canada and the US, may visit Lithuania for up to three months without a visa. Other nationals require a visa, which is usually also valid for the other Baltic States. Foreign nationals remaining in Lithuania for more than 90 days must apply for a temporary residence permit. For further visa information see page 19.

Residence Permits: Temporary residence permits are required for all foreigners staying for more than 90 days. Non-EU nationals are usually issued a residence permit in conjunction with a work permit from outside the country.

International Dialling Code: 370.

Time Difference: GMT +2.

Weights & Measures: Metric.

Reference

Useful Addresses

British Embassy, Antakalnio 2, 2055 Vilna (☎ 5-246 2900, 🖳 www.britain.lt).

Lithuanian Embassy, 84 Gloucester Place, London W1H 6AU, UK (☎ 020-7486 6401).

Lithuanian Embassy, 2622 16th Street NW, 20009 Washington DC, USA (☎ 202-234 5680, 🖳 www.ltembassyus.org).

US Embassy, Akmenu 6, 2600 Vilna (☎ 5-266 5500, 🖳 http://vilnius.usembassy.gov).

Useful Websites

Baltics Worldwide (🖳 www.balticsww.com) – A useful guide to many aspects of the Baltic States.

Lithuanian Development Agency (🖳 www.leda.lt) – Publishes factsheets and a guide to doing business.

Visit Lithuania (🖳 www.visitlithuania.net) – Useful information about the country.

LUXEMBOURG

General Information

Capital: Luxembourg.

Population: 441,300.

Foreign Community: Almost one-third of the Luxembourg population is comprised of expatriates and many Belgian, French and German nationals commute daily to work there. Half the workforce is made up of non-Luxembourg nationals.

Area: 2,590km² (1,000mi²).

Geography: Luxembourg is the smallest country in Europe and lies landlocked between the borders of Belgium, north-eastern France and western Germany. The north of the country lies in the wooded Ardennes and the south in the agricultural plains of Lorraine. The Moselle flows through the south of the country where the capital is situated, home to over a third of the population.

Climate: Luxembourg has a temperate climate with mild winters and warm summers. Rainfall is high in autumn and winter. Average temperatures are 5°C (41°F) in January and 23°C (73°F) in July.

Language: The official language is Luxembourgian (a German dialect), but English, French and German are also widely spoken.

Government: Constitutional monarchy with a bicameral legislature.

Political Stability: Excellent. Luxembourg is Europe's last independent duchy and, together with Belgium and the Netherlands, forms the economic union known as Benelux. Luxembourg is a founder member of NATO and the EU, and is home to the Secretariat of the European Parliament, the European Court of Justice and the European Monetary Cooperation Fund.

EU Accession: Founder member.

Economy

Overview: Luxembourg is one of the world's most prosperous countries and has one of the highest standards of living. The economy is based on banking, insurance, telecommunications and the steel industry, and is extremely stable. Inflation and unemployment are consistently low. Luxembourg is heavily dependent on foreign trade and the foreign workforce from neighbouring countries.

GDP Per Head: US$44,000 (the highest in the world).

Growth (2003): 0.75 per cent.

Forecast Growth For 2004: 2 per cent.

Main Industries: Finance, insurance, manufacture (aluminium, cement, computers glass and magnetic tapes) and steel.

UK Trade Partner Ranking: 50+.

US Trade Partner Ranking: 50+.

Working

Overview: The workforce is generally highly skilled and with a strong work ethic. Labour costs are lower than in neighbouring countries.

Unemployment Rate (2003): 3.9 per cent. Unemployment has been consistently low for several years (the lowest in Europe).

Employment Opportunities: Prospects are generally very good and mainly concentrated in the financial sector and in the various EU institutions situated in Luxembourg City. Although English is widely spoken, most positions require a working knowledge of French or German.

Work Permits: Nationals from the original EU member states don't require a work permit. EU citizens from new member states must obtain a permit in order to start work but may visit the country and seek work for up to six months under the same conditions as other EU nationals. Regulations are expected to change in May 2006 and you should check with the authorities for the latest information. All non-EU citizens require work permits. Employment in the Duchy is subject to obtaining a provisional residence permits (*autorisation de séjour provisoire*) and work permits **before** arrival. You should apply for these at a Luxembourg consulate or embassy in your home country.

Labour Relations: Excellent: Luxembourg claims not to have had a strike for the last 80 years! Regular consultation and bargaining between employers, trade unions and the government, known as the 'Luxembourg Model', are the norm.

Employment Conditions: Working conditions are very good in Luxembourg, where the working week is 40 hours and employees are entitled to 25 days annual paid holiday. Salaries and conditions are decided by collective bargaining and are tied to the cost of living index.

Salaries: Salaries are generally the highest in the EU and executives and professionals can expect to earn up to 100 per cent more. Many employees also receive generous benefits such as housing or a car.

Minimum Monthly Wage (2003): €1,369.

Social Security: All employees and employers must contribute to the social security fund. Employees pay 10.65 per cent of gross salary and employers between 11.33 and 16.65 per cent. Benefits are numerous and include retirement pension, accident cover and healthcare.

Business Hours: Banks open from 8.30am to 4.30pm Monday to Friday. Offices (including government) open from 8am to noon and from 2pm to 5pm Monday to Friday.

Public Holidays: Six per year:

- 1st January
- 15th August
- 1st September
- 1st November
- 25th & 26th December

Business Etiquette: Business is usually conducted in a formal manner and punctuality is very important. Business cards are exchanged. It's best to avoid doing business during holiday periods, particularly in August.

Finance

Currency: Euro (€).

Exchange Controls: None.

Banks: Luxembourg has the largest concentration of banks in the EU with around 220 represented. The Association of Banks and Bankers supervises banking activity, which is efficient and secure. Non-residents and residents can open bank accounts with little formality.

Cost/Standard Of Living: In general, because of the high number of executives and professionals among the population, the standard and cost of living are high.

Loans: Loans are available from banks in Luxembourg.

Interest Rate (Early 2004): 2 per cent (European Central Bank).

Taxation

While Luxembourg isn't considered a tax haven, the country does have some low tax rates, particularly for businesses. All taxpayers require a tax card obtainable from the tax authorities.

Corporate Tax: Corporate income tax is levied at 22 per cent on annual profits in excess of €15,000. A municipal business tax of 7.5 per cent is also payable.

Personal Income Tax: Income tax rates depend on your status and range from zero to 38 per cent. All taxpayers also pay a 2.5 per cent surcharge for the unemployment fund. There are numerous tax allowances for families, pensioners and special expenses plus deductions.

Capital Gains Tax: CGT is levied at the same rates as income tax on gains from all assets except a principal residence.

Wealth Tax: Luxembourg currently levies a wealth tax of 0.5 per cent on a resident's worldwide wealth, but this is expected to be abolished by 2005.

Inheritance & Gift Tax: None.

Value Added Tax: The standard rate of value added tax is 15 per cent, plus reduced rates of 3 per cent on certain services and 6 per cent on art objects.

Withholding Taxes: Dividends are subject to 20 per cent withholding tax and interest to 15 per cent for EU residents and 10 per cent for Luxembourg residents.

Tax Filing: The tax year is the calendar year. Whether you need to file a tax return depends on your annual earnings, where you earned them and your residence status in Luxembourg. Check with an expert. Returns can be filed online and must be completed by 31st March.

Accommodation

Building Standards: Very high.

Restrictions On Foreign Ownership: None.

Cost Of Housing: The cost of accommodation reflects the country's high standard of living and it's difficult to find low-cost housing. A two-bedroom apartment costs around €200,000 and a three-bedroom house from €250,000. Prices are higher in the capital (where apartments cost from €270,000 and houses from €500,000) and in town centres. Most foreigners who work in Luxembourg find it considerably cheaper to live in France and commute.

Fees: Fees total around 7 per cent of the purchase price and include registration tax of 6 per cent and transcript tax of 1 per cent. If you declare in the purchase deed your intention to resell the property, the registration tax is 7.2 per cent, 5 per cent of which can be recovered if the property is resold within four years. Taxes in Luxembourg City can be higher.

Local Mortgages: Mortgages are available from local banks and up to 80 per cent is usually available over negotiable periods with a maximum of 30 years.

Property Taxes: Property tax rates vary according to the area, with the highest rates in the capital. Between 0.7 and 1 per cent of the rateable value is payable annually.

Renting: Rental property is in short supply and houses, in particular, are very difficult to find. Apartments cost from €1,000 a month.

Personal Effects: Personal and household effects can be imported duty-free, provided they've been in your possession for at least six months.

Utilities: The electricity supply (220V) is reliable and charges are reasonable. Mains gas is available in the capital and other main towns. Tap water is drinkable and of good quality.

Services

Getting There: Luxembourg is strategically placed and well connected with its neighbouring countries. Luxembourg airport, close to the capital, has frequent flights to major European cities and you can also reach the country by train, including the Eurostar from London and Brussels. There are also good coach connections from many European cities.

Public Transport: Generally excellent. There are extensive electrified railway and bus networks covering all corners of the country and the capital has an efficient public transport service. The Moselle River was 'canalised' in 1964 and has ferry links with other European waterways.

Motoring: Roads are excellent and are all toll-free, although traffic congestion is a problem, particularly in the capital. Speed limits are 50kph in built-up areas, 90kph outside built-up areas, including dual carriageways, and 130kph on motorways. Maximum permitted alcohol level is 80mg per 100ml of blood. A warning triangle must be carried in all vehicles. Petrol is the cheapest in Western Europe. No leaded petrol is available. Foreigners may drive with existing licences for up to one year, after which time EU licence holders are required to register their licence with the authorities and non-EU licence holders must exchange their licence for a Luxembourg one (this may entail taking a driving test).

Medical Facilities: Healthcare is excellent and facilities are of a high standard. Those entitled to social security benefits have most of their healthcare bills reimbursed, but you must pay for treatment before you're reimbursed. Otherwise healthcare is expensive and private insurance is recommended.

Education: Education is free and compulsory for children aged from 4 to 15 years, and standards are high. The vast majority of children are educated in the state sector and there are few private schools. There are three international schools in Luxembourg, including one for EU employees; however, you should apply well in advance, as all three schools are oversubscribed.

Postal Services: The postal service is efficient and fast, and there are post offices throughout the country. Prospective recipients must first register for a PO Box.

Telephone: The telephone service is currently a monopoly held by PTT, although privatisation is about to be introduced for long-distance calls. Call charges are reasonable. Mobile phones are popular and rates are competitive.

Internet: The internet is readily available and has become very popular in recent years. There are numerous ISPs providing pay or free subscription options.

English TV & Radio: English-language programmes (with subtitles) are available if you can receive Belgian or Dutch channels, and cable and satellite TV are also available. A TV licence isn't required.

Miscellaneous

Crime Rate: Luxembourg has a relatively low crime rate and violent crime is rare.

Pets: Pets require an up-to-date health certificate, which must include proof of vaccination against rabies.

Visas: Nationals from many countries, including the EU, Canada, Japan and the US, don't require a visa for visits for any purpose for up to three months. Business visas for visits up to three months are available for many non-EU countries under the same conditions as the Schengen Visa (see page 20). For further visa information see page 19.

Residence Permits: Residence permits are a formality for EU nationals, although a permit (*carte d'identité*) from the Administration Communale is necessary for stays over three months. Non-EU nationals must apply for a residence permit from a Luxembourg embassy or consulate in their home country **before** arrival.

International Dialling Code: 352 (There are no area dialling codes in Luxembourg).

Time Difference: GMT +1.

Weights & Measures: Metric.

Reference

Useful Addresses

British Embassy, 14 Boulevard Roosevelt, 22450 Luxembourg (☎ 229864, 🖳 www.britishembassy.gov.uk/luxembourg).

Employment Office, Administration de l'Emploi (ADEM), 10 Rue Bender, 1229 Luxembourg (☎ 478 5300, 🖳 www.etat.lu/ADEM).

Luxembourg Embassy, 27 Wilton Crescent, London SW1 X 8SD, UK (☎ 020-7235 6961, ✉ embassy@luxembourg.co.uk).

Luxembourg Embassy, 2200 Massachusetts Ave NW, Washington DC 20008, USA (☎ 202-265 4171, 🖳 www.luxembourg-usa.org).

US Embassy, 22 Boulevard Emmanuel Servais, 2535 Luxembourg (☎ 460123, 🖳 www.amembassy.lu).

Further Reading

Living & Working in Holland, Belgium and Luxembourg, Beverly Laflamme (Survival Books Ltd, 🖳 www.survivalbooks.net).

Living in Luxembourg (available from the American Women's Club of Luxembourg, 7 Rue de Luxembourg, 8184 Kopstal).

Useful Websites

Business Directory (🖳 www.abc-d.lu) – Comprehensive listing of businesses.

Government Online (🖳 www.gouvernement.lu) – General official information in French only.

Tourist Office (🖳 www.luxembourg.co.uk) – Tourist and general information about Luxembourg with some excellent links.

MALTA

General Information

Capital: Valletta.

Population: 397,000.

Foreign Community: Malta has a significant expatriate community, mainly comprised of British retirees.

Area: 316km² (122mi²).

Geography: Malta is in the Mediterranean south of Sicily and east of Tunisia. It consists of the islands of Malta, Gozo, Comino and the smaller uninhabited islands of Cominotto and Filfla. The landscape is mainly an undulating limestone plateau with no mountains, woodland, rivers or lakes, and all available land is under cultivation. The coastline is indented with natural harbours, sandy beaches and rocky coves.

Climate: Malta has hot, dry summers and mild, damp winters. The temperature ranges from 10°C to 21°C (50°F to 70°F) in winter in January and 25°C to 33°C (77°F to 91°F) in summer in July, which is usually very humid. Malta enjoys an average of eight hours sunshine a day. Most rain falls in winter and spring.

Language: The official languages are Maltese and English.

Government: Parliamentary democracy.

Political Stability: Excellent. Malta is a member of the Commonwealth.

EU Accession: The Maltese are enthusiastic advocates of the EU and voted overwhelmingly in favour of joining in a referendum held in March 2003. Malta has negotiated generous financial aid and extended transitional periods to enable the island to fulfil the necessary reforms, particularly the restructuring of domestic business organisations. Experts predict it will be some 10 years before Malta experiences tangible economic growth, although accession to the EU in 2004 will on the whole be beneficial to the island. Malta is one of only two new member states to allow free movement of workers from the original EU countries.

Economy

Overview: The Maltese economy is based on a thriving industrial sector (many multinational companies have established their Mediterranean base on the island) and tourism. The economy is stable and heavily reliant on foreign trade, particularly since the island has limited freshwater supplies and no domestic energy sources. The country's main trading partners (after the EU) are the US, Singapore and Libya.

GDP Per Head: US$9,497.

Growth (2003): 1 per cent.

Forecast Growth For 2004: 2.3 per cent.

Main Industries: Electronics, export-oriented business, IT, services industries, telecommunications and tourism.

UK Trade Partner Ranking: 50+.

US Trade Partner Ranking: 50+.

Working

Overview: The workforce is well trained and motivated, and has a strong work ethic. Unemployment has traditionally been high, but the rate has dropped in recent years.

Unemployment Rate (2003): 8.1 per cent.

Employment Opportunities: Education and training, electronics, export-related business, healthcare, IT, telecommunications and tourism. Since the Maltese economy is heavily orientated towards to the export market, fluency in other European languages – particularly French, German and Italian – is advantageous.

Work Permits: Malta has in principle agreed to have no transitional period for the employment of EU nationals from the original member states. It does, however, have the right to safeguard its own employment market and enforce restrictions should the market become saturated. Check with the authorities for the latest information.

EU citizens from new member states must obtain a permit in order to start work but may visit the country and seek work for up to six months under the same conditions as other EU nationals. Regulations are expected to change in

May 2006 and you should check with the authorities for the latest information. Work permits are difficult to obtain for non-EU citizens and are issued only on express permission from the Maltese government, when there's no Maltese national available to do a job.

Labour Relations: Generally good.

Employment Conditions: Good. The working week is 40 hours from Monday to Friday and employees are entitled to 24 days annual paid leave. Most employees receive a bonus several times a year.

Salaries: Labour costs are generally very low and this is reflected in the salaries.

Minimum Monthly Wage (2003): €535.

Social Security: Social security contributions are compulsory and calculated on a weekly basis. Both employers and employees pay 10 per cent of gross salary with a minimum amount of LM5.31 and maximum amount of LM12.90 per week. The self-employed contribute 15 per cent with a minimum of LM9.49 and maximum of LM19.35 per week and payments must be made three times a year. Malta has few reciprocal agreements (in 2003 with Australia, Canada, Libya, the Netherlands and the UK only).

Business Hours: Offices open from 8am to 12.30pm and from 1.30pm to 5pm Monday to Friday.

Public Holidays: Around 14 a year, plus other local holidays:

- 1st January
- 10th February
- 19th & 31st March
- 9th April
- 1st May
- 7th & 29th June
- 15th August
- 8th & 21st September
- 8th, 13th & 25th December

Business Etiquette: Business is conducted formally, although first-name terms may be used from early on in the relationship, and punctuality is expected. Business cards are always exchanged. The best months for conducting business are from October to May.

Finance

Currency: Maltese lira (LM).

Exchange Rate: €1= LM0.43 (February 2004).

Exchange Controls: Permission is required for non-residents. Residents are subject to no controls.

Banks: Banking activity in Malta is modern and secure, and controlled by the Central Bank of Malta. The island is also an offshore banking centre. Many foreign banks are present.

Cost/Standard Of Living: Malta enjoys a relatively low cost of living, around 10 to 15 per cent lower than northern European countries. However, although food and essential services are good value, imported luxury goods are expensive.

Loans: Maltese banks provide personal loans of a maximum of around LM10,000.

Interest Rate (Early 2004): 3 per cent.

Taxation

Corporate Tax: Corporate income tax is levied at 35 per cent. Malta provides many generous tax incentives for foreign investment.

Personal Income Tax: Income tax rates for single individuals and married couples declaring separately are from 0 per cent (up to LM3,100) to 35 per cent (on income over LM6,750). Married couples declaring jointly are subject to rates ranging from 0 per cent (on amounts up to LM4,300) to 35 per cent (on income over LM10,000).

Residence permit holders (1988 scheme) are entitled to a flat income tax rate of 15 per cent, subject to a minimum annual tax liability of LM1,800 (after double taxation relief). Income tax is levied on income and capital gains arising in Malta and on foreign income remitted to Malta. Non-residents are liable for income tax at rates from 0 per cent (up to LM300) to 35 per cent (income in excess of LM3,300).

Capital Gains Tax: CGT is payable at the same rates as income tax (see above).

Wealth Tax: None.

Inheritance & Gift Tax: None. The transfer of immovable property as part of an inheritance is, however, subject to stamp duty.

Value Added Tax: The standard rate is 15 per cent. There's a reduced rate of 5 per cent levied on hotel and approved tourist accommodation, and solar water heaters.

Withholding Taxes: Rates depend on double taxation treaties and range from 0 to 15 per cent for both dividends and interest. Malta has double tax treaties with many countries including Australia, Canada, most EU countries and South Africa, but not with the US.

Tax Filing: Individuals (both salaried and self-employed) must present an annual tax return by 30th June. Residence permit holders must file an annual tax declaration by 30th April. The self-employed are required to file three provisional tax payments a year (30th April, 1st September and 22nd December).

Accommodation

Building Standards: Good, although the design of new buildings, particularly apartment blocks, is uninspiring.

Restrictions On Foreign Ownership: Non-Maltese nationals are allowed to own only one property, which must exceed LM15,000 in value. To qualify as a permanent resident, the minimum cost must be LM30,000 for an apartment and LM50,000 for a house. Permission to purchase property must be obtained from the Ministry of Finance, although this is generally a formality.

Cost Of Housing: Small apartments start at €50,000 in most areas, although those in prime areas start at €100,000. Large apartments start at €130,000 and you can expect to pay from €180,000 upwards for a house. Traditional village properties start at around €100,000.

Fees: Fees include stamp duty at 5 per cent of the market value as set by government authorities. Residents pay 3.5 per cent on the first LM20,000.

Local Mortgages: Mortgages from local banks are available, often on attractive terms including a maximum loan of 90 per cent of the price for up to 40 years. Monthly repayments are a maximum of 25 per cent of gross income.

Property Taxes: None.

Renting: Rental accommodation is inexpensive in Malta, where a furnished two-bedroom apartment can be rented from €230 to €400 a month. A small house costs from €500 to €700 a month.

Personal Effects: Personal effects and household goods (including one car) imported within six months of arrival in Malta are exempt from duty and tax if you have a residence permit.

Utilities: The electricity supply (240V) is reliable and charges reasonable. Tap water is safe to drink, but bottled water tastes considerably better and has the advantage of much lower levels of chlorine. Water rates are high and the island suffers from drought periodically.

Services

Getting There: Malta's international airport at Valletta is well connected by flights from mainland Europe and the Middle East. There are ferry services during the summer from Sicily and Genoa.

Public Transport: Getting around Malta is easy and there's a comprehensive bus service and taxis. Ferries operate between Malta and Gozo as well as between Comino and other islands. The two main islands are also connected by a helicopter service, which takes 10 minutes and runs eight times a day.

Motoring: There's a good road network on Malta, although Maltese driving leaves much to be desired. Cars drive on the left and the maximum permitted speed is 65kph (40mph). Maximum permitted alcohol level is 80mg per 100ml of blood. Leaded petrol is available. If you drive a hire car, you must have your driving licence endorsed by the Department of Transport. Foreign licence holders may drive for up to three months, after which the foreign licence must be exchanged for a Maltese one.

Medical Facilities: Medical facilities are generally very good (the WHO ranks Malta tenth in the world for its medical standards) and there's a major general hospital in Malta (with mostly British-trained medical staff) and a number of 24-hour health centres. Free healthcare is provided for permanent residents and reduced hospital charges for holders of temporary residence permits. Residents and visitors who aren't covered by reciprocal agreements require private health insurance.

Education: Education is free and compulsory for children aged from 5 to 16. Teaching is in English and Maltese. Private education, where the teaching medium is English, is also available in a number of international schools.

Postal Services: The postal service is reliable and efficient.

Telephone: The telephone service is modern and call charges are reasonable. Mobile phones are popular.

Internet: Internet is increasingly popular on the island and service providers are available.

English TV & Radio: Maltese television and radio broadcast regularly in English, and cable and satellite TV are also available.

Miscellaneous

Crime Rate: Malta has a very low crime rate, although house burglary and theft from cars are on the increase

Pets: All pets require an import licence and are subject to quarantine. Animals from countries with rabies cannot be imported. Quarantine for animals from Australia, Norway, Sweden and the UK are subject to 21 days quarantine. Pets from some other EU countries are subject to one month's quarantine on arrival in Malta. Otherwise quarantine is six months.

Visas: Nationals from many countries, including all EU member states, Australia, Canada, Japan, New Zealand and the US, don't require a visa for visits for less than three months. Non-EU nationals require a visa for longer visits or for employment purposes. Nationals not included on the 'visa-free' list may require an entry visa. Consult the Maltese representative in your home country for up-to-date details.

Residence Permits: All foreigners require a residence permit and to qualify they must either own assets outside Malta of at least LM150,000 or have an annual income of at least LM10,000. They must import a minimum annual income of at least LM6,000 plus LM1,000 for each dependent (these remittances may not be re-exported out of Malta). Once the residence permit is issued, the holder must take up residence within 12 months and either purchase a residence in Malta at a cost of at least LM30,000 for a flat or LM50,000 or rent a residence costing at least LM1,800 per year. Residence permit holders are required to submit an annual declaration stating they've complied with the annual remittance conditions. Residence permit holders may not undertake any form of employment or business activity unless duly authorised by the Office of the Prime Minister.

International Dialling Code: 356 (There are no area codes on the island).

Time Difference: GMT +1 (+2 from the end of March to the end of October).

Weights & Measures: Metric.

Reference

Useful Addresses

British Embassy, Whitehall Mansions, Ta'Xbiex Seafront, Ta'Xbiex MSD 11 (☎ 2323-0000, 🖥 www.britain.com.mt).

Embassy of Malta, 2017 Connecticut Ave, NW, Washington DC 20008, USA (☎ 202-462 3611, ✉ malta_embassy@compuserve.com).

Maltese High Commission, Malta House, 36-38 Piccadilly, London W1V 0PQ, UK (☎ 020-7292 4800, 🖥 http://malta.embassyhomepage.com)

US Embassy, 3rd Floor, Development House, Saint Anne Street, Floriana (☎ 2561-4000).

Useful Websites

Government Online (🖥 www.gov.mt) – Comprehensive official information on all aspects of living in Malta.

Malta Investment Agency (🖥 www.investinmalta.com) – Useful information on doing business as well as good links.

THE NETHERLANDS

General Information

Capital: The Hague.

Population: 16 million.

Foreign Community: Around 5 per cent of the population is comprised of foreigners, including some Europeans, but mainly immigrants from Morocco and the former Dutch colonies of Indonesia and Surinam.

Area: 41,863km² (16,163mi²).

Geography: The Netherlands is a small country in the west of Europe, bordering on the North Sea, Germany and Belgium. In spite of its small size, it's the third most densely populated country in the world, although most people live in the major cities stretching from Amsterdam in the centre to Rotterdam in the south. Much of the agricultural land has been reclaimed from the sea and around two-fifths of the country lies below sea level protected by an extensive system of dykes and sand dunes. The vast port of Rotterdam and the neighbouring industrial area of Europoort form the largest industrial complex in the world.

Climate: The Netherlands has a temperate maritime climate with cool winters, when the inland waterways occasionally freeze over, and mild summers. It rains a lot, particularly in spring and autumn, and the weather can be extremely changeable. Average temperatures are 2°C (35°F) in winter and 20°C (68°F) in summer.

Language: The official language is Dutch, but English is widely spoken.

Government: Constitutional monarchy with bicameral legislature.

Political Stability: Excellent. The Netherlands joined Belgium and Luxembourg in 1948 in the Benelux Customs Union, the foundation of the EU.

EU Accession: Founder member.

Economy

Overview: The Netherlands has a stable and prosperous economy, and growth has been steady and unemployment low for the last few years. The country has strong industries and its agricultural exports are the third largest in the world after the US and France. The Netherlands attracts around a quarter of Foreign Direct Investment (FDI) in the EU, mainly because of its steady economic environment, highly trained workforce, well-developed financial sector and excellent infrastructure. In the first quarter of 2003, however, GDP growth was negative and the Netherlands, along with France, Germany and Italy, entered a recession which lasted for the rest of 2003.

GDP Per Head: US$21,740.

Growth (2003): -0.3 per cent.

Forecast Growth For 2004: 1.5 per cent.

Main Industries: Agriculture, chemicals, financial services, food processing, natural gas, oil, property services, retail and transport.

UK Trade Partner Ranking: 4.

US Trade Partner Ranking: 50+.

Working

Overview: The Netherlands' stable economy generally ensures low unemployment. The workforce is highly skilled and well educated, although there are labour shortages in some areas. Temporary employment is high.

Unemployment Rate (2003): 4 per cent.

Employment Opportunities: There are currently shortages in the financial services sector and of people with technical qualifications. Agencies recruit for a variety of posts. Many multi-national companies are in the Netherlands.

Work Permits: Nationals from the original EU member states don't require a work permit. EU citizens from new member states must obtain a permit in order to start work but may visit the country and seek work for up to six months under the same conditions as other EU nationals. Regulations are expected to change in May 2006 and you should check with the authorities for the latest information. Nationals from non-EU countries may have difficulty in getting a work permit, which must be obtained from a Dutch consulate or embassy **before** arrival in the Netherlands.

Labour Relations: Generally excellent: relations are characterised by a high degree of cooperation between management and workers. The Netherlands has one of the lowest strike rates in the EU.

Employment Conditions: Very good, with a working week of 38 hours and 14 to 21 days annual paid holiday. Extensive employment legislation is heavily biased in favour of employees and all employment is subject to a minimum wage, which is revised at least annually for workers aged over 23. Benefits such as housing and travel are common. Most job offers are temporary and contracts are of one-year duration.

Salaries: Salaries are slightly higher than the EU average and professional salaries are on a par with Ireland and Spain.

Minimum Monthly Wage (2003): €1,249.

Social Security: Social security payments are very high in the Netherlands, where contributions depend on your age and income level. Coverage and premiums vary and, above certain income levels, you cannot join the national health plan and must contribute to a private health plan.

Business Hours: Offices open from 8.30am to 5pm or 5.30pm Monday to Friday and banks open from 9am or 10am to 4pm or 5pm Monday to Friday.

Public Holidays: Nine per year:

- 1st January
- Good Friday & Easter Monday
- 30th April
- 5th May
- Ascension Day
- Whitsun (May/June)
- 25th & 26th December

Business Etiquette: Punctuality is extremely important in Dutch business and you should always make an appointment first. Dress is formal. Try to avoid doing business in July and August when many people are on holiday. Most Dutch speak very good English.

Finance

Currency: Euro (€).

Exchange Controls: None.

Banks: The banking system in the Netherlands is modern and extremely efficient, and dominated by four main banks: ABN AMRO, Fortis, ING and Rabobank, while the Postbank (post office bank) is used by many people for day-to-day transactions. Opening an account can be time-consuming and usually involves a number of visits to a bank, although the process is speeded up if you can provide a letter of introduction from a bank where you have an existing account. Banks may be reluctant to open an account for non-residents. Dutch banks have among the lowest costs in the world.

Cost/Standard Of Living: The standard of living in the Netherlands is higher than the EU average, although the cost of living is similar to that of the UK.

Loans: Loans are available from Dutch banks, but banks may be reluctant to lend to non-residents.

Interest Rate (Early 2004): 2 per cent (European Central Bank).

Taxation

Corporate Tax: Corporate income tax is levied at 29 per cent on annual profits under €22,689 and at 34.5 per cent on amounts above this.

Personal Income Tax: Income tax rates go up to 52 per cent, although there are many tax credits depending on your age, status and number of children. Expatriates working in non-Dutch companies in positions that cannot be filled by a Dutch national qualify for a 30 per cent tax credit, and employers can reimburse international school fees, tax-free. The top rate for expatriates qualifying under this scheme is 36.4 per cent, although there are strict conditions to be fulfilled.

Capital Gains Tax: CGT is levied at a flat rate of 25 per cent.

Wealth Tax: None.

Inheritance & Gift Tax: None.

Value Added Tax: The standard rate of value added tax (known as BTW) is 19 per cent for most goods and services. There's a reduced rate of 6 per cent for food, medicine and other essentials.

Withholding Taxes: Dividends derived from a foreign subsidiary are generally exempt from withholding taxes.

Tax Filing: The Dutch tax year is the calendar year and returns must be filed before 1st April of the following year. Companies and the self-employed are generally required to make advance payments of estimated additional tax in quarterly tax returns.

Accommodation

Building Standards: Standards range from excellent in modern buildings to variable in older buildings.

Restrictions On Foreign Ownership: None. However, to discourage speculators, property purchase outside your area of residence may be prohibited.

Cost Of Housing: Outside Amsterdam, a two-bedroom apartment costs around €130,000 and an average three-bedroom town house in the region of €225,000. Property prices in Amsterdam are at least twice these amounts. Given the rising cost of rental accommodation and the substantial tax deductions available on a mortgage, property purchase is a viable option for stays of longer than around two years.

Fees: The fees connected with a property purchase are around 12 per cent of the purchase price and include 6 per cent transfer tax, 2 per cent estate agency commission, notary fees and 2 per cent local taxes.

Local Mortgages: Local mortgages are available from Dutch banks for residents, although obtaining a mortgage may be difficult for foreigners and you'll be charged a slightly higher rate. There are substantial tax deductions on mortgages.

Property Taxes: Annual property taxes vary from community to community, although the average is around 0.5 per cent of a property's rateable value.

Renting: Rental accommodation isn't generally hard to find, although in Amsterdam rental properties are in short supply and rents are twice as high as in the rest of the country. In Amsterdam, Utrecht and Rotterdam, rents rose sharply in 2000 and are now almost on a par with London or Paris. Average monthly rents outside Amsterdam are €500 for an apartment and €700 for a small house.

Personal Effects: Personal and household effects can be imported duty-free, provided they've been in your possession for at least six months and that you import them within 12 months of your arrival in the country.

Utilities: Electricity (220V) and mains gas are available throughout the country and prices are reasonable, although gas prices are linked to oil prices and are rising. The quality of water is excellent and relatively inexpensive, although the cost has risen in recent years.

Services

Getting There: KLM, the Dutch airline, provides an extensive service to most European and worldwide destinations, and Amsterdam airport is served by most major international airlines. The Netherlands can also be easily reached by rail and road from the rest of Europe, as well as by ferry (car and passenger) from the UK and Scandinavia.

Public Transport: There is an excellent network of public transport and frequent train and bus services link the main towns and cities, although fares are quite expensive. Canals are used for freight transportation and the port of Rotterdam is one of the world's largest and busiest.

Motoring: The road network is modern and well-maintained, and driving standards good. Speed limits are 50kph in built-up areas, 80kph or 100kph outside built-up areas, including dual carriageways, and 120kph on motorways. Maximum permitted alcohol level is 50mg per 100ml of blood. A warning triangle must be carried in all vehicles. No leaded petrol is available. Driving licence regulations for foreign residents are complicated and depend on your nationality or whether you're entitled to the 30 per cent tax credit (see Personal **Income Tax** on page 329). EU nationals are generally permitted to continue to drive with an EU licence for up to 10 years, but other nationalities must exchange their licence for a Dutch one and possibly take the driving test. Check with the transport authorities in your locality for up-to-date information.

Medical Facilities: The standard of healthcare is high but expensive and, if you don't qualify for healthcare under the compulsory social security scheme, private medical insurance is essential.

Education: Education is free and compulsory for children aged from 5 to 16. Standards are generally high with particular emphasis placed on the learning of foreign languages. There are several international schools in The Hague and other major cities.

Postal Services: The postal service in the Netherland is one of the best in the world and post offices offer banking and exchange facilities.

Telephone: Four companies provide telephone services and the service is reliable and prices competitive. Telephone infrastructure is excellent.

Internet: The internet is highly popular (more than half the population has internet connection) and there are numerous service providers, many of which offer a free service.

English TV & Radio: All foreign programmes are shown in their original language with Dutch sub-titles, which means that around half of all programmes are in English. The Netherlands has among the highest density of cable TV in the world (over 90 per cent) and satellite TV reception is excellent.

Miscellaneous

Crime Rate: Low.

Pets: Pets require a 'Pet Passport' (*Dierenpaspoort*) available from vets in the EU, which includes a certificate of good health and proof of immunisation. Dogs must be registered at the local town hall and there's an annual dog tax ranging from €55 to €105.

Visas: Nationals from many countries, including the EU, Canada, Japan and the US, don't require a visa for visits for any purpose for up to three months. Business visas for visits up to three months are available for many non-EU countries under the same conditions as the Schengen Visa (see page 20). For further visa information see page 19.

Residence Permits: Foreigners residing in the Netherlands for more than three months require a temporary residence permit (*verblijfsvergunning*), which must be applied for at the Dutch embassy or consulate in your home country. People from countries except the EU, Australia, Canada, Japan, New Zealand, Switzerland and the US must apply for an authorisation visa for temporary stay (MVV) **before** arrival. EU nationals must apply within three days of arrival for a residence permit from the Foreign Police. Permanent residence permits are very expensive.

International Dialling Code: 31.

Time Difference: GMT +1.

Weights & Measures: Metric.

Reference

Useful Addresses

British Embassy, Lange Voorhout 10, 2514 ED, The Hague (☎ 070-427 0427, 🖳 www.britain.nl).

Royal Netherlands Embassy, 38 Hyde Park Gate, London SW7 5DP, UK (☎ 020-7590 3200, 🖥 www.netherlands-embassy.org.uk).

Royal Netherlands Embassy, 4200 Linnean Avenue, NW, Washington DC 20008, USA (☎ 202-244 5300, 🖥 www.netherlands-embassy.org).

US Embassy, Lange Voorhout 102 2514 EJ, The Hague (☎ 070-310 9209, 🖥 http://thehague.usembassy.gov).

Further Reading

Living & Working in Holland, Belgium and Luxembourg, Beverly Laflamme (Survival Books Ltd, 🖥 www.survivalbooks.net).

Useful Websites

Expatica (🖥 www.expatica.com) – A useful site for expatriates.

Netherlands Foreign Investment Agency (NFIA, 🖥 www.nfia.com) – Provides assistance for foreign investors including tailor-made information as well as a wealth of information about doing business and working in the country.

POLAND

General Information

Capital: Warsaw.

Population: 38.6 million.

Foreign Community: The foreign community in Poland is quite large, particularly in the capital and in the industrial areas of Gdansk and Szczecin, and is comprised mainly of Germans and Americans. Most expatriates agree that Poland is one of the most pleasant and welcoming countries in central and Eastern Europe.

Area: 312,684km² (120,736mi²).

Geography: Poland is a large country on the Baltic Sea bordering on Germany in the west, the Czech Republic and Slovakia in the south, and the Ukraine, Belarus and Lithuania in the east. The landscape is mainly flat and forested with many rivers and lakes, although the west of the country, particularly around the ports of Gdansk and Szczecin, is heavily industrialised.

Climate: Poland has a continental climate with long, often very cold winters and mild summers. Average temperatures are -2°C (29°F) in January and 18°C (64°F) in July.

Language: The official language is Polish. German and Russian are widely spoken and English is often used in business.

Government: Parliamentary democracy.

Political Stability: Good. Since the unsettled days of Solidarity in the '80s and the economic difficulties of the early '90s, Poland now has an established democracy and a stable economy backed by steady foreign investment. Poland looks very much to the west, is a member of NATO and on joining the EU in 2004, it will be the dominant country in Central Europe. The Poles overwhelmingly approved EU entry in the nationwide referendum held in June 2003.

EU Accession: Poland's large population (bigger than the other nine new members together) and strategic location between Germany and Russia make it the most important new member state of the EU. Its huge and underdeveloped agricultural sector, unrestructured heavy industry and regional poverty mean, however, that it is the most problematic and most expensive state to integrate. Experts claim it will take Poland more than 30 years to reach 75 per cent of the EU's average GDP per capita (currently 39 per cent), although accession will undoubtedly contribute substantially to improving Poland's infrastructure and educational standards. Poland's main problem once it joins the EU will be large-scale unemployment. In early 2004, Poland was the member state with most accession problems and there was concern that lack of progress in many EU criteria (agriculture particularly) would mean Poland would be unable to participate as a full member of the EU in May 2004.

Economy

Overview: Poland's economy has grown rapidly over the last decade and has sustained steady growth although in 2002 the economy weakened and budget deficit and high inflation are two main problems facing the country. The country has rich natural resources, particularly in coal, although the coal mining industries are inefficient and cost the Polish government billions of dollars annually in subsidies. Privatisation is well underway and one of the government's top priorities.

GDP Per Head: US$5,120.

Growth (2003): 3.5 per cent.

Forecast Growth For 2004: 4.2 per cent.

Main Industries: Agriculture and heavy industry dominate the Polish economy, although other industries such as the services sector are gradually emerging.

UK Trade Partner Ranking: 32.

US Trade Partner Ranking: 50+.

Working

Overview: Poland has a well trained workforce but unemployment figures have remained high over the last decade, although figures are considerably lower in the capital. Restructuring in industry and agriculture is expected to push figures even higher in the near future. One of the government's top priorities is the reduction of unemployment and it is in the process of introducing fiscal reforms to this effect. There are generally no shortages in the labour market, although training is often required.

Unemployment Rate (2003): 19.1 per cent (the highest in the EU).

Employment Opportunities: Business specialists and management consultants are in short supply. Most opportunities are found, however, in TEFL, although pay rates are low.

Work Permits: EU citizens must obtain a permit in order to start work but may visit the country and seek work for up to six months. Regulations are expected to change in May 2006 and you should check with the authorities for the latest information. All non-EU citizens require a work permit to work in Poland. This permit, accompanied by a firm offer of employment, must be obtained from a Polish consulate or embassy in your home country, and **cannot** be obtained if you're already in Poland.

Labour Relations: Poland is home to Solidarity, the trade union **per se**, and trade union membership is high in the country, although labour relations are generally peaceful with few strikes. Unions tend to be active at all levels and in both public and private sectors, and tend to present demands directly to the government.

Employment Conditions: A Labour Code regulates working conditions and collective bargaining is common. There's a national minimum salary. The working week is 42 hours and employees are entitled to 18 to 26 days annual paid holiday.

Salaries: Very low compared to Western European countries.

Minimum Monthly Wage (2003): €201.

Social Security: Social security contributions are obligatory for all employers and employees to four state funds: retirement, disability, sickness and occupational hazards. Employers contribute from 17 to 20 per cent and employees contribute 18.71 per cent of gross monthly salary up to a maximum annual income of PLN65,850. Contributions on income in excess of this amount are 2.45 per cent for employees and between 0.97 and 3.86 per cent for employers.

Business Hours: Businesses and offices generally open from 8am to 4pm and banks from 9am to 6pm Monday to Friday.

Public Holidays: Ten a year:

- 1st January
- Easter Monday
- 1st & 3rd May
- Corpus Christi (June)
- 15th August
- 1st & 11th November
- 25th & 26th December

Business Etiquette: Business is conducted formally and handshakes are the accepted form of greeting. Business cards should be exchanged. Many Polish business people speak English, but it's worth making the effort to learn a few simple phrases in Polish.

Finance

Currency: Zloty (PLN).
  Exchange Rate: €1= PLN4.74 (February 2004).
  Exchange Controls: None.
  Banks: Polish banks have been restructured and the country now has a well developed and efficient banking system, one of the best regulated in Central Europe. Many foreign banks are present. Foreigners can open a bank account in local or foreign currency, although the latter is advisable.
  Cost/Standard Of Living: Poland is no longer the cheap country it once was and prices of almost everything are rising and on a par with western European countries. Salaries aren't, however, rising as fast.
  Loans: Loans are available from local banks but interest for credit loans may be high.
  Interest Rate (Early 2004): 5.25 per cent.

Taxation

Corporate Tax: Corporate tax is levied at 24 per cent and Poland has no permanent establishment concept, therefore all income generated within Poland is taxable in Poland. Polish taxes are generally considered to be an impediment to foreign investment.
  Personal Income Tax: Income tax is deducted at source (PAYE) and there are various rates ranging from 19 per cent (on annual income up to PLN37,024) to 40 per cent (on annual income over PLN74,048). There are numerous tax deductions for items such as accommodation, relocation, work clothing, cars and company loans.
  Capital Gains Tax: Capital gains from the sale of real estate or movables are taxed at the flat rate of 10 per cent. There is no CGT if the sale of real estate occurs five years after the purchase.
  Wealth Tax: None.
  Inheritance & Gift Tax: None.
  Value Added Tax: Polish VAT rates are being brought into line with EU regulations and there are at present two rates: a standard rate of 22 per cent on most goods and services, and a reduced rate of 7 per cent on most foodstuffs, medicines and transport. Some foodstuffs and certain services such as accounting and data processing are exempt.
  Withholding Taxes: Dividends are subject to 15 per cent and interest and fees subject to 20 per cent withholding tax.

Tax Filing: Individuals are not generally required to file a tax return unless they are self-employed or receive remuneration from outside Poland. Tax returns must be filed before 30th April.

Accommodation

Building Standards: Variable, although they are generally poor in apartment blocks in the main cities.

Restrictions On Foreign Ownership: Foreigners wishing to purchase property in Poland must apply for a permit from the Ministry of Internal Affairs. If you're a permanent resident in Poland and have lived there for at least five years, a permit isn't necessary. These regulations may change for EU nationals after Poland enters the EU.

Cost Of Housing: Property prices are rising in Poland as foreign investment increases, particularly in Warsaw where there was a property boom in 2000. Prices are often quoted per m² in US$ or PLN and property is classified per number of rooms. An average two-bedroom apartment costs from US$135,000.

Fees: Fees include transfer tax of 10 per cent, which is payable by the vendor unless the money is reinvested in another property within five years of the sale, stamp duty of 2 per cent, a registration fee of around PLN1,000; plus legal and notary fees.

Local Mortgages: Local mortgages are available, although the market is limited. For more flexibility, it's advisable to take out a loan with a foreign bank (if possible).

Property Taxes: Property taxes vary from region to region, but they cannot be higher than the maximum rates set by the Ministry of Finance. In 2003, this was up to PLN0.62 per m² for land, up to PLN17.31 per m² of useable area in buildings and 2 per cent of the value of buildings. Exact rates are established by local authorities.

Renting: Rental accommodation is increasingly difficult to find in Warsaw and Krakow, and rents are high. It's also sometimes difficult to find accommodation that isn't small and cramped, although most apartments usually have good heating. Rental prices for a two-bedroom apartment range from US$1,500 per month. Rentals are usually quoted in US$.

Personal Effects: Personal effects can be imported duty-free into Poland.

Utilities: Electricity (220V) is reliable although very expensive and subject to continual price rises. Mains and bottled gas are widely available and are a popular and cheap form of energy. Tap water is usually safe to drink, but in cities in the south of the country high levels of pollution mean bottled water is a safer option.

Services

Getting There: Communications to Poland are reasonable, although air travel is expensive and the number of flights limited. Poland can also be reached by road and rail from Western Europe, but train fares are also expensive. Ferry services from the UK and Scandinavia to Poland are also available.

Public Transport: Poland generally has good communications. There are several domestic airports with good connecting flights within the country, the train service is efficient and inexpensive, and several national bus companies serve all corners of the country. Warsaw has a good public transport system.

Motoring: Driving conditions in and around the large cities are good but poor elsewhere. Warsaw is extremely congested because of the very high car density in the capital. Driving standards are generally extremely poor and driving is definitely **not** for the faint-hearted in Poland! Spare parts for cars are in short supply and there are few petrol stations. Speed limits are 60kph in built-up areas, 90kph outside built-up areas, 110kph on dual carriageways and 130kph on motorways. Alcohol tolerance is zero. A warning triangle, first aid kit and fire extinguisher must be carried in all vehicles. No leaded petrol is available. All foreign residents must exchange their driving licences for a Polish one within six months of residence. Some nationalities may have to take a driving test. Regulations for EU nationals are expected to change shortly after Poland joins the EU. Check with the transport authorities for up-to-date information.

Medical Facilities: Medical facilities are adequate but below western standards in the state sector, although private facilities are generally good. Doctors and hospitals often expect immediate cash payment and comprehensive health insurance is strongly advised.

Education: Education is free and compulsory for all children aged from 7 to 15, the vast majority of whom attend state schools. There are a few international schools in Warsaw.

Postal Services: The Polish postal service has a reputation for slowness and inefficiency, although this is gradually changing. Many people still prefer to use courier services for postal deliveries, particularly for items of value or importance. The post office provides a limited range of banking services.

Telephone: Poland's telephone service has recently been modernised, including the installation of digital lines and fibre optic networks, and is now very efficient, although call charges are high unless you phone at off-peak times. There's also a popular mobile phone service.

Internet: The internet is gradually making headway in Poland, although usage is low compared to other countries in the area (6.4 million users in 2002) and the vast majority of Polish companies have internet access and use email communication.

English TV & Radio: English-language programmes are available only via cable or satellite TV. Reception is generally good.

Miscellaneous

Crime Rate: In general, lower than in many western countries. Petty crime is, however, a problem in the cities and you should take good care of your belongings. Violent crime is rare.

Pets: Dogs and cats require a bilingual health certificate (available from Polish consulates abroad) that must state that the animal has been vaccinated against rabies within four weeks and no longer than six months before the certificate was issued. The health certificate should also state that there were no rabies incidents in the previous three months within a 13km (8mi) radius of the pet's residence.

Visas: UK nationals don't require a visa to enter Poland for visits of less then 180 days. EEA, Canadian and US citizens require a visa for visits over 90 days. If you wish to work or study in Poland, you must apply for a visa whatever the length of your stay. Visas are obtainable from a Polish consulate or embassy in your home country.

Residence Permits: All foreigners require a residence permit to stay in Poland for longer than six months. EU nationals should apply to the regional office of the provincial governor for the permit. Other foreigners should apply for a permit **before** arrival in the country. Temporary permits are issued for a period of up to two years and are renewable for a maximum of ten.

International Dialling Code: 48.

Time Difference: GMT +1.

Weights & Measures: Metric.

Reference

Useful Addresses

British Embassy, Aleje Roz 1, 00-556 Warsaw (☎ 22-628 1001, 💻 www.britishembassy.pl).

Polish Embassy, 47 Portland Street, London W1B 1JH, UK (☎ 0870-774 2700, 💻 http://home.btclick.com/polishembassy).

Polish Embassy, 2640 16th Street, NW, Washington DC 20009, USA (☎ 202-234 3800, 💻 www.polandembassy.org).

US Embassy, Aleje Ujazdowskie 29-31, 00-540 Warsaw (☎ 22-604 2000, 💻 www.usinfo.pl).

Useful Websites

British Polish Chamber of Commerce (💻 www.bpcc.org.pl) – Good expat advice and information including an 'Expert Forum'. Registration is required, but this is quick and free.

Polish Agency for Foreign Investment (💻 www.paiz.gov.pl) – Useful information on doing business and working in Poland.

Travel Poland (💻 www.travel-poland.pl) – Good general and tourist information.

PORTUGAL

General Information

Capital: Lisbon.

Population: 10 million.

Foreign Community: There's a sizeable expatriate community in Portugal, particularly in the Algarve and other resort areas where many British, German and Scandinavians have made their homes. There's also a large expatriate business community in Lisbon and a sizeable number of Brazilians.

Area: 92,000km² (32,225mi²).

Geography: Portugal is situated in the extreme south-west corner of Europe, occupying around one-sixth of the Iberian Peninsula, with an Atlantic coastline of over 800km (500mi). It has a huge variety of landscapes, including sandy beaches, rugged mountains, rolling hills, vast forests (over a quarter of the country is forested) and flat grasslands. Portugal also possesses the island of Madeira (pop. 300,000), situated off the West African coast north of the Canary Islands, and the nine islands in the Atlantic that comprise the Azores (pop. 250,000).

Climate: Portugal is noted for its generally moderate climate with mild winters and long, warm summers, with the notable exception of the north-east which has long, cold winters and hot summers. The Algarve has one of the best year-round climates in Europe, with hot summers tempered by cooling sea breezes from the Atlantic and mild winters. Average temperatures in the Algarve are 12°C (54°F) in January and 24°C (75°F) in July. Madeira is sub-tropical with wet winters and hot summers.

Language: The official language is Portuguese. English is widely spoken, particularly in resort areas.

Government: Democratic republic.

Political Stability: Excellent. In 1974 a 'velvet' revolution ended almost 50 years of military dictatorship and since then Portugal has established a strong democracy.

EU Accession: 1986

Economy

Overview: Over the last 15 years, Portugal has experienced one of the highest growth rates within both the EU and OECD countries and, although both 2002 and 2003 registered low economy growth after several years of steady increases, Portugal is becoming a rich nation. The economy is currently based on traditional industries, although this is changing rapidly as the country widens its economic base to include energy, tourism and telecommunications. Portugal hosts the 2004 European Football Championship and in preparation is investing around €1,150 million in construction and renovation.

GDP Per Head: US$14,070.
Growth (2003): -1 per cent.
Forecast Growth For 2004: 1 per cent.
Main Industries: Glassware, oil products, paper, pottery and ceramics, textiles and tourism.
UK Trade Partner Ranking: 29.
US Trade Partner Ranking: 50+.

Working

Overview: The employment market in Portugal is extremely regulated, with little flexibility over the hiring and dismissal of employees. There is little part-time employment. Unemployment in Portugal is one of the lowest in the EU, although the trend is now reversing because of low economic growth. The workforce is known for its dedication, flexibility and hard work. Labour costs are by far the cheapest in the original EU and considerably cheaper than in the US.

Unemployment Rate (2003): 6.9 per cent.

Employment Opportunities: Job opportunities are not particularly good in Portugal, where national companies are somewhat reluctant to hire foreign workers. Jobs are mainly concentrated in infrastructure projects, TEFL and tourism.

Work Permits: Nationals from the original EU member states don't require a work permit. EU citizens from new member states must obtain a permit in order to start work but may visit the country and seek work for up to six months under the same conditions as other EU nationals. Regulations are expected to change in May 2006 and you should check with the authorities for the latest information. All non-EU citizens require work permits, which must be obtained from a Portuguese consulate or embassy in your home country **before** arrival. Work permits can be difficult to obtain since companies employing more than five workers must limit foreign workers from outside the EU to 10 percent of the workforce, although exemptions are granted if the foreign workers have special technical expertise.

Labour Relations: Although labour relations are generally good, strikes and stoppages are relatively common in Portugal, but tend to be of short duration and generally limited to the public sector.

Employment Conditions: Generally good, with extensive labour legislation mainly protecting employees and, in particular, providing equal rights for women in the workplace. The working week is usually 38 hours, although this is flexible and employees are entitled to 28 days annual paid holiday. Most employees are paid a 13th and sometimes a 14th month's salary.

Salaries: Generally lower than the EU average for most professionals, although top executives and professionals can expect to earn a similar salary to those in France or Italy.

Minimum Monthly Wage (2003): €416.

Social Security: Contributions are compulsory for all employees and the self-employed. For employees, rates depend on profession and age, and range from

8 to 11 per cent of gross monthly salary. Employers contribute rates ranging from 20.7 to 24.5 per cent of the employee's gross monthly salary. The self-employed pay contributions under either the mandatory regime (25.4 per cent) or an enlarged regime (32 per cent), depending on the benefits required. Benefits covered by social security contributions include healthcare and retirement and disability pensions.

Business Hours: Office hours are generally from 9am to 1pm and from 3pm to 7pm, and banks open from 8.30am to 3pm Monday to Friday in large towns.

Public Holidays: 13 per year:

- 1st January
- Carnival (March)
- Good Friday
- 25th April
- 1st May
- 10th June
- Corpus Christi (June)
- 15th August
- 5th October
- 1st November
- 1st, 8th & 25th December

Business Etiquette: Business meetings tend to be formal and formal address is generally used. English is widely spoken in large companies, but may not be in smaller ones.

Finance

Currency: Euro (€).

Exchange Controls: None. However, if you import funds to pay for the purchase of a property you must obtain a licence from the Bank of Portugal (*Boletim de Autorizacao de Capitals Privados*).

Banks: There are many banks in Portugal and banking is efficient (if a bit slow) and secure. Several foreign banks have branches, mainly in Lisbon and resort areas, and supermarket banking is popular. To open a bank account in Portugal you require a fiscal number from the local tax office.

Cost/Standard Of Living: Portugal has a relatively low cost of living and is one of the cheapest countries in the EU, although prices have increased considerably in recent years. Food and wine are cheap, but imported goods are expensive.

Loans: Loans are available from Portuguese and foreign banks, although some Portuguese banks may be reluctant to lend to non-resident entities.

Interest Rate (Early 2004): 2 per cent (European Central Bank).

Taxation

Corporate Tax: Corporate income tax is levied at 25 per cent (plus local levies in some areas). Capital gains are calculated minus losses arising on tangible fixed assets, and are taxed as part of normal income. From 2006, corporate income tax will be reduced to 20 per cent.

Personal Income Tax: Income tax is levied at rates from 12 per cent (on annual income over €4,100) to 40 per cent (on annual income over €51,251). There are numerous allowances and tax deductions. Non-resident employees are subject to income tax at a flat rate of 25 per cent.

Capital Gains Tax: Capital gains tax is levied at income tax rates, although there are various exceptions – e.g. shares acquired prior to 1st January 2001 are taxed at 10 per cent; principal residences are exempt provided the proceeds are invested in a new home within two years of the sale.

Wealth Tax: None.

Inheritance & Gift Tax: None. Inheritance and gift tax were abolished in January 2004. Stamp duty is levied at 10 per cent on gifts, but exemptions apply for transfers to spouses, descendants and ascendants.

Value Added Tax: VAT (IVA in Portugal) is levied at a standard rate of 19 per cent on most goods and services, except those included in the intermediate rate of 12 per cent (certain foodstuffs and restaurants) and the reduced rate of 5 per cent (essential foodstuffs, printed matter, utilities, public transport and medicines). These rates are 13, 8 and 4 per cent in the Azores and Madeira. Healthcare, educational services, postal services and banking and insurance are exempt from VAT.

Withholding Taxes: 20 per cent on interest and income from securities and 25 per cent on income from shares and non-resident income earned in Portugal.

Tax Filing: The tax year in Portugal is the calendar year. At the beginning of the year residents are sent a tax return, which should be filed between 1st February and 15th March, if your income is from employment or pensions only, and between 16th March and 30th April otherwise. Non-residents with rental income or capital gains from property must file a tax return before 30th April.

Accommodation

Building Standards: Generally very good.

Restrictions On Foreign Ownership: None.

Cost Of Housing: Property prices vary considerably in Portugal and are generally more expensive in Lisbon and the Algarve, with lower prices in the north and east of the country. Prices in Lisbon and the Algarve for a two-bedroom apartment are from €150,000 and from €180,000 for three bedrooms. On the Algarve, three-bedroom villas cost from €600,000.

Fees: The fees when buying a property are usually between 10 and 15 per cent of the purchase price. Notary fees are from €153, registration fees between 0.75 and 1 per cent of the property's value and legal fees between 1 and 2 per cent. VAT (at 19 per cent) is included in the price of new properties. The main fee is stamp duty or transfer tax (SISA), which is calculated according to the price of property and ranges from 0 to 10 per cent. Under new legislation introduced in 2004, transfer tax is increased to 15 per cent if the property is bought by an offshore company.

Local Mortgages: Local mortgages are available from Portuguese banks but can be difficult to obtain, particularly if you are non-resident. You may get better terms from a foreign lender.

Property Taxes: Property or municipal tax is based on a property's value, location and the standard of local services. New rates were introduced in December 2003 and now range from 0.4 to 0.8 per cent of a property's fiscal value per year. They can be paid in full in April or in two instalments in April and September. Tax on property owned by offshore entities has been increased to 5 per cent.

Renting: Rental accommodation is generally easy to find, although long-term rentals may be difficult to find in resort areas. Rental prices for Lisbon are from €750 per month for an apartment and from €1,200 per month for a small house, although houses for rent are in short supply.

Personal Effects: Personal effects can be imported duty-free, provided they've been owned for over six months.

Utilities: Electricity is provided by *Electricidade de Portugal*, which has a monopoly and charges among the highest prices in the EU. The electricity supply (220V) is generally reliable, although power cuts are frequent during bad weather. Mains gas is available only in Lisbon, although bottled gas is in widespread use elsewhere. Water is expensive and shortages are commonplace in the south during the summer.

Services

Getting There: Portugal has good international air connections to its three main airports in Lisbon, Faro and Porto, as well as to the Azores and Madeira. The country can also be reached by train and ferry via Spain. The road connection with the south of Spain has been greatly improved in recent years and is now all-motorway.

Public Transport: Portugal has a good domestic air service including flights to the Azores and Madeira from the mainland, although fares are high. Public transport varies considerably from good in Lisbon (where metro, buses, trams and funiculars operate) and Porto to poor in rural areas. The train service is somewhat limited, although there's an excellent countrywide express coach service. There are numerous transport infrastructure projects currently underway in preparation for the 2004 European Football Cup.

Motoring: Private transport is essential in many parts of Portugal, where main highways are good and minor roads can be terrible. Driving standards are very poor and Portugal has the highest accident rate in the original EU. Traffic congestion and parking are major problems in most towns and cities. Speed limits are 50kph in built-up areas, 90kph or 100kph outside built-up areas, including dual carriageways, and 120kph on motorways. Maximum permitted alcohol level is 50mg per 100ml of blood. A warning triangle must be carried in all vehicles. No leaded petrol is available. You can drive in Portugal for up to six months with an international licence. EU licence holders are not required to exchange their driving licence for a Portuguese one, but other foreigners are, once they become resident.

Medical Facilities: Healthcare has greatly improved in the last decade or so and is generally of a high standard. There are many English-speaking and foreign doctors in resort areas and major cities, although hospital facilities are limited in many rural areas. If you contribute to social security, you pay only a small percentage of the cost of treatment. Emergency treatment is free for everyone. Residents who aren't covered by social security require private health insurance.

Education: Education standards are reasonable and schooling is free and compulsory for children aged from 6 to 14. There are private schools, usually of a religious denomination, and international schools in Lisbon and the Algarve.

Postal Services: The postal service is generally slow and unreliable, although there have been improvements in recent years. However, it's advisable to send valuable or urgent post by courier. The post office doesn't provide banking services.

Telephone: Telecommunications have improved greatly in recent years and in 2000 the market was fully liberalised, resulting in some welcome competition for Telecom Portugal and a fall in prices. Mobile phones are very popular.

Internet: The internet has been slow to take off in Portugal, although demand has grown significantly in recent years and many companies are now on-line. Personal usage still isn't widespread, but is expected to grow in the near future. There are many ISPs, mainly in Lisbon and on the Algarve, offering a range of services.

English TV & Radio: Satellite TV is popular in Portugal, particularly in the capital and expatriate areas. Cable TV is also available, although it isn't as popular. There are several English-language radio stations, mainly on the Algarve.

Miscellaneous

Crime Rate: Portugal has a relatively low crime rate and little serious or violent crime. However, burglary and thefts from cars are problems in resort areas and major cities.

Pets: Pets require a health certificate showing the animal has been examined within 48 hours of shipment and showed no signs of disease. The certificate must also show the animal has been vaccinated against rabies no less than six months and no more than one year prior to shipment. The health certificate must be officially translated into Portuguese.

Visas: Nationals from many countries, including the EU, Canada, Japan and the US, don't require a visa for visits for any purpose up to three months.

Business visas for visits up to three months are available for many non-EU countries under the same conditions as the Schengen Visa (see page 20). For further visa information see page 19.

Residence Permits: Residence permits are required by all foreigners in Portugal who wish to stay for more than 60 or 90 days at a time and non-EU nationals should apply for a residence visa **before** arrival in Portugal. EU nationals should apply for a residence permit from the nearest Foreigners Department (*Serviço de Estrangeiros e Fronteiras*/SEF).

International Dialling Code: 351.

Time Difference: GMT.

Weights & Measures: Metric.

Reference

Useful Addresses

British Embassy, 33 Rua de Sao Bernardo, 1249-082 Lisbon (☎ 21-392 4000, 💻 www.uk-embassy.pt).

Portuguese Embassy, 11 Belgrave Square, London SW1X 8PP, UK (☎ 020-7235 5331, 💻 www.portembassy.gla.ac.uk).

Portuguese Embassy, 2125 Kalorama Road, NW, Washington DC 20008, USA (☎ 202-462 3726, 💻 www.portugalemb.org).

US Embassy, Av das Forcas Armadas, 1600-081 Lisbon (☎ 21-727 3300, 💻 www. american-embassy.pt).

Useful Websites

Algarve Net (💻 www.algarvenet.com) – Comprehensive information about visiting and living in the Algarve, including business listings.

General information (💻 www.portugal-info.net) – Good general information about Portugal.

Madeira Information (💻 www.madeira-island.com) – A wealth of information about the island as well as news items and events listings.

Trade & Tourism (💻 www.portugal.org) – Official investment site with comprehensive information about doing business as well as tourist information.

SLOVAKIA

General Information

Capital: Bratislava.
Population: 5.4 million.

Foreign Community: A small foreign community is concentrated in the capital, mainly consisting of Germans and some British and Americans.

Area: 49,000km² (18,920mi²).

Geography: Slovakia is a small landlocked country in central Europe bordering with Poland in the north, the Czech Republic and Austria in the east, Hungary in the south and Ukraine in the west. The north of the country is mountainous and includes the Carpathian and Tatra Mountains, while the south consists mainly of lowlands drained by the Danube. Bratislava in the south is one of four European capitals on the banks of the Danube.

Climate: Slovakia has a typically continental climate with long, often very cold winters, and mild, warm summers. Average temperatures are 2°C (36°F) in January, although in the mountains it's considerably colder, and 18°C (64°F) in July.

Language: The official language is Slovak and Hungarian is widely spoken. English and German are spoken in the capital and some other areas.

Government: Unicameral parliamentary democracy.

Political Stability: Slovakia claimed its independence from the former Czechoslovakia in 1993, although the country still maintains close links with its former partner and many Slovaks work in the Czech Republic. However, Slovak economic progress has been much slower and less successfulthan in the Czech Republic. Slovakia became a member of NATO in 2002.

EU Accession: Slovakia, due to join in May 2004, was a latecomer to the accession process and serious reform, although progress in recent months has been spectacular, particularly in heavy industry, banking and agriculture. Accession should bring immediate positive effects to the country – particularly funds for regional infrastructure – and do much to alleviate current regional poverty.

Economy

Overview: Slovakia introduced an extensive programme of restructuring and austerity in 1999 in an attempt to overhaul the country's economy. Some progress has been made, although the reforms have been unpopular with the people. Growth has been slow over the last few years and Slovakia faces several major problems such as budget deficit, endemically high unemployment and dependence on heavy industry.

GDP Per Head: US$4,900.

Growth (2003): 3.9 per cent.

Forecast Growth For 2004: 4 per cent.

Main Industries: Ceramics, chemical products, food processing, machinery and metal products, mining, oil and chemical refining, paper/wood processing and textiles.

UK Trade Partner Ranking: 50+.

US Trade Partner Ranking: 50+.

Working

Overview: The workforce is generally highly skilled and productive. The higher education system is one of the best in Europe and there is no shortage of executive staff. The services sector is the largest employer, although industry still employs only slightly fewer people. Unemployment levels are very high and the government has introduced several programmes aimed at reducing these figures.

Unemployment Rate (2003): 16.5 per cent (one of the highest in the EU).

Employment Opportunities: Consulting, exports, investment, managerial positions, retail and tourism. Austria, Germany, Italy and the UK are major investors in Slovakia and, as a result, numerous firms from these countries are represented there. Many British start in English language teaching and then move into other areas of employment.

Work Permits: EU citizens must obtain a permit in order to start work but may visit the country and seek work for up to six months. Regulations are expected to change in May 2006 and you should check with the authorities for the latest information. Work permits are necessary for all non-EU nationals wishing to work in Slovakia. You must apply for a long-stay visa from the Slovak Republican consulate or embassy in your home country and enclose a preliminary job agreement issued by the Slovak Republic Labour Centre with your application.

Labour Relations: Unions exist in Slovakia and membership is high at around 75 per cent. In recent years there have been few strikes. Unions have up until now been tolerant of the effects on labour costs of economic transformation, although some experts suggest this may change as new union leadership is more aggressive.

Employment Conditions: The working week is 42.5 hours and employees are entitled to at least 15 days annual paid holiday.

Salaries: Generally low.

Minimum Monthly Wage (2003): €118.

Social Security: Slovakia has introduced a comprehensive social security system, to which employees contribute 12 per cent of their gross monthly salary up to maxima of Skk24,000 for health insurance and Skk32,000 for social security. Employers must contribute (a high) 38 per cent of the employee's gross salary. The self-employed contribute 50 per cent of the prorated monthly tax base from their business activities up to a maximum of Skk24,000. Benefits include healthcare, unemployment subsidies and retirement pensions.

Business Hours: Offices and businesses generally open from 8am to 4.30pm Monday to Friday. Banks open from 9am to 6pm Monday to Friday and from 9am to noon on Saturday.

Public Holidays: 15 a year:

- 1st & 6th January
- Good Friday & Easter Monday

- 1st & 8th May
- 5th July
- 29th August
- 1st & 15th September
- 1st & 17th November
- 24th, 25th & 26th December

Business Etiquette: Business is formal in Slovakia for introductions and attire. Business cards should be exchanged.

Finance

Currency: Koruna (Skk). The Skk is a convertible currency and very stable.
   Exchange Rate: €1= Skk40.90 (February 2004).
   Exchange Controls: There are still some foreign currency exchange regulations in place.
   Banks: There are 24 banks and some 12 foreign banks represented in the country, all of which provide a comprehensive range of banking services. The banking sector has been extensively restructured recently.
   Cost/Standard Of Living: The standard and cost of living are much lower than in Western Europe, although prices have been rising in recent years. Imported goods are expensive and food and accommodation prices have increased markedly, although local salaries have yet to catch up.
   Loans: Loans are available from local and foreign banks in the country, although interest rates are higher than most other EU countries.
   Interest Rate (Early 2004): 6.25 per cent.

Taxation

Corporate Tax: As from January 2004, corporate tax is levied at 19 per cent and all companies are taxed on their worldwide income.
   Personal Income Tax: Income tax is generally deducted at source (PAYE) and, as from January 2004, is levied at a flat rate of 19 per cent. There are annual personal and dependent allowances.
   Capital Gains Tax (CGT): CGT is levied at the taxpayer's marginal rate, although the disposal of assets not used for commercial purposes and held for specific minimum periods are exempt – e.g. a property used as a primary residence for over two years or owned for over five years; securities held for over 3 years; or movable assets held for more than one year.
   Wealth Tax: None.
   Inheritance & Gift Tax: The tax rates are progressive from 1 to 40 per cent depending on the value of the estate or gift and the relationship between the recipient and the deceased or donor.

Value Added Tax: VAT (DPH) is levied at a standard rate of 23 per cent and there's a reduced rate of 6 per cent for certain goods and services, e.g. food and energy. Some exports are exempt.

Withholding Taxes: Dividends and interest are subject to 15 per cent withholding tax.

Tax Filing: The Slovak tax year is the calendar year and for annual income in excess of Skk10,000 returns must be filed by 31st March although, if the income is from one source of employment only, filing is not necessary.

Accommodation

Building Standards: Variable. New property is of very good quality.

Restrictions On Foreign Ownership: Restrictions have recently been lifted and foreigners may now own property.

Cost Of Housing: There's currently a housing shortage, particularly of good quality property, and prices have risen considerably in recent years in Bratislava, where property costs from Skk30,000 to 35,000 per m². Prices outside the capital are around Skk14,000 to 18,000 per m².

Fees: Fees include 10 per cent transfer tax plus legal fees.

Local Mortgages: The mortgage market is still very much in its infancy and currently not user-friendly. It's therefore advisable to take out a mortgage with a foreign lender if possible.

Property Taxes: The amount payable for property tax depends on the area, although it's usually around Skk1 per m².

Renting: Rents are relatively high in Bratislava and similar to Prague, but much lower in rural areas. A two-bedroom apartment costs from Skk15,000 a month.

Personal Effects: No duty is payable on the import and export of personal effects, provided that they're exclusively for personal use and aren't sold in Slovakia.

Utilities: The electricity supply (220V) is generally reliable, but charges are quite high. Mains gas is available in the cities. Tap water isn't generally safe to drink owing to high levels of chlorination and pollution.

Services

Getting There: Bratislava has few direct international flights, so many travellers fly to Vienna (connected by a good bus service to the capital) or to Prague. Slovakia can also be easily reached by road and rail from Western Europe. A hydrofoil service connects the capitals of Bratislava, Budapest and Vienna along the Danube.

Public Transport: At present communications are generally poor, but are currently being improved under an extensive programme of modernisation due to be completed by 2005, by which time train travel will be faster and more efficient, and the road network vastly improved and increased. There's no domestic flight service.

Motoring: The road network is currently under ambitious expansion and road conditions are now generally good. Speed limits are 50kph in built-up areas, 90kph outside built-up areas, including dual carriageways, and 130kph on motorways. Alcohol tolerance is zero. A warning triangle and first aid kits must be carried in all vehicles. No leaded petrol is available. All foreign residents must exchange their driving licence for a Slovak licence after six months of residence.

Medical Facilities: Healthcare facilities are adequate in Slovakia, although standards are below those expected by westerners. There's a reciprocal health agreement with the UK, but comprehensive health insurance is highly recommended. There are no international hospitals. **Health warning: Vaccination against Hepatitis B is recommended and if you plan to visit any forested areas, you should be vaccinated against tick-borne encephalitis.**

Education: Education standards are excellent in Slovakia, particularly primary schools and higher education establishments. The country trains a large number of specialists every year. Education is free and compulsory for children aged from 6 to 14 or 15.

Postal Services: The postal service is inefficient and slow. Post offices are found in most cities and towns, and provide postal and currency exchange services only.

Telephone: At present, telecommunications aren't very efficient; however, a huge programme of modernisation is underway which should bring the telephone system into line with western standards. Call charges are high.

Internet: The internet has got off to a slow start in Slovakia mainly because of poor telecommunications, although companies are adapting and several have websites and email. There are a number of service providers.

English TV & Radio: Satellite and cable TV are the only means of watching English-language programmes. Reception is generally good

Miscellaneous

Crime Rate: Petty crime, particularly against tourists, is commonplace, as is theft from hotels. You should take good care of your valuables and avoid crowded places. Only use official taxis and beware of bogus plain-clothes policeman who may ask to see your foreign currency and passport, only to disappear with them. Violent crime is rare.

Pets: Animals require an International Vaccination Certificate issued no more than three days before departure. Dogs and cats are inspected by veterinary surgeons at the border.

Visas: Visits without visas are limited to 30 days for US nationals, 90 days for, Australian and Canadian nationals and 180 days for UK nationals. For longer stays or to work or study in Slovakia, a long-term stay permit is necessary, together with a visa, which must be obtained from a Slovak embassy or consulate **outside** the country – visas cannot be obtained at the border. You must provide evidence of financial support and accommodation, and a certificate proving that you have no contagious diseases with your visa application. Visa processing can be lengthy and you should allow several months.

Residence Permits: You must register at the local office of the Border and Aliens Police within three days of your arrival, where you will be issued with an identity card that you must carry at all times.

International Dialling Code: 421.

Time Difference: GMT +1.

Weights & Measures: Metric.

Reference

Useful Addresses

British Embassy, Panská 16, 81101 Bratislava (☎ 2-5996 2000, 🖥 www.britemb.sk).

Slovak Embassy, 25 Kensington Palace Gardens, London W8 4QY, UK (☎ 020-7243 0803, 🖥 www.slovakembassy.co.uk).

Slovak Embassy, 3523 International Court, NW, Washington DC 20008, USA (☎ 202-237 1054, 🖥 www.slovakembassy-us.org).

US Embassy, Hviezdoslavovo Námestie 5, 81102 Bratislava (☎ 2-5443 3338, 🖥 http://bratislava.usembassy.gov).

Further Reading

Slovak Spectator – English-language newspaper published weekly and also available online (🖥 www.slovakspectator.sk).

Useful Websites

Foreign Trade Support Fund (🖥 www.fpzo.sk) – Provides useful information on investment in the country.

General guide (🖥 www.slovakia.org) – Good information and links.

Slovak Tourist Board (🖥 www.sacr.sk) – Official tourist site.

Spectacular Slovakia (🖥 www.spectacularslovakia.sk) – Internet tourist guide with a wealth of useful information about living and working in the country.

SLOVENIA

General Information

Capital: Ljubljana.

Population: 2 million.

Foreign Community: There's a relatively small foreign population and westerners tend to be concentrated around the capital.

Area: 20,252km² (7,820mi²).

Geography: Slovenia is a small, almost landlocked, country bordering on Austria in the north, Italy to the west, Croatia to the south and Hungary to the east. Much of the country is mountainous with alpine scenery and a small stretch lies on the Adriatic, where the port of Koper provides important trade links with the rest of landlocked central Europe.

Climate: Slovenia has three climatic zones: the Adriatic coast has a mild, sunny climate; the north has long cold winters and wet summers; and the eastern plains have cold winters and hot summers. Average temperatures are 0°C (32°F) in January and 20°C (68°F) in July.

Language: The official language is Slovene. German is widely spoken and English to a lesser extent.

Government: Democratic republic.

Political Stability: Excellent. Slovenia gained independence from the former Yugoslavia in 1991 and had the immense good fortune of being relatively unaffected by the violent civil war that overtook much of the other former Yugoslav states. Since independence, Slovenia has made creating a market economy its top priority. The country joins NATO in May 2004 as well as the EU.

EU Accession: Slovenia is by far the wealthiest of the new member states – its GDP per capita is nearly 70 per cent of the EU average, higher than Greeceand not far from Portugal. The country's wealth is expected to increase once it joins the EU and Slovenia will eventually become a net contributor to the EU budget. As a member of the EU, Slovenia will be forced to facilitate foreign investment and the business environment is expected to improve markedly.

Economy

Overview: Slovenia has a strong and steady economy and the highest per capita income and standard of living in Central Europe. GDP and purchasing power now exceed those of some EU countries. The economy is characterised by a high and balanced level of trade, and growth over the last few years has been steady. Slovenia is considered to be the country with the brightest economic future in the area.

GDP Per Head: US$10,462.

Growth (2003): 2.2 per cent.

Forecast Growth For 2004: 3.6 per cent.

Main Industries: Automotive parts, chemicals, electronics, food processing, glass products, metal, textiles, tourism and transport.

UK Trade Partner Ranking: 50+.

US Trade Partner Ranking: 50+.

Working

Overview: The workforce in Slovenia is generally well educated and skilled. Unemployment is generally low, although in areas such as Maribor figures are considerably higher than the national average. In areas with little unemployment, e.g. Idrija, there are shortages of skilled labour. Employment contracts are compulsory and all employees must be hired on a temporary or permanent basis.

Unemployment Rate (2003): 6.2 per cent.

Employment Opportunities: Consultancy and management, retail, TEFL and tourism.

Work Permits: EU citizens must obtain a permit in order to start work but may visit the country and seek work for up to six months. Regulations are expected to change in May 2006 and you should check with the authorities for the latest information. All non-EU nationals require a work permit, which is usually possible only if you have a firm offer of work from an employer in Slovenia. This offer must be sent with your visa application.

Labour Relations: Generally good with few strikes.

Employment Conditions: Working conditions are generally good and most professions are regulated by collective bargaining. Employers are obliged to provide certain benefits such as meal and transport allowances, and a holiday bonus. The working week is 40 to 42 hours and employees are entitled to a minimum of 20 days annual paid holiday. Maternity (or paternity) benefits are among the most generous in Europe, with one parent's salary paid for one year.

Salaries: Salaries are the highest of the new member states, but significantly lower than those in most other EU countries.

Minimum Monthly Wage (2003): €451.

Social Security: All employees and employers are obliged to make monthly social security contributions to the five separate national schemes: pension and disability insurance, healthcare, unemployment insurance, maternity benefit and injury and illness. Employees contribute 22.1 per cent of their gross monthly salary and employers pay 15.9 per cent.

Business Hours: Offices and businesses generally open from 8am to 4pm Monday to Friday. Banking hours are from 8am to 5pm Monday to Friday and from 8am to noon on Saturday. Many banks close between 1pm and 2pm.

Public Holidays: 13 per year:

- 1st & 2nd January
- 8th February
- Easter Monday
- 27th April
- 1st & 2nd May
- 25th June

- 15th August
- 31st October
- 1st November
- 25th & 26th December

Business Etiquette: Business is conducted formally and punctuality is important. Most Slovenes speak English.

Finance

Currency: Slovene Tolar (SIT). The Tolar is fully convertible.
  Exchange Rate: €1= SIT237.20 (February 2004).
  Exchange Controls: None, provided that the relevant taxes have been paid.
  Banks: Some 24 banks operate in Slovenia of which seven are foreign (Austrian and French), all controlled by the Bank of Slovenia. Banks are efficient and offer a full range of banking services. Foreigners can open a bank account with any bank in Slovenia with no restrictions. Non-residents need permission from the Bank of Slovenia to withdraw more than SIT500,000 monthly from a Slovenian bank account.
  Cost/Standard Of Living: The standard and cost of living are low by EU standards and comparable to those of Greece or Portugal. Imported goods are expensive.
  Loans: Some eight banks in Slovenia currently hold licences for business and investment services and as such can provide loans. Check with the Slovenian embassy or consulate in your home country for up-to-date information.
  Interest Rate (Early 2004): 4.8 per cent.

Taxation

Corporate Tax: Corporate income and capital gains tax is levied at 25 per cent, and Slovene-registered companies are subject to income tax on their worldwide income.
  Personal Income Tax: Income tax is deducted at source (calculated as the difference between the total tax payable and the total amount of advance payments) by employers and tax returns must be filed annually. Rates range from 17 to 50 per cent. Deductions and allowances (11 per cent of the annual average wage for individuals) are available.
  Capital Gains Tax: CGT is levied at the same rates as income tax. Profits on real estate, securities and shares are subject to 25 per cent CGT after three years.
  Wealth Tax: None.
  Inheritance & Gift Tax: None.
  Value Added Tax: The standard rate of value added tax is 20 per cent and the reduced rate 8.5 per cent, which is levied on food, medicine, public transport

and holiday accommodation. Certain services such as postal, education and some cultural activities are exempt.

Withholding Taxes: Dividends are subject to 40 per cent withholding tax.

Tax Filing: The Slovenian tax year is the calendar year and all taxpayers including businesses and companies must file an annual return by 31st March. Non-residents present in Slovenia for at least six consecutive months in a calendar year must file an annual tax return.

Accommodation

Building Standards: Variable.

Restrictions On Foreign Ownership: Non-resident foreigners can own property in Slovenia only if they inherit it. EU nationals can buy property if they can provide proof of three years of permanent residence in Slovenia. Companies registered in Slovenia can buy with no restrictions. **Warning: Previous titles to ownership occasionally aren't properly registered, therefore you should check the property registration carefully.**

The Denationalisation Act provides for the restitution of land and buildings to former owners. The employment of a lawyer is absolutely essential when buying property in Slovenia.

Cost Of Housing: Property is generally expensive, particularly in the capital where you would expect to pay from €100,000 for a small two-bedroom apartment and from €200,000 for a house.

Fees: Fees include 2 per cent transfer tax for all residential properties except new properties, on which 8 per cent VAT is levied.

Local Mortgages: Local mortgages are available, but uncommon. It's advisable to take out a mortgage with a foreign lender if possible.

Renting: Rental accommodation can be difficult to find in the capital. Monthly rents for a two-bedroom apartment are around €500 and from €1,250 for a small house, plus maintenance fees.

Personal Effects: Personal and household effects can be imported duty-free, provided you're in possession of a residence permit.

Utilities: The electricity supply (220V) is reliable and charges are inexpensive. Mains and bottled gas are widely available and are a popular and very cheap form of energy. Tap water is safe to drink throughout the country.

Services

Getting There: Slovenia can be easily reached from European cities and the country's three international airports have frequent flights. You can also get there by road and rail from Western Europe.

Public Transport: Slovenia's transport network is generally excellent and is currently being modernised and upgraded to improve connections to the rest of Europe. There are daily flights to most major European cities. The port of Koper on the Adriatic is an important gateway from Europe to the Middle East and Asian markets.

Motoring: The road network is generally good and distances within the country are short. Major traffic congestion is a problem between the capital, Celje and Kranj during peak times. Speed limits are 50kph in built-up areas, 90kph outside built-up areas, 100kph on dual carriageways and 130kph on motorways. Maximum permitted alcohol level is 50mg per 100ml of blood. A warning triangle must be carried in all vehicles. No leaded petrol is available. Resident foreigners are required to exchange their driving licence for a Slovene one (a process that involves taking the practical test) within a year of arrival. It's expected that EU licences will be valid for residents by 2005.

Medical Facilities: Healthcare facilities are adequate, although below western standards. Doctors and hospitals often expect immediate payment in cash. Comprehensive health insurance is essential.

Education: Standards are generally high and education is free and compulsory for children aged from 7 to 15.

Postal Services: The postal service is reliable, although a little slow.

Telephone: Telekom Slovenia has a monopoly on telecommunications, which have been modernised and are good. Call charges are high.

Internet: An internet service is provided by Telekom Slovenia and is efficient with ISDN lines available, although connection charges are high. Many Slovene companies have websites and email, and uptake in private usage is on the increase.

English TV & Radio: Radio Slovenia has occasional news and weather broadcasts in English, but otherwise there are no TV or radio programmes in English. Satellite TV is available and reception is good.

Miscellaneous

Crime Rate: Slovenia has a low crime rate and is generally a safe country, although petty crime can be a problem for foreigners in the capital. Violent crime is rare.

Pets: Pets require an international health certificate, a vet's certificate (issued no earlier than 10 days before entry) stating the animal is healthy, and proof of rabies vaccination administered between 14 days and 12 months before entry.

Visas: Nationals from Australia, Canada, New Zealand, Switzerland and the US don't require a visa to enter Slovenia for visits of up to 90 days. Nationals from other countries require a visa for stays exceeding one month. All foreigners require a visa for longer stays or to work or study in Slovenia. Slovene bureaucracy is extremely slow and you may have administrative (i.e. red tape) problems obtaining a visa. If you plan to stay in Slovenia for longer than three months, you must obtain an extended-stay visa from a Slovene consulate or embassy in your home country before your arrival. Visas for business purposes usually require an invitation from a business within Slovenia.

Residence Permits: All foreigners must report to the local police to obtain a residence permit once they've entered the country.

International Dialling Code: 386.

Time Difference: GMT +1.

Weights & Measures: Metric.

Reference

Useful Addresses

British Embassy, 4th Floor, Trg Republike 3, 1000 Ljubljana (☎ 1-200 3910, 🖥 www.british-embassy.si).

US Embassy, Presernova 31, 1000 Ljubljana (☎ 1-200 5500, 🖥 www.us embassy.si).

Slovenian Embassy, 10 College Street, London SW1P 3SH, UK (☎ 020-7222 5400, 🖥 http://slovenia.embassyhomepage.com).

Slovenian Embassy, 1525 New Hampshire Avenue, NW, Washington DC 20036, USA (☎ 202-667 5363, 🖥 www.embassy.org/slovenia).

Useful Websites

Chamber of Commerce and Industry of Slovenia (🖥 www.gzs.si/eng) – The website provides excellent business and legal information as well as directories and government contacts.

Slovenia Online (🖥 www.slovenia-online.com) – A wealth of useful information about Slovenia including business, economy and legislation

Slovenia Tourism (🖥 www.slovenia-tourism.si) – Official tourism guide.

Trade and Investment Promotion Office/TIPO (🖥 www.gov.si/tipo) – Comprehensive information is provided for businesses wishing to set up in Slovenia.

SPAIN

General Information

Capital: Madrid.

Population: 42 million.

Foreign Community: Spain has a large expatriate community in its major cities and resort areas, including many Americans, British, Germans, Scandinavians and assorted other Europeans.

Area: 510,000km^2 (197,000mi^2).

Geography: Spain is the second largest country in Western Europe after France and its territory includes the Balearic Islands off the eastern coast, comprising the islands of Mallorca, Ibiza, Menorca and Formentera, the Canary Islands, situated 97km (60mi) off the west coast of Africa, and two North African enclaves, Ceuta and Melilla. The Pyrenees in the north form a natural barrier between Spain and France, while to the west is Portugal. To the north-west are the Bay of Biscay and the province of Galicia with an Atlantic coast. In the east and south is the Mediterranean. The southern tip of Spain is just 16km (10mi) from Africa across the Strait of Gibraltar, a British territory claimed by Spain and a constant source of friction between the countries. Spain's mainland coastline totals 2,119km (1,317mi). The country consists of a vast plain (*meseta*) surrounded by mountains and is the highest country in Europe after Switzerland, with an average altitude of 650m (2,132ft) above sea level. The vast plateau of the meseta covers an area of over 200,000km^2 (77,000mi^2) at altitudes of between 600 and 1,000m (2,000 and 3,300ft). Mountains hug the coast on three sides, with the Cantabrian chain in the north (including the Picos de Europa); the Penibetic chain in the south (including the Sierra Nevada which has the highest peaks in mainland Spain); and a string of lower mountains throughout the regions of Catalonia and Valencia in the east.

Climate: Spain is the sunniest country in Europe, where the climate (on the Costa Blanca) has been described by the World Health Organisation as among the healthiest in the world. The Mediterranean coast, from the Costa Blanca to the Costa del Sol, enjoys an average of 320 days sunshine each year. Continental Spain experiences three climatic zones: Atlantic, Continental and Mediterranean, in addition to which some areas, particularly the Balearic and Canary Islands, have their own distinct microclimates. Most of inland Spain has little rainfall and experiences cold winters and hot summers. The average temperatures in Madrid are 9°C (49°F) in January and 31°C (88°F) in July, and on the Mediterranean coast 12°C (53°F) in January and 27°C (80°F) in July.

Language: The official language is Spanish, although Basque, Catalan and Galician are also official languages in the regions of the Basque country, Catalonia and Galicia respectively. There are also a number of regional dialects. English is widely spoken in resort areas and the major cities.

Government: Parliamentary democracy.

Political Stability: Excellent. Although Spain has been free from dictatorship for only a relatively short time (since Franco's death in 1975), democracy is well established in the country. Spain has been a member of NATO since 1982.

EU Accession: 1986.

Economy

Overview: Since 1997, Spain's economy has shown one of the highest growth rates in the EU, owing mainly to the rapid expansion of industry and tourism. Growth, although slower, is still continuing and remains higher than the EU average. The main economic centres are Madrid and Barcelona, and the country has strong economic ties with Central and South America.

GDP Per Head: US$18,710.

Growth (2003): 2.25 per cent.

Forecast Growth For 2004: 3 per cent.

Main Industries: Aerospace, airports, clothing, communications, food and drink, healthcare, power, software and computer services, and tourism.

UK Trade Partner Ranking: 9.

US Trade Partner Ranking: 50+.

Working

Overview: The Spanish workforce is generally skilled and well qualified, and labour costs are among the lowest in the original EU. Successive attempts to liberalise rigid labour laws have failed and these remain responsible in part for consistently high unemployment figures. However, overall figures mask regional divides where in some areas (e.g. Catalonia and Almería) employers hire immigrants because of the labour shortage whilst in others (such as Galicia and many rural areas) unemployment is extremely high.

Unemployment Rate (2003): 11.3 per cent.

Employment Opportunities: construction, engineering, IT, management, retail, telecommunications and tourism.

Work Permits: Nationals from the original EU member states don't require a work permit. EU citizens from new member states must obtain a permit in order to start work but may visit the country and seek work for up to six months under the same conditions as other EU nationals. Regulations are expected to change in May 2006 and you should check with the authorities for the latest information. Non-EU nationals must apply for a work permit **before** arrival and may have difficulty obtaining one since a work permit is issued to non-EU nationals only if there are no EU nationals available for the job.

Labour Relations: Trade unions are strong in Spain, although membership is considerably higher in the public sector than the private. Labour relations are generally good, although there are occasional general strikes. Collective bargaining is commonplace and there's a minimum legal wage (currently the lowest in the EU except for Portugal).

Employment Conditions: Working conditions in Spain are good and legislation is generally heavily slanted in the employee's favour. Minimum salaries as well as collective rights are compulsory conditions for most jobs. Most employees receive 14 months' salary and are entitled to one calendar month's holiday annually. A working knowledge of Spanish is essential outside major resort areas.

Salaries: Salaries are generally lower than the EU average, although professionals can expect to earn salaries on a par with those in Ireland and the Netherlands.

Minimum Monthly Wage (2003): €526 (the second lowest in Western Europe).

Social Security: All employees make compulsory monthly contributions to the social security system of 6.4 per cent of their gross monthly salary (the employer pays a high 32.8 per cent). Benefits include healthcare, sickness and maternity leave, unemployment and housing benefits, and pensions. The self-employed pay a minimum of around €220 a month (the maximum is around €2,575) and all self-employed people, even those working part-time, must contribute to the social security system.

Business Hours: Office hours vary, but are generally 9 or 10am to 2pm and 5pm to 8pm Monday to Friday. Government offices open from 9am to 2pm. Banking hours are from 8.30am to 2pm Monday to Friday and from 8.30am to 1pm on Saturday between October and March. Many Spaniards take their annual holidays during the month of August and it's advisable to avoid doing business at this time.

Public Holidays: Ten national holidays per year, plus other regional and local holidays:

- 1st & 6th January
- Good Friday
- 1st May
- 15th August
- 12th October
- 1st November
- 6th, 8th & 25th December

Business Etiquette: Spanish business is generally conducted in a formal manner to start with, although a friendly relationship is usually quickly established. You should shake hands at the beginning and end of a meeting, and exchange business cards. Dress is formal. English is widely spoken in business circles.

Finance

Currency: Euro (€).

Exchange Controls: None.

Banks: There are two types of banks in Spain: clearing banks and savings banks, which are controlled by the Bank of Spain. Banking services are generally reasonably efficient and banking via the internet is increasingly popular. Foreign banks are well represented, mostly in Madrid and Barcelona, although British and other foreign banks operate in resort areas.

Cost/Standard Of Living: The cost of living in Spain is generally lower than most western European countries, although in major cities it's much higher. Quality clothing is relatively expensive, as are consumer goods such as electronic equipment, cameras and computers, but food, alcohol and tobacco are cheaper than in most other EU countries. Spain, along with Italy and Portugal, is rated one of the cheapest countries in the eurozone.

Loans: Loans are available from Spanish and foreign banks, although Spanish banks may be reluctant to lend to non-resident entities.

Interest Rate (Early 2004): 2 per cent (European Central Bank).

Taxation

Corporate Tax: Corporate income tax is levied on resident companies at 35 per cent and on non-resident entities at 25 per cent.

Personal Income Tax: Income tax rates in Spain are lower than in most other European countries, although recent reforms have increased the levels of taxation. Employees have their income tax deducted at source (PAYE) and rates range from 15 per cent (on the first €4,000) to 45 per cent (on amounts over €45,000). There are generous allowances for families and mortgage holders. All taxpayers, including non-resident property owners, require a fiscal number.

Capital Gains Tax: CGT is payable on the profit made from the sale of certain assets such as antiques, stocks and shares, and real estate. CGT for non-residents is levied at a flat rate of 35 per cent and residents are subject to 18 per cent CGT. Primary residences are exempt from CGT.

Wealth Tax: All residents in Spain are subject to wealth tax levied on assets. Residents are exempt from wealth tax on the first €108,182 of assets and there's an additional allowance of €150,253 for the principal residence. Non-residents have no allowances and, if they own assets in Spain, including property, must file an annual wealth tax declaration. Tax is levied at 0.2 per cent of the value of property.

Inheritance & Gift Tax: Inheritance and gift tax rates range from around 8 to 34 per cent and inheritance tax is payable by the beneficiaries of the deceased. For direct descendants and close relatives there are allowances of €15,956. The amount payable depends upon the relationship between the donor and the recipient, the amount inherited, and the current wealth of the recipient, and varies from 7.65 to 34 per cent. The government has plans for the gradual abolition of inheritance tax and in several regions of Spain there are lower rates.

Value Added Tax: Value added tax (IVA) is levied at a standard rate of 16 per cent on all goods and services not attracting the reduced rate of 7 per cent (drink, fuel, communications, new homes) or the super reduced rate of 4 per cent (basic foodstuffs, books and newspapers). Certain goods and services are exempt, including healthcare, educational services, insurance and banking.

Withholding Taxes: Interest and dividends received by residents are subject to 15 per cent tax and non-residents are subject to rates of 15 or 25 per cent only if their home country does not have a tax treaty with Spain.

Tax Filing: All companies and the self-employed must file quarterly and annual tax returns in Spain. Annual returns must be file by 30th June. Many employed individuals are not now required to present a tax return unless they qualify for allowances that are not deducted at source (e.g. mortgage interest).

Accommodation

Building Standards: For new properties and developments, standards are generally good to excellent, while for older properties they vary considerably.

Restrictions On Foreign Ownership: None.

Cost Of Housing: Home ownership is high in Spain and a considerable number of Spaniards also own second homes. In resort areas, home ownership by foreigners is very high. Property prices in Spain vary considerably from region to region and have risen spectacularly in all areas in recent years. Madrid and Barcelona are the most expensive places to buy property, although some resort areas, such as Marbella or the Balearic Islands, also have high property prices. A small apartment in Madrid or Barcelona costs at least €200,000 and a three-bedroom house from around €300,000. However, in rural and resort areas, prices can be up to 50 per cent lower.

Fees: The fees payable when buying a property in Spain amount to around 10 per cent of the purchase price and include VAT (IVA) or transfer tax (6 or 7 per cent); legal fees (1 to 2 per cent for the lawyer and around €600 for the notary); and a property registration fee (up to €300). A land tax (*plus valía*) is also payable when a property is sold, which should be paid by the vendor.

Local Mortgages: Local mortgages are available to both residents and non-residents although Spanish banks are somewhat restrictive on their lending to non-residents. Loans are available for up to 25 years although loans of 15 years are the most popular, and are usually for up to 80 per cent of the price. Non-residents may be limited to a 50 per cent loan from 10 to 15 years.

Property Taxes: Property tax in Spain is based on the fiscal value (*valor cadastral*) of a property, which may be higher than a property's actual market value. It's important that the fiscal value of your property is correct, as a number of taxes are linked to it, including income tax, wealth tax, transfer tax on property sales, and inheritance tax. In general, property tax rates in Spain are 0.5 per cent for urban properties and 0.3 per cent for those living on agricultural properties although, in some municipalities, they are as high as 1.7 per cent. Most municipalities also charge an annual fee for rubbish collection.

Renting: Rental accommodation is in short supply in the main cities, but is relatively easy to find in resort areas, although long-terms rentals may be difficult to find. Tenants are well protected by Spanish law and contracts are usually in generous terms. For a two-bedroom apartment, rents range from €600 per month in a resort area to up to €1,000 or more per month in a major city. A three-bedroom house costs from around €1,000 per month in a resort area and up to €1,500 per month in a major city.

Personal Effects: Personal and household effects can be imported duty-free, provided they've been owned for at least six months.

Utilities: Electricity (220V) is provided in Spain by different companies, according to the region. Costs have risen considerably in recent years and are now among the highest in the EU. Mains gas is available only in the major cities, but bottled gas is used extensively throughout the country. Tap water is safe to drink throughout Spain and is relatively inexpensive. It is scarce in most parts of Spain, where drought is commonplace and often a constant problem, particularly in the east and south of the country. In some areas, water supplies may be limited or cut off during dry periods. In some rural areas, water is provided by wells and may not be safe to drink

Services

Getting There: Spain has numerous international airports served by flights from cities worldwide, although most non-European flights go to Madrid or Barcelona. Charter and budget flights from the UK and Germany are very competitively priced. Spain can also be easily reached by road and rail from France, and there are ferry services to and from the UK and Morocco.

Public Transport: Communications are generally good and there's currently a huge investment programme, particularly in the road and high-speed rail networks. There's a comprehensive domestic flight service and increased competition has reduced fares considerably, although you have to book early to take advantage of discounts. Public transport within cities is generally good and economical. The rail network isn't particularly extensive and many areas have no connections at all. The high-speed train (AVE) is currently under massive expansion and by 2007 the south and east of Spain will be connected to Madrid. The Balearics and Canaries are connected to mainland Spain by ferry.

Motoring: Motorways (often toll) and other main roads are generally well maintained, but in rural areas roads are often in dreadful condition. Traffic congestion is a major problem in all large cities and parking is a challenge everywhere except in rural areas. Speed limits are 50kph in built-up areas, 90kph or 100kph outside built-up areas, including dual carriageways, and 120kph on motorways. Maximum permitted alcohol level is 50mg per 100ml of blood. **Two** warning triangles and a reflective jacket must be carried in all vehicles. No leaded petrol is available. Foreigners can drive in Spain for up to six months with an international driving licence. EU licence holders resident in Spain must have their licence stamped and registered by the local traffic authorities. Non-EU nationals who become resident in Spain must exchange their licence for a Spanish one, a process that usually involves taking the theoretical and practical tests.

Medical Facilities: The quality of healthcare and hospital facilities in Spain is generally good and medical staff is highly trained. Those who contribute to social security are entitled to free healthcare, although payment is required for prescriptions (40 per cent) and dental treatment. However, private health insurance is advisable to circumvent waiting lists for operations and is popular among both Spaniards and foreign residents.

Education: Education in Spain is free and compulsory for children aged from 6 to 16. The vast majority of children attend state schools where standards are generally high, but there are also many private schools, mainly run by the Catholic Church, and international schools in major cities and resort areas.

Postal Services: There's a post office in most towns, offering the usual postal services, as well as a limited range of other services such as money orders and transfers. The Spanish postal service has historically been one of the least efficient and slowest in Western Europe – it's slowly improving but services remain erratic. It also manages to lose many thousands of items of post a year and anything important should be sent by courier.

Telephone: The telephone service is dominated by Telefónica, although there are around ten other telephone companies in Spain. The introduction of competition in the market has reduced prices dramatically in recent years and there's a continual price war. Standards of telecommunications are generally very good and there's considerable investment in fibre optic lines. Mobile phone usage has expanded spectacularly in recent years and there are now more mobile phones than fixed lines.

Internet: The use of the internet has taken off in recent years, although the number of households on-line is well below the EU average. There's intense competition for clients between the many ISPs and prices for flat rates are reasonable.

English TV & Radio: Spanish TV broadcasts exclusively in Spanish (or in the local language) and there's little available in English apart from the occasional film with sub-titles. Cable TV is available in the major cities and satellite TV reception is excellent in most regions. In resort areas, there are a number of expatriate radio stations broadcasting in English (and other languages) for the foreign population.

Miscellaneous

Crime Rate: Spain's crime rate is among the lowest in Europe although, in major cities, crime (particularly theft) is on the increase.

Pets: Animals require two certificates in Spanish and English available from Spanish consulates abroad. One states that the animal has been vaccinated against rabies at least one month and no more than one year before shipment, and the other must be signed by the owner certifying that the animal has been under his supervision for three months prior to import. All dogs must be identified (microchip or tattoo) and registered in Spain.

Visas: Nationals from many countries, including Australia, Canada and the US, don't require any form of permit or visa to enter Spain and may remain in the country for up to three months. EEA nationals may remain for up to six months. Nationals from many countries may enter Spain without a visa and stay for up to 90 days and business visas for visits up to three months are available for many non-EU countries under the same conditions as the Schengen Visa (see page 20).

Residence Permits: EEA nationals intending to reside in Spain should apply for a residence permit within 15 days of arrival. Under new legislation, EEA nationals who are employees or self-employed in Spain **and** paying Spanish taxes no longer require a residence permit. Non-EU nationals should apply for a residence permit within 15 days of arrival.

International Dialling Code: 34.

Time Difference: GMT +1.

Weights & Measures: Metric.

Reference

Useful Addresses

British Embassy, C/ Fernando El Santo 16, 28010 Madrid (☎ 913-190200, 💻 www.ukinspain.com).

Spanish Embassy, 39 Chesham Place, London SW1X 8SB, UK (☎ 020-7235 5555, 💻 www.uk.tourspain.es).

Spanish Embassy, 2375 Pennsylvania Avenue, NW, Washington DC 20037, USA (☎ 202-452 0100, 💻 www.spainemb.org).

US Embassy, Serrano 75, 28006 Madrid (☎ 915-872200, 💻 www.embusa.es).

Further Reading

Living & Working in Spain, David Hampshire (Survival Books Ltd, 💻 www.survivalbooks.net).

Useful Websites

Ideal Spain (💻 www.idealspain.com) – Information about many aspects of living in Spain.

Invest in Spain (💻 www.investinspain.org) – Official investment website run by the Ministry of Economy.

Madrid Man (💻 www.madridman.com) – A wealth of useful information about living and working in Madrid.

Spanish Forum (💻 www.spanishforum.org) – Comprehensive and continually updated information about all aspects of living and working in Spain.

SWEDEN

General Information

Capital: Stockholm.

Population: 8.9 million.

Foreign Community: There isn't a large expatriate population in Sweden and most foreigners tend to be other Scandinavians, although there are some 25,000 North American residents.

Area: 449,964km² (173,744mi²).

Geography: Sweden is the largest of the Scandinavian countries and occupies the eastern half of the Scandinavian peninsula bordering with Norway in the west along practically all its length and with Finland in the north-east. In the south, Sweden is close to Denmark, separated by the Kattegat Strait (now spanned by a road bridge). Sweden can be divided geographically into two regions: the north consists mainly of forested plateaux crossed by rivers and narrow lakes; while the south (where most of the population is concentrated) comprises lowlands with several large lakes.

Climate: The south of the country has an Atlantic climate with cool and wet summers and cold winters. The eastern region has warmer, drier summers but severe winters. Average temperatures for Stockholm are -3°C (27°F) in January and 20°C (68°F) in July. There's little daylight during winter in the north of the country, although in summer the sun hardly sets.

Language: The official language is Swedish. English is widely spoken.

Government: Parliamentary monarchy.

Political Stability: Excellent. The Swedes have one of the most stable governments in the world.

EU Accession: 1995.

Economy

Overview: Sweden has a strong and stable economy based mainly on its high-tech and information-based industrial sector. The economy is heavily export-based with liberal corporate legislation and emphasis on free trade. Sweden has one of the highest tax burdens in the western world and there is concern that this is forcing some foreign investment abroad. Small and medium enterprises also find the tax burden excessive.

GDP Per Head: US$32,800.

Growth (2003): 1.3 per cent (much recovered from -0.5 per cent in 2002).

Forecast Growth For 2004: 2.3 per cent.

Main Industries: Automobile and vehicle safety, design (creative industries), food and drink, metals and minerals, real estate, retail, textiles, software and computer services, and wood processing.

UK Trade Partner Ranking: 14.

US Trade Partner Ranking: 19.

Working

Overview: Sweden has a well-disciplined and highly skilled workforce. Unemployment is consistently low and there's high participation in the labour market from women and older people. In recent years, the percentage of the workforce employed in foreign firms has grown steadily and now stands at around 20 per cent.

Unemployment Rate (2003): 5.9 per cent.

Employment Opportunities: IT and candidates with technical skills are in high demand. Most investment comes from the EU (the UK is the top investor), although there are also important investment projects from the US.

Work Permits: Nationals from the original EU member states don't require a work permit. For EU citizens from new member states, a work permit must be obtained in order to start work but they may visit the country and seek work for up to six months under the same conditions as other EU nationals. Regulations are expected to change in May 2006 and you should check with the authorities for the latest information. Non-EU nationals require a work permit, which is normally valid for one year. You must apply for the appropriate visa and need a firm offer of employment from a Swedish-based company who must obtain permission from the immigration authorities. If you're granted a work permit for longer than six months, your spouse is also entitled to a work permit.

Labour Relations: Nearly 90 per cent of the workforce belongs to labour unions (among the highest in the world), although relations between unions and management are generally excellent and non-confrontational. Swedish unions have helped to implement business rationalisation and strongly favour employee education and technical progress.

Employment Conditions: Working conditions are excellent in Sweden, where the working week is 40 hours and employees are entitled to 35 days annual paid holiday. Salaries are set by collective bargaining and there is no minimum wage.

Salaries: Salaries are among the highest in the EU, although taxes are also high and, once these have been deducted, salaries are on a par with the EU average.

Minimum Monthly Wage (2003): Not applicable.

Social Security: Social security contributions are compulsory for all employees and total 7 per cent of gross monthly salary. Benefits, including health insurance, retirement and disability pensions, and unemployment allowances are generous. Employers pay 33.03 per cent and companies pay an additional 6-7.4 per cent for pensions under collective agreements.

Business Hours: Flexible working hours are now the norm in offices and shorter hours are worked during June, July and August. Normal hours are 8.30am to 5pm with one-hour for lunch. Banks generally open from 9.30am to 3pm or 5.30pm Monday to Friday.

Public Holidays: 14 per year:

- 1st & 6th January
- Good Friday, Easter Thursday & Easter Monday
- 1st May
- Ascension

- Whitsun (May/June)
- 6th June & 21st June
- 1st November
- 24th, 25th & 26th December

Business Etiquette: The Swedes are formal and punctuality is extremely important. Dress is also formal and business is conducted directly with straight talking. Handshakes are the correct form of greeting and departure. Business is often conducted in English and business cards are widely used.

Finance

Currency: Swedish Krona (SEK).

Exchange Rate: €1= SEK9.19 (February 2004). Sweden voted in referenda in both 2000 and 2003 not to join the euro.

Exchange Controls: None.

Banks: The Swedish banking system is well developed and secure. There are several large Pan-Nordic Banks and subsidiaries of foreign-owned banks offering a full range of banking services. Internet banking is popular.

Cost/Standard Of Living: Sweden, along with other Scandinavian countries, has one of the highest standards and costs of living in the EU. Salaries are well above the EU average, but taxation is also very high. Almost all goods and services are considerably more expensive than in other EU countries.

Loans: Loans are available from Swedish banks.

Interest Rate (Early 2004): 2.75 per cent.

Taxation

Corporate Tax: Swedish companies are subject to corporate income and capital gains tax at 28 per cent on their worldwide income.

Personal Income Tax: Individual income tax is levied mainly by the municipality of residence, at rates ranging from 27 to 34 per cent (averaging around 31 per cent). On taxable earnings over SEK273,800, an additional 20 per cent is levied and a further 5 per cent is levied on taxable earnings over SEK414,200. Most Swedish taxpayers pay only municipal income tax plus a general SEK200 national tax. Expatriates whose stay in Sweden doesn't exceed five years may be eligible to benefit from a special income tax concession, whereby only 75 per cent of their income is taxed during a three-year period.

Capital Gains Tax: Flat rate of 30 per cent.

Wealth Tax: A personal wealth tax (including bank accounts, real estate and vehicles) is levied at a rate of 1.5 per cent on assets above the value of SEK1.5 million (SEK2 million for a couple).

Inheritance & Gift Tax: None.

Value Added Tax: Value added tax (MOMS) is levied at a standard rate of 25 per cent on most goods and services. A reduced rate of 12 per cent is levied on food and hotel charges, and a super-reduced rate of 6 per cent on newspapers and tickets for sporting and cultural events.

Withholding Taxes: Interest is exempt from withholding tax. Dividends are taxed at 30 per cent, although there are exceptions (e.g. exempt if the company is from the EU and owns at least 25 per cent of the capital).

Tax Filing: The Swedish tax year is the calendar year and individuals must file by 5th May and businesses by 31st March. Most tax filing in Sweden is done via the internet.

Accommodation

Building Standards: Excellent.

Restrictions On Foreign Ownership: Generally none, although there are certain regulations applying to both Swedish and foreign nationals, and you should seek legal advice before buying.

Cost Of Housing: Property in Stockholm costs from SEK2.3 million for a small apartment in the centre and from SEK2.2 million for a small house with three bedrooms on the outskirts of the city. Prices outside the capital are lower.

Fees: Fees for property purchase are low, where you pay 3 per cent transfer tax (apartments are exempt) and a maximum of SEK1,000 for registration fees.

Local Mortgages: Local mortgages are available and banks usually lend 75 per cent of a property's value and will often finance a further 20 per cent. Loan periods are generally 10 to 15 years on the first 25 per cent of the loan and up to 30 years on the remainder.

Property Taxes: Annual property tax is 0.5 per cent of the rateable value on houses, while property tax on apartments is included in the monthly management fee.

Renting: Regulation of the housing market in Sweden means that there's little available rental accommodation and waiting lists for accommodation in Stockholm can be as long as ten years. You're therefore advised to use a relocation company to help you find accommodation. A two-bedroom apartment costs around SEK16,000 per month in the capital (SEK13,000 outside) and a small house near an international school from SEK22,000 per month.

Personal Effects: Personal and household effects can be imported duty-free, provided they've been owned for at least six months.

Utilities: The electricity supply (220V) is reliable and covers the whole country. Charges are lower than the EU average. Water is of a high quality and is inexpensive.

Services

Getting There: Sweden has three international airports, two in Stockholm and one in Gothenburg, served by frequent flights from cities worldwide. Ferry services operate from the ports of Malmö and Stockholm across the Baltic and to other Scandinavian countries.

Public Transport: Sweden has generally excellent communications. The domestic air service is comprehensive and flights are cheap. The rail system is excellent and, although concentrated mainly in the south, has routes throughout the country. Public transport within Stockholm is very good with bus, tram, metro and rail services.

Motoring: Road conditions are excellent and roads are relatively uncrowded. Speed limits are 50kph in built-up areas, 70kph outside built-up areas, including dual carriageways, and 110kph on motorways. Maximum permitted alcohol level is 20mg per 100ml of blood. A warning triangle must be carried in all vehicles. No leaded petrol is available. Resident foreigners with EU driving licences are not required to exchange them. Non-EU driving licence holders must exchange their licence within a year of becoming resident. They may have to take the practical test.

Medical Facilities: Healthcare facilities are of a very high standard in Sweden and are free to foreigners with a residence permit. Private healthcare is also available, but is very expensive.

Education: The Swedes are generally highly educated and have the third largest per capita population in the world educated to tertiary level. Education is free and compulsory for all children aged from 6 to 16, and foreign children may benefit from free education if their parents have a residence permit. Practically all schools are state and co-educational, and private schools are rare, although there are a few international schools in Stockholm.

Postal Services: Postal services are provided by some 50 different companies, although the main company is Swedish Post. The service is efficient and reliable, and post offices also provide a comprehensive banking service.

Telephone: Telecommunications are efficient and call charges are competitive. Mobile phones are extremely popular in Sweden and are operated by three companies, all offering competitive rates.

Internet: Sweden is a European leader in internet use and a world leader in personal computer ownership. Most companies use the internet on a regular basis and there's a wide range of ISPs, some of which offer free connection.

English TV & Radio: English-language programmes are shown with Swedish subtitles and all films are shown in their original languages. English-language programmes are also available via cable and satellite TV.

Miscellaneous

Crime Rate: Very low and violent crime is practically unknown.

Pets: Legislation regarding the import of pets into Sweden is complex. Quarantine may be necessary, depending on the country of origin. Check with the Swedish consulate in your home country for up-to-date information.

Visas: Nationals from many countries, including the EU, Canada, Japan and the US, don't require a visa for visits for any purpose for up to three months.

Business visas for visits up to three months are available for many non-EU countries under the same conditions as the Schengen Visa (see page 20). For further visa information see page 19.

Residence Permits: EEA nationals must apply for a residence permit after three months and other nationals must obtain a work and residence permit **before** arrival in Sweden.

International Dialling Code: 46.

Time Difference: GMT +1.

Weights & Measures: Metric.

Reference

Useful Addresses

British Embassy, Skarpogatan 6-8 (PO Box 27819), 11593 Stockholm (☎ 8-671 9000, 🖥 www.britishembassy.com).

Swedish Embassy, 11 Montagu Place, London W1H 2AL, UK (☎ 020-7917 6400, 🖥 www.swedish-embassy.org.uk).

Swedish Embassy, 1501 M Street, NW, Washington DC 20005, USA (☎ 202-467 2600, 🖥 www.swedenemb.org).

US Embassy, Dag Hammarskjolds Vag 31, 11589 Stockholm (☎ 783-5300, 🖥 http://stockholm.usembassy.gov).

Useful Websites

Invest in Sweden Agency/ISA (🖥 www.isa.se) – A very helpful and informative government body mainly orientated towards business but also providing expatriate information.

Official Gateway to Sweden (🖥 www.sweden.se) – Comprehensive information about all aspects of living and working in Sweden.

UNITED KINGDOM

General Information

Capital: London.

Population: 60 million.

Foreign Community: Around 5 per cent of the British population is made up of immigrants from British Commonwealth countries and their descendants. There's also a large foreign population from throughout the world, particularly in London, the world's most ethnically diverse city.

Area: 242,432km^2 (93,600mi^2).

Geography: The term United Kingdom (UK) comprises Great Britain (the island which includes England, Wales and Scotland) and Northern Ireland. The UK is often referred to as Britain. The UK is about the size of New Zealand and half the size of France. It has a varied landscape and most of England is fairly flat and low lying with the exception of the north and south-west, while much of Wales and Scotland is mountainous. The country can be roughly divided into a highland region in the north and west, and a lowland region in the east, approximately delimited by the mouth of the River Exe (Exeter) in the south-west and the River Tees (Teeside) in the north-east. The central belt, which stretches across England from London to North Yorkshire, contains around half of the UK population. Some 90 per cent of the population live in urban areas.

Climate: The UK has a generally mild and temperate climate, although it's extremely changeable and usually damp at any time of year. The west of the country tends to be wetter and milder than the east, while the north-west is the wettest region. Winters are often harsh in Scotland and the north, where snow is common in winter. The south-east of the country has the best and warmest weather, although even here winters can be long, cold and wet. Average temperatures are 4°C (39°F) in January and 18°C (64°F) in July, although in the south-east temperatures can reach around 26°C (79°F) in summer.

Language: The official languages are English, Welsh and Scots-Gaelic although the latter two are spoken only in their respective countries and by a relatively small minority.

Government: Constitutional monarchy.

Political Stability: Excellent: one of the most politically stable countries in the world.

EU Accession: 1973

Economy

Overview: The UK has the world's fourth-largest economy and started the 21st century with strong economic growth and relatively low unemployment. Forecasts are strong for beyond 2003.

GDP Per Head: US$29,360.

Growth (2003): 1.75 per cent.

Forecast Growth For 2004: 2.5 per cent.

Main Industries: Finance, manufacturing and service industries.

US Trading Partner Ranking: 43.

Working

Overview: The UK has the second largest workforce in the EU after Germany and education is generally of a high standard with strong emphasis on vocational training. There's a current shortage of skilled employees, particularly in the high technology sector

Unemployment Rate (2003): 4.9 per cent.

Employment Opportunities: Opportunities abound in the services sector, particularly for casual work in restaurant and hotel services. There are also shortages of doctors, IT specialists, nurses and veterinary surgeons.

Work Permits: Nationals from the original EU member states don't require a work permit. EU citizens from new member states must obtain a permit in order to start work but may visit the country and seek work for up to six months under the same conditions as other EU nationals. Regulations are expected to change in May 2006 and you should check with the authorities for the latest information. There are several work permit-free categories in the UK, including EU nationals, Commonwealth citizens with a parent born in the UK, and Commonwealth citizens aged 17 to 27 seeking a holiday job (maximum duration two years). Business investors may also qualify for work permit-free entry provided they've obtained entry clearance from the British embassy in their home country. For other categories you should obtain advice from a British consulate or embassy in your home country **before** arrival in the UK. Those who don't come under a permit-free category may have difficulty obtaining a work permit. In 2002, the Highly Skilled Migrant Programme (HSMP) was introduced in order to attract individuals with exceptional personal skills and experience to the UK to find work. Current qualifying criteria can be found on 🖳 www. workpermits.gov.uk.

Labour Relations: Generally very good and working days lost to strikes and absences are among the lowest in Europe.

Employment Conditions: Working conditions are generally good in the UK and employees work the longest average hours in the EU (over 40 hours per week), although the official working week is 37 hours. Most employees are entitled to four weeks annual paid holiday and can expect some sort of bonus or commission on top of their salary. A working knowledge of English is essential for most jobs and there are plenty of short-term job opportunities in large cities, particularly London.

Salaries: Salaries in the UK are slightly higher than the EU average and you can expect to earn more than in Finland, France and Italy, but less than in Austria and Germany.

Minimum Monthly Wage: £4.85 an hour for employees over 17. There are plans to introduce a minimum wage for the under-18s in 2004.

Social Security: Social security payments are mandatory for most employees in the UK and contributions are calculated as a percentage of your salary and depend on which of five classes you come under. Rates range from 12.8 per cent paid by the employer and 11 per cent paid by the employee on a monthly wage of at least £385, below which you're exempt from contributions, and there are reductions depending on your status. Contributions for the self-employed are generally lower. Social security provides a range of benefits, including healthcare, family allowances, sick and unemployment pay, and pensions.

Business Hours: Offices and businesses open from 9am to 5pm Monday to Friday and banking hours are generally from 9.30am to 4.30pm. Some banks open on Saturday.

Public Holidays: There are eight annual public holidays in England, Scotland and Wales, and there are ten in Northern Ireland, as shown in the following lists:

England & Wales

- 1st January
- Good Friday & Easter Monday
- May bank holiday (first Monday)
- Spring bank holiday (last Monday in May)
- Summer bank holiday (last Monday in August)
- 25th & 26th December

Scotland

- 1st & 2nd January
- Good Friday
- May bank holiday (first Monday)
- Spring bank holiday (last Monday in May)
- Summer bank holiday (first Monday in August)
- 25th & 26th December

Northern Ireland

- 1st January
- 17th March
- Good Friday & Easter Monday
- May bank holiday (first Monday)
- Spring bank holiday (last Monday in May)
- 12th July
- Summer bank holiday (last Monday in August)
- 25th & 26th December

Business Etiquette: Business is conducted in a formal manner and personal contacts are very important. Punctuality is essential.

Finance

Currency: Pound Sterling (£).

Exchange Rate: €1= £0.69 (February 2004). Although the British prime minister, Tony Blair, is in favour of the euro, many politicians and the Bank of England are not, and a referendum on joining the euro zone isn't expected until 2005 at the earliest.

Exchange Controls: None.

Banks: There are a number of major banks in the UK and most towns have branches of one or more of them, although branch networks have been reduced in recent years through mergers and rationalisation. Telephone and internet banking are provided by most banks and building societies (similar to savings banks). In recent years, there has been a flood of new-style 'banks' often run by supermarkets or stores offering innovative accounts and services. Bank accounts can be opened by both residents and non-residents.

Cost/Standard Of Living: The UK has a high cost of living, particularly food and consumer goods, making it one of the most expensive places to live in the world. There's a huge disparity between the wealthy, expensive south and the relatively poor (and much less expensive) north of England, Scotland, Wales and Northern Ireland. Duty and taxes on cars, petrol, alcohol and tobacco are high. However, salaries are also relatively high, particularly in the south of England.

Loans: Loans are available from British and foreign banks, and other financial institutions.

Interest Rate (Early 2004): 3.75 per cent.

Taxation

Corporate Tax: The UK has very attractive corporate income and capital gains tax rates which range from 0 per cent (on annual profits up to £10,000) to 30 per cent (on annual profits in excess of £1.5 million). UK resident companies are taxed on their worldwide income.

Personal Income Tax: Income tax is among the lowest in Europe and is collected at source from employees (PAYE). There are three rates of income tax: a lower rate of 10 per cent on the first £1,960, a basic rate of 20 per cent on income from £1,961 to £30,500, and a higher rate of 40 per cent payable on income above £30,500. The self-employed pay their tax in arrears in two annual instalments. There's a basic personal allowance of £4,615.

Capital Gains Tax: CGT is payable by individuals on any asset with profits in excess of £7,900. Net gains over £7,900 are taxed at the same rates as income tax. Main residences are exempt from CGT.

Wealth Tax: None.

Inheritance & Gift Tax: Inheritance tax of 40 per cent is payable on any bequests above £255,000 when left to anyone other than your spouse or a registered charity. Up to £3,000 a year may be donated tax-free. Inheritance and gift tax is complicated and professional advice should be sought.

Value Added Tax: The standard rate of VAT is 17.5 per cent on all goods and services except domestic fuels and power, on which the rate is 5 per cent. Most food (not catering), new buildings, young children's clothes and footwear, books and newspapers are exempt.

Withholding Taxes: Withholding tax is levied on income from savings at the same rates as income tax and on dividends at 10 per cent on income up to £29,900 and at 40 per cent on higher amounts.

Tax Filing: The UK tax year runs (unusually) from 6th April to 5th April. Tax returns (known as 'self-assessment') must be filed by all individuals and businesses, generally by 31st January.

Accommodation

Building Standards: Generally excellent.

Restrictions On Foreign Ownership: None.

Cost Of Housing: Property prices in the UK vary widely according to the area of the country, although the average price for a three-bedroom house in 2003 was £136,000. London (one of the world's most expensive cities for property) and the south-east are the most expensive areas and prices have been steadily rising in recent years (by between 15 and 20 per cent). The average property price in London in 2003 was £233,200. Prices in the north of England or Scotland (except Edinburgh) are generally lower.

Fees: The fees for buying a property in the UK are among the lowest in the EU and total around 3 to 6 per cent of the purchase price. They include legal fees, land registry fees and stamp duty (from 1 to 4 per cent, depending on the purchase price).

Local Mortgages: Mortgages are easy to obtain in the UK and repayments are relatively low owing to the long repayment period, typically 25 to 30 years. Mortgages of up to 95 per cent are widely available and discounts are provided for first-time buyers and those switching lenders, with interest rates up to two percentage points lower than the standard rate for a number of years. The availability and terms of mortgages mean that it's usually cheaper to buy a home than rent one.

Property Taxes: There's no property tax in the UK but instead residents pay 'council tax', which is calculated according to the value of a property, the number of people who live there and the area where the property is situated. Annual rates range from £400 in a rural area to £900 in a major city. Payment can be made in instalments.

Renting: The UK has one of the most unregulated letting markets in Western Europe and the consumer has little protection against voracious landlords. There isn't a strong rental market and there's a chronic shortage of rental properties throughout the country, particularly in London and the south-east. Average rental costs in the counties (excluding London and the south-east) are from £500 a month for a two-bedroom apartment and from £650 to £1,200 for a small three-bedroom house. London rents are around 50 per cent higher, but those paid in the north of England and Scotland are substantially lower.

Personal Effects: Household goods purchased within the EU can be imported duty-free and don't need to be retained for a minimum period. However, goods (including vehicles) purchased outside the EU must have been owned for at least six months and cannot be sold for 12 months after importation.

Utilities: Electricity (240V) is provided by many companies in the UK, most of which provide a countrywide service. The supply is generally good in most parts of the country and relatively inexpensive. Mains gas is available in all but the remotest areas of the UK and is supplied by some 26 companies. Gas is a relatively cheap form of energy in the UK, particularly for central heating and hot water. Tap water is safe to drink throughout the country and charges are usually based on the rateable value of a property and included in the council tax (few homes in the UK have water meters). In spite of the very wet climate, water charges can be high and there are often water shortages in many areas, particularly the south-east.

Services

Getting There: The UK has numerous international airports which serve a comprehensive network of international destinations. London's Gatwick and Heathrow airports are among the world's busiest airports. Airfares to and from the UK are the most competitive in Europe and there's fierce competition between airlines offering discount fares. Regular (and expensive) car and passenger ferries operate all year round to Ireland and continental ports in Europe.

Public Transport: Communications in the UK are generally good but very congested. The domestic flight service is comprehensive and prices competitive. The public transport system varies from excellent to poor, according to the region or city. The railway network, once the pride of the UK, is currently being rescued by the government from its state of abandonment and lack of investment in private hands.

Motoring: British roads are generally very good, but are among the most crowded in Europe. Traffic jams are commonplace in towns and cities, and roads in the south, particularly around London, are practically saturated. Cars are generally more expensive in the UK than in the rest of Europe. Driving standards are good and cars drive on the left. Speed limits are 48kph (30mph) in built-up areas, 96kph (60mph) outside built-up areas, including dual carriageways, and 112kph (70mph) on motorways. Maximum permitted alcohol level is 80mg per 100ml of blood. No leaded petrol is available. EU driving licence holders are not required to exchange their licence. Foreign residents with non-EU licences must exchange their licence for a British one and take the practical test within a year of arrival in the UK.

Medical Facilities: The UK is renowned for its National Health Service, which provides healthcare to all British citizens and most foreign residents. Standards of training for health professionals and treatment are generally very good, but underfunded NHS hospitals struggle to cope with demand in many areas, although a huge cash injection from the government is hoped to alleviate the problem. Healthcare is provided free to most residents, although patients must pay a charge for prescriptions and dental care. Private healthcare is excellent and increasingly popular.

Education: Education is free and compulsory in the UK for children aged from 5 to 16. Over 90 per cent of children attend state schools, most of which are co-educational and where standards are generally high (but extremely variable). There are some 2,500 private schools in the UK, including American, international and foreign schools. British universities have an excellent reputation worldwide and over 40 per cent of school-leavers attend university.

Postal Services: The British postal service is one of the most efficient and modern in the world. Most towns and villages have a post office, at which you can use banking services, pay bills and licences, in addition to the usual postal services.

Telephone: The phone market in the UK is dominated by British Telecom (BT), although some 100 other telephone companies also have licences to operate in the country, making it one of the most competitive and relatively inexpensive markets in the world (at least for international calls). The telephone system is generally excellent and the UK is at the forefront of telecommunications technology and a world leader in the use of mobile phones.

Internet: The internet has really taken off in the UK in the last few years and a large number of homes and companies are on-line. There are hundreds of ISPs to choose from offering a range of services for the avid surfer, including flat rate deals.

English TV & Radio: British TV is generally recognised as the best (or least worst) in the world and British TV companies, particularly the BBC, produce many excellent programmes. There are five national channels as well as dozens of cable and satellite stations, an increasingly popular option in the UK. An annual TV licence is payable (which finances the BBC). British radio is split between the BBC and commercial stations, which provide a wide range of music, discussion (chat), sport and other entertainment.

Miscellaneous

Crime Rate: The crime rate in the UK has gone down in recent years and it's a relatively safe place to live, although there has been an escalation in crimes against property and violent crime, usually drug-related, in the major cities.

Pets: The UK has strict quarantine regulations and you should check with a British representative abroad for up-to-date information. A Pet Travel Scheme (PETS) exists for animals imported from some 22 European countries, Bahrain, Canada and the US, under which animals don't have to undergo quarantine if they are microchipped, vaccinated against rabies, undergo a blood test proving this and have a health certificate. Animals entering the UK under PETS can enter only through certain ports or Gatwick or Heathrow airports. Further information is available from DEFRA (⊠ pets.helpline@ defra.gsi.gov.uk) and on page 199.

Visas: Nationals from many countries, including the EU, Canada, Japan and the US, don't require a visa for visits for any purpose for up to three months. For further visa information see page 19.

Residence Permits: EU nationals don't require a residence permit. Other foreigners do and should acquire them **before** arrival in the UK. **In late 2003 the immigration authorities introduced new entry clearance requirements for foreigners from some countries wishing to spend longer than six months in the UK.** At the time of writing (early 2004) nationals from the following countries require entry clearance **before** arrival: Australia, Canada, Hong Kong, Malaysia, New Zealand, Singapore, South Africa, South Korea and the US. Check with the British embassy or consulate in your home country for the latest information.

International Dialling Code: 44.
Time Difference: GMT.
Weights & Measures: Metric.

Reference

Useful Addresses

British Embassy, 3100 Massachusetts Avenue, NW, Washington DC 20008, USA (☎ 202-588 7800, 💻 www.britainusa.com).

US Embassy, 24 Grosvenor Square, London W1A 1AE (☎ 020-7499 9000, 💻 www.usembassy.org.uk).

Further Reading

Living & Working in Britain, David Hampshire (Survival Books Ltd, 💻 www. survivalbooks.net).

Living & Working in London, Joe Laredo ed. (Survival Books Ltd, 💻 www. survivalbooks.net).

Useful Websites

American Expats in the UK (▣ www.americanexpats.co.uk) – A site designed for Americans living and working in the UK, but with information useful for all foreigners there.

Invest UK (▣ www.invest.uk.com) – Official government body promoting foreign investment in the UK. The website is comprehensive with numerous useful downloadable factsheets.

Trade Partners (▣ www.tradepartnersuk-usa.com) – Useful business information and good links.

Visit Britain (▣ www.visitbritain.com) – Official tourism site.

APPENDICES

Appendix A: USEFUL ADDRESSES

American Citizens Abroad (ACA), 5 Rue Liotard, CH-1202 Geneva 12, Switzerland (☎ 022-340 0233, 🖳 www.aca.ch).

Assist-Card (☎ USA 1800-874-2223, UK 0800-3580080, 🖳 www.assist-card.com). Helps members with travel crises such as illness, loss of passport, legal trouble and theft.

The British Association of Removers (BAR) Overseas, 3 Churchill Court, 58 Station Road, North harrow, Middx. HA2 7SA, UK (☎ 020-8861 3331, 🖳 www.removers.org.uk).

The British Council, 10 Spring Gardens, London SW1A 2BN, UK (☎ 020-7930 8466, 🖳 www.britishcouncil.org).

The Centre for International Briefing, Farnham Castle, Farnham, Surrey GU9 0AG, UK (☎ 01252-721194, 🖳 www.farnhamcastle.com). Organises briefing courses for people moving overseas.

Corona Worldwide, Commonwealth Institute, Kensington High Street, London W8 6NQ, UK (☎ 020-7610 4407). Provides information for women expatriates and a useful *Notes for Newcomers* series on many EU countries.

Employment Conditions Abroad, Anchor House, 15 Britten Street, London SW3 3TY, UK (☎ 020-7351 5000, 🖳 www.ecainternational.com). Publishes information for Expatriates' on over 75 countries.

English Contacts Abroad, PO Box 126, Oxford OX2 6UB, UK.

European Council of International Schools (ECIS), 21b Lavant Street, Petersfield, Hants. GU32 3EL, UK (☎ 01730-268244, 🖳 www.ecis.org).

The Experiment in International Living, PO Box 595, Putney, VT 05346, USA (☎ 802-387 4210, 🖳 www.experiment.org).

Federation of Overseas Property Developers, Agents and Consultants (FOPDAC), Lacey House, ST Clare Business Park, Holly Road, Hampton, Middlesex TW12 1QQ, UK (☎ 020-8941 5588, 🖳 www.fopdac.com).

Going Places, 84 Coombe Road, New Malden, Surrey KT3 4QS, UK (☎ 020-8949 8811). Organises tailor-made expatriate briefing courses.

Homebuyer Events Ltd., Mantle House, Broomhill Road, London SW18 4JQ, UK (☎ 020-7069 5000, 🖳 www.homebuyer.co.uk). Organises property shows.

International Living, 5 Catherine Street, Waterford, Ireland 5 (☎ 800-643 2479, 🖳 www.internationalliving.com). Useful source of advice and information on living abroad (outside the USA).

Medical Advisory Service for Travellers Abroad (MASTA), Moorfield Road, Yeadon, Leeds LS19 7BN, UK (☎ 0113-238 7575, 🖳 www. masta.org). Provide a 24-hour Travellers E-line ⊠ enquiries@ masta.org).

Voluntary Service Overseas, 317 Putney Bridge Road, London SW15 2PN, UK (🖳 www.vso.org.uk).

Wexas International, 45-49 Brompton Road, London SW3 1DE, UK (☎ 020-7589 3315, 🖳 www.wexas.com). Useful source of travel information.

Major Property Exhibitions

Property Exhibitions are common in the UK and Ireland, and are popular with prospective property buyers who can get a good idea of what's available in a particular area and make contact with estate agents and developers. Below is a list of the main exhibition organisers in the UK and Ireland. Note that you may be charged a small admission fee.

Homes Overseas (☎ UK 020-7939 9852, 🖳 www.blendoncommunica tions.co.uk). Homes Overseas are the largest organisers of international property exhibitions and stage a number of exhibitions each year at a range of venues in both the UK and Ireland.

Incredible Homes (☎ UK 0800-652 2992, Spain 952-924 645, 🖳 www. incredible-homes.com). Incredible Homes are based on the Costa del Sol and organise several large exhibitions a year in both the UK and Ireland.

International Property Show (☎ UK 01962-736712, 🖳 www.inter nationalpropertyshow.com). The International Property Show is held several times a year in London and Manchester.

Spain on Show (☎ UK 0500-780878, 🖳 www.spainonshow.com). Spain on Show organises several annual property exhibitions at venues around the UK.

Town & Country (☎ UK 0845-230 6000, 🖳 www.spanishproperty. uk.com). This large estate agency organises small Spanish property exhibitions at venues around the UK twice monthly.

World Class Homes (☎ UK 0800-731 4713, 💻 www.worldclass homes.co.uk). Exhibitions organised by World Class Homes are held in small venues around the UK and mainly include only UK property developers.

World of Property (☎ UK 01323-726040, 💻 www.outbound publishing. com). The *World of Property* magazine publishers (see **Appendix B**) organise three large property exhibitions a year, two in the south of the UK and one in the north.

Appendix B: FURTHER READING

The books listed below are just a small selection of the many books written for those planning to live, work or retire in the EU. Some titles may be out of print, but may still be obtainable from bookshops and libraries. Books prefixed with an asterisk (*) are recommended by the author. See also the list of books published by Survival Books (see page 414).

Living & Working In The EU

*Americans Living Abroad, J. Kepler (Praeger)

*Buying a Home Abroad, David Hampshire (Survival Books)

*Buying a Home in Britain, David Hampshire (Survival Books)

*Buying a Home in France 2003-4, David Hampshire (Survival Books)

*Buying a Home in Greece/Cyprus, Joanna Styles (Survival Books)

*Buying a Home in Ireland, Joe Laredo (Survival Books)

*Buying a Home in Italy, David Hampshire (Survival Books)

*Buying a Home in Portugal, David Hampshire (Survival Books)

*Buying a Home in Spain 2003-4, David Hampshire (Survival Books)

*Directory of Jobs and Careers Abroad, E. Roberts (Vacation Work)

Executives Living Abroad, Deloitte Touche Tohmatsu International (Kluwer Law)

Getting a Job Abroad, Roger Jones (How To Books)

*Getting a Job in Europe, Mark Hempshell (How To Books)

Guide to Living Abroad, Michael Furnell & Philip Jones (Kogan Page)

Guide to Working Abroad, Godfrey Golzen & Helen Kogan (Kogan Page)

International Jobs: Where They Are and How to Get Them, E. Kocher (Perseus Press)

Living & Working Abroad: A Parent's Guide, Robin Pascoe (Kuperard)

Living & Working Abroad: A Wife's Guide, Robin Pascoe (Kuperard)

*Living & Working in Britain, David Hampshire (Survival Books)

*Living & Working in France, David Hampshire (Survival Books)

*Living & Working in Germany, Nick Daws (Survival Books)

*Living & Working in Belgium, Holland & Luxembourg, Bev Laflamme (Survival Books)

*Living & Working in Ireland, Joe Laredo (Survival Books)

*Living & Working in Italy, Nick Daws (Survival Books)

*Living & Working in Spain, David Hampshire (Survival Books)

Look Ahead: A Guide to Working Abroad, Alan Vincent (Heinemann)

*Money Mail: Moves Abroad, Margaret Stone (Kogan Page)

Moving and Living Abroad, Sandra Albright, Alice Chu & Lori Austin (Hippocrene Books, Inc.).

Opportunities in Overseas Careers, B. Camenson (Vgm Opportunities Series)

Relocation: Escape from America, R. Gallo (Manhattan Loft Publishers)

Summer Jobs Abroad, David Woodworth (Vacation Work)

Survival Kit For Overseas Living: For Americans Planning to Live and Work Abroad, L. Robert Kohis (Nicholas Brealey)

*US Expat Handbook Guide to Living & Working Abroad, John W. Adams

*Work Your Way Around the World, Susan Griffith (Vacation Work)

Working Abroad, Alan Vincent (Heinemann)

Working Abroad, Jonathan Golding (How To Books)

*Working Abroad, Peter Gartland (Financial Times)

*Working Abroad, William Essex (Bloomsbury)

*Working Holidays Abroad, Mark Hempshell (Trotman)

Working Overseas, Bryan Havenhand (Global Exchange)

*Your Own Business in Europe, Mark Hempshell (How To Books)

Health & Safety

The ABC of Healthy Travel (British Medical Journal)

Business Smarts – Business Travel Safety Guide, Aura Lee O'Banion (Safety First)

*How to Stay Healthy Abroad, Dr. R. Dawood (Oxford University Press)

International Travel and Health 2004 (World Health Organization)

Keeping Your Life, Family and Career Intact While Living Abroad, Cathy Tsang-Feign (Hamblan)

*Travellers' Health, Richard Dawood (Oxford Paperbacks)

*A Travellers' Medical Guide, Paul Zakowich (Kuperard)

Immunization – Childhood and Travel Health, Kassianos (Blackwell)

*Merck Manual of Medical Information: Home Edition (Merck)

*Rough Guide to Travel Health, Dr. Nick Jones (Rough Guides)

*Safety and Security for Women Who Travel, Sheila Swan (Travellers' Tales)

*Survivor's Guide to Business Travel, R. Collins (Kogan Page)

Travel Can be Murder: A Business Traveler's Guide to Personal Safety, Terry Riley (Applied Psychology Press).

*Travel with Children, Mike Wheeler (Lonely Planet)

Travel in Health, Graham Fry & Vincent Kenny (Gill and Macmillan)

Travel and Health in the Elderly, I.B. McIntosh (Quay)

*Travel Medicine and Migrant Health, Cameron Lockie MBE (Churchill Livingstone)

*Travel Safety, Adler (Hippocrene)

*The Travellers Handbook (Wexas)

*Travellers' Health, Dr. R. Dawood (OUP)

Understanding Travel and Holiday Health, Bernadette Carroll (Family Doctor)

*World Wise - Your Passport to Safer Travel, (Thomas Cook)

Information About The EU

The EC/EU Fact Book: A Complete Question & Answer Guide, **Alex Roney (Kogan Page)**

The European Union: A Very Short Introduction, **John Pinder (Oxford Paperbacks)**

*The Penguin Companion to the European Union, **Timothy Bainbridge and Anthony Teasdale (Penguin)**

Retirement

*The Good Retirement Guide, Rosemary Brown (Kogan Page)

How to Retire Abroad (How To Books)

*Life in the Sun, Nancy Tuft (Age Concern England)

Making the Most of Retirement, Michael Barratt (Kogan Page)

Retirement Abroad, Robert Cooke (Robert Hale)

*Retiring Abroad, David Hampshire (Survival Books)

*The World's Top Retirement Havens, Margaret J. Goldstein (John Muir)

Your Retirement: How to make the Most of It, Rosemary Brown (Kogan Page)

English-Language Publications

France

France Magazine, Cumberland House, Oriel Rd, Cheltenham, Glos. GL50 1BB, UK (☎ 01242-216 080, ▣ www.francemag.com). Monthly lifestyle magazine.

France Magazine, 4101 Reservoir Rd., Washington DC 20007, USA (☎ 202-944 6069, ▣ www.francemagazine.org). Bi-monthly lifestyle magazine published in the USA.

France-USA Contacts, FUSAC, PO Box 115, Cooper Station, New York, NY 10276, USA (☎ 212-777 5553, ▣ www.fusac.com). Free weekly magazine.

Living France, Picture House Publishing Ltd., 9 High Street, Olney MK46 4EB, UK (☎ 01234-713203, ▣ www.livingfrance.com). Monthly lifestyle/property magazine.

Greece

Greece Magazine (UK ☎ 01225-786 834, ▣ www.greece-magazine. co.uk). Monthly lifestyle/property magazine.

Italy

Italy Italy, Italy Italy Enterprises, Via Salana 71, Rome 00198 (▣ www. italyitalymagazine.com). Bi-monthly glossy lifstyle and culture magazine.

Italy Magazine, Poundbury Publishing Ltd., Prospect House, Peverell Avenue East, Poundbury, Dorchester, Dorset DT1 3WE, UK (☎ 01305-266 360, 💻 www.italymag.co.uk). Bi-monthly lifestyles/property magazine.

Spain

Living Spain, Albany Publishing, High Street, Olney MK46 4EB, UK (☎ 01234-710 992, 💻 www.livingspain.co.uk). Bi-monthly lifestyle/property magazine.

Spain Magazine, The Media Company Publications Ltd, 21 Royal Circus, Edinburgh EH3 6TL UK (☎ 0131-226 7766, 💻 www.spain magazine.info). Monthly lifestyle/property magazine.

Miscellaneous

Condé Nast Traveller, Vogue House, 1 Hanover Square, London W1S 1JU, UK (☎ 020-7499 9080, 💻 www.cntraveller.com). Glamorous travel magazine for the well-heeled.

Expat World, Expat World (💻 www.expatworld.net). Monthly relocation magazine available in print or by e-mail subscription.

Homes Overseas, Blendon Communications Ltd, 207 Providence Square, Mill Street, London SE1 2EW, UK (☎ 020-7939 9888, 💻 www.homesoverseas.co.uk). Bi-monthly international property magazine.

International Homes, 3 St. Johns Court, Moulsham Street, Chelmsford, Essex CM2 0JD, UK (☎ 01245-358877, 💻 www.international-homes.com). Bi-monthly magazine.

National Geographic, National Geographic Society, PO Box 89199, Washington, DC 20090-8199, USA (☎ 813-979 6845, 💻 www.national geographic.com). Also publish National Geographic Traveller.

Nexus Expatriate Magazine, Expat Network Limited, First Floor, 5 Brighton Road, Croydon CR2 6AE, UK (☎ 020-8760 5100, 💻 www.expatnetwork.co.uk).

Official Airlines Guides, OAG Publications (☎ 01582-695050, 💻 www.oag.com). Monthly airline timetables.

Relocation Today, BR Anchor publications (💻 www.branchor.com). Monthly relocation magazine available online.

Thomas Cook Magazine, 7 St Martin's Place, London WC2H 4HA, UK (☎ 020-7747 0700).

TNT Magazine, 14–15 Child's Place, Earls Court, London SW5 9RX, UK (☎ 020-7373 3377, 💻 www.tntmag.co.uk). Free weekly magazine for expatriate Australians. Also publish TNT Magazine New Zealand.

Transitions Abroad, (☎ 866-760 5340, 💻 www.transitionsabroad.com). Online magazine.

Traveller, Wexas International, 45–49 Brompton Road, Knightsbridge, London SW3 1DE, UK (☎ 020-7589 3315, 💻 www.travelleronline.com). Long-established, quality travel magazine published quarterly.

Wanderlust, PO Box 1832, Windsor SL4 6YP, UK (☎ 01753-620426, 💻 www.wanderlust.co.uk). Excellent monthly practical magazine for avid travellers.

World of Property, Outbound Publishing, 1 Commercial Road, Eastbourne, East Sussex BN21 3XQ, UK (☎ 01323-726040, 💻 www. outboundpublishing.com). Quarterly property magazine. Also publish the quarterly *Focus on France* magazine published monthly.

APPENDIX C: USEFUL WEBSITES

There are literally dozens of expatriate websites and as the internet increases in popularity the number grows by the day. Most information is useful and websites generally offer free access, although some require a subscription or payment for services. Relocation and other companies specialising in expatriate services often have websites, although these may only provide information that a company is prepared to offer free of charge, which although it can be useful may be rather biased. However, there are plenty of volunteer sites run by expatriates providing practical information and tips. A particularly useful section found on most expatriate websites is the 'message board' or 'forum', where expatriates answer questions based on their experience and knowledge, and offer an insight into what a country or city is **really** like.

Below is a list of some of the best expatriate websites. **Note that websites are listed under headings in alphabetical order and the list is by no means definitive.** Websites relating to specific countries can be found in **Chapter 9 – Country Profiles.**

General Websites

International Living

ExpatBoards (🖳 www.expatboards.com) – The mega site for expatriates, with popular discussion boards and special areas for Britons, Americans, expatriate taxes, and other important issues.

Escape Artist (🖳 www.escapeartist.com) – An excellent website and probably the most comprehensive, packed with resources, links and directories covering most expatriate destinations. You can also subscribe to the free monthly online expatriate magazine, *Escape from America.*

Expat Exchange (🖳 www.expatexchange.com) – Reportedly the largest online community for English-speaking expatriates, provides a series of articles on relocation and also a question and answer facility through its expatriate network.

Expat Forum (🖳 www.expatforum.com) – Provides interesting cost of living comparisons as well as 7 EU country-specific forums and chats (Belgium, the Czech Republic, France, Germany, the Netherlands, Spain and the UK).

Expat Network (⌨ www.expatnetwork.co.uk) – The leading expatriate website in the UK, which is essentially an employment network for expatriates, although there are also numerous support services plus a monthly online magazine, *Nexus*.

Expat World (⌨ www.expatworld.net) – 'The newsletter of international living.' Contains a wealth of information for American and British expatriates, including a subscription newsletter.

Expatriate Experts (⌨ www.expatexpert.com) – A website run by expatriate expert Robin Pascoe, providing invaluable advice and support.

Expats International (⌨ www.expats2000.com) – The international job centre for expats and their recruiters.

Gap Year (⌨ www.gapyear.co.uk) – A website mainly targeted at students doing a gap year, but full of useful information and advice about countries and travelling.

Global People (⌨ www.peoplegoingglobal.com) – Provides interesting country-specific information with particular emphasis on social and political aspects.

Living Abroad (⌨ www.livingabroad.com) – Provides an extensive and comprehensive list of country profiles, although they are available only on payment.

Outpost Information Centre (⌨ www.outpostexpat.nl) – A website containing extensive country specific information and links operated by the Shell Petroleum Company for its expatriate workers, but available to everyone.

Real Post Reports (⌨ www.realpostreports.com) – Provides relocation services, recommended reading lists and plenty of interesting 'real-life' stories containing anecdotes and impressions written by expatriates in just about every city in the world.

Travel Documents (⌨ www.traveldocs.com). – Useful information about travel, specific countries and documents needed to travel.

World Travel Guide (⌨ www.wtgonline.com) – A general website for world travellers and expatriates.
American Websites

Americans Abroad (⌨ www.aca.ch) – This website offers advice, information and services to Americans abroad.

Americans In Britain (⌨ http://groups.yahoo.com/group/americans inbritain) – A website providing a support and advice for Americans living and working in the UK.

American Teachers Abroad (⌨ www.overseasdigest.com) – A comprehensive website with numerous relocation services and advice plus teaching opportunities.

Australians Abroad (⌨ www.australiansabroad.com) – Information for Australians concerning relocating plus a forum to exchange information and advice.

US Government Trade (⌨ www.usatrade.gov) – A huge website providing a wealth of information principally for Americans planning to trade and invest abroad, but useful for anyone planning a move abroad.

British Websites

British In America (⌨ www.britishinamerica.com and www.british-expats.com) – Two websites designed for Britons in the USA.

British Expatriates (⌨ www.britishexpat.com) – This website keep British expatriates in touch with events and information about the UK.

Southern Cross Group (⌨ www.southern-cross-group.org) – A website for Australians and New Zealanders providing information and the exchange of tips.

Trade Partners (⌨ www.tradepartners.gov.uk) – A government sponsored website whose main aim is to provide trade and investment information on just about every country in the world. Even if you aren't planning to do business abroad, the information is comprehensive and up to date.

Worldwise Directory (⌨ www.suzylamplugh.org/worldwise) – This website run by the Suzy Lamplugh charity for personal safety, providing a useful directory of countries with practical information and special emphasis on safety, particularly for women.

Websites For Women

Family Life Abroad (⌨ www.familylifeabroad.com) – A wealth of information and articles on coping with family life abroad.

Foreign Wives Club (⌨ www.foreignwivesclub.com) – An online community for women in bi-cultural marriages.

Third Culture Kids (⌨ www.tckworld.com) – A website designed for expatriate children living abroad.

Travel For Kids (⌨ www.travelforkids.com) – Advice on travelling with children around the world.

Women Of The World (⌨ www.wow-net.org) – A website designed for female expats anywhere in the world.

Travel Information & Warnings

The websites listed below provide daily updated information about the political situation and natural disasters around the world, plus general travel and health advice and embassy addresses.

Australian Department of Foreign Affairs and Trade (⌨ www.dfat. gov.au/travel)

British Foreign and Commonwealth Office (⌨ www.fco.gov.uk)

Canadian Department of Foreign Affairs (⌨ www.dfait-maeci. gc.ca). – They also publish a useful series of free booklets for Canadians moving abroad.

New Zealand Ministry of Foreign Affairs and Trade (⌨ www.mft. govt.nz)

SaveWealth Travel (⌨ www.save wealth.com/travel/warnings)

The Travel Doctor (⌨ www.tmvc.com.au) – Contains a country by country vaccination guide.

US State Government (⌨ www.state.gov/travel) – US Government website.

World Health Organization (⌨ www.who.int)

APPENDIX D: WEIGHTS & MEASURES

Most EU countries use the international metric system of measurement, which has superseded the old imperial measures in most countries. However, some countries, e.g. the USA and the UK, still refer to Fahrenheit temperatures, inches, miles, gallons and pounds, while in others you can expect to find goods sold in imperial (and other old measures), metric or marked in both metric and imperial measures. Therefore, many people will find the tables on the following pages useful. Some comparisons shown are approximations only, but are close enough for most everyday uses.

Women's Clothes

Continental	34	36	38	40	42	44	46	48	50	52
UK	8	10	12	14	16	18	20	22	24	26
USA	6	8	10	12	14	16	18	20	22	24

Pullovers

Pullovers	Women's						Men's					
Continental	40	42	44	46	48	50	44	46	48	50	52	54
UK	34	36	38	40	42	44	34	36	38	40	42	44
USA	34	36	38	40	42	44	sm	med	lar	xl		

Men's Shirts

Continental	36	37	38	39	40	41	42	43	44	46
UK/USA	14	14	15	15	16	16	17	17	18	-

Men's Underwear

Continental	5	6	7	8	9	10
UK	34	36	38	40	42	44
USA	sm	med		lar	xl	

Note: sm = small, med = medium, lar = large, xl = extra large

Children's Clothes

Continental	92	104	116	128	140	152
UK	16/18	20/22	24/26	28/30	32/34	36/38
USA	2	4	6	8	10	12

Children's Shoes

Continental	18 19 20 21 22 23 24 25 26 27 28 29 30 31 32
UK/USA	2 3 4 4 5 6 7 7 8 9 10 11 11 12 13
Continental	33 34 35 36 37 38
UK/USA	1 2 2 3 4 5

Shoes (Women's and Men's)

Continental	35 36 37 37 38 39 40 41 42 42 43 44
UK	2 3 3 4 4 5 6 7 7 8 9 9
USA	4 5 5 6 6 7 8 9 9 10 10 11

Weight

Avoirdupois	Metric	Metric	Avoirdupois
1oz	28.35g	1g	0.035oz
1lb*	454g	100g	3.5oz
1cwt	50.8kg	250g	9oz
1 ton	1,016kg	500g	18oz
2,205lb	1 tonne	1kg	2.2lb

Length

British/US	Metric	Metric	British/US
1in	2.54cm	1cm	0.39in
1ft	30.48cm	1m	3ft 3.25in
1yd	91.44cm	1km	0.62mi
1mi	1.6km	8km	5mi

Capacity

Imperial	Metric	Metric	Imperial
1 UK pint	0.57 litre	1 litre	1.75 UK pints
1 US pint	0.47 litre	1 litre	2.13 US pints
1 UK gallon	4.54 litres	1 litre	0.22 UK gallon
1 US gallon	3.78 litres	1 litre	0.26 US gallon

Note: An American 'cup' = around 250ml or 0.25 litre.

Area

British/US	Metric	Metric	British/US
1 sq. in	0.45 sq. cm	1 sq. cm	0.15 sq. in
1 sq. ft	0.09 sq. m	1 sq. m	10.76 sq. ft
1 sq. yd	0.84 sq. m	1 sq. m	1.2 sq. yds
1 acre	0.4 hectares	1 hectare	2.47 acres
1 sq. mile	2.56 sq. km	1 sq. km	0.39 sq. mile

Temperature

°Celsius	°Fahrenheit	
0	32	(freezing point of water)
5	41	
10	50	
15	59	
20	68	
25	77	
30	86	
35	95	
40	104	
50	122	

Notes: The boiling point of water is 100°C / 212°F.

Normal body temperature (if you're alive and well) is 37°C / 98.6°F.

Temperature Conversion

Celsius to Fahrenheit: multiply by 9, divide by 5 and add 32. (For a quick and approximate conversion, double the Celsius temperature and add 30.)

Fahrenheit to Celsius: subtract 32, multiply by 5 and divide by 9. (For a quick and approximate conversion, subtract 30 from the Fahrenheit temperature and divide by 2.)

Oven Temperatures

Gas	Electric	
	°F	°C
-	225–250	110–120
1	275	140
2	300	150
3	325	160
4	350	180
5	375	190
6	400	200
7	425	220
8	450	230
9	475	240

Air Pressure

PSI	Bar
10	0.5
20	1.4
30	2
40	2.8

Power

Kilowatts	Horsepower	Horsepower	Kilowatts
1	1.34	1	0.75

APPENDIX E: MAP

The map opposite shows the 25 countries in the European Union, numbered alphabetically. The countries are listed below with details of when they joined the EU.

1. Austria	14. Latvia
2. Belgium	15. Lithuania
3. Cyprus	16. Malta
4. Czech Republic	17. Luxembourg
5. Denmark	18. Netherlands
6. Estonia	19. Poland
7. Finland	20. Portugal
8. France	21. Slovakia
9. Germany	22. Slovenia
10. Greece	23. Spain
11. Hungary	24. Sweden
12. Ireland	25. United Kingdom
13. Italy	

March 1957: Belgium, France, Germany, Italy, Luxembourg and the Netherlands establish the European Economic Community (EEC).

January 1973: Britain, Denmark and Ireland become members of the European Community (EC).

January 1981: Greece becomes the tenth member of the EC.

January 1986: Spain and Portugal join the EC.

January 1995: Austria, Finland and Sweden join the European Union (EU).

May 2004: Cyprus, the Czech Republic, Estonia, Hungary, Latvia, Lithuania, Malta, Poland, Slovakia and Slovenia join the EU.

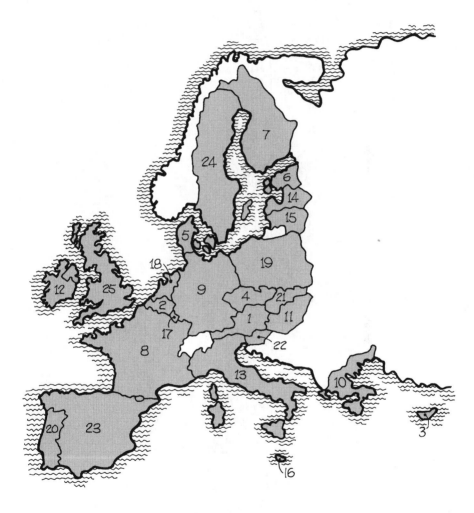

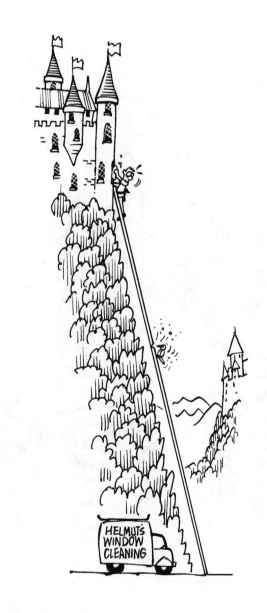

INDEX

D

E

F

J

K

L

M

O

P

Q

R

LIVING AND WORKING SERIES

Living and Working books are essential reading for anyone planning to spend time abroad, including holiday-home owners, retirees, visitors, business people, migrants, students and even extra-terrestrials! They're packed with important and useful information designed to help you **avoid costly mistakes and save both time and money.** Topics covered include how to:

- Find a job with a good salary & conditions
- Obtain a residence permit
- Avoid and overcome problems
- Find your dream home
- Get the best education for your family
- Make the best use of public transport
- Endure local motoring habits
- Obtain the best health treatment
- Stretch your money further
- Make the most of your leisure time
- Enjoy the local sporting life
- Find the best shopping bargains
- Insure yourself against most eventualities
- Use post office and telephone services
- Do numerous other things not listed above

Living and Working books are the most comprehensive and up-to-date source of practical information available about everyday life abroad. They aren't, however, boring text books, but interesting and entertaining guides written in a highly readable style.

Discover what it's *really* like to live and work abroad!

Order your copies today by phone, fax, mail or e-mail from: Survival Books, PO Box 146, Wetherby, West Yorks. LS23 6XZ, United Kingdom (☎/▤ +44 (0)1937-843523, ✉ orders@ survivalbooks.net, 🖥 www.survivalbooks.net).

BUYING A HOME SERIES

Buying a Home books are essential reading for anyone planning to purchase property abroad and are designed to guide you through the jungle and make it a pleasant and enjoyable experience. Most importantly, they're packed with vital information to help you **avoid the sort of disasters that can turn your dream home into a nightmare!** Topics covered include:

- Avoiding problems
- Choosing the region
- Finding the right home and location
- Estate agents
- Finance, mortgages and taxes
- Home security
- Utilities, heating and air-conditioning
- Moving house and settling in
- Renting and letting
- Permits and visas
- Travelling and communications
- Health and insurance
- Renting a car and driving
- Retirement and starting a business
- And much, much more!

Buying a Home books are the most comprehensive and up-to-date source of information available about buying property abroad. Whether you want a detached house, townhouse or apartment, a holiday or a permanent home, these books will help make your dreams come true.

Save yourself time, trouble and money!

Order your copies today by phone, fax, mail or e-mail from: Survival Books, PO Box 146, Wetherby, West Yorks. LS23 6XZ, United Kingdom (☎/▤ +44 (0)1937-843523, ✉ orders@ survivalbooks.net, 🖳 www.survivalbooks.net).

ORDER FORM 1

Qty.	Title	Price (incl. p&p)*			Total
		UK	Europe	World	
	The Alien's Guide to Britain	£6.95	£8.95	£12.45	
	The Alien's Guide to France	£6.95	£8.95	£12.45	
	The Best Places to Buy a Home in France	£13.95	£15.95	£19.45	
	The Best Places to Buy a Home in Spain	£13.95	£15.95	£19.45	
	Buying a Home Abroad	£13.95	£15.95	£19.45	
	Buying a Home in Florida	£13.95	£15.95	£19.45	
	Buying a Home in France	£13.95	£15.95	£19.45	
	Buying a Home in Greece & Cyprus	£13.95	£15.95	£19.45	
	Buying a Home in Ireland	£11.95	£13.95	£17.45	
	Buying a Home in Italy	£13.95	£15.95	£19.45	
	Buying a Home in Portugal	£13.95	£15.95	£19.45	
	Buying a Home in Spain	£13.95	£15.95	£19.45	
	Buying, Letting & Selling Property	£11.95	£13.95	£17.45	
	Foreigners in France: Triumphs & Disasters	£11.95	£13.95	£17.45	
	Foreigners in Spain: Triumphs & Disasters	£11.95	£13.95	£17.45	
	How to Avoid Holiday & Travel Disasters	£13.95	£15.95	£19.45	
	Costa del Sol Lifeline	£11.95	£13.95	£17.45	
	Dordogne/Lot Lifeline	£11.95	£13.95	£17.45	
	Poitou-Charentes Lifeline	£11.95	£13.95	£17.45	
					Total

Order your copies today by phone, fax, mail or e-mail from: Survival Books, PO Box 146, Wetherby, West Yorks. LS23 6XZ, UK (☎/▤ +44 (0)1937-843523, ✉ orders@ survivalbooks.net, ▣ www.survivalbooks.net). If you aren't entirely satisfied, simply return them to us within 14 days for a full and unconditional refund.

Cheque enclosed/please charge my Amex/Delta/MasterCard/Switch/Visa* card

Card No. __ __ __ __   __ __ __ __   __ __ __ __   __ __ __ __

Expiry date _____   Issue number (Switch only) _____

Signature _____   Tel. No. _____

NAME _____

ADDRESS _____

_____

* Delete as applicable (price includes postage – airmail for Europe/world).

ORDER FORM 2

Qty.	Title	Price (incl. p&p)*			Total
		UK	Europe	World	
	Living & Working Abroad	£14.95	£16.95	£20.45	
	Living & Working in America	£14.95	£16.95	£20.45	
	Living & Working in Australia	£14.95	£16.95	£20.45	
	Living & Working in Britain	£14.95	£16.95	£20.45	
	Living & Working in Canada	£16.95	£18.95	£22.45	
	Living & Working in the European Union	£16.95	£18.95	£22.45	
	Living & Working in the Far East	£16.95	£18.95	£22.45	
	Living & Working in France	£14.95	£16.95	£20.45	
	Living & Working in Germany	£16.95	£18.95	£22.45	
	L&W in the Gulf States & Saudi Arabia	£16.95	£18.95	£22.45	
	L&W in Holland, Belgium & Luxembourg	£14.95	£16.95	£20.45	
	Living & Working in Ireland	£14.95	£16.95	£20.45	
	Living & Working in Italy	£16.95	£18.95	£22.45	
	Living & Working in London	£13.95	£15.95	£19.45	
	Living & Working in New Zealand	£14.95	£16.95	£20.45	
	Living & Working in Spain	£14.95	£16.95	£20.45	
	Living & Working in Switzerland	£16.95	£18.95	£22.45	
	Renovating & Maintaining Your French Home	£13.95	£15.95	£19.45	
	Retiring Abroad	£14.95	£16.95	£20.45	
	Rioja and its Wines	£11.95	£13.95	£17.45	
	The Wines of Spain	£13.95	£15.95	£19.45	
					Total

Order your copies today by phone, fax, mail or e-mail from: Survival Books, PO Box 146, Wetherby, West Yorks. LS23 6XZ, UK (☎/▤ +44 (0)1937-843523, ✉ orders@ survivalbooks.net, 🖥 www.survivalbooks.net). If you aren't entirely satisfied, simply return them to us within 14 days for a full and unconditional refund.

Cheque enclosed/please charge my Amex/Delta/MasterCard/Switch/Visa* card

Card No. __ __ __ __   __ __ __ __   __ __ __ __   __ __ __ __

Expiry date _____   Issue number (Switch only) _____

Signature _____   Tel. No. _____

NAME _____

ADDRESS _____

_____

_____

* Delete as applicable (price includes postage – airmail for Europe/world).

OTHER SURVIVAL BOOKS

The Alien's Guides: *The Alien's Guides to Britain and France* provide an 'alternative' look at life in these popular countries and will help you to appreciate the peculiarities (in both senses) of the British and French.

The Best Places to Buy a Home in France/Spain: The most comprehensive and up-to-date homebuying guides to France or Spain.

Buying, Selling and Letting Property: The most comprehensive and up-to-date source of information available for those intending to buy, sell or let a property in the UK and the only book on the subject updated annually.

Foreigners in France/Spain: Triumphs & Disasters: Real-life experiences of people who have emigrated to France and Spain.

How to Avoid Holiday and Travel Disasters: This book will help you to make the right decisions regarding every aspect of your travel arrangements and to avoid costly mistakes and disasters that can turn a trip into a nightmare.

Lifelines: Essential guides to specific regions of France and Spain, containing everything you need to know about local life. Titles in the series currently include the *Costa del Sol*, *Dordogne/Lot*, and *Poitou-Charentes*.

Renovating & Maintaining Your French Home: The ultimate guide to renovating and maintaining your dream home in France.

Retiring Abroad: The most comprehensive and up-to-date source of practical information available about retiring to a foreign country – contains profiles of the 20 most popular retirement destinations.

Wine Guides: *Rioja and its Wines* and *The Wines of Spain* are the most comprehensive and up-to-date sources of information available on the wines of Spain and of its most famous wine-producing region.

Broaden your horizons with Survival Books!

Order your copies today by phone, fax, mail or e-mail from: Survival Books, PO Box 146, Wetherby, West Yorks. LS23 6XZ, United Kingdom (☎/🖷 +44 (0)1937-843523, ✉ orders@ survivalbooks.net, 🖳 www.survivalbooks.net).

NOTES

NOTES